S0-AJM-745

WITHDRAWN

NUCLEAR
STRATEGIZING

NUCLEAR STRATEGIZING

Deterrence
and
Reality

STEPHEN J. CIMBALA

PRAEGER

New York
Westport, Connecticut
London

Library of Congress Cataloging-in-Publication Data

Cimbala, Stephen J.
   Nuclear strategizing.

   Includes indexes.
     1. Nuclear warfare. 2. Deterrence (Strategy)
I. Title.
U263.C49   1988   355'.0217   87–38496
ISBN 0–275–92987–6 (alk. paper)

Copyright © 1988 by Stephen J. Cimbala

All rights reserved. No portion of this book may be
reproduced, by any process or technique, without the
express written consent of the publisher.

Library of Congress Catalog Card Number: 87–38496
ISBN: 0–275–92987–6

First published in 1988

Praeger Publishers, One Madison Avenue, New York, NY 10010
A division of Greenwood Press, Inc.

Printed in the United States of America

The paper used in this book complies with the Permanent
Paper Standard issued by the National Information Standards
Organization (Z39.48–1984).

10 9 8 7 6 5 4 3 2 1

U
263
.C49
1988

To Betsy

CONTENTS

Acknowledgments   ix

Introduction   1

1   Nuclear Strategizing   11

2   Strategy and Control in the Nuclear Age   29

3   Nuclear Scientism and Nuclear Strategism   51

4   Deterrence, Rationality, and Nuclear Weapons   75

5   De-Escalation and War Termination   97

6   Missile Defense: Rationality or Escapism   115

7   Deterrence, Rationality, and Political Consistency   137

8   Expected and Unexpected Wars   155

9   Nuclear Surprise   175

10   Arms Control and U.S. Nuclear Strategy   211

11   Force and Policy in the Nuclear Age   231

12   Conclusion   253

Epilogue   273

Index   291

About the Author   307

ACKNOWLEDGMENTS

The author gratefully acknowledges the extensive comments and criticisms of this manuscript provided by Professor David W. Tarr, University of Wisconsin, Madison. His careful reading of the text prevented many errors of omission and commission. In addition, I am most grateful to those who have given their time and expertise to explain the more complicated aspects of their disciplines to my simple mind, including Richard Betts, Bruce G. Blair, Paul Bracken, Paul K. Davis, Keith A. Dunn, Colin S. Gray, Richard Ned Lebow, William C. Martel, Keith B. Payne, Alan N. Sabrosky, Leon Sloss, and John Allen Williams. Among those who have struggled, sometimes against great odds, to educate the author about Soviet military doctrine and strategy are Joseph D. Douglass, Jr., Mary Fitzgerald, Daniel Goure, Leon Goure, John G. Hines, Benjamin S. Lambeth, Phillip Stewart and Edward L. Warner III. Michael N. Pocalyko insists, after exposure to this writer, that landlubbers can understand maritime strategy only after repeated and painful doses. The author also wishes to express appreciation to Daniel Goure, Richard Ned Lebow, and Scott Sagan for extensive and helpful comments on earlier drafts, and to Michael Handel for suggested reference sources. None of them bears any responsibility for errors or points of views herein. Finally, I am grateful to Susan Pazourek and Frank Welsch at Praeger Publishers for their encouragement to complete this manuscript.

Some personal debts for encouragement through thick and thin must also be acknowledged here: Michael Altfeld, Vincent Davis, Charles Hermann, Lawrence Korb, Sam Sarkesian, David Segal, William J. Taylor,

Jr., and Gregory Treverton. I am also grateful to Edward Tomezsko, Lynn M. Haskin, and Diane Wolf of Penn State University for administrative support for this project. Finally and most important, I apologize to my family for still another academic imposition.

NUCLEAR
STRATEGIZING

INTRODUCTION

The discussion that follows pivots around the concept of rationality. So it is well to spell out that issue, in order that the reader who may disagree will at least know where we are coming from. Rationality is a charged word in the social sciences, and, in addition, political scientists, economists, and psychologists use the term with somewhat different emphases.

The generic meaning of rationality is the successful adjustment of a group or individual—even a system—to the environment. Perhaps this means dominating the environment, like successful dictators or prehistoric monsters, but even they sooner or later face environmental adaptation or obsolescence. The term "adjustment," however, connotes something quite subjective, and not all environments involve the kinds of situations of which we would approve. A concentration camp, for example, is certainly an environment of sorts, but not one, we hope, that people would tolerate by adapting to it, but would rebel against. Inherent in the very notion of social rebellion is a cry by the disadvantaged against the privileged, by the oppressed against the oppressor.

This problem of adjustment to an essentially sick or depraved environment is often thought to describe our situation in the nuclear age. The environment is one of malice and dread, to which we adapt to the mechanism of deterrence, or war prevention by threat of reprisal. Here there is a divide. Experts tell us that nuclear deterrence is the only way to cope with this environment, but the lay audience keeps smelling a rat. Of course, there is the usual coterie of world government and world disarmament advocates, but they have little hope of electing politicians who will promote such views through national legislation. Instead, force structures and defense policies of both the United States and other countries are built on the edifice of deterrence, presumed to be the most rational adjustment to the prevailing situation.

When we say "rational," we may mean any number of things. It is argued here that there are three meanings of rationality that might be applied to U.S.–Soviet nuclear deterrence relationships. The first two are the meanings that most Western writers about deterrence have used. The third offers an alternative, which is believed by this writer to be more descriptive of what actually takes place.

The first of these kinds of rationality is heuristic rationality. This is the rationality of the perfect logician or philosopher king. It serves the useful purpose of providing a benchmark against which to measure relative success or failure, according to some social scientists. In the model of heuristic rationality, all alternatives are known to the policy maker. There are no appropriate options that have been omitted from consideration. In addition, all consequences that can follow from each of these alternatives are also known. Finally, and most demanding, the decision-making individual or group has a unique preference ordering, such that a transitive hierarchy of preferred consequences can be established. If, for example, A is preferred to B, and B is preferred to C, then C cannot be preferred to A. Ideally, rational decision makers would also know the exact distance from A to B, and B to C, so that with regard to the various alternatives, degrees of comfort and misery could be established.[1]

It will be noted by the reader that if it is anything at all, this is a model of how people ought to decide, instead of a description of how they actually do it, but it has also served as a standard of reference for deterrence theory and other social science studies of war and peace. The question is not whether the ideal type of heuristic rationality applies literally, but whether its influence on our understanding of policy making is contributory or pernicious.

The second kind of rationality is conditional rationality, meaning that it is an approximation of heuristic rationality, following the same road map. Conditional rationality is the preferred model for many social scientists, including deterrence theorists, who acknowledge that heuristic rationality is not attainable in practice. So conditional rationality is endorsed instead, with the decision makers wanting to come as close to perfect or heuristic rationality as they can, while recognizing that they can never get there. The seminal works of Herman Kahn and other deterrence theorists of the later 1950s and early-to-middle 1960s are based upon this insight—that conditional rationality is within the state of the art, even if heuristic rationality is not.[2] Note, however, that conditional rationality imposes the same standard of perfection that is explicit in heuristic rationality, while lamenting the inability of individuals and decision-making groups to perform up to the higher standard.

As applied to nuclear strategy and the logic of deterrence, this has interesting implications. Conditional rationality, like the inhabitants of the Garden of Eden, has tasted the forbidden fruit of miserable reasoning and illogical policy compromises. Conditional rationality knows that the world cannot be force-fed into a heuristically rational model, except perhaps by theoretical physicists. Because they endorse the standards of perfection inherent in heuristic rationality, however, conditional-rationality theorists adopt the same basic frame of reference. Justifiably, deterrence theorists and other social scientists ask, What else are we to do? and the responses have been inadequate. Conditional rationality holds sway as the dominant approach to deterrence and strategy, at least in the West and certainly in the United States.

According to the logic of conditional rationality, policy makers are faced with more problems than they can handle in a perfectly logical or sequential way. Not all relevant alternatives will be known or their consequences understood. National leaders will do the best they can with the information they have available at the time, recognizing that much is missing. Frequently they must adopt the first alternative that gets them some of what they want, instead of attempting to maximize their preferred values. Deterrence theory partakes of this kind of rationality quite extensively, with the cost-benefit calculus limited by imperfect knowledge and the sunken costs of previous decisions. Then, too, organizational process and bureaucratic politics, so characteristic of government, lead to compartmentalized knowledge and fragmented accountability for decision making. Graham T. Allison, in his extensive study of the Cuban missile crisis in October 1962, has shown how these syndromes affect national security policy.[3]

Conditional rationality purports to escape from the limitations of heuristic rationality, recognized as too demanding for causal explanation or prediction about the real world. And the escape may well succeed in areas of research that are less policy oriented than is nuclear strategy, and in which the consequences of mistakes are less gruesome. Conditional rationality would work very well with rats and mazes, or professors making tenure decisions (no symmetry implied). It would also work very well with the logic of deterrence as it applies to conventional wars, including some that have not yet happened but are distinct possibilities, and others that have, for which the record has been established. John J. Mearsheimer's important study, *Conventional Deterrence*, applies the logic of conditional rationality quite successfully, and shows that deterrence will usually hold, and war thus be averted, if prospective attackers are denied the opportunity for a rapid and relatively inexpensive victory, as opposed to a costly war of attrition.[4]

This logic of conditional rationality does not, however, apply in such a straightforward way to nuclear strategy. Nuclear weapons, at least in the size and diversity in which they exist in superpower arsenals, are not like other weapons. They can destroy civilizations in the twinkling of an eye, and perhaps more than that. Of course, they can be used in small amounts, and the prospect of limited and controlled nuclear wars is advocated by some very competent strategists, using arguments that are variants of conditional rationality.[5] The logic of conditional rationality can also be applied, and has been, to the problem of deterring deliberate Soviet attack against the United States with nuclear weapons, or vice versa. According to the logic of conditional rationality, deterrence of nuclear war should look exactly like deterrence of conventional war, except that national leaders will be more nervous about the consequences— but the same logic will still hold. In order to prevent nuclear war, as for conventional war, the trick is to reduce the probability of a decisive first strike that will disable the retaliatory forces of the opponent. If each side's second-strike capability is secure from surprise attack, then it is illogical for either side to attack. Nuclear strategists who make these kinds of arguments are aware of the enormous consequences of super-power conflict, but the reasoning about nuclear deterrence is otherwise similar to the reasoning about deterring war without nuclear weapons: The defender should be able at all times to prevent a *blitzkrieg* or successful strategic military surprise by the opponent.

This notion of conditional rationality sounds very appealing, and it is, for those with long memories of the nuclear age, for the second-strike theory of deterrence called attention to the instability of a world in which both sides have large but vulnerable forces. The other implication of conditional rationality, however, as applied to nuclear deterrence, does not hold. Survivable forces are a necessary condition for deterrence, but not a sufficient one. And the sufficiency problems of conditional-deterrence rationality are considerable. Three will be discussed at some length in subsequent chapters. The first is the problem of command and control; the second, the issue of extended deterrence; and the third, the matter of societal support for national strategy. The burden of ensuing arguments is that conditional rationality, as applied to superpower nuclear deterrence, on all three counts leaves too much out.

This leaves us with the task of identifying the kind of rationality that would apply to superpower deterrent relationships. No elegant terminology is needed or preferred. It is, quite simply, the rationality of coping. Coping means that policy makers are seeking to avoid those military or political happenings that spell trouble for themselves or for their nation. There is no logic of preferred value hierarchies operating, or even an approximate logic. Such logic as exists is the logic of national interest as seen crudely through policy makers' hunches about external threats, selective memories of national historical experiences, and expectations about public reactions to their decisions.[6] Coping is what Margaret Thatcher did when she undertook a seemingly odds-against cause in the

Falkland Islands, what Kennedy did in Cuba, or what Churchill did in the locust years of World War II and especially prior to U.S. entry. Coping implies a recognition that one must live with certain conditions instead of expecting to triumph over them, and that policy makers get to choose within very bounded historical time periods. For several successive U.S. presidents, for example, their perceived choice was neither to get into Vietnam nor get out of it, but simply to pass the problem along to their successors.[7]

If we assume that policy makers facing a nuclear war or peace decision are coping more than they are engaging in heuristic or conditional rationality, interesting things follow. One implication is that they will not be searching for options but will have options inflicted upon them by organizations that have preplanned those options. In other words, peacetime planning by persons well below the level of accountable policy makers will limit the menu from which they select retaliatory options. This observation goes beyond the observation by conditional rationality strategists, to the effect that bureaucracies scan selectively for information and transmit that information to policy makers already lubricated with the bureaucracies' own perceptions and biases. This much is true. The problem, however, is more serious than conditional rationality suggests.

What is more serious than tendentiously edited information is the possibility of loss of control by political or military leaders during the early stages of war. Although this has happened in wars of the past, its occurrence in a superpower nuclear war would have far greater consequences. Loss of control might come about during the process of nuclear alerts, when the principal concern of government officials becomes not that of preventing accidental war, but that of providing for assured retaliation under all circumstances. Policy makers will enter a crisis armed with nuclear forces built according to the dictates of conditional rationality, so that the forces and their command, control, and communications will be progressively more poised to retaliate, once an attempted surprise attack has been detected. The management of these forces, once the crisis has passed a certain point, will not take place, however, according to the logic of conditional rationality, but of coping. Beyond a certain point in any crisis, if history is any indication, scanning for alternatives is replaced by fixation upon any choice that resolves the anxiety of policy makers.[8] Mistakenly, in my judgment, some writers have termed this kind of behavior on the part of political and military leaders "irrational," and perhaps it is by the standard of heuristic or conditional rationality. But those standards of reference are themselves misleading, because policy makers facing nuclear war or peace decisions are facing the loss of everything that matters, not some things that matter. Again, the conditional rationality theorist would object, noting that small nuclear wars are possible, and this author agrees. They are possible, but once the United

States and the Soviet Union are committed to war, even conventional war involving U.S. forces in direct contact with Soviet forces, eventual escalation to the employment of one or both sides' strategic nuclear forces cannot be ruled out. There are several reasons for this, among them that it is NATO's declaratory strategy to engage in nuclear escalation, if the only alternative appears to be losing a conventional war in Europe.

Now consider the absurdity of that choice, according to the logic of heuristic or conditional rationality. Having to choose between nuclear escalation and conventional defeat is a proverbial no-win situation that the heuristic or conditional rationality model would not accept. So, deterrence theorists for the most part would recommend increasing NATO's conventional forces in order to reduce reliance upon nuclear weapons, perhaps even renouncing first use or early first use of those weapons. The reality of European domestic politics and economics is such, however, that NATO is unlikely to be able to increase its conventional capabilities relative to those of the Warsaw Pact, which are, of course, not standing still. So, the U.S. president faced with a failure of conventional deterrence will have an illogical choice, which should have been avoided by his or her predecessors, according to the logic of heuristic or conditional rationality. And avoiding the choice is exactly what some strategists in the United States and abroad recommend, with proposals as varied as withdrawal of U.S. forces from Europe, or, at the opposite end of the continuum, creating a NATO conventional deterrent that is sufficient to deny Soviet attackers their objectives unless they (the Soviets) use nuclear weapons. A real U.S. president faced with the decision about what to do after conventional deterrence has failed will not be so fortunate as to have either of these options, in all likelihood. Instead, the task will be that of deciding between escalation and concession or, said with less delicacy, between suicide or surrender.

A U.S. president faced with a plausible warning of strategic nuclear surprise attack against the homeland will be coping in the same way. Conditional rationality might have dictated that the United States never be in this position, by having forces survivable against even theoretically perfect attacks, perhaps even those capable of "credible first strike" or other performances meeting the purported standard of "nuclear superiority." No defense budget that Congress will pass can build such forces, however, nor is it necessary, if we relax the requirements of conditional rationality for both U.S. and Soviet leaders. Conditional rationality requires that Soviet leaders, if they have decided that war is highly probable or inevitable, consider preemptive attack, in order to limit damage to their homeland from a U.S. retaliatory strike and in order to maximize the effectiveness of their attack by using surprise as a force multiplier.

With regard to nuclear as opposed to conventional attacks, however, the logic of conditional rationality, favorable to preemption under these circumstances, is misleading. If leaders are coping instead of trying to fulfill the requirements of rationality, they will never strike first, at least not until the opponent's warheads are detonating on their soil or well on their way. It simply makes no sense to follow the dictates of rationality to an irrational result, that is, irrational by the standards that are meaningful to policy makers. What are those standards? They are intangibles, including the instincts of the policy maker about human life and death, national honor, and one's place in history. These gut feelings will be more compelling at the time of decision than a well-calibrated decision tree of the kind that rationality theorists suggest. Leaders will be staring into Nietzsche's abyss, and the abyss will be staring back.

Robert Jervis has, I think, identified an important part of the missing link in heuristic or conditional rationality, as it applies to nuclear strategy, by noting the tendency among some U.S. strategists and policy makers to "conventionalization" of nuclear strategy.[9] Undoubtedly some deterrence theorists have drawn misleading analogies from the experience of conventional wars, given the probable consequences of any nuclear war, even a less than total one, involving superpower forces. However, the faulty reasoning attributable to "conventionalization" is only part of the misleading pattern of inference here. Not only wrongly cited historical examples but also misexplained expectations of policy makers' behavior are at work. The expectation by rationality theorists that U.S. or Soviet policy makers, faced with nuclear war, will follow a clear decision calculus, even a restricted one, contradicts what we have seen of individual and group behavior when the stakes are so high that they defy measurement. The closest analogies are the natural disasters that sometimes afflict parts of the planet, or the human-technology fiascoes such as Three Mile Island or Chernobyl. The most impressive thing about the behavior of local, state, and national officials during the Three Mile Island crisis is that for days, they had no clear information about what had happened and no clear understanding of why for even longer.[10] The issue was not the goodness or badness of their decision calculus, but the fact that they had none at all, beyond stalling for time and providing misleading—and contradictory—information to the public.

In the midst of a U.S.–Soviet nuclear crisis with a high expectation that war was possible, how policy makers on either side would react is simply unknown. Deterrence theorists can apply rationality models to tell us how the policy makers' problem might be solved around a conference table, or in a classroom, without any expectation of real consequences for failure. It will be different in the Situation Room when the expectation is not hypothetical. Two polar problems often cited by deterrence theorists have received too much emphasis in this regard. The first is the possibility that a national leader would jump the gun and launch a first strike without compelling evidence that the other side had already launched. This can happen in simulations when the participants are most concerned with postattack tabulations of paper gains and losses, but it will not happen in the real world if policy makers are coping as is suggested here. The second possibility, also much discussed, is that the U.S. strategic nuclear arsenal could be completely eliminated in a surprise counterforce attack, or the command system paralyzed, thus precluding effective retaliation. Again, rationality theories might recommend such an attack to Soviet leaders if they believed in such notions, but any Soviet leader who proposed today to launch his nuclear forces against North America would meet resistance from other Politburo members, unless a U.S. attack was already thought to be under way. Again, this contradicts the standard U.S. analysis, which argues for a determined Soviet interest in preemption, expressed in their military writings. Discussing the possibility of nuclear preemption in the Voroshilov Military Academy, however, is one thing, and doing it is quite another, as the apocryphal story about former Soviet General Secretary Nikita Khrushchev ordering a nuclear attack makes quite clear. According to the story, Khrushchev tells his military commanders to fire, although the USSR is not actually under attack. His military chief responds, "What did you say? There must be a bad connection on the phone." Khrushchev repeats, "I said you should fire our missiles." The response is, "I still cannot hear you." Finally an exasperated Khrushchev says; "If you don't fire those missiles, I will have you court-martialed and shot." To which his military leader responds; "I heard you that time—don't fire."

Against this, it may be objected that technology can override the human and group decision-making attributes that we have described as coping. Two assertions of this kind involve arguments for and against missile defenses. The first assertion is that very capable nonnuclear strategic defenses will eventually make offensive nuclear weapons obsolete and thus change the basis of nuclear deterrence. The second assertion, opposite to the first, is that mutual assured destruction is not a policy choice of a preferred deterrent strategy, but one dictated by technology, which makes protection of populations infeasible, but protection of retaliatory forces plausible.

Both arguments are rationality arguments, of a kind that we will discuss under the heading of scientism, but scientism is a specific form of a more general fallacy, which is called strategizing, or strategism, here and later. I am torn between the two terms because strategism is less awkward, but it also has another and quite respectable connotation. So strategizing will be used most frequently, with occasional references to strategism only when the term cannot be confused with its commonly accepted meaning. Strategizing, then, is strategy based on heuristic or conditional rationality when those rationalities, as applied to the problem at hand, lead to misleading or wrongheaded conclusions. This specification is important, because some problems are quite amenable to heuristic and conditional rationality; in fact, most probably are. Nuclear strategy presents special problems, however, so brackets must be drawn around those areas where rationality models lead to mistaken inferences and policy disasters. For the most part the discussion will be about how conditional rationality does this, for conditional rationality is most commonly used in Western deterrence theory. Unless otherwise specified, references to rationality refer to conditional rationality.

It should be noted, in conclusion that any work builds upon its predecessors, including works with which it is in substantial disagreement. Intellectual disagreements are part of a professional growth process, so criticism of preexisting theories is not meant as a negative judgment about the capabilities of the authors of those theories. To the contrary, I am more indebted to those whose arguments I dispute than I am to those who automatically agree with me, for the former have forced me to consider more carefully my arguments, including some persons noted in the acknowledgments. That having been said, and with sincerity, complete closure between mainstream views and some of my own is neither expected nor necessary. It is the job of professors to stir the pot, not to rejoice in received wisdom.

NOTES

1. My distinctions between types of rationalities is much influenced by Patrick M. Morgan, *Deterrence: A Conceptual Analysis*, 2d ed. (Beverly Hills, CA: Sage Publications, 1983), Ch. 4.

2. Herman Kahn, *On Escalation: Metaphors and Scenarios* (New York: Praeger, 1965).

3. See Graham T. Allison, *Essence of Decision* (Boston: Little, Brown, 1971).

4. John J. Mearsheimer, *Conventional Deterrence* (Ithaca, NY: Cornell University Press, 1983), esp. p. 63.

5. Albert Wohlstetter and Richard Brody, "Continuing Control as a Requirement for Deterring," in *Managing Nuclear Operations*, ed. Ashton B. Carter, John D. Steinbruner, and Charles A. Zraket (Washington, DC: Brookings Institution, 1987), pp. 142–96, make an argument to this effect.

6. A very interesting exploration of these and other factors that influence policy makers is Richard E. Neustadt and Ernest R. May, *Thinking in Time: The Uses of History for Decision-Makers* (New York: The Free Press, 1986).

7. For an authoritative account of U.S. Vietnam decision making, see Robert W. Komer, *Bureaucracy at War* (Boulder, CO: Westview Press, 1986).

8. See Richard Ned Lebow, *Between Peace and War* (Baltimore, MD: Johns Hopkins University Press, 1981).

9. This theme is developed in Robert Jervis, *The Illogic of American Nuclear Strategy* (Ithaca, NY: Cornell University Press, 1984). See also Jervis, Richard Ned Lebow, and Janice Gross Stein, Psychology and Deterrence (Baltimore, MD: Johns Hopkins University Press, 1985).

10. Charles Perrow, *Normal Accidents* (New York: Basic Books, 1984), Ch. 1.

1

NUCLEAR STRATEGIZING

The thesis here is that nuclear strategy is not strategy but strategizing. Strategizing is what one does when unable to use strategy. Strategy is an exacting art in theory and in practice. Noteworthy academic strategists and military commanders stand out in a crowd. Thus, the discussion begins with a notion of what strategy consists of, and moves on to the consideration of its less competent approximation—strategizing.

Strategy is the art of relating military means to the ends of policy—a definition that should not be confused with its sum total. *Grand* strategy must order national priorities on the world stage. *Military* strategy must provide for deterrence without yielding important values to opponents. Military strategy must also provide, if deterrence fails, for preferred war outcomes with available resources. Relating military means to political ends is at least a four-dimensional enterprise, as Michael Howard has recently reminded us: There are operational, societal, technical, and logistical components of the means to wage war on behalf of policy.[1] If these are not in harmony, then the policy that military strategy is designed to support will fail. A poor policy cannot be redeemed by a good strategy, but a good policy can be undone by a poor strategy.

Most U.S. nuclear strategy has had little to say about some of these dimensions compared to others. It has been dominated, for the most part, by technical discussion of the "how many warheads can dance on the head of a pin" variety. U.S. technical virtuosity has extended to the rest of the Western alliance in terms of the pride of place given to technology by policy makers and policy analysts. This has led to fixation upon the military balance as the key to successful deterrence of Soviet aggression in Europe and, ultimately, a direct Soviet attack against North America.

Thus, in Western and U.S. strategizing in particular, there are many discussions of the balance of terror, as if the balance of power can somehow be equated to the numbers of nuclear-weapons delivery vehicles deployed on either side. But a balance of terror is not a balance of power, and the difference between the single-mindedness of the one concept and the subtlety of the other illustrates the difference between strategy and strategizing.

Strategy must be grounded in an appreciation of the international system within which states conduct their foreign polices. By international system is meant the complex interactions among states and other international actors, as they accumulate into patterns over time. The international system can be discussed at a very high level of abstraction, such that policy makers find nothing useful in it. Or it can be addressed in terms of middle-range theories that attempt to fit diplomatic history into meaningful patterns. An example of the latter, which is very informative, is the study by Gordon A. Craig and Alexander L. George, *Force and Statecraft*.[2] The authors examine the process by which the Holy Roman Empire ceased to be an important international actor and was replaced by the domination of Europe in the eighteenth century by the five major national states: Britain, France, Austria, Prussia, and Russia. This is, of course, a very large question, but Craig and George are interested in the relationship between force and policy, and what that has to do with the rise of the modern European state system. They analyze the role of war in bringing about that system. Their analyses focus upon three principal effects of the wars fought for several centuries in Europe: the development of modern armed forces, competent bureaucracies, and a new theory of state.[3]

Of these, the last is fundamental. It is to Machiavelli, as much as to Clausewitz, that we owe the self-conscious development of *raison d'état*, of theories of the state that attribute to it a self-interest of its own.[4] Although students of military strategy have been properly attuned to Clausewitz, at least in the West, Machiavelli provides the highway on which the battalions of Clausewitz can proceed with such velocity. The modern armies of Europe were necessary but not sufficient conditions for the emergence of the contemporary state system. The theory of the state, as contributed to by Bodin, Hobbes, and Machiavelli, provided another necessary condition for the emergence of new ideas about the relationship between force and policy. So, too, did the French Revolution and the aftermath of the Napoleonic wars, for they produced new ideas about the nature of citizenship and new methods of raising and supporting armies.[5]

Machiavelli is the beginning of a consciousness that the state may have an enduring interest in foreign policy making distinct from the interest of the ruler, and that the international system of the day might dictate to rulers choices that in other circumstances they would not necessarily abide. Reason of state might even require that the ruler adopt a pose at home and abroad that was inconsistent with previously established images or policies. This was not, as was suggested at the time by Machiavelli's critics, intended by him as an endorsement of duplicity and violence for their own sake. Instead, Machiavelli endorsed the concept of *necessità* or a requirement that circumstances might impose on a ruler on behalf of his or her state, regardless of personal proclivities. Centuries later the French Revolution and Napoleon would provide evidence that European rulers had learned some of these lessons and not others. Those other than Napoleon learned that wars could involve stakes higher than the adjustment of territorial boundary disputes, and that one must sometimes choose sides when one would prefer to stand aside. Observers of Napoleon also learned that military and political ambition unchecked by any recognition of the friction attendant on war, as Clausewitz termed it, would eventually bring down the most imposing of edifices.[6] Napoleon's experiences also suggested that a nation's strategic reach could easily exceed its grasp, either in a military sense of resources available to do the job, or in the sense of a proper understanding of the political and military obstacles to success.

The balance of power as a central organizing concept in politicomilitary affairs grew out of the modern nation–state system in Europe and the consciousness of that system of its history. It was a concept for wars of limited aim and continuing diplomatic adjustment between wars. It required subtlety in its application to a "multipolar" power system that would characterize Europe until at least the end of World War II.[7] Wars were fought for limited ends, generally territorial gains, which were subject to being overturned in the next conflict. With the notable exception of Napoleon, the victor did not seek to overturn the system, or to rewrite the basic rules of the game. Napoleon did, and so he was removed from the board, not only once, but twice.

The Napoleonic wars, with their ideological hatred, prefigured twentieth-century wars, especially the ideological conflict between fascism and communism that marked the period preceding World War II, as well as the war itself. But this ideological hatred, severe as it was, did not totally negate the functioning of a balance-of-power system, as indicated by the temporary *rapprochement* between Nazi Germany and the USSR in the Molotov–Ribbentrop pact of 1939.[8] The postwar world was very different. Now conflicting ideologies were superimposed on nuclear weapons, or vice versa. The result is something very different from the relationship among major powers in the prenuclear era.

ABSOLUTE WAR AND THE BALANCE OF TERROR

The conjunction of absolute weapons and absolutist approaches to politics marks off the period following World War II from historical precedent. For the first time, two and only two major powers could destroy the entire society of their opponent without first defeating its army. Eventually, and even more historically unique, both became able to do this even after absorbing an attack from their presumed opponent. That is, both the United States and the Soviet Union eventually developed a "survivable" arsenal (an interesting anthropomorphism), and neither could protect its population against retaliatory strikes, even after attacking the other's arsenal first. This came to be known as the balance of terror and was thought by some writers to have become the modern equivalent to the balance of power.[9]

The balance of terror, however, was not a modern version of the balance of power. It was missing some of the key ingredients of that former system, and in some ways it turned those ingredients inside out. Politically this was most obvious in the replacement of five or six major powers by two whose nuclear forces dominated the others, even other nuclear powers. The military implications of the nuclear revolution were also discouraging for the balance of terror as a replacement for the balance of power, for a number of reasons.

First, the balance of power depended upon intentional limitation in the political objectives of warring states. England and France might go to war over territory in North America or struggle for position in Africa, but with the Napoleonic exception, they did not contest the viability of their forms of government or seek to control the entire continent of Europe. In the case of nuclear-armed superpowers, their arsenals became their own self-imposed restraints. Bloc politics developed, in which other powers and lesser lights gravitated around the nuclear centers in Washington and Moscow. For much of the postwar period, what leaders of one side perceived as their gain, they perceived as the other side's loss. There was no "spare" territory to be traded without risking a collision, with nuclear exchanges against one another's homelands. This condition so characteristic of the early cold-war years has since relaxed somewhat, and the Third World has obviously become a battleground of anxieties for U.S. and Soviet planners. Nevertheless, their involvements in the developing societies of Asia, Africa, and Latin America have for the most part been indirect, in the form of military and economic assistance to client states. Vietnam and Afghanistan are the atypical cases in which superpowers have tasked their forces to engage in direct combat in Third World situations, and in both cases the reach proved to be longer than the effective grasp. In neither case, however, was the possibility of counterintervention by the opposing superpower considered probable, and therefore the risks of war between major powers was slight to nonexistent. Thus, wars in the Third World, with the exception of the 1973 Arab–Israeli war and the attendant U.S.–Soviet crisis diplomacy, have been fought without the threat of direct conflict between U.S. and Soviet forces. The United States and the USSR cannot risk going to war directly with their own conventional forces, because the war might escalate into mutual nuclear exchanges and so remove any limitation on political objectives. This point can be taken to extremes; there is certainly a distinction between several low-yield nuclear weapons detonated in Europe or the Persian Gulf and a furious exchange of the greater number of U.S. and Soviet missiles against one another's cities. But, and this is a crucial but, policy makers, having experienced the first exchanges, will immediately begin to contemplate the possibility of escalation to the worst case. Thus, they are very fearful of crossing the threshold from nonnuclear to nuclear use, and with good reason. This caution, however, has not necessarily meant caution about the size of arsenals, the qualities of weapons, or the investments in science and technology made by the superpowers.

We have said that the first major distinction between the balance of power and the balance of terror is that the balance of terror makes wars between major powers unlikely to be limited wars. A second major difference follows from the first and from the capabilities of nuclear weapons per se, and revisits the important concept of reason of state, noted earlier. This second difference is that, in the presence of superpower nuclear forces and their awesome potential for destruction, reason of state is not obviously related to the use of force. This statement is carefully put—using "not obviously" as opposed to "irrelevant," even though the case for irrelevancy has been argued since the nuclear age began. It has been contended by many that nuclear weapons are irrelevant to diplomacy and political objectives other than mutual suicide. It is understandable that this has been the viewpoint of many critics of U.S. and Soviet policies, given the consequences, should deterrence fail. The perspective taken here, however, leads to a different conclusion.

Under present conditions, reason of state is not obviously related to the use of force, because the use of force in the traditional state system had as its mission the postwar improvement of the state's position, relative to its prewar position. Now, this statement must immediately be qualified by two amendments. First, there is a nonphysical use of force, for coercive purposes. Force may be held in the background as a plausible threat, in order to persuade the opponent not to do something (deterrence) or to induce him to stop doing something that is already under way (compellence). Second, if attacked, the state must defend itself, and so the ratio between its pre- and postwar positions is in part imposed upon it, and not entirely an abstraction of its own. Nevertheless, the differences between pre- and postnuclear conditions are more marked than their similarities. The mission of armed forces prior to nuclear weapons was to advance the territorial security of the state, to make it less vulnerable to destruction by the forces of the enemy. Nuclear weapons make this traditional logic inapplicable in some circumstances. Unconstrained nuclear attacks by U.S. and Soviet forces, and even some constrained ones, could bring about such societal destruction that the postwar military balance would be unimportant, or even unknown. This means that, if superpower nuclear war were to begin, however it occurred, it would be important to terminate it as soon as possible. There was not much thought given to terminating wars between states in the classical balance-of-power system, because they were felt to be self-terminating when one side's armies or navies prevailed over another's, and because war objectives were consensually limited. Neither self-terminating wars nor limited objectives could be assumed for a U.S.–Soviet global conflict involving their respective allies, even if nuclear weapons were not used. Writing an endgame for nuclear war between U.S. and Soviet adversaries is a task that might seem grisly, or quixotic. Unless and until it can be done, however, a key ingredient of the balance-of-power system, which stabilized that system most of the time, remains missing from the system of the present day. If wars cannot be terminated short of mutual national destruction, then they should not be fought. They can only be deterred. Deterring them, however, presupposes that they can be fought; for deterrence to work, the prospective opponent must believe that the defender has both the capability and the will to retaliate. If either is in question, deterrence is weakened.

This brings us to a third difference between a balance of power and the present balance of terror. Under the balance of power, as it obtained in the eighteenth and nineteenth centuries, wars were fought in order to deter future wars. Skirmishing with the forces of the major powers was frequently done, and major-war fighting often but less frequently, in order to impress the opponent with one's resolution to defend a certain territory or other valued objective. Under present nuclear-armed conditions, wars cannot be fought by the strongest powers in the system in order to deter. In fact, deterrence has become a substitute for war and crisis management a putative substitute for nuclear warfare. The term "crisis" has itself taken on a sanctity in the writings of U.S. behavioral scientists, and whole volumes have been devoted to its understanding. For present purposes, the point is that the management of crises by superpower nuclear antagonists has superseded the conduct of wars for the purpose of deterrence, because the latter has disproportionate risks and costs.

A fourth difference between the balance of power and the balance of terror follows from this. The nuclear-armed giants have a shared interest in avoiding nuclear war and any direct clash of arms with a significant probability of escalating into a nuclear war, which is stronger than their opposed interests in expanding their peripheral control. This shared interest in avoiding nuclear war has important implications for their relations with other states. In times of crisis it might mean that the United States would be opposed to West European perspectives, or the USSR to Chinese ones. During the Suez crisis of 1956 the United States sided with the Soviet Union and against Britain, France, and Israel, in reaction to these allies' untoward and possibly illegal action against Egypt. U.S. officials might also, however, have had in mind the need to avoid a U.S.– Soviet confrontation so contemporaneous with the Hungarian revolution. A similar pattern of U.S.–Soviet cooperation was also apparent in October 1973, when the USSR threatened unilateral intervention to rescue the beleaguered Egyptian Third Army.[10]

This shared interest in avoiding nuclear war is a mixed blessing from the standpoint of Western interests. Avoiding nuclear war is not the only political objective of the United States or the Western alliance. And nuclear weapons are depended upon by Americans and Europeans to help deter Soviet conventional attack on Europe. Contemporary NATO strategy, for example, was incorporated in NATO policy MC 14/3 in 1967, calling for a "flexible response" strategy in which both conventional and nuclear forces play a part, including U.S. strategic nuclear forces based on land, on sea, and on aircraft.[11] The strategy calls for initial resistance to a Warsaw Pact attack by NATO conventional forces alone. If NATO appears to be losing the conventional war, then it may choose deliberate escalation to the use of short- or medium-range nuclear forces based in Europe. Ultimately, continued Soviet aggression will result in the use of U.S. strategic nuclear forces. It is thought that this coupling of nuclear and conventional forces makes deterrence more stable and war less likely, although it also makes war more destructive if it occurs.

Flexible-response strategy is about as much as NATO can do politically, given the complexity of negotiating strategy among 16 diverse and democratic participants. What is consensual about NATO strategy may be as problematic as what is disputatious within the alliance. The alliance argues incessantly about who is bearing what share of the burden for ground forces, or about budgetary contributions to the common defense effort, and so forth. Fundamental strategic assumptions, however, are harder to tackle, if only because of the enormous political capital expended by all governments in getting to the strategy already agreed upon.

Acknowledging that NATO strategy is not necessarily as coherent as a textbook might be, there are still problems with the role of nuclear weapons in that strategy. These problems, as others have noted previously, result from some of the differences between a balance of power and a balance of terror. Under a balance of power, the use of force to back up diplomacy was more a matter of practicality than of intimidation. Forces were deployed or sent into combat in order to attain an objective, more than they were used as signaling devices or bargaining chips. The role of nuclear forces in NATO strategy, although they are obviously tasked for fighting if need be, is primarily that of coercive diplomacy. They are going to be introduced in order to persuade the Soviet Union to desist from continuing an attack that would otherwise succeed. And, if the attack persists, then they are going to destroy attacking armies while serving as detonators to the larger theater and intercontinental nuclear weapons that may come after them.[12]

This bargaining and escalation requirement for the use of nuclear weapons in NATO strategy partakes of two different, although somewhat related, modes of coercion. The first is the threat that is created by the semi-automatic stumbling of two combatants into a conflict they would prefer to avoid, or, if not avoid, at least confine to a lower level. The second is the threat of being able to trump an opponent with superior forces at one or more critical points during the war itself. The first of these is called "manipulation of risk" with some optimism, because it may be the risk takers who are manipulated by events, rather than the reverse. The second is called "escalation dominance," and refers somewhat vaguely to Herman Kahn's famour "ladder of escalation" metaphor, in which combatants gradually introduce more and more pressure until one subsides.[13]

There is more to say about bargaining and escalation, but the present discussion aims to tease out the ambiguity in NATO strategy with regard to the use of nuclear weapons. The shared-risk potential lies inherent in the deployment of nuclear weapons amid conventional forces that are astride the inter-German border and at other potential flashpoints. Shared risk does not involve any assumptions about decision makers' resolve under fire, once the weapons have begun to go off. On the other hand, the escalation-dominance perspective does require that policy makers have a very well defined set of objectives for which they are fighting and a clearly defined set of costs they are willing to pay for each. In the absence of either a clear hierarchy of objectives or a sensible reckoning of costs, control may be lost and policy objectives unfulfilled. Failure on both counts can be found in the U.S. strategy for conduct of the war in Vietnam. A relatively successful use of U.S. coercive diplomacy and escalation dominance occurred in the Cuban missile crisis, in which Khrushchev agreed to withdraw the missiles he had introduced.[14] It was less frequently remarked that, despite this apparent U.S. success, Khrushchev's willingness to deploy the missiles in the first place was a dramatic failure of deterrence, occurring in the face of apparent U.S. superiority in intercontinental systems.[15] It might be contended that the Soviet leader's decision to put missiles in Cuba was not a failure of deterrence in the strictest sense, since no attack on the U.S. resulted; but if deterrence is supposed to prevent provocations that could lead to nuclear war, as the installation of missiles in Cuba almost did, then Cuba is properly classified as a deterrence failure.

Under a balance-of-terror system, then, the use of the most destructive weapons becomes more political in one sense, and less in another. A nuclear war seems to have little meaningful relationship to the interests of the state. If deterrence fails, however, the control of escalation assumes paramount importance. The absolutist qualities of nuclear weapons, their unprecedented destructive power to obliterate entire societies within minutes or hours, seems to preclude a logical connection to national policy objectives. In the present day, however, U.S. and NATO allies' policy objectives cannot be attained in "peacetime" without the deployment of weapons whose use, if introduced into war, would be potentially self-destructive. Whether these potentially self-destructive nuclear forces would become actually so is very dependent upon important political variables, such as who is attacking whom, and for what. But regardless of who started a nuclear war, once it began, both participants and spectators would have an overriding interest in controlling it, if they could, if they recognized this shared interest as more important than "victory" by whatever definition. However, they might not be able to control the war, or they might not be persuaded that control was in their interest.

Much will depend upon prewar policies, if superpower antagonists or their allies are to recognize their interest in controlling war in Europe, including nuclear war, after it has begun. If, for example, U.S. and Soviet military strategists and political leaders have declared that the control of nuclear war is highly improbable, then it may diminish expectations that war can be controlled in the event. If, in addition, either side believes that it can "prevail" or win a nuclear war, even if it expands into U.S.–Soviet exchanges against their respective homelands, its prospective opponent will take heed and be motivated to increase its prewar preparedness. U.S. and Soviet leaders have said many misleading or dangerous things during the nuclear age, but these two—that nuclear war is controllable, or that it can be won in the traditional sense that conventional wars were won—are among the most misleading. The issue of fightable, controllable, and winnable nuclear wars receives further consideration later. The reason that these statements are so dangerous does not lie in the probability of their truth or falsity, but in their ability to influence the perceptions and expectations of those who will have to deter wars and fight them: the U.S. and Soviet political and military leaderships. The opposing arguments, however, that nuclear war is controllable or that victory is possible, must not be taken as simplistic debating points or propagandistic volleys for the sake of intimidating the opponent. Nuclear war is not controllable in the way that prenuclear war was, at least not between superpowers and not in Europe. And victory in the traditional sense is not possible unless the war is deliberately controlled, which in the event may mean that one side is prepared to concede more than the other.[16] As we will see later, this is one of the important differences that active defenses, including ballistic missile defenses, such as the Reagan-proposed SDI, might make. A side equipped with defenses might mistakenly believe that victory was possible or war controllable; in other words, it might believe that we had returned to the conditions of the balance of power, escaping from the limitations of the balance of terror. Were we to do so, it is not obvious that we would be better off. It depends upon the yardstick, as we shall see.

This point about defenses brings us to another difference between balance-of-power systems and the present balance of terror. The emergence of the modern national state in Europe, and the eventual spread of that model of territorial sovereignty and *raison d'état* elsewhere, allowed for the replacement of a relatively anarchic European system by a relatively predictable one. Now, predictable does not mean peaceful, and the role of war in the making of the modern state system has been noted by eminent historians.[17] But predictability does have its virtues, and keeping track of the interests of five or six major powers that are relatively consensual about ideological issues is far easier than keeping track of several thousand autonomous fiefdoms and principalities. All other things being equal, a more predictable international system, in terms of the accuracy of knowledge among major actors about one another's intentions, is apt to be less bellicose than a less predictable one.

The present balance of terror seems superficially to have the virtue of improved predictability relative to the balance-of-power system, because there are now two major powers instead of five or six. This appearance of predictability under the balance of terror is deceiving, however, because the aims of states are known only in general ways, and because U.S. and Soviet interests are so widely dispersed globally. In addition, the potential unpredictability of the balance-of-terror system is enormous, should the spread of nuclear weapons bring diverse nuclear arsenals into the hands of "threshold" states, many of which have their own regional scores to settle.[18] The Nuclear Non-Proliferation Treaty gives evidence of the superpowers' awareness of their shared interest in limiting the spread of nuclear weapons to countries that do not already have them. Nuclear arsenals in the hands of India and Pakistan, Israel and Arab neighbors, Iraq and Iran, or other regional antagonists could prove to be destructive to their users, victims, and perhaps to the system itself. This prospect of catalytic war, in which the United States and the Soviet Union are drawn into conflict with one another, growing out of a nuclear war begun by regional combatants outside Europe, can be exaggerated, but it is a realistic and growing concern for the international community.[19] The nuclear arsenals of Britain, France, and the People's Republic of China represent cases of horizontal proliferation to which we have already grown accustomed, and some argue that additional dispersion of nuclear weapons throughout the world would supplement a multipolar nuclear-power condition that is already in place. It can still be argued, however, that the superpower arsenals are unique and that the prospect of catalytic war growing out of newly minted nuclear-armed states with regional grudges to settle is stronger than it is for those states whose arsenals are now deployed.

There is another way in which the predictability of the present balance-of-terror system is more apparent than real. No one can predict the reactions of U.S. or Soviet leaders under the stress of nuclear crisis. Our best example of a two-sided superpower nuclear showdown is the Cuban missile crisis, which occurred in a period of extreme imbalance (in favor of the United States) in strategic nuclear forces and in the two sides' conventional forces that could be brought to bear in the immediate theater of operations. A future nuclear crisis would take place under the shadow of two forces, neither of which could be annihilated preemptively by the other. This mutual survivability of forces might help to defuse the crisis by facing each prospective attacker with the apparent hopelessness of knocking out the other side's retaliatory arsenal; but it might have the opposite effect. If national leaders are not calculating, rational actors, but are prone to launch into war for reasons of pride or fear, then calculations of the prewar balance might not deter them, but attract them to war. There is a fine line between deterrence and provocation. Forces felt to be secure deterrents in normal peacetime conditions may, during a crisis with potentially ultimate values at stake, turn into provocations in the minds of opponents. Now, there are those who will argue that U.S. and Soviet forces are so colossal that no sane leader could ever contemplate a successful first strike, and they are right, if by "successful" is meant a sober, contemplative calculation made in the armchair by the fire.

Neither Soviet nor U.S. leaders, however, would go to war in this fashion. Perfectly sane leaders who perceived a nuclear threat to destroy military forces or societal values might make erroneous calculations that seemed to have mitigating force. For example, leaders might calculate that, although their arsenal was large, it was not entirely survivable against the worst attack that an opponent could launch. Therefore, they must launch some of their force against the opponent "on warning" or "under attack" on the basis of indicators suggesting that deterrence has failed.[20] Launch on warning means on tactical warning that an attack has actually begun, as opposed to strategic warning that an attack is being planned or is probably imminent.[21] The (tactical) survivability of the U.S. strategic "Triad" of land-based intercontinental ballistic missiles (ICBMs), submarine-launched ballistic missiles (SLBMs), and bombers carrying cruise missiles has been a matter of dispute within the U.S. defense community since the Carter administration. The Scowcroft Commission may have found a political solution to the issue of land-based missile vulnerability (lack of prelaunch survivability) in its 1983 package of MX, Midgetman, and arms control, but the current U.S. ICBM force remains dubiously survivable, even launched under attack.[22]

Not too much should be made of these statistical vulnerabilities, for they are fine calculations, pale in comparison to the gross levels of fear that would grip policy makers who were forced to contemplate using nuclear weapons in anger for the first time since Hiroshima. Again, this might argue for a predictable self-deterrence of both sides in all but the most desperate circumstances.[23] The interest here and in Washington or Moscow, however, will be primarily in those situations in which self-deterrence is not operative and attack becomes an option actually being considered by policy makers. In those situations, as previously noted, the apparent predictability of peacetime nuclear decision making may give way to crisis or wartime unpredictability.

One of the reasons for this possible gap between peacetime and crisis or wartime decision making becomes apparent if we consider not just the top policy-making levels of either superpower, but the lower levels as well. These are usually called "administrative" or "organizational" levels, implying that they are sub-cabinet-level and below the level at which presidents, prime ministers, and other key leaders formulate policy with their principal advisors. It is well to recognize, however, that the organizational or bureaucratic forces in a democratic government, and possibly in autocratic ones as well, may be "below" the political principals, but are rarely "beneath" them in lasting influence. Mr. Gorbachev is now discovering this unhappy fact as he attempts to reform the Soviet economy, and many a U.S. president or British prime minister has also learned it the hard way.[24] The permanent bureaucracy remains in place, while the temporary bureaucracy of political appointees comes and goes. This sometimes means that the bureaucracy (meaning the permanent civil service one) develops political interests at variation with those of the administration in power, although this happens less frequently in Great Britain than it does in the United States. But something more subtle takes place when political decision is translated into bureaucratic implementation, even when political interests at the top are not opposed by those below.

The more subtle problem is that large bureaucratic organizations cannot be moved very rapidly to do anything, and especially to improvise. Moreover, the organizations that are entrusted with the command, control, and communications (C3) of nuclear forces have special properties that make even more uncertain how the complex interaction of parts of the organization, under unexpected stress and possible destruction, would function. It would not do to misrepresent this as a problem of refusal to obey orders, as such. This happens infrequently in military organizations, compared to their civilian counterparts, although it does occur. The problem with complex organizations, especially those that are technically highly complex, is that they are charged with combining apples and oranges into a composite whole that is supposed to work with utmost predictability. The apples are those things that an organization must do to deal with standard operational problems, the kinds of problems that occur on a day-to-day basis and for which personnel and software are preprogrammed.[25] These apples can be built into organizational repertoires and so dealt with summarily, without, as it were, thinking.

Oranges, on the other hand, are things that organizations must do when the environment does not conform to expectations and rapid changes in stimuli cross the threshold of preestablished routines. These nonroutine stimuli can cause disruptions of organizational performance in two ways. First, component failure in one or more parts of the organization may occur separately. Thus, land-based missiles might take off, but bombers, for whatever reason, might be grounded. Second, and more complex than parts in isolation, the interdependency of the system may defeat itself. The relationships established among the various parts of the system may have failed to anticipate the actual conditions that are now taking place, so that the management system makes wrong inferences. This problem of organizationally maladroit inferences could take place not only after war began, but also during the alerting of nuclear forces, especially if nuclear forces were kept on high levels of alert for too long.[26] Consider, for example, the problem of attack assessment. In order to terminate a nuclear war before it escalated out of control, we would want to be able to ascertain how much damage, and to what targets, the United States or its allies had sustained. We would also want to know this information about the Soviet Union. The fidelity of postattack assessment, however, is quite different from that of peacetime assessment. Mechanistic models of nuclear combat often presuppose information environments that are unrealistic, given the probable stresses to command and control systems that even limited nuclear strikes will cause.[27]

These observations about the apparent, but misleading, sense of predictability in the balance of terror might seem to be rooted in intrastate rather than systemic causes. This is not altogether so. Bureaucratic behavior has its internal dynamics and causes, but the behavior of nuclear command and control systems of the superpowers is also responsive to their shared strategic and structural predicament. That predicament derives from a system in which the most carefully planned first strike can probably (one can never speak with certainty in these things) not bring about outcomes very different from a poorly coordinated retaliation. It might be thought that either a "splendid" counterforce first strike that disarmed the opponent, or a "decapitation" of its political and military leadership, could provide something very close to a superior outcome in nuclear combat.[28] These are more strategies for the blackboard than they are realistic paths to victory with current or imminently foreseeable superpower strategic nuclear forces. Drastic reductions in force size, changes in their character, or the deployment of defenses might change that calculation. Therefore, those steps should not be taken lightly without careful estimation of their fallout with regard to the stability of the U.S.–Soviet strategic balance. In addition, systemic forces affect the performances of command systems in a direct way. U.S. and Soviet systems are obviously sensitive to the behaviors and performances of one another, on a continuing basis in peacetime and with acute sensitivity during crisis. The command systems are tightly coupled to sensors, communications, and data-fusion centers, which monitor the opposite number's activities to determine which are routine and which are atypical. U.S. and Soviet command and control systems are thus synergistic in a peculiar way, in that each is somehow dependent upon steady-state feedback about the status of the other. Notice that either side, for example, obviously raising its level of alert, might provoke immediate reaction from the opposite side, with the first side then counterreacting, and so on, *ad infinitum*. Awareness does not necessarily mean a deterioration in relations or a crisis getting out of control. What is suggested here is that the superpower command systems are in the habit of observing what the other will do and attempting to preformat that expectation into the standard operating procedures of each system. As a result, the two national systems are coupled interactively because the behavior of each system is responsive to changes in the expected or actual behavior of its counterpart.[29]

The preceding paragraph referred to the stability of the strategic nuclear balance. This is a term of reference in military studies that implies that crises are manageable and/or that arms races are not accelerating beyond control. Crisis stability resides in the short-term expectation that neither side has a credible first-strike capability or a willingness to attack preemptively for fear of being struck first. Arms-race stability lies in the long-run expectation that neither side can gain a significant advantage from deploying newer technologies or more weapons of the same kind, relative to the preexisting baseline. U.S.–Soviet Strategic Arms Limitation Talks (SALT) during the 1970s are an example of an effort to support arms-race stability. The "Hot Line" or Direct Communications Link between Washington and Moscow contributes to crisis stability.

Herein lies a difference between balance-of-power and balance-of-terror systems that should also be noted. In the classical European balance-of-power system, the forces conducive to arms-race stability or instability also tended to have the same effects with regard to crisis stability. One could fight numerous small wars without necessarily disturbing the balance of the whole. Flexible alignment and limited means for warfare meant that a collapse of crisis stability did not mean the collapse of the system, until 1914, when those two conditions, in addition to other balancing conditions, disappeared. Under present conditions, powers fearful of losing the arms race will also assume that such a loss jeopardizes their prospects with regard to crisis stability. Worst-case assessments can always posit that a putative advantage in the hands of the opponent of the future adds to the coercive power of that opponent in the present. Thus, both U.S. and Soviet spokesmen have argued that the development of strategic ballistic missile defenses (BMD) by the other superpower will destabilize the arms race and might bring about crisis instability. Each, however, sees its own defenses as stabilizing, because each puts the best face on its own intentions, which are obviously not threatening. The largest misunderstandings between the United States and the Soviet Union during the past several decades have developed over this issue of the impact of defenses on stability. As will be seen later, much depends on whether one takes a one-sided or a two-sided view of the problem, and on what is assumed to be happening to other parts of the nuclear arsenals. There is also the issue of the political relations between the superpowers, frequently too neglected in atomic discourse. The point here is that, in the balance-of-terror system that we have been discussing, defenses are not obviously defensive in the way that castles and moats were. They may have offensive strategic implications when combined with other force components. This does not mean that any and all active defenses are undesirable—more on that will follow; but it does mean that the balance-of-terror system is unique and that certain things follow from that, which are disregarded at our peril.

CONCLUDING OBSERVATIONS

Prenuclear and nuclear strategy contrast markedly. This is not surprising, given the differences between a prenuclear balance-of-power system and a postnuclear balance-of-terror system. Perhaps the two systems and strategies have been contrasted too much in this discussion. Later it will be noted that some strategists feel that the difference between preatomic and postatomic military thinking is not as great as has been alleged.

Two endnotes might qualify the seemingly skeptical and one-sided view presented above, relative to the difference between a balance of power and a balance of terror. First, it is not that *a* nuclear weapon is incommensurate with any conceivable political objective, or a few weapons. The number of weapons available and their sheer destructive potential make them incommensurate with plausible policy objectives. If the superpowers were to reduce their arsenals of nuclear weapons by orders of magnitude—through arms control, for example—then the aggregate numbers might not make the prospect of war so daunting. Those numbers would have to be very close to zero, however, if not at zero, before unprotected publics would feel that nuclear weapons were continuous in evolution with their predecessors, whatever professional strategists declared to be the case.[30]

Second, in terms of arms-race stability, the balance of terror is more predictable than the classical prenuclear balance-of-power system. At least on a day-to-day basis, the two-way relationship between the United States and the Soviet Union is certainly more stable than the relationship among the great powers of Europe, say, in the eighteenth century. The balance of terror becomes less predictable when the relationship between or among major powers changes from routine to crisis conditions. Crises, even if fumbled, did not destroy the international political system, although World War I did result in the dismantling of at least three major empires in Europe. Mishandling of a superpower nuclear crisis could bring about unprecedented societal destruction, for combatants and bystanders. Thus, the costs of crisis instability in the nuclear age mitigate against too much optimism about the problem of arms-race stability, compared to the balance of terror.

Third, nuclear weapons do not make conventional forces or conventional-force balances less important. Exactly the opposite is true. Because nuclear weapons are used for coercion instead of fighting, conventional forces are the instruments with which war must be waged if it is to be waged at all. But conventional war involving superpower interests, even if their own forces are not committed to it, takes place under a nuclear shadow. One must be careful here not to endorse some kind of mystical argument that the quantity of violence in the international system is a universal constant—less nuclear war must mean more conventional war, and so forth. The problem is not so simple. Conventional forces for nuclear powers serve two purposes. Like traditional conventional forces, they are instruments for denying the opponent physical possession of one's territory or other objectives, or for attaining through direct application of force one's own objectives. Unlike conventional forces before the nuclear age, however, superpower armies, navies, and fleets are also fuses that are lighted as soon as they are engaged in conflict with nuclear-armed opponents or their surrogates. And the end of those fuses is the annihilation of the societies of nuclear combatants, regardless of how well their conventional forces perform.

NOTES

1. See Michael Howard, "The Forgotten Dimensions of Strategy," reprinted in Howard, *The Causes of Wars*, (Cambridge, MA: Harvard University Press, 1984), pp. 246–64.

2. Gordon A. Craig and Alexander L. George, *Force and Statecraft* (New York: Oxford University Press, 1983).

3. Craig and George, p. 5.

4. See Felix Gilbert, "Machiavelli: The Renaissance of the Art of War," in *Makers of Modern Strategy: From Machiavelli to the Nuclear Age,* ed. Peter Paret (Princeton, NJ: Princeton University Press, 1986), pp. 11–31.

5. A. J. P. Taylor, *From Napoleon to Lenin* (New York: Harper Torchbooks, 1966), pp. 1–11.

6. Karl Von Clausewitz, *On War,* ed. and trans. Michael Howard and Peter Paret (Princeton, NJ: Princeton University Press, 1976), Ch. 7, pp. 119–21.

7. The concept of the balance of power is explicated in Hans J. Morgenthau and Kenneth W. Thompson, *Politics Among Nations* (New York: Knopf, 1985), Chs. 11–14. This is the sixth edition of Morgenthau's widely used book, revised by Professor Thompson.

8. The balance-of-power system was often supported by ineffective intelligence systems, leading to surprising changes of alignment, which ironically provided flexibility for the system. See Ernest R. May, "Capabilities and Proclivities," in *Knowing One's Enemies: Intelligence Assessment before Two World Wars,* ed. Ernest May, (Princeton, NJ: Princeton University Press, 1984), pp. 503–42.

9. An interesting discussion of the development of nuclear strategy, including its early years, is found in Lawrence Freedman, *The Evolution of Nuclear Strategy* (New York: St. Martin's Press, 1981).

10. Barry M. Blechman and Douglas Hart, "The Political Utility of Nuclear Weapons: The 1973 Middle East Crisis," in *Strategy and Nuclear Deterrence,* ed. Steven E. Miller (Princeton, NJ: Princeton University Press, 1984), pp. 273–97.

11. On NATO strategy, see Stanley R. Sloan, *NATO's Future: Toward a New Transatlantic Bargain* (Washington, DC: National Defense University Press 1985).

12. For more discussion of this, see Stephen J. Cimbala, *Extended Deterrence: The U.S. and NATO Europe* (Lexington, MA: D. C. Heath/Lexington Books, 1987).

13. See Herman Kahn, *On Escalation: Metaphors and Scenarios* (New York: Praeger, 1965).

14. See Graham T. Allison, *Essence of Decision* (Boston: Little, Brown, 1971).

15. For counterorthodox interpretations of the Cuban crisis, see Richard Ned Lebow, "The Cuban Missile Crisis: Reading the Lessons Correctly," *Political Science Quarterly* 98, No. 3 (Fall 1983):431–58.

16. On this issue see Colin S. Gray, "Escalation Control and Crisis Management," in *Nuclear Strategy and National Style,* ed. Colin Gray (Lanham, MD: Hamilton Press, 1986), Ch. 6, pp. 169–200.

17. See the excellent pieces anthologized in Paret, ed., *Makers of Modern Strategy,* above.

18. Leonard S. Spector, *Nuclear Proliferation Today* (New York: Vintage Books, 1984).

19. Henry S. Rowen, "Catalytic Nuclear War," in *Hawks, Doves and Owls: An Agenda for Avoiding Nuclear War,* ed. Graham T. Allison, Albert Carnesale, and Joseph S. Nye, Jr. (New York: Norton, 1985), Ch. 6, pp. 148–66.

20. For a discussion of launch under attack, see Office of Technology Assessment, *MX Missile Basing* (Washington, DC: U.S. GPO, September 1981), Ch. 4, pp. 147–64.

21. See Richard K. Betts, *Surprise Attack: Lessons for Defense Planning* (Washington, DC: Brookings Institution, 1982), pp. 248–49.

22. There is some hair splitting in distinctions among launch on warning, launch under attack, and other variations of the same decision. Ashton B. Carter provides the sensible guidance: "LUA is simply taken to mean launch of some or all ICBMs before the attack on them is complete, with a variety of precise sequences possible." See Carter, "Assessing Command System Vulnerability," in *Managing Nuclear Operations*, ed. Ashton B. Carter, John D. Steinbruner, and Charles A. Zraket (Washington, DC: Brookings Institution, 1987), p. 579. It is generally assumed that Soviet submarines patrolling off the U.S. Atlantic and Pacific coasts could detonate warheads above ICBM fields and so pin down missiles in their silos, at least temporarily, thus precluding a coordinated LUA. See Carter, "Assessing Command System Vulnerability," pp. 580–81.

23. I am indebted to Donald M. Snow for this very à propos terminology.

24. See Stephen M. Cohen, *Sovieticus: American Perceptions and Soviet Realities* (New York: Norton, 1986), esp. pp. 73–98.

25. For an excellent discussion of this as it applies to strategic nuclear command organizations, see Bruce G. Blair, *Strategic Command and Control: Redefining the Nuclear Threat* (Washington, DC: Brookings Institution, 1985), pp. 65–78.

26. See Paul Bracken, *The Command and Control of Nuclear Forces* (New Haven, CT: Yale University Press, 1983), esp. pp. 5–73.

27. Bracken, *The Command and Control of Nuclear Forces*, pp. 105–28.

28. See John D. Steinbruner, "Nuclear Decapitation," *Foreign Policy* 45 (Winter 1981–82):16–28.

29. Bracken, *The Command and Control of Nuclear Forces*, pp. 59–68.

30. I am grateful to David W. Tarr for calling my attention to this point. See also Michael Mandelbaum, *The Nuclear Revolution* (Cambridge: Cambridge University Press, 1985).

2

STRATEGY AND CONTROL IN THE NUCLEAR AGE

The development of nuclear weapons spawned the notion that there is something in general called a "nuclear strategy," distinct from strategy in general. If strategy in general is the plausible connection of military means to political ends, then nuclear strategy is not unique. Only the role of nuclear weapons is, because of their unprecedented destructiveness. Nuclear strategy divorced from strategy proper is strategizing, a self-contained and poorer approximation of strategy. Strategizing, as opposed to strategy, commits the following disservices: It confuses the logic of nonmilitary affairs, especially economics, with the logic of war; it assumes that war can be treated with a degree of precision and exactitude that is, in fact, impossible under the circumstances; it ignores the reciprocal relationship between war and policy; and it fails to ground the phenomena of war and coercion in the societies from which they are generated, so that the analysis of war is asocietal and ahistorical.

There are as many ways to group nuclear strategies as there are strategies themselves. Almost all groupings are to some extent arbitrary. Here we offer a taxonomy based on the relationship between nuclear flexibility, or the degree to which we can expect that control will be exercised over forces during alerts and wars, and the scope of the conflict, or its longevity. These two dimensions, longevity and flexibility, can be used to characterize assumptions about nuclear deterrence and warfare in military strategy.

Nuclear wars can, at least the principle, be long or short. And political leaders can exercise tight or loose control over their forces during crises and wars. Much of the nuclear strategizing in the West, however, ignores the possibility of long wars or of attenuated control. Somehow, planners frequently assume that wars will be short and the control of policy makers over events fine tuned. Consider, as an illustration, the proliferation of game-theory analyses of nuclear combat during the 1950s and 1960s.[1] Game theory was originally intended as a tool for helping to think abstractly about the choices that might have to be made in a conflict situation. It assumed a common frame of reference, based upon shared cultural expectations between antagonists. Within this common frame of reference, one could deduce the preferred course of action in a crisis or war. A "payoff matrix" would tell the analyst whether the marginal utility of not striking back was preferable to the marginal cost of retaliation. Two popular games applied to nuclear strategy were "chicken" and "prisoner's dilemma," in which the payoff tables resembled very stark choices in a two-person game.

Gradually, what had been intended as an academic tool became a substitute for political and military thinking. The admonitions of Clausewitz about the effects of friction, the wear and tear of crises and wars on military and political organizations and their leaders, were somehow omitted from the calculations. In counterpoint, many mathematical Luddites decided to ignore altogether the lessons of game theory and other applied statistical decision models. Especially after Vietnam and the notoriety about "body counts" and other irrelevant measurements of military effectiveness, the statistical analysis of military conflicts was fighting a rearguard action. There is, in fact, a very lively tradition in the United States and elsewhere of statistical analysis within the framework of historical study of military campaigns. Trevor N. Dupuy is probably its best-known U.S. contributor.[2]

It was easy to take cheap shots at the statistical analysis of combat, especially nuclear combat, for which (in the case of U.S.–Soviet conflict or any nuclear war in Europe) there was no historical precedent. And some analysis was so simplistic as to invite derision. Neither policy makers nor military strategists, however, could escape the requirement to think more rigorously about what they would be prepared to do if nuclear war ever really broke out. Taking deterrence out of the laboratory and into the field was what the credibility of nuclear strategy was all about.

"Into the field" in this instance meant developing war plans for the use of nuclear weapons, including strategic nuclear weapons. The history of U.S. strategic nuclear war planning has been told in other places and will not be fully recounted here.[3] The short form of this history is a continuing struggle to develop war plans that are credible to opponents (thus deterring them) and to ourselves (avoiding self-deterrence). The issues that have been most confounding for U.S. war planners have been the two issues noted above: maintaining control over nuclear forces during crises and war, and coping with the possibility of a war that extends beyond the first few exchanges on both sides.

In both cases, the subject matter lends itself to misstatement, sometimes in a good cause. Some academic students of deterrence theory rightly fear that policy planners might become too enthralled with the pursuit of extended war capabilities, to the detriment of crisis stability and deterrence credibility. Also, expectations that nuclear war would be easy to control might be disappointed in the event, and policy makers could find themselves in a war for which they lacked the command, control, and communications (C3) capabilities. Although pertinent, these fears of extended war capabilities detrimental to crisis stability and of exaggerated expectations for postattack control can be overstated. The requirements for continuing control of nuclear war can probably be met only if the war is limited. An extended or protracted war between superpowers would require that substantial forces be withheld for coercive bargaining. Otherwise, the war could not be ended on any acceptable terms. So, a short war in which arsenals are rapidly exhausted is very different from a long war, which by definition requires that capabilities be used very selectively and discriminately. Deterrence theorists have tended to argue that preparedness for the short war is good, and for the longer, bad, on account of their assumption that preparing for extended nuclear war is mischievous. The assumption is valid if the extended nuclear war is conceived of as a total war, but if not, then extended war may be compatible with expectations of continuing control, instead of contradictory to them.

MAINTAINING CONTROL

The nominal solutions to the problems of maintaining control over nuclear forces seem readily apparent. In the U.S. case, nuclear weapons can be fired only on the express authorization of the president, who is the constitutionally established commander in chief of all U.S. military forces. This is the legalistic premise on which U.S. war planning must be based. The premise, however, must be qualified, for various reasons. The president might be killed in the early phases of a war, during a surprise attack and before he could authorize retaliation. Presidential successors are specified in the U.S. Constitution and in the Presidential Succession Act of 1947; however, they must somehow be identified in sequence as the successors and be given the information about what is happening to their military forces and other assets that are under attack.

It can be assumed that neither the United States nor the Soviet Union has failed to provide *de facto* for the possibility of leaders being presumed dead or unavailable to make decisions.[4] How the lapse of control can be prevented without a slippage of authority, which is a legal and judicial concept, is a problem that the two systems will undoubtedly solve in very different ways. If only because more has been disclosed about how the

U.S. system is likely to operate, we can speculate with more confidence about it.

Paul Bracken uses the analogy of nuclear "safety catch" and a "trigger" to describe what might be the kind of arrangement made by the United States and possibly other Western states to prevent decapitation. In this analogy, the U.S. president is not a nuclear trigger, without whose orders the force lies paralyzed. Instead, she or he functions as a safety catch that prevents retaliation.[5]

While the authority to order nuclear retaliation remains inherent in the president and the president's lawful successors, the capability to retaliate can be delegated as the circumstances dictate. And the circumstances might so dictate. There is substantial evidence that the Soviet Union sees suppression of the opponent's command and control system as an inviting target, once their political leadership has decided that war is necessary or unavoidable.[6] Articles in U.S. newspapers and academic studies have suggested that, if necessary, the United States is including plans to return the favor, although attacks against the highest-ranking Soviet officials might be withheld until the later stages of a war.[7]

In practice, then, the capacity to launch in retaliation is distributed at multiple points in the U.S. command system, and arrangements have probably been made for those military commanders of U.S. forces that have been assigned nuclear weapons in peacetime to use them in lieu of tolerating their destruction. This means that there are many fingers on the trigger and a single safety catch, the U.S. National Command Authority (the president, the secretary of defense, and/or their successors in the military chain of command). If the NCA is destroyed, the nuclear deterrent is not paralyzed.

This is small consolation, however, assuming that we want nuclear forces that can do more than execute a large thermonuclear dump on Soviet cities. Execution of strikes that are more subtle and more complicated than that requires the continuing control of forces, even during war. Here the lay understanding of how nuclear war might be fought differs from that of the strategist, who is more likely to assume that U.S.–Soviet nuclear conflict would begin with a regional and limited nuclear exchange and then escalate into war against Soviet and U.S. homelands. The "bolt from the blue" attack is deemed less probable, although it is a worst-case benchmark against which preparations should be made for caution's sake.[8] Even more probable than a general nuclear war that grew from a limited nuclear war would be a conventional war in Europe that then escalated into regional nuclear war, or strategic homeland exchanges, or both.[9]

Even before war broke out, U.S. and allied NATO leaders would want to ensure control over the process for alerting conventional and nuclear forces. The management of alerts is a tricky business. A provocative alert would bring about the very opposite of what policy makers are trying to accomplish: a winding down of tension and the avoidance of war. A less visible alert, or an unwillingness to go on alert when it is obviously called for, suggests weakness and indecision. But alerts cannot always be fine tuned.[10] During the Cuban missile crisis of 1962, U.S. naval forces executed standard operating procedures, which tracked, and in some cases forced to the surface, Soviet submarines in the Atlantic, Caribbean, and Pacific oceans.[11] During the Arab–Israeli war of 1973, U.S. carrier task forces in the Mediterranean were shadowed by Soviet maritime forces, which were obviously poised for imminent attacks against the U.S. carrier groups.[12] In the same crisis, an apparent threat from the Soviet Union to intervene unilaterally if the Egyptian Third Army was destroyed by Israel prompted a U.S. Defense Condition 3 (Defcon 3) alert for its forces worldwide.[13] If the United States has difficulty in managing the details of its own alerts, the process would be even more cumbersome for NATO. The NATO alliance has never gone fully on alert, and its procedures are such that political authorization for the use of nuclear weapons might require a bureaucratic hopscotch that consumed from 24 to 60 hours.[14]

Reviewing some of the findings from academic literature on nuclear command and control systems, there are several cautions that must be advised in relying upon those sources for information about this topic. First, many of the persons most knowledgeable about command and control systems are not in a position, either legally or bureaucratically, to write about what they know. Second, much of the academic literature is written by former government officials or defense consultants who have assembled in their minds a picture of how things work, based on access to classified materials, and then retrofitted the picture onto a template of open sources for publication. Third, on account of the second factor, and because of the normal herding instincts of academics and policy analysts, there is a circle of persons writing about nuclear command and control for public consumption, whose bona fides cannot be challenged because admission to the group is by cooptation. Fourth, we know very little that is reliable about Soviet nuclear command and control, and much of our guesstimation is a projection of what we would do in the same circumstances onto Soviet planners.

Allowing for these cautions, one can translate from the academic and bureau jargon about U.S. strategic and other nuclear command and control to some contestable, although interesting, propositions.

The first of these is that the U.S. nuclear command system operates very well in peacetime, when it is subjected to few if any stresses. How it would operate in wartime, even before nuclear detonations began occurring on U.S. soil, is uncertain. Few of the experts are willing to venture a guess in the open literature. Among those who are, Desmond

Ball has suggested that control over any U.S.–Soviet nuclear exchange, once more than a few tens of weapons have been fired into Soviet or U.S. territory, is improbable.[15] Ashton B. Carter distinguishes the command system that would have to survive a comprehensive attack against U.S. forces and C3 systems from the system that would have to provide for flexible and continuous prosecution of a nuclear war. The former system need not be very supple; it suffices if it can guarantee retaliation against a large but perhaps not comprehensive Soviet target set. The latter system, designed for flexibility during a war of uncertain duration, need not survive a comprehensive attack, which by definition would not be occurring in a protracted war.[16]

One can quibble with these estimates, although they are as good as any available to the public. The difficulty is that there have been no critical experiments to test the hypotheses, as scientists like to say. Hopefully this lack of experience will continue; it is a happy omission. In the absence of data, one can turn to simulation through the use of computers and human interaction games designed by experts. Or scenarios can be developed that are limited only by the limits of human imagination. Military services play both classified and unclassified war games, which are designed to inject more realism into an otherwise routine and stultified planning process.

There is, however, no substitute for the real thing. The closest the United States and the Soviet Union have come to the real thing has been the Cuban missile crisis of 1962. Authoritative accounts of that episode do not provide much reassurance about how well we would get through a similar crisis today.

First, in the Cuban case, the United States had overwhelming nuclear- and conventional-force superiority relative to the forces of the USSR at that time. Khrushchev did not have sufficient cards even for credible bluffing. His entire strategy depended on not being caught. Once his strategy was exposed, he was forced to back down, although the Kennedy administration was careful not to humiliate him in an obvious way. The United States could afford to start with a "quarantine" or blockade, because we knew that, should this initial move fail, the ante could be increased with conventional forces capable of invading Cuba and/or isolating it, although not without some significant costs in the case of invasion.

Second, the performances of U.S. policy makers, including the president, left much to be desired. Kennedy assembled an *ad hoc* team of "Executive Committee" members picked for personal reasons, as well as for their expertise. The president's brother was a key player in decision making throughout the crisis (imagine presidential brothers in other administrations being assigned such a role). The ExCom deliberations first resulted in a recommendation for air strikes against Cuba, to be followed by an invasion if necessary; only belatedly and under presidential pressure did they finally resolve upon the blockade as a first step.[17] Several intelligence mishaps during the crisis almost resulted in its getting out of control, including the inability to coordinate the timing of U–2 reconnaissance flights over Cuba and elsewhere with the political requirements of the president for careful signaling to the USSR.

Third, and further to our consideration of present-day organizational behavior, what was desired at the top of the organizational pyramid was not always perceived in the same way by those at the middle or lower levels. This might seem to be typical bureaucratic behavior, as indeed it is, but it has special consequences for nuclear command organizations. Most organizations are not dealing with matters in which there is no time to correct mistakes, especially mistakes of certain kinds. Nuclear command organizations are both especially dependent upon technology and especially prone to short-term information glut. The result is that they may fall victim not only to errors of the external policy-making system over which they have no control; they may also fall prey to their own self-generated and self-sustaining errors. This is significant because the second kind of mistake is harder to detect, especially in time to do any good. A well-known illustration, from the Cuban crisis, was the Air Force response to policy makers' inquiries about the possibility of conducting a "surgical" air strike. The Air Force responded with a plan for a strike that was anything but surgical, thus following the well-known practice among astute college students: If you do not care for the question as asked, answer the question you wanted.

Why these slippages between top and bottom (or middle) of organizations occur is a matter of some dispute among theorists and managers. Some frequent explanations include the following: Organizational guerrillas have their own incentives and capabilities to sabotage plans developed higher up; strategic planning, or planning of long range and broad scope, almost always occurs in ignorance of many short-term forces; top-level planners estimate the future environment within very stable ranges of variation, and any deviation from this standard expectation makes plans irrelevant. There is also the well-documented fact that organizations do not really have consensual goals, except at a very broad level of abstraction. Military organizations, for example, are divided into communities of professional expertise and interest, although all may wear the same basic service uniform. U.S. naval aviators, surface-ship sailors, and submariners would all fight on the same side in wartime, but in peacetime they fight professionally and bureaucratically against one another. The same holds true for U.S. Air Force tactical versus strategic air planners and pilots. Nor are these differences in perspective attributable solely to bureaucratic malicious mischief. The diversity of intra-service perspectives results from morale-boosting efforts to develop group identification, which is directly related to group cohesiveness, and thus combat effectiveness. This is perhaps the largest difference between professional military organizations and other bureaucratic organizations; in the most stressful conditions, the execution of plans and procedures is as competent, and only as competent, as the cohesion of small groups and the self-motivation supplied by intraprofessional norms.

The reliance upon motivation for the execution of war plans would be most acute during the latter stages of a crisis preceding nuclear war or during war itself. There is insufficient research to make reliable estimates of the performance of nuclear commanders in chief and their subordinates in nuclear war. Some authoritative studies have been done on the psychological and social consequences of nuclear bombing attacks, among survivors of the bombings of Hiroshima and Nagasaki.[18] Studies of strategic bombing in World War II (other than nuclear bombing) found that prewar estimates of its effectiveness were considerably in error. In particular, the terror bombing of civilians in major European cities during that war proved to be less coercive of enemy leaders and less discouraging of public support for continuation of the war than airpower enthusiasts had estimated.[19] There is also the motivational issue for those who must carry out missions that might be considered repugnant, including the use of nuclear, chemical, or biological weapons against civilian noncombatants. In a bolt-from-the-blue scenario in which the United States or the Soviet Union awoke one day to find missiles raining down on its forces or major cities, without any previous warning or crisis, an automatic, preprogrammed, and furious response is almost assured. Time would permit little else. The problem of reaction, however, based on possible reservations at various points in the chain of command, becomes more subtle if and when a crisis is building to a boiling point and people have time to think about conflicting values. If war breaks out after a prolonged crisis, cognitive dissonance, or a value conflict, which individuals are unable to resolve within their existing frames of reference, might induce hesitancy and confusion within the highest circles.

Suppose, for example, that instead of our proverbial bolt-from-the-blue instantaneous surprise, a crisis builds into the outbreak of tactical nuclear exchanges in Europe, but not yet in Soviet or U.S. territory. The first exchanges might involve packages of low-yield weapons against military targets on both sides, in order to reduce the opponent's military capabilities, and also in order to signal willingness to escalate. Suppose, then, that a NATO response is authorized for airbursts over several East European cities, as a reaction to assumed Soviet strikes that have just been launched. The effort to even up firepower ratios soon gives way to competition in risk taking and damage acceptance. It would be a contrast of nerve and will, or of resolve and commitment, instead of a competition in destruction for its own sake, however mindless it would seem compared to peace, or even conventional war. Limited nuclear exchanges against cities would then have the status of tacit messages to the opponent (and to one's own side) of the following sorts: "We can do worse" or "To continue this is self defeating" or "We are as steadfast as you are, regardless of how much we must suffer." How those messages were interpreted by the opponent would be extremely important.[20]

At just this time, it would be of fundamental importance for U.S. and NATO leaders, who were attempting to end the war in some fashion without surrendering decisive political objectives, to be able to count on the prompt execution of orders, and only those orders, throughout the chain of command. There is all the difference in the world between options that are included in peacetime war planning and those that would be executed exactly as they were planned in wartime. The possibility that they will not be executed as planned does not occur on account of insubordination, but because of the rapidly changing expectations of commanders who are under fire and whose damage assessments will be imperfect, if they are available at all. The "fog of war" refers not only to the gap between prewar plans and their execution but also to the reciprocal effect of execution on subsequent plans. If the results of execution are as uncertain as the results of limited nuclear exchanges are apt to be, then the feedback into decisions for subsequent attacks will provide mostly noise. The ability of decision makers to control escalation under these conditions will be difficult, depending as it does on communicating clearly to the opponent that we will go this far, and no farther, contingent on its cooperation in reciprocal targeting restraint. The indeterminacy of whether we can control our own strikes in order to send the proper messages or proposals is compounded by our imperfect and perhaps grossly inadequate knowledge of how the opponent controls its forces and interprets our messages. If we understand poorly the opponent's interpretive framework, we will send messages that are misdirected, and misread.

PROLONGED WAR

Loss of control is an inherent risk in nuclear war. So, too, is the possibility that the war will not end quickly. Of all prewar expectations that might be disappointed, this one would cause the most drastic deviation from Western scenarios of nuclear war. Whether the Soviets would be equally surprised is not clear. Some Western analysts argue that the USSR would expect either a short or a long nuclear war and be equally prepared for either. We can be cynical about such assertions, if they are made as scientific estimates of Soviet capabilities; nonetheless, if the USSR expected to be able to fight an extended war, and to win it in some politically acceptable fashion, then they might not be as deterred as their U.S. opponents expected or hoped.

One difficulty standing in the way of contemplating an extended or protracted nuclear war is the fact that, in any U.S. or Soviet strikes against their respective homelands, unprecedented levels of physical destruction and human suffering would follow quickly. Although in theory such a war could go on for a long time, in practice it seems likely that even full counterforce exchanges by the superpowers against one another would be severely limited by the contents of their arsenals and the collateral effects of thousands of nuclear detonations. The importance of distinguishing between war, in the proper sense of a politically conscious use of force, and continuation of attacks for revenge, or for want of finding a way to stop them, is vital here. The concept of an extended nuclear war assumes that this war is about something politically important, including the possible surrender of important political values by one side. This concept thus implies that relative degrees of social and political deprivation are more meaningful to national leaders, and to the public in democratic societies, than absolute losses. In the case of massive U.S. or Soviet attacks against their respective homelands, it seems that reactions would be the other way around: The absolute level of damage would be so colossal, compared to previous experience, that relative misery might seem insignificant. (Whether missile defenses would make a difference in this expectation—that absolute destruction will be deemed more important than relative destruction—is a separate and arguable issue.)

Thus, an extended war is as likely as not to involve limited rather than comprehensive attacks and probably attacks outside U.S. and Soviet territory. Such a war, however, will not be limited from the European standpoint. This difference, between Soviet warheads detonating on European soil versus those that would strike the continental United States, has plagued NATO scenario writers since the U.S. nuclear umbrella was first extended to Europe. Europeans fear two contradictory things: that the United States might propel them into a war that they would rather avoid, and the direct opposite—that the United States would not use nuclear weapons against Soviet territory, even if the USSR exploded them in Europe. The second fear is probably the more pronounced among the political leadership, whereas the first, of provoking an unnecessary war, exists among much of the public. Michael Howard has correctly stated that this is the problem of making deterrence and reassurance work together.[21]

From the standpoint of European fears, the United States and the USSR might conduct a conventional and regional nuclear war, sparing their own homelands from destruction while doing so. And such a war could be prolonged by pauses for negotiation, followed by continuation of the fighting. Even during a conventional war limited to Europe, and excluding attacks into Soviet territory, fighting would take place under the imminent expectation that the nuclear threshold could be crossed. From the U.S. standpoint, policy exhortation has called for several decades for improvements in NATO conventional forces, in order to raise the nuclear threshold higher than it now is thought to be. European strategists who might agree with this objective, in theory, are careful not to applaud it too loudly in practice. The message it conveys to skeptical politicians and publics is that, in the event deterrence failed, the United States might take advantage of a higher nuclear threshold in order to limit the war to the conventional level, and in Europe. It is an exaggeration, to which apologists for the low-threshold deterrent position are sometimes prone, to contend that Europeans perceive no difference between the consequences of conventional war and those of nuclear war. The debate surrounding the NATO "572" decision to deploy Pershing II and cruise missiles in Europe should give the lie to that exaggeration.

Where the exaggeration touches upon truth, however, is in the unwillingness of most Europeans to believe that conventional forces, by themselves, can deter Soviet aggression. It can be argued that the mere presence of U.S. troops in Europe, and close to the inter-German border, would be enough to trigger U.S. intervention in any war, including if necessary the use of U.S. strategic nuclear forces. This argument, however, is very dependent upon the actual pattern of events at the time deterrence fails. If the Soviet attack is with conventional forces only and grows out of a crisis of misperception in which either side might be thought at fault, then U.S. willingness to respond, especially with nuclear escalation, could be ambivalent. On the other hand, an obvious Soviet attempt to conquer and to subjugate all of Western Europe, even with conventional forces alone, would be a strategic war in two senses: the comprehensive nature of the Soviet war aim, and the catastrophic costs if they accomplish it. Such a war really has, as its fundamental objective, the determination of whether the United States can be isolated from the sustainment of other developed and democratic societies in the postwar world. If it can be, whether nuclear weapons are involved or not, both it and Europe have lost the war. Therefore, it may be more important for NATO planners to ask when a war is strategic, in scale and consequences, than to ask when it is going to be nuclear.

An extended war in Europe, and elsewhere, could be conducted without nuclear escalation, at least at first. The U.S. maritime strategy promulgated in 1986 is based on the presumption that, during war in Europe or even globally, U.S. maritime superiority provides an alternative to nuclear escalation to induce Soviet willingness to conclude a peace on some mutually acceptable terms.[22] All the intricacies of U.S. maritime strategy cannot be covered here. Basically, it offers to provide a conventional warfighting capability that also raises the expected costs and risks for the USSR, should the nuclear threshold be crossed. The U.S. maritime strategy wants to do this in two ways: by destruction of the Soviet fleet and penetration of its protected bastions, especially those of the Northern Fleet in Murmansk and Polyarny; and by gradual attrition of Soviet ballistic missile submarines (SSBNs), which adjusts their anticipated nuclear "correlation of forces" in an unfavorable way, should nuclear escalation later occur.[23] The Soviets are thus induced to terminate the war on terms acceptable to NATO, by virtue of their already sustained maritime losses and their expectation that they cannot prevail in any nuclear exchange.

Of course, the major risk inherent in this strategy is that the first part, global maritime pressure on the USSR to induce war termination without nuclear escalation, is not subverted by the second part, attrition of the Soviet SSBN fleet. The U.S. strategy involves a manipulation of the risk of escalation, which (we are telling the USSR) we might not be able to control with complete confidence. Therefore, should they persist, they are rocking the boat in which both sides are standing. This assumption, which borrows much from Thomas Schelling's work already cited, depends upon the gradual and somewhat ambiguous mustering of a threat to Soviet objectives, as the USSR perceives them. It is a sliding scale of menace, which they and their U.S. opponents can only partially control.

The partial control creates the problematic aspect of the strategy, however. At the very time that it might be most important for political leaders to preserve control, including control over maritime operations in progress, inadvertent nuclear escalation could take place.[24] In fact, were inadvertent nuclear war not possible, the threat to influence the Soviet perception of the nuclear correlation of forces would not be meaningful. Thus, U.S. policy makers could have built into their repertoire two conflicting expectations: that maritime escalation can be controlled short of nuclear war, and that, if it cannot, the Soviets will recognize it in advance and capitulate. According to Admiral James D. Watkins, U.S. chief of naval operations in 1986, the objective of the maritime strategy is war termination, and preferably without nuclear escalation.[25] The problem, however, of turning off the war before the nuclear threshold is crossed will be compounded by U.S. uncertainty about Soviet value hierarchies. Will the USSR consider nuclear war to have occurred only when a dedicated nuclear weapon is launched against one of their seaborne or shore-based targets? Or will the Soviet Union decide that they are in a nuclear war when a Soviet vessel carrying nuclear charges is destroyed? In other words, is nuclear war defined by the attacker's weapons, or the defender's losses?

These questions pertaining to maritime strategy are related to the issue of whether protracted war is in the interest of either side, or to which, relatively speaking, it might be of greater interest. Peter H. Vigor, a widely regarded Soviet specialist, argues that for the USSR the prospect of a protracted (conventional) war must be very discouraging.[26] He lists a number of factors that would influence the Soviet calculus of risks, in a negative way for them, prior to a decision to engage in a long war against NATO. Included in this list of cautionary factors are the following, among others: the larger size and productive capacity of the economies of the United States and its allies, compared to the Soviet Union and its allies; the possibility of Chinese intervention on another flank, should the USSR become bogged down in an extended war against NATO; the greater opportunity for things to go wrong in the Soviet game plan, the longer the war is stretched out; and the emphasis placed in Soviet doctrine upon the importance of surprise and fast tempo of operations.[27]

John G. Hines, Phillip A. Petersen, and Notra R. Trulock are among U.S. analysts who contend that the Soviet Union is now more interested in limiting war, including war with the Western alliance, below the nuclear threshold.[28] According to these and other respected analysts, the USSR has examined the implications of nuclear strikes for the progress of its own ground and tactical air forces. It is becoming more concerned that the use of nuclear weapons may be counterproductive to the tasking of Soviet ground forces, and it is also possible that the USSR will not want to destroy property and other assets that would be the spoils of victory in a conventional war in Europe. Moveover, the Soviet Union apparently has not disregarded the possibility that chemical weapons could be used as a force multiplier in Europe or elsewhere, and, in some circumstances, they could substitute for the shock effects of nuclear weapons.[29] Other analysts caution, however, that Soviet interest in getting greater mileage out of its conventional forces does not preclude a willingness to escalate to the use of nuclear weapons, if it is deemed advantageous to do so. Soviet military and political leaders would go to war in Europe in the expectation that, even if the opening salvos were nonnuclear, no guarantee could be given that eventual escalation was avoidable. Two polar models of the escalation process in Europe, from conventional through theaterwide nuclear war, have widespread currency. One is that the first crossing of the inter-German border immediately trips NATO nuclear forces and thus Soviet nuclear reprisals, which then escalate unavoidably into theater-strategic warfare using all kinds of weapons. The other model is optimistic that important thresholds of escalation, including the "firebreak" between conventional war and nuclear first use, can be maintained.[30]

It would probably be foolish to assume that escalation could easily be controlled after nuclear weapons begin detonating, at least in Europe.[31] Albert Wohlstetter, one of the original architects of U.S. nuclear strategy and a thinker whose views must be respected under all conditions, argues that continuing control is not improbable.[32] According to Wohlstetter and Richard Brody, escalation could be controlled, because policy makers would have every incentive to do so once war began, despite their expressed skepticism beforehand. Moreover, the tools for limitation of nuclear war to less than total attacks are available, provided C3 is not too seriously degraded. This, however, is quite a proviso, and there are reasons to suppose that even during conventional war in Europe, both NATO and Warsaw Pact C3 would be among the earliest and most decisive targets.[33] It is pointed out by students of Soviet military doctrine that doctrinal statements of years ago, arguing for the inevitable escalation of any nuclear war into total war, have been significantly modified in recent years.[34] This, too, is scenario dependent and dependent upon NATO incentives for tacit cooperation, once the shooting starts. There are scenarios for Soviet restraint in the use of nuclear weapons that can be painted in the abstract, but fail to convince when they are run against NATO as it is presently constituted. To this argument, advocates of stronger NATO conventional forces respond, "Well, of course. This is why we want to raise the nuclear threshold." Mostly these advocates are found in the United States, which historically has been relatively more interested in reducing the consequences of war in Europe than have Europeans, who have been more interested in prevention per se. This difference is not an abstract matter of doctrine, because it is rooted in fundamental differences of geography and politics, which cannot be swept away with strategic rhetoric.

This issue of the controllability of war in Europe has already been touched upon, and more will be said about it. For the moment, let us suppose that somehow nuclear exchanges are avoided and an extended war is taking place with U.S. and Soviet forces, plus their allies, in Europe, the Pacific, and in Southwest Asia (Persian Gulf). To whose advantage or disadvantage is it to engage in horizontal escalation of a regional war into a global war, by extending the geographical scope of a conflict? And to whose advantage, or disadvantage, is the extension in time, or temporal escalation?

On these grounds there has been a spirited argument in the United States, between self-declared continental strategists, such as Robert W. Komer, and a variety of spokesmen categorized under the maritime-emphasis school of thought.[35] Keith A. Dunn and William O. Staudenmaier have identified several varieties of maritime emphasis, including unilateralist and multilateralist schools of thought (going it alone versus going with allies).[36] Of course, in a war in Europe the United States is by definition fighting with allies, so the unilateralist school is more artificial than real. And the maritime versus continental debate is more about emphasis than it is about the virtue of sea power over and against land power; virtually all schools of thought recognize that war in Europe will occur in both media.

What is at issue is the matter of force structure pertinent to the scenarios that U.S. planners judge most probable. The continentalists regard improved ground and tactical air forces on the Central Front as the highest priorities among general-purpose-forces (conventional forces) needs. The U.S. Navy, in their view, should devote less of its budget to the creation of new carrier battle groups and more of it to missions that would aid allied ground forces in carrying out their missions in Europe, especially fast sea lift and protection of the sea lanes of communication (SLOCs) between Europe and North America.[37] The Navy, for its part, is reluctant to divert more resources to ferrying the ground forces to their points of embarkation at the perceived cost of being able to conduct forward, aggressive maritime operations in the Norwegian and (perhaps) Barents seas.

Additional force structure for conventional ground, tactical air, or maritime forces would not necessarily buy an improved U.S. or NATO capability to fight a protracted war. In strategy the opponent must also be taken into account. If an extended conventional war seemed to be advantageous to the West, then this is the very war the USSR will be be reluctant to fight. The prospect of an extended conventional war may therefore be deterring to the USSR, replacing or supplementing the nuclear threshold with a temporal threshold that promises to exhaust Soviet resources and to gradually debilitate Soviet control over parts of its imperium.

For this substitution of extended conventional war for vertical escalation to work as a deterrent, however, is not the same issue as whether it might work after the fact of deterrence failure. Deterrence via temporal escalation requires that the Soviet leadership perceive, before the fact, that NATO is able to turn any conflict into an extended war. There can be no recipe apparent to the Politburo for a rapid and decisive victory in Europe without using nuclear weapons. In order to deter the Soviet long-war plan, the Soviet short-war plan has got to look unpromising.

Can NATO make the prospect of conventional war in Europe unappealing to Soviet planners under normal peacetime conditions? Probably it can. The Soviets are having sufficient difficulties keeping under control their fraternal allies in Eastern Europe and hostile insurgents in Afghanistan, and in the latter case they are now committed to withdrawal. A lurch into the heartland of Western Europe by them seems inconceivable as the result of any rational game plan to accomplish Soviet geopolitical objectives. The USSR has much more to gain in Europe by détente and trade agreements than it has by making war against Europe. Moreover, as good Marxists, Soviet leaders must believe that the health of Western democratic societies internally is the key to their defeat by external forces, especially external Soviet forces. Based on a proper Marxist reading of its own history, the USSR must count on internal political and economic forces in Western Europe to prepare the way for its invading armies. Otherwise, they are likely to meet with resistance, which could pose for the Soviet Union a stalemate tantamount to a denial of its political objectives. Of course, too much can be made of the literal Marxist script, by which capitalism first dies of its own internal rot, and then is helpfully pushed over by the fraternal assistance of the Red Army. Even periodic "defection" on specific NATO policies, or the dropping out of one or more members in a particular conflict, does not necessarily paralyze the alliance as a whole militarily, or make Soviet war planning uncomplicated.

This analysis just presented is logical as far as it goes into the thoughts of Soviet war planners who are thinking in peacetime about their options in the abstract. Many wars, however, do not begin as plausible constructs from peacetime situations. They grow from crises that spin out of control. In those situations, a princess-and-the-pea phenomenon results, in which great perturbations are felt from an apparently small and insignificant source. This source may not be a sufficient cause for war by itself, but it can add some contributory negligence at the right time to help bring down the house.

Such was the case, apparently, in the assassination of Archduke Francis Ferdinand immediately prior to the outbreak of World War I. Certainly, the assassination of a solitary political figure, however weighted with the symbolism of anti-imperialist nationalism, did not cause World War I. The causes of the war go much deeper, into nineteenth-century politics of the great powers in Europe. These deeper structural causes cannot, however, account for the timing of the outbreak of war or for the character of what is now called "crisis management" on the part of national leaders. Instead, one must look at the persons who were involved in the decision making in August 1914, as Barbara W. Tuchman has done, and at their choices as they perceived them, in order to understand the proximate causes of the war.[38]

As the Soviet plan for conventional war in Europe might do today, so the German plan for World War I (the Schlieffen Plan) emphasized a rapid and decisive knockout blow against the West before it became necessary to fight a two-front war. And, just as this problem of having to fight a two-front war bedeviled German planners prior to World War I, so it must confound Soviet planners who may be contemplating World War III. In the contemporary Soviet case, the fear is a war against China while the USSR is still fighting in Europe. Of course, fears of two-front war work both ways. The West must fear simultaneous conflict in the Persian Gulf and in Europe, with the Gulf theater of operations beginning first and tying down critical forces and supplies, while then become scarce when Europe erupts. This scenario is a problematic one for the United States, and is recognized in its attempt to develop a Rapid Deployment

Force (now Central Command) for dispersal to the Indian Ocean, if national interests dictate military intervention.

The West has its problems with two-front war, but the task facing the USSR, should China initiate its own moves during war in Europe, is equally formidable. There is no hope of conquering China in any war that remains below the threshold of nuclear exchanges, and probably not much chance of doing it with nuclear weapons. Assuming war remains conventional, the Soviets lack the forces to do more than push their border with the PRC in a favorable direction, and even then, it is not clear that they can hold it. The prospect of a long war between NATO and the Warsaw Pact will almost certainly tempt Chinese irredentism, with or without a formal declaration of war by the PRC against Moscow (which might be withheld for reasons of ideological consistency that Communist states do not war against one another). Taking into account the Chinese factor, NATO gains still more if it can halt a rapid and decisive Soviet offensive in Europe and prolong the war into a costly attrition for the Warsaw Pact.

This possibility of protracted conventional war, however, in which the West, with or without Chinese "assistance," might preserve its territorial integrity and political values, is not altogether reassuring for the United States and its NATO allies. A protracted war requires that the NATO alliance resist Soviet political strategy as well as the Red Army. And that political strategy, which will obviously begin in prewar peacetime, will offer to the various states of Western Europe the opportunity to exercise their unilateral rights of noncommitment (for the proffered benefit of being omitted from Soviet targeting coordinates, among other inducements). Two or three defections from the NATO order of battle just prior to the outbreak of war would be the best force multiplier the Kremlin could ask for, and probably the decisive factor in victory or defeat. Thus, NATO political cohesion becomes the most important military indicator of probable success or failure for the Soviet (short) war plan. Equally significant for the USSR will be its degree of control over its East European satellites and its fears or expectations of revolt after war begins.

Thus, temporal escalation plays a role in deterring war in Europe if the USSR can be convinced that the short war cannot be won. There are several ways to convince her. One way is to maintain tight coupling of NATO conventional forces to nuclear escalation, in order that any conventional war will almost automatically detonate the U.S. strategic nuclear deterrent. A second way is to provide for the Soviet Union the prospect that Nato conventional forces can avoid losing the short war, and that other factors will result in Soviet defeat in a long war, including Western maritime superiority, possible Chinese intervention, and U.S. industrial potential, once it is mobilized. A third way to maintain effective

NATO political cohesion in the face of any Soviet intimidation, so that even during a crisis, no member of the Soviet general staff or Politburo could expect to split the alliance along the lines of "accommodationists" and "stalwarts" or some such. This third way might be viewed as the political base, without which either of the first two methods of denying Soviet objectives will not work.

Even with the requisite political cohesion assumed by NATO, however, it is still problematic whether the vertical or horizontal/temporal escalations could be turned into something called victory or even prevailing. In the case of vertical (nuclear) escalation, no one can guarantee that it will not totally escape control by the responsible authorities. In the case of horizontal/temporal escalation, it offers an alternative to vertical escalation, but an exhausting one. It will be a Pyrrhic victory to prevail in a protracted war of attrition fought globally between NATO and Warsaw Pact coalitions. The best that can be said for the strategy of protracted conflict is that it offers the hope, albeit desperate, of avoiding the defeat, conquest, and occupation of Western Europe, while preserving some semblance of a postindustrial society. Better that deterrence should work in order to prevent any war, which means the political cohesion noted earlier, which in turn depends upon the credibility of NATO deterrent strategies. The chicken-and-egg quality of the relationship between political and military factors is all too obvious, and how the Soviets see that relationship is more important for deterrence than how NATO sees it. All things considered, NATO is probably more pessimistic about its own faults than Soviet net assessors are apt to be, because the Soviets, if they underestimated NATO, would be risking everything on a losing bet.

NOTES

1. See Steven J. Brams, *Game Theory and Politics* (New York: The Free Press, 1975), esp. Ch. 1 on international relations games, and pp. 30–39.

2. Col. T. N. Dupuy, *Numbers, Prediction and War* (Indianapolis, IN: Bobbs-Merrill, 1979).

3. See Desmond Ball, "The Development of the SIOP, 1960–1983," in *Strategic Nuclear Targeting*, ed. Desmond Ball and Jeffrey Richelson (Ithaca, NY: Cornell University Press, 1986), Ch. 3, and David Alan Rosenberg, "U.S. Nuclear War Planning, 1945–1960," Ch. 2 in the same volume. Also important is Rosenberg, "The Origins of Overkill: Nuclear Weapons and American Strategy, 1945–1960," in *Strategy and Nuclear Deterrence*, ed. Steven E. Miller (Princeton, NJ: Princeton University Press, 1984), pp. 113–82.

4. In the U.S. case, see Paul Bracken, *The Command and Control of Nuclear Forces* (New Haven, CT: Yale University Press, 1983), pp. 199–206; for the Soviets, see Stephen M. Meyer, "Soviet Nuclear Operations," in *Managing Nuclear Operations*, ed. Ashton B. Carter, John D. Steinbruner, and Charles A. Zraket (Washington, DC: Brookings Institution, 1987), Ch. 15.

5. Bracken, *The Command and Control of Nuclear Forces*, p. 202, discusses the concept of the presidential center as a safety catch.

6. Fritz W. Ermarth, "Contrasts in American and Soviet Strategic Thought," in *Soviet Military Thinking*, ed. Derek Leebaert (London: Allen and Unwin, 1981), pp. 50–72.

7. See Ball, "Development of the SIOP, 1960–1983," pp. 78–83, and Walter Slocombe, "The Countervailing Strategy," in *Strategy and Nuclear Deterrence*, ed. Steven Miller, pp. 245–54.

8. Richard K. Betts, *Surprise Attack: Lessons for Defense Planning* (Washington, DC: Brookings Institution, 1982), p. 229.

9. Fen Osler Hampsen, "Escalation in Europe," in *Hawks, Doves and Owls: An Agenda for Avoiding Nuclear War*, ed. Graham T. Allison, Albert Carnesale, and Joseph S. Nye, Jr. (New York: Norton, 1985), pp. 80–114.

10. Bruce G. Blair, "Alerting in Crisis and Conventional War," in *Managing Nuclear Operations*, ed. Carter et al., Ch. 3, pp. 75–120; Scott D. Sagan, "Nuclear Alerts and Crisis Management," *International Security* 9 (Spring 1985): 99–139.

11. Graham T. Allison, *Essence of Decision* (Boston: Little, Brown, 1971), p. 138; John D. Steinbruner, "Choices and Trade-Offs," in *Managing Nuclear Operations*, ed. Carter et al., pp. 542–43.

12. Barry M. Blechman and Douglas Hart, "The Political Utility of Nuclear Weapons: The 1973 Middle East Crisis," in *Strategy and Nuclear Deterrence*, ed. Steven Miller, pp. 273–97.

13. U.S. experiences in the Jordanian crisis of 1970 may have suggested to policy makers that an alert would signal U.S. intentions to the Soviet Union more effectively than other options. See Seymour M. Hersh, *The Price of Power: Kissinger in the Nixon White House* (New York: Summit Books, 1983), pp. 234–49.

14. Catherine McArdle Kelleher, "NATO Nuclear Operations," in *Managing Nuclear Operations*, ed. Carter et al., p. 457.

15. Desmond Ball, "Can Nuclear War Be Controlled?" *Adelphi Papers*, No. 169 (London: International Institute for Strategic Studies, Autumn 1981).

16. Ashton B. Carter, "Assessing Command System Vulnerability," Ch. 17 in *Managing Nuclear Operations*, ed. Carter et al. pp. 556–60.

17. The most delicate day of the Cuban crisis was Saturday, October 27. The preceding Tuesday the ExCom had decided that if U.S. U–2 reconnaissance aircraft were shot down over Cuba by Soviet surface-to-air missiles (SAMs), the United States would retaliate by striking at a single SAM site. When the event took place Saturday, the president hesitated and reconsidered. The U.S. Air Force, however, had taken Tuesday's *contingent* decision for retaliation as the equivalent of an expedient order, unless higher officials acted to prevent it from attacking. According to Allison, a series of rapid calls "just managed to intercept Air Force implementation" of what their officers took to be an open-ended go-ahead, "not without strenuous objections" from uniformed personnel. See Allison, *Essence of Decision*, p. 140.

18. See Committee for the Compilation of Materials on Damage Caused by the Atomic Bombs in Hiroshima and Nagasaki, *Hiroshima and Nagasaki: The Physical, Medical and Social Effects of the Atomic Bombings* (New York: Basic Books, 1981).

19. See David MacIsaac, "Voices from the Central Blue: The Air Power Theorists," in *Makers of Modern Strategy: From Machiavelli to the Nuclear Age*, ed. Peter Paret (Princeton, NJ: Princeton University Press, 1986), pp. 624–47.

20. For perspective on this and related issues, see Thomas C. Schelling, *Arms and Influence* (New Haven, CT: Yale University Press, 1966).

21. Michael Howard, "Reassurance and Deterrence: Western Defense in the 1980s," in *The Causes of War* (Cambridge, MA: Harvard University Press 1984), pp. 246–64.

22. Admiral James D. Watkins, "The Maritime Strategy," *Proceedings* of the U.S. Naval Institute, January 1986, pp. 3–17.

23. See Linton Brooks, "Conflict Termination Through Maritime Leverage," in *Conflict Termination in Military Strategy*, ed. Stephen J. Cimbala and Keith A. Dunn (Boulder, CO: Westview Press, 1987), Ch. 10 pp. 161–74.

24. Barry R. Posen, "Inadvertent Nuclear War? Escalation and NATO's Northern Flank," in *Strategy and Nuclear Deterrence*, ed. Steven E. Miller (Princeton, NJ: Princeton University Press, 1984), pp. 85–112.

25. Watkins, "The Maritime Strategy."

26. P. H. Vigor, *Soviet Blitzkrieg Theory* (New York: St. Martin's Press, 1983).

27. Vigor, *Soviet Blitzkrieg Theory*, Ch. 1.

28. John G. Hines, Phillip A. Petersen, and Notra Trulock III, "Soviet Military Theory from 1945–2000: Implications for NATO," *Washington Quarterly* 9, No. 4 (Fall 1986): 117–37.

29. See Hugh Stringer, *Deterring Chemical Warfare: U.S. Policy Options for the 1990s* (New York: Pergamon Brassey's/Institute for Foreign Policy Analysis, April 1986).

30. Western and Soviet notions of escalation are compared in Paul K. Davis and Peter J. E. Stan, *Concepts and Models of Escalation*, Rand Strategy Assessment Center (Santa Monica, CA: Rand Corporation, May 1984).

31. For background, see Stephen J. Cimbala, *Extended Deterrence: The U.S. and NATO Europe* (Lexington, MA: D. C. Heath/Lexington Books, 1987).

32. Albert Wohlstetter and Richard Brody, "Continuing Control as a Requirement for Deterring," in *Managing Nuclear Operations*, ed. Carter et al., Ch. 5, pp. 142–96.

33. Wohlstetter and Brody, "Continuing Control," p. 181, note how much C3 relevant to nuclear weapons might be destroyed or attenuated in the nonnuclear phase of a conflict.

34. I am grateful to Notra Trulock for the opportunity to read an unpublished manuscript of his on this point. See also Christopher N. Donnelly, "Soviet Operational Concepts in the 1980s," in *Strengthening Conventional Deterrence in Europe: Proposals for the 1980s* (New York: St. Martin's Press, 1983), pp. 105–36.

35. For an interesting appraisal of the maritime versus continental emphases in U.S. and NATO strategy, see Captain Roger W. Barnett, U.S. Navy (Retired), "The Maritime-Continental Debate Isn't Over," *Proceedings* of the U.S. Naval Institute, June 1987, pp. 28–34.

36. See Colin S. Gray, *Maritime Strategy, Geopolitics and the Defense of the West* (New York: National Strategy Information Center, 1986).

37. An argument that the U.S. maritime strategy should emphasize defensive

sea control and SLOC protection instead of offensive sea control and riskier operations is made by John J. Mearsheimer, "A Strategic Misstep: The Maritime Strategy and Deterrence in Europe," *International Security* 11, No. 2 (Fall 1986): 3–57.

38. Proximate causes of war based upon study of historical crises are addressed in Richard Ned Lebow, *Between Peace and War* (Baltimore, MD: Johns Hopkins University Press, 1981).

3

NUCLEAR SCIENTISM AND NUCLEAR STRATEGISM

Scientism is to science as strategism is to strategy. Scientism is a self-contained and self-defeating approximation of science. Like strategism, it is a policy-oriented commingling of facts, values, and biases. Perhaps the best way to begin a discussion of scientism is to introduce an auto-biographical note. The author's first teaching job was at the State University of New York, Stony Brook. In those days the word "revolution" was very much in the air, since the late 1960s and early 1970s were turbulent periods in the United States. Among the revolutions that were promised by never materialized was the behavioral revolution in the social sciences.

According to the pronouncements of leading political scientists then and now, the study of politics was akin to the study of physics, biology, and other physical or natural sciences. All that was necessary was the accumulation of enough raw data (presumably analogous to raw sewage), and the proper scientific generalizations would follow. Of course, political scientists had to be trained in the appropriate experimental (scientific) methods, else they would not do the research necessary to establish the discipline in the ranks of true sciences. Thus, entire graduate curricula were given over to the training, as opposed to the education, of future political scientists, who now dominate the academic establishment, at least in the United States. Although a supposed postbehavioral revolution took place later in the 1970s, it never really influenced an entire generation of researchers the way the behavioral revolution did.

This undoubtedly selective history would be irrelevant, were it not so tragic. The tragedy was that political science forgot political philosophy. Now, leading political scientists will deny that this is so. They will say that all the appropriate gestures were made to political philosophy, by which they mean the writings of persons who are assigned to panels at conventions entitled "Ancient and Medieval Western Political Thought," but political philosophy is more than this. Philosophy is an approach to inquiry, not a body of writing. A philosophical mind insists that more than one conceptual model or dominant paradigm guide research and inquiry. And a truly scientific spirit, in the proper sense, tries to disprove its null hypothesis instead of finding evidence to support orthodoxy. There was little of this kind of philosophical and scientific approach in the social sciences in the 1970s. There is little now.

Consider, for example, the war in Vietnam. The U.S. academic establishment, then and now, is unable to say anything very useful about how and why the United States failed to accomplish its political objectives there. More fundamentally, it failed for the most part to examine the entire concept of revolutionary civil war and its social context. A proliferation of think-tank studies and postwar *exposés* were as predictable as they were uninformative. The truth is that we still do not have a political science that can tell us much that is very useful about very important questions, which is why, not surprisingly, policy makers pay very little attention to it.[1] Although science had little to do with Vietnam, however, scientism had a great deal. Progress in the war was measured from Washington by indicators that included ammunition expended, body counts, sorties flown, and other quantifiable irrelevancies. The quantity of information actually proved to be qualitatively self-defeating, as the glut of messages moving through the system made it impossible to maintain coherent command and control of forces in the Vietnam theater of operations.[2] Indicators told policy makers and military advisors that the United States was winning the war, although journalists reporting from the front said the opposite, and the latter, in some cases to their obvious delight, were proved correct. Among all schemes attributed to U.S. policy planners for using science and technology as substitutes for strategy, the most notorious was the electronic barrier to separate North and South Vietnam. This was (allegedly) a Pentagon project for denying to North Vietnamese infiltrators the security of secret border crossings; they would be greeted by electronic sensors and mine fields. This proposal died of its own weight, but it speaks volumes about the propensity of high-technology societies to resort to scientism when the art of war is wanting.

If science was displaced by scientism in Vietnam, it followed that strategy could be displaced by strategism. It is conceivable that scientism could be mated to good strategy instead of bad, but unlikely. U.S. Vietnam strategy was based on the assumption that superior technology and firepower could substitute for the incompetency of the South Vietnamese government and armed forces. No politicomilitary strategy was needed, because the North Vietnamese would eventually tire of the war (although they had been fighting it off and on since World War II). Nor was the U.S. military and political establishment going to be distracted by the real history of revolutionary civil wars, as opposed to the fictional history. Real revolutionary civil wars require that the government set up a more competent and loyal police and intelligence establishment than its opponents, and that it not become fundamentally dependent on outside assistance for its survival. In the case of the South Vietnamese government, neither condition was fulfilled. Nor were U.S. military tactics designed to succeed in the environment of Vietnam. Heavy bomber attacks on North Vietnamese "industry" and search-and-destroy missions within South Vietnam combined the worst of both worlds. The ground forces of the opponents were awarded a sanctuary behind which they could take as much or as little of the fighting as they wanted. And the U.S. bombing of North Vietnam became Ho Chi Minh's favorite citation in the public-relations war against the U.S. involvement, which he eventually won. Scientism and strategism triumphed over doubters, however, and as recently as 1972, or even today, U.S. advocates assert that just a little more bombing of additional targets in North Vietnam would have brought that country to its knees and forced its acquiescence to any terms of settlement the United States might offer.

As it was in theorizing about revolutionary civil war, so it is in thinking about nuclear war, or deterrence based on the threat of nuclear war. Scientism replaces science, and strategism becomes the new strategy. Several examples of this substitution of scientism for science, and thus strategism for strategy, are noted now. Perhaps the combination should be called strategic scientism.

The first example of strategic scientism is provided by the debates that took place during the 1970s, and especially during the presidential campaign of 1980, over the "window of vulnerability" for U.S. strategic nuclear forces. According to presidential candidate Ronald Reagan in 1980, drawing from strategic analysis and campaign documents, the U.S ICBM force would at some time during the 1980s become vulnerable to a Soviet surprise first strike that could destroy most of it, if not all of it. The United States would be left with the option of retaliation against Soviet cities or other social and economic targets, purely for revenge. Retaliation would not be logical, however, since the USSR could then retaliate with the remainder of its strategic forces and destroy U.S. cities. Knowing this, the president's hand would be paralyzed, and the United States deterred from retaliation.[3] This window-of-vulnerability argument survived as an important topic of scholarly and public discourse, until the report of the Scowcroft Commission in 1983 effectively disarmed most of the public debate.[4] Thereafter, the public debate became more muted, although the debate among specialists continued. Experts continue to offer contending analyses of this issue of ICBM vulnerability, as if the stability of the strategic balance between the superpowers depended upon it.

In fact, as the debate heated up, the ICBM was becoming progressively more irrelevant and obsolete with regard to the question of strategic stability, at least in its fixed basing mode (as in the U.S. Minuteman II and III and the Soviet Union's fourth generation SS–17, SS–18, and SS–19). The nuclear balance was being challenged fundamentally, and not by ICBM vulnerability, which could easily have been fixed if anyone had wanted to do so. Clearly, neither Reagan conservatives nor Washington liberals wanted to solve the problem, and the Scowcroft Commission provided a face-saving compromise for Congress in the form of interim MX/Peacekeeper deployments in Minuteman silos and a research and development program to deploy the Small ICBM (Midgetman) in the 1990s. This decision was a harbinger of the obsolescence of the fixed-based ICBM as the weapon of the future, with important implications for strategy.

That the U.S. ICBM based in fixed silos was on its way out was confirmed by the Carter administration's acknowledgment of improvements in Soviet ICBM accuracy. The Soviet SS–18 force, thought to be targeted against the U.S. ICBM force, and its progeny would eventually win the race between the attacker's accuracy and the defender's silo hardness. In recognition of this, the Carter administration reviewed extensively possible basing modes for MX, other than the fixed silo.[5] Carter eventually endorsed a complicated scheme for basing MX which would have moved the missile on transporter-erector-launchers from one silo/garage to another on a schedule that would not be known to Soviet observers. Some 200 of these missiles would be shuffled among 23 holes each, thus creating 4,600 potential aim points for Soviet targeters. This was thought to be an arms-control asset as well as a survivability measure, for the plan would encourage the USSR to agree to arms reductions or face an unending race between U.S. concrete pouring and Soviet warhead proliferation. That such a Rube Goldberg scheme as MX/MPS (as it was called, for Multiple Protective Shelters) could be favored by some of the most prominent strategists and technologists in the Carter administration showed the importance of scientism and strategism. MX/MPS was a sponge that would soak up a lot of Soviet warheads, thereby, if deterrence failed, assuring a more devastating attack on the U.S. homeland than otherwise. What the entire MX/Peacekeeper fiasco demonstrated was the attractiveness of options other than additional land-based strategic missiles, including cruise missiles and submarine-launched ballistic missiles.

Indeed, the land-based, immobile missile was probably headed for obsolescence the day the first submarine-launched ballistic missile (SLBM) was deployed aboard a U.S. submarine. Given the accuracies of current and foreseeable Soviet and U.S. ballistic and cruise missiles, it is only a matter of time until both sides' fixed, land-based missiles become out-moded dinosaurs. Notice, again, that military experts step forward to deny that this is so. Representative is the statement of the Scowcroft Commission that ICBMs have unique properties that other strategic weapons do not, including flexibility in command/control and hard target accuracies.[6] Technology is making this argument less and less pertinent to the facts of the future, even if it did apply in the past. Future sub-marine-launched ballistic missiles will have accuracies approaching cur-rent generations of ICBMs. The newest U.S. SLBM, the Trident II (D–5), scheduled to begin deployment at the end of the 1980s, will have estimated accuracies sufficient to destroy protected counterforce targets, including Soviet ICBM silos.[7] And, although the problems of communi-cating with submarines cannot be trivialized, they are not necessarily worse, given the submarines' mission, than the problems of command and control for other retaliatory forces.[8] Given their assumed missions, U.S. ballistic missile submarines need not receive communications as urgently as ICBMs, or with the flexibility required by the bomber force.

Then, too, the development and deployment of cruise (air-breathing) missiles on bombers, surface ships, and attack submarines provide an entirely new component to U.S., and eventually Soviet, strategic nuclear forces. Cruise missiles can be armed with conventional or nuclear war-heads and delivered from a variety of airborne, ground-based, or sea-based platforms. They blur the distinction between nuclear and conven-tional forces, and between retaliatory and first-strike weapons. Although slow compared to ballistic missiles, under the right circumstances cruise missiles could be critical components of a surprise attack. If the defender's radar cannot see the cruise missile coming, its slow speed is not neces-sarily a drawback. U.S. defenses against bombers and cruise missiles (so-called atmospheric defenses or air defenses) are acknowledged to be porous and obsolete. A Soviet surprise attack on U.S. bomber bases and command centers might employ submarine-launched cruise and ballistic missiles; SLBMs launched from Soviet submarines on routine patrol could strike about half of the 400 primary and secondary command and control targets in the continental United States.[9]

Recognition of the growing importance of cruise missiles and SLBMs has led the United States to conduct research aimed at eventual deploy-ment of an Advanced Cruise Missile and Advanced Technology Bomber ("Stealth") in the 1990s. In both cases, the objective is to reduce the radar cross-section ("observables") in order to evade detection by the Soviets' land-based and airborne radar detection systems. This will be a race of U.S. measures, Soviet countermeasures, and U.S. counter-countermea-sures during the 1990s. As to the growing importance of SLBMs, the British have given their own witness, having agreed to obtain from the United States the Trident II missile for deployment in their own ballistic

missile submarine (SSBN) force. The French have also deployed significant numbers of warheads on ballistic missile submarines, and both the
U.K. and French forces could threaten the Soviet Union with the destruction of many of its major cities, and much of its industrial capacity,
by the middle of the 1990s (assuming no deployment of territorial ballistic-
missile defenses by the Soviet Union).[10]

As for the Soviets, they are deploying cruise missiles on a bomber
force, which is being modernized after a long period of apparent disinterest in bomber modernization, compared to ICBM development. This
may be because the USSR feels more confident now of its ICBM capability
than it did in earlier decades, or it may be that the Soviets wish to
diversify their arsenal and increase its survivability. Most interesting in
this diversification of the Soviet strategic portfolio is the deployment of
the mobile, strategic land-based missile SS–25 (thought to carry a single
warhead) and the planned deployment of the mobile SS–24 ICBM (expected by U.S. intelligence to carry multiple warheads).[11] This addition
of mobile ICBMs to an already substantial armada of fixed land-based
missiles indicates apparent Soviet interest in the problem of ICBM survivability, relative to other strategic forces. So, too, does the modernization of Soviet bomber forces and their deployment of strategic cruise
missiles on bombers and attack submarines.

Both superpowers, then, are headed in the direction of diversified deterrence, including mobile land-based, sea-based, and air-launched missiles of various kinds. Unmentioned for the moment are the possible
complications of space defenses, which we turn to presently. Enough has
been said to see that the window of vulnerability never existed in quite
the way it was presented in U.S. policy debates. As U.S. and Soviet
ICBMs became progressively more vulnerable, technologists were at
work inventing delivery systems and basing modes that made the entire
controversy largely irrelevant. Moreover, even this imminent technological irrelevance of the ICBM vulnerability debate, relative to the strategic
importance of other issues, was not the only error committed by policy
advocates. This scientism was compounded by strategism.

Strategism was committed by those who supposed that the Soviet
Union, in a nuclear crisis, would attack the U.S. homeland in the hope
of destroying the U.S. ICBM force, even if the numbers seemed to imply
that such an attack could succeed (mathematically). The obvious question
was, What would the USSR do then? The answer would be that the
USSR would absorb a U.S. retaliation from U.S. submarine and bomber
forces that would bury the Soviet Union in the proverbial rubble. If
nuclear weapons are perceived to be artillery, then the USSR ICBM
force, relative to that of the United States might come out ahead in the
postattack boxscore. Soviet society, however, could not escape unprecedented and perhaps economically fatal devastation. And the Kremlin's

hold on its subject populations and nationalities might be attenuated in the extreme.

Now, much has been said, with some justice, about the relevance of a warfare capability to the credibility of deterrence. This is true up to a point, and we return to the point when we consider Soviet strategy. There is, however, warfare with the expectation of victory, and there is warfare out of desperation and revenge, promising, at best, Pyrrhic victory. The first kind of warfare, that to which a meaningful expectation of victory is attached in war between the United States and the Soviet Union, is not impossible, but highly improbable. Only if nuclear war between superpowers were confined to very few and limited (in destructiveness) exchanges, would anything approximating victory be possible, although it would be far from certain. Uninhibited exchanges of U.S. and Soviet nuclear firepower would spell devastation of both societies and economies to an extent that precluded victory in politically meaningful terms.[12]

Since the USSR cannot expect to escape devastating retaliation against its society, following a (successful) attack on the U.S. ICBM force, why, then, the concern about ICBM vulnerability? The assertion that ICBMs have unique strategic properties has already been noted, but it carries little weight in the face of future innovations in other forces. Instead, the silo-based ICBM hangs onto prominence because so much psychological and organizational capital has been invested in it. It represents decades of sunken costs and military traditions. Like the horse cavalry, it has become more ceremonial than utilitarian. It could be disutilitarian, however; vulnerable ICBMs invite attack by a desperate opponent. Best bet would be a joint U.S. and Soviet decision to consign their immobile ICBMs to a binational aerospace museum, presumably with fixed basing.

SOVIET STRATEGY

The second representative sampling of scientism and strategism lies in U.S. analyses of Soviet strategy. Of particular interest are misattributions to the Soviet Union of strategic and military perspectives developed in the West. We have already noted the behavioral revolution and its impact on political science. This also had implications for U.S. understanding of Soviet strategy. The tendency to see Soviet strategy through U.S. eyes resulted, however, from political rather than methodological forces.

For understandable reasons, the nature of Soviet strategy is a bone of contention among various factions in the U.S. policy debate. It would be misleading to characterize these factions as liberals and conservatives, since those terms mean something very different in Europe, and meant something different still in the nineteenth-century United States. With regard to perceptions of Soviet strategy, it would be more accurate to say that there are U.S. absolutist and U.S. relativists. U.S. absolutists believe that Moscow takes literally its Marxist–Leninist rhetoric about world revolution. The USSR will not be satisfied until the West is militarily subjugated or politically impotent (for example, "Finlandized"). Accordingly, the Soviet view of arms-control negotiations is that they are weapons in a struggle to disarm the West, while Soviet buildups of their own defenses continue apace. Moreover, in the absolutist view, the USSR cannot be satisfied with any partial military conquests or piecemeal political gains. Its relentless pressure to expand its imperium will relent only when the regime that rules Moscow is deposed by forces from outside or by pressures within the society. Thus, U.S. policy should, according to the absolutist view, attempt to create chronic stress in the Soviet system by presenting to them a full-court press of U.S. military and economic confrontation. This pressure will show the inferiority of the Soviet system, weaken its economy, and ultimately force it to change, or capitulate.

U.S. pragmatists do not consider the prospects for making fundamental changes in the character of the Soviet regime, as opposed to its behavior, to be very promising. The Kremlin is, in their view, more interested in holding onto what it has, than it is in expanding its imperial reach. In the pragmatist view, the USSR has already overextended its politico-military grasp, and Afghanistan is evidence that the Soviet leadership is aware of it. So, too, are events in Poland from the early 1980s to the present, and elsewhere in Eastern Europe. Most ominously for any Soviet aspirations for global or even regional hegemony, the People's Republic of China is no longer a fraternal Socialist ally, but a competitive Socialist antagonist and a potential superpower in the next century. The economy that the Cultural Revolution had placed in drydock has now been freed of its fetters, and capitalist experiments are being attempted by the regime in Beijing. Factional struggles continue within the Chinese leadership, but the modernizations of industry, agriculture, education, and defense are certainly going to continue. This raises the possibility of a Sino–Japanese trade or larger economic association, creating further distance between Soviet economic performance and that of its leading Asian competitors. Nor is this all. Capitalism also rears its ugly head in Taiwan, South Korea, and Singapore, with dramatic results. From an economic standpoint, Mr. Gorbachev is well aware that, far from global or regional hegemony, he will do well if he does not lose ground in the next two decades, relative to the competition in Europe and Asia.

If so, the Soviet leadership must "bite the bullet" on the reallocation of resources from military production to civilian economic and technology investment. Although some of these investments will have military spillovers, such as "enhanced technology" weapons, the larger implication of a relative loss of influence by the "metal eaters" (military and heavy industry) is clear. Gorbachev and other Soviet leaders have little choice. The performance of the economy under Brezhnev was dismal, and not coincidentally because of a steady increase in military spending during the Brezhnev years.[13] Brezhnev's long tenure did bring some much needed stability to a turbulent system, but, in the end, it also led to an ossified and geriatric bureaucracy that could not innovate. Gorbachev must dismantle much of the Brezhnev-era party and state bureaucracy without appearing to do so too openly, or in a way that obviously contradicts party or ideological imperative. These domestic constraints on the Soviet leadership, according to U.S. pragmatists, are related to the success or failure of its foreign policy, and especially to the success or failure of détente. Relaxation of tensions with the West is a prerequisite for any reform-minded Soviet leadership; conversely, deterioration of relations, as happened following the Soviet invasion of Afghanistan in 1979, makes innovation directed from the Kremlin more controversial within its own leadership hierarchy.[14]

Notice that no particular person has been identified with either the absolutist view or the pragmatist perspective. That would be unfair, because these perspectives are ideal types, caricatures, which are not necessarily found in exactly that form "in nature." However, the ideal types can be defended as such, and it can be argued that the U.S. electoral process is often polarized between the two ideal-typical sets of views. Certainly the U.S. presidential election of 1980 pitted against one another candidates whose perspectives on the Soviet Union fitted the caricatures of absolutist (Reagan) and pragmatist (Carter) rather well. This is not a prejudgment of the validity of those assessments, for academics are by nature pragmatically biased, at least in public. The point is that campaigns organized around these thematically centered perspectives on Soviet objectives then reverberate into subsequent policy decisions. As has been seen, for example, the Reagan administration, having diagnosed a window of vulnerability with regard to the U.S. ICBM force, decided that closing it was a priority, although the Scowcroft Commission at least significantly amended the vulnerability thesis. It said that ICBMs might be vulnerable, but that the U.S. triad of strategic forces, taken as a whole, was not. Reagan also came to regret early assessments of the USSR as an "evil empire" (no doubt some allowance must be made for the fact that this utterance was pronounced at Orlando, Florida, home of Disney World). U.S. conservatives later wondered why it was imperative to negotiate arms-control agreements with the evil empire, if it could not be trusted to keep those agreements, as Reagan claimed, and if its basic intentions could not be changed. Jimmy Carter also offered assessments of the U.S.– Soviet political relationship that came back to haunt him later. Early on he pronounced that the people of the United States needed to get over their "inordinate fear of communism" and concentrate on North–South instead of East–West issues. After the Soviet invasion of Afghanistan in 1979, Carter in his January 1980 State of the Union address defined the Persian Gulf as a vital interest that the United States would defend by force against Soviet aggression, if necessary. The Soviets were to all appearances not planning any conquest of Iranian oil fields in the near term, having their hands full coping with rebellious Afghans, and needing no protracted war in Iran in order to accumulate further casualties on their southern flank. Having been defined as altogether meaningless in the early Carter years, the Soviets were reinvented as altogether malevolent by 1980 (in time for the presidential campaign). One wonders whether, if the USSR was not so malleable relative to U.S. campaign images, campaigns could be at all interesting, since U.S. politicians have ceased to say anything important about the economy for many years (everybody is for a bigger pie and for cutting it up among more and more diverse interest groups).

The Soviets do have military power and military problems, however, and it is important to appreciate both realistically. Their military power is significant, most notably in their ground forces, the best of which are poised for westward attack in Eastern Europe.[15] These Soviet forces in Eastern Europe also symbolize a problem for the Kremlin. They are constabulary forces with which the armies of the Warsaw Pact are connected for obvious reasons: to suppress any workers' revolts against the workers' paradises that are run more or less according to Kremlin dictates. Of particular interest to the USSR is the possibility that one of the workers' paradises in Eastern Europe might defect to neutralism or to the West. Now, there are paradises and paradises. Rumania has declared its disinterest in some Warsaw Pact maneuvers and asserted itself quite independently on other issues, seemingly pushing Soviet leaders well beyond their threshold of tolerance. Ceaucescu, however, the ruler of Rumania, is no threat to the USSR in the way that Dubcek was in Czechoslovakia in 1968. The Rumanian party chairman is not the head of a popular reform movement that threatens to spill over to other East European countries, or even to the USSR. He is as unappealing a figure as the Kremlin could find to rule a portion of its continguous empire, and as long as he keeps Rumania securely under his heel, this heel will satisfy his fraternal allies in Moscow. Hungary, Czechoslovakia, and Poland are different stories, and most especially East Germany. There, the possibility of discontent with Moscow-style rule must be stifled, and quickly. The withholding of Soviet intervention in 1980 until Polish forces were ready to do the job in 1981 was based in part on the assumption that when they did, Jaruzelski and company would do the job well. Otherwise Big Brother would step in behind, a possibility that is still not foreclosed.

So, the Soviet political glacis in Eastern Europe is rickety, and its military power formidable. The second paradox of power and problems relates to China. The USSR cannot reasonably hope to wage war in the West, and perhaps not deter war in a crisis, unless it can feel confident about the absence of a two-front war, with the second front along the Sino–Soviet border. This would not, on its face, seem an impossible problem to solve. The issues that prevent a Soviet–PRC *rapprochement* are more subject to resolution by negotiation than some of the issues that divide Moscow from Washington. It is improbable that Western rights in Berlin could be renegotiated, but disputed areas along the Sino–Soviet border might be. Similarly, the Soviet invasion of Afghanistan soured relations with Beijing, perhaps one incentive for the Soviet decision to withdraw their combat forces from Afghanistan during 1988 and 1989. Changes in leadership, since the mutual antagonism between Khrushchev and Mao, would seem to permit adjustment of other disputes without personal recrimination between leaders, especially if the Gorbachev leadership is as reform minded as some U.S. observers have judged it to be. Left to fester without détente, the Sino–Soviet hostility will limit what the USSR can do in security policy, and in particular, it will limit Western incentives to cooperate with the Soviet Union in strategic and European-theater arms control. Knowing the Soviets to be weaker with a Chinese opponent than with a possible Chinese ally, the West will be less likely to accommodate Soviet geopolitical ambitions.

However, and here is the paradox for the USSR, accommodation with post-Mao China brings with it one danger of the pro-Mao period, and that is the danger of two claims to the Communist papacy, one in Moscow and one in Beijing. Moreover, the claim of the PRC might be more palatable in the Third World of developing societies than that of Moscow, and Chinese footprints have been visible in the sands of Soviet surrogate wars, aiding the other side. Worst of all, the Chinese competitor for Third World influence might combine a Marxist rhetorical appeal with successful capitalist (really socialized marketing) experiments. A Chinese polyglot economic success story, which Third World socialist states would want to emulate, would turn the tables on the USSR and force reconsideration of its internal as well as its external strategy. Moreover, a Chinese papacy is an ideological threat to the Soviet claim that the USSR is the true standard-bearer of philosophical Marxism. This last point is extremely important within the Soviet Union, although it is too casually pooh-poohed by Western readers who are raised in an allegedly deideologized society (the behavioral revolution strikes again). Soviet leaders do take their ideology seriously, seriously enough to go to war if their papacy appeared to be crumbling to a challenger on their border. This appearance could become reality if, for example, the USSR began to lose the allegiance of non-Soviet nationalities on its southern and western borders. Thus the dilemma for the Soviet leadership is that it cannot have détente with the

West without some tolerance for it with the East, but détente with the PRC is more than "good business"; it risks ideological concessions and intrasocialist community power sharing that the Kremlin will be very reluctant to acknowledge.

The third paradox of power and problems that Moscow confronts lies in its relations with Europe, especially NATO Europe. The Soviet political strategy in the long run must be to wean Western Europe away from the U.S. alliance security system. To do this, the Soviets must not appear to be too menacing, for fear of reinvigorating NATO into additional military expenditures and political resolution. No menace at all, however, is not necessarily contributory to Soviet interests, because then East Europeans ask why military preparedness against the West is necessary. The USSR must somehow convince the West Europeans that the United States and its military alliance in NATO are the real threats to peace in Europe. If Europe would only separate from the United States, a fraternal bear hug would be safe. Thus, Soviet influence in Western Europe grows during period of détente, as it did during the 1970s following the SALT I agreement. Citizens and governments of Eastern and Western Europe, and especially the two Germanies, feel that détente has led to material and social benefits that they do not want to give up. The entire process surrounding the Conference on Security and Cooperation in Europe (CSCE), including the Helsinki accords of 1975, has led to improved East–West trade, investment, and other economic and political benefits, which are seen by most Europeans as net pluses. The United States is not sufficiently sensitive to the post-*Ostpolitik* climate in Europe, in which resolution of the most important issues relative to the status of the two Germanies was felt by many to be a permanent adjustment in the temperature of East–West relations. The Soviets can and have manipulated this U.S. lack of sensitivity—or, when sensitivity is not lacking, timing. Carter's handling of the neutron-bomb fiasco and the outbreak of a European "peace offensive" against the Pershing II and cruise missiles showed disparate assessments and perspectives on both sides of the Atlantic by leaders and interest groups who were previously thought to have been satisfied, or pacified.[16]

The fine line the Soviets must walk between provocation and passivity with regard to NATO Europe, and hence the United States also, echoes within the Soviet economic planning hierarchy as well. Future military strength may lie in the fields of computers and electronics, the "smarts" of warfare instead of the brawn indicated by numbers of tanks and field artillery pieces. If so, this represents an especially insidious challenge from the capitalist world to the internal control of Soviet socialism over its dominions. How will the USSR cope with the microelectronics revolution without undergoing a proliferation of computer terminals and electronic data banks that make secrecy much harder to protect against inquisitive dissidents and others? Can ideas suppressed by administrative fiat remain beneath the surface, when the average shopkeeper or elementary school pupil has access to a terminal? This has not happened yet, but the dilemma is a foreseeable one. It will be insufficient for the Soviet leadership to keep pace with the West (and Japan) by sponsoring competitive developments in engineering and computer science research. They will also have to contemplate diffusion of the results of this research and the development of knowledge bases and data inventories tailored to the needs of individual users. If they do not, they will be left hopelessly behind by the middle of the twenty-first century, and not only in their civilian economy and its performance relative to that of the West. They will also be left out of the competition militarily. This is not as hopeless a competition for the USSR as Western Sovietophobes sometimes suppose; their space program attests to their ability to solve problems when their minds are made up to do so, despite bureaucratic rigidity. The Soviet space program, however, has not presented a fundamental ideological challenge to the regime in the same way that decentralized electronic data processing will. It may then occur to Soviet leaders that Mr. Lenin and Mr. Marx provided no fair warning of this postindustrialist, capitalist revolution, in which information and electronics become the force multipliers that make or break economies and armies. Consider, for example, the impact of a battlefield almost totally open to observation from remarkably accurate sensors based in space, at sea, and on land. These sensors will, in turn, be able to interpret information by preprogrammed artificial intelligence almost instantaneously, referring it upward to higher-level commanders, or downward to lower ones. True, this is a mixed blessing, for presidents and premiers may be tempted to play sergeant at the most inopportune times;[17] but they will also know what is going on very far down in the chain of command, which means that politically significant deviation from orders will be easier to detect, and that may be important in the management of nuclear crises.[18]

Faced with this possibility, the Kremlin will have not only to adjust its allocative priorities but also to alter its definition of what behavior is politically acceptable and what is not. This does not mean a revolt of the masses against the Soviet elites, but more controversy within the elite, and the possibility of an elite more sensitive to where the consumer's shoe pinches, or the corporal's boot. In this regard, there is the inevitable propensity for Western commentators who visit the USSR, no doubt from boredom as much as anything else, to prophesy a decade-hence return to Stalinism, or a rebirth of nineteenth-century Russian religious nationalism based on the writings of Dostoevsky and Tolstoy. Such developments, if they occur, will come as artistic and literary epiphenomena, and they will not necessarily cast much of a shadow over the political system or its foreign-policy objectives. At the level of exhortation or pacification of the non-Communist Soviet intelligentsia (always a discontented lot), such a revival of old Russian nationalism and nationalistic religion may have significance, but overthrow of the regime, or its conversion into an orthodox theocracy, is not in the cards. Besides, demographic trends seem to be moving away from, instead of toward, a Russification of Soviet culture.

All of these political and social fundamentals argue against a Soviet lurch through the Fulda Gap or across the North German plain. If they did take place, the USSR would most probably be motivated by a "defensive surprise," that is, the desire to attain the tactical initiative as a result of a deteriorating crisis in Eastern Europe from which the Soviets concluded that war was inevitable.[19] NATO is understandably concerned with planning for the worst case, which is assumed to be a prepared Soviet invasion against a numerically inferior Western alliance. This planning scenario, however, is itself the victim of scientism and strategism. Depending on how the numbers are derived, NATO can be shown to have sufficient, insufficient, or uncertain readiness for a Warsaw Pact attack with conventional forces on the Central Front in Europe.[20] Barry Posen has shown that by making assumptions favorable to NATO strategy, NATO has adequate forces to contain a Soviet attack; equally, by making assumptions favorable to Soviet strategy, NATO has inadequate numbers.[21] William W. Kaufmann, in an analysis published by the Brookings Institution, compares the Reagan force, the Carter administration force projected into the future, and a "combat force" of his own devising in terms of their performance in conventional war in Europe. Kaufmann's comparisons are designed to illustrate the probable combat proficiency of different force structures. They also, however, illustrate the relative importance of strategy, as opposed to structure. By using forces in more efficient ways in hypothetical battles, Kaufmann can get more mileage out of them.[22]

What all of this number crunching leads to, then, is the conclusion that NATO has a good chance of not being defeated (that is, stalemating a Pact attack and then bringing about war termination short of nuclear escalation), if it follows a sensible strategy. This, however, the alliance is reluctant to do, for reasons of politics and economics. Politics dictates that top-of-the-line forces be massed far forward near the inter-German border, under the policy of forward defense, in which not one morsel of West German territory can be yielded to Pact attackers. This political imperative of forward deployment, however, is not supported by permanently fortified positions that are militarily defensible. The reason for this second decision, effectively a refusal to implement the first, is that it will bring about a Maginot-Line mentality in the covering forces and not a concept of an aggressive fighting force. This is pure malarkey, and everybody in the NATO military loop knows it. The real reason for the lack of permanent fortifications is the symbolism it raises for the Germans, who want to believe, it is alleged, in the eventual possibility of unification of their nation, however remote. While this argument has some truth, it should be given no encouragement by the political and military leadership of Western Europe today. If the West Germans want to be defended far forward, not only by their own troops but also by allied NATO ground forces, then they can face the political reality that the German *volk* will never be reunited without a drastic realignment of system bipolarity. And, if Europeans outside of Germany remember their history, they will decide that this permanent division of the German nation is not such a bad outcome for preserving the peace in Central Europe.

Here scientism has appeared again, suggesting that NATO can compensate for poor strategy with improved gadgetry. The Follow-on Forces Attack (FOFA) strategy based on the use of sophisticated conventional deep-attack munitions will allow NATO to raise the nuclear threshold, while still containing the Pact offensive.[23] Although NATO does need to exploit new technology in order to improve its conventional defenses, technology is not a panacea. It will not compensate for an inferior strategy. And NATO's current strategy, if deterrence fails, invites the very kind of attack that might be most problematical for the alliance: a rapid and decisive air offensive against NATO's rear, followed by Soviet ground forces moving rapidly through selected defense zones to establish control over the operational zone of combat within a few days to a week.[24] Caught off balance, and facing the prospects of surrendering important territory or escalating to the use of nuclear weapons (if those weapons have not been overrun or destroyed), NATO might well capitulate. Whether it did would depend more on its political cohesion than it would on the force balance when war began, or upon the exploitation of new technology that will certainly be available to both sides.

Enough has been said on the subjects of scientism and strategism relative to the prospect of Soviet attack on the Western alliance. The arguments made earlier to not imply that attack is impossible, simply that if it happens, it will be motivated not by perceived force imbalances, but by political causes, including possible panic in Moscow over the potential loss of its control in Eastern Europe. Lech Walesa probably frightens Moscow more than five NATO divisions do, and the timing of uprisings in Poland or Czechoslovakia might be very hard to predict with mathematical models of crisis behavior. The study of crisis is important; the danger lies in seeing crises as their own causes. Contrary to much conventional wisdom in the social sciences, crisis does not just happen, and it is frequently foreseeable. Of course, some crises can be better managed than others, and those poorly managed can lead to wars that are not wanted, at least not then.[25]

Two other illustrations of scientism pertinent to the discussion of nuclear strategy, come to mind. In both instances scholars or scientists were motivated by the loftiest objectives, sounding the tocsin against possible danger to motivate a bovine public to pay attention. The illustrations come from opposite ends of the U.S. political spectrum. The first is the thesis of nuclear winter and the second, the argument that the Soviet Union expects to fight and win a nuclear war.

The first issue, nuclear winter, was the thesis that nuclear war between superpowers could produce by-products that would be destructive of the global climate, and potentially the entire habitat.[26] Carl Sagan and his colleagues attempted to define thresholds beyond which nuclear winter would be triggered and the effects of blocked sunlight and lower temperatures. This, however, was advocacy of a position that has much to commend it in its own right, but not science. And when the advocacy, rather than the scientific character, of nuclear-winter studies became apparent to other researchers, the findings about nuclear winter were somewhat discredited.[27]

This does not dispose of the problem, however, for the nuclear-winter thesis was not really a scientific argument to begin with. It was a well-intended effort to awaken public consciousness to the dangers of nuclear wars, even limited nuclear wars in which the United States and the Soviet Union might use only small proportions of their total delivery vehicles or warheads. It is important to reinforce this warning, and the reinforcement is a kind of advocacy that does contribute to science. The reason for the claim that the advocacy is scientifically respectable, even if the science of nuclear winter is not, lies in the difference between existential awareness and scientific findings. Scientific findings may or may not penetrate into the public consciousness, as studies of the habits of cigarette smokers will attest. The nuclear-winter studies are a necessary corrective against the pseudoscience of limited nuclear war, which became a preoccupation of think tanks on both sides of the Atlantic in the 1970s. Limited-nuclear-war theories grew out of Western unwillingness to spend the funds and the sacrifices to provide credible conventional defense: So, find a way to make nuclear weapons usable in smaller packages, like elephants reduced to the size of gnats. This was the ultimate perversion of science into scientism, as if the repackaging of nuclear weapons into more discrete components would lead naturally into a more restrained political conflict, once the warheads began flying. So nuclear winter has its place, as a reminder that the idea of controlled or limited nuclear war between superpowers, in Europe, is an idea whose time has come, and gone.[28]

On the other hand, one cannot defend the motives or political objectives of nuclear-winter advocates without reservation and at the same time criticize those of persons who advocate preparedness for limited nuclear war. The difference is one of degree, not of kind. The advocates of nuclear

winter want to avoid complacency among policy planners; the proponents
of limited nuclear war do not prefer that condition to peace, but only to
total war, and relatively speaking, the preference is correct as stated.
The polemical character of nuclear-winter and limited-nuclear-war studies
must be extracted to isolate the grains of analysis, and the result is an
enhanced appreciation for the paradox of limited nuclear options. If war
cannot be avoided, they offer an alternative to prompt societal extinction.
Control of escalation after nuclear weapons have been exchanged, however, is tenuous, and the distinction between no nuclear weapons and
some is more meaningful than the distinction between some and more.
This last point is now much disputed among U.S military strategists, and
some argue that the United States or NATO may not get to make the
choice, if the Soviets initiate nuclear strikes. True enough, but our declaratory doctrines and war plans do condition the choices available to us
if and when deterrence fails. And those doctrines and war plans, in recent
years, have tended to emphasize how much better limited options are,
compared to total war, than an emphasis upon war avoidance. Indeed,
there is something close to a schism in the academic and policy scientific
literature on this subject, with a "psychology of deterrence" school providing focuses on crisis stability and war prevention, and a "how to do
it" school examining the credibility of war plans and arguing for more
refinements.

The second illustration of well-intended but dubiously scientific advocacy is Richard Pipes's thesis that the Soviet Union thinks it can fight
and win a nuclear war.[29] Pipes, like Sagan, desired to set in motion a
turbulent debate to jar complacency, and like Sagan, he succeeded.[30]
Pipes, too, was overstating the case to make a point. Soviet strategy is
different from Western military strategy. One could make this argument
on the basis of doctrinal citations, Soviet historical experience, or simple
common sense. As an educator, it strikes this author as very telling that
there are literally hundreds of institutions of higher military education
throughout the Soviet Union, equivalent in societal prestige to U.S. graduate schools. Imagine proposing to the typical U.S. or British university
that they confer a master's or doctoral degree in military science. Now,
the point is not that the Soviet system should be copied in the West; but
it is a statement of societal priorities and the seriousness with which
military history is studied in the Soviet Union. Moreover, the Soviet
knowledge of their military history is buttressed by the remembrances
of citizens who were civilian victims or military participants in the Great
Patriotic War. Soviet generals, too, are a special breed. Where in the
West could one find a parallel for Marshal Zhukov or Rokossovsky? We
are not talking of skills in this instance, but of mind set, in which the
view is inculcated that war and deprivation must be suffered stoically

and eventual triumph is assured, provided adherence to the right political and military principles is supported by the proper mixture of social control.

The Soviet view of military strategy is quite properly Leninist in its connection of war with politics, and follows Clausewitz in its insistence upon politics as the determining factor by which military means are assigned. This view of a holistic relationship between strategy and politics does not, contrary to some arguments, make the Soviets more optimistic about fighting a war successfully, especially if they have started it by attacking someone else. To the contrary, the USSR has followed a very cautious policy in which it prefers to attack victims that are smaller in size and military capability, internally divided, and not capable of drawing upon outside allies to resist Soviet encroachment.[31] The USSR fights much more effectively on the defensive than it does on the offensive, if the campaigns of Napoleon and Hitler are any indication. If the Soviet leadership is cautious about getting into conventional war in Europe, for fear of uncertainty about war outcome even without nuclear escalation, would the same leaders be optimistic about getting into a nuclear war? Even without nuclear weapons, Soviet uncertainties loom large during any war in Europe. Soviet forces have trained for the conduct of a rapid and decisive theater offensive; if it bogged down and NATO counterattacks began to achieve momentum, the USSR would be fighting on the operational defensive under conditions very different from those of World War II. Without invading the Soviet Union proper, NATO counteroffensives could play havoc with Soviet control over fraternal Socialist allies in Eastern Europe.

It hardly seems so, and Soviet expressions of hubris about winning a nuclear war should be taken in the spirit of Sunday sermons for the congregation to repent. The sermon is undoubtedly sincere, and the congregation may sincerely want to repent, at least of some things. Human nature being what it is, however, total repentance does not come about. In the same fashion, Soviet leaders exhort the faithful with a secular version of religion that promises them fulfillment, even in the aftermath of nuclear war; but in their writings and scripts for military students who will become future military leaders, Soviet experts tell a different and more sobering story. They tell students of the ways in which nuclear weapons could interfere with the movements of their own forces as well as those of the enemy. Soviet political and military leaders write in classified as well as unclassified journals about their preferences for keeping war conventional, including war in Europe.[32] For students of military history, as the Soviets are, the most important difference between conventional and nuclear war is that, in the latter case, we have no experience with it since Hiroshima and Nagasaki. Thus, conservative assumptions about its effects (that they may be worse than expected) and its controllability (that it may escape control) have an obvious appeal, and the Soviets do find them appealing. Their entire operational art for the ground forces depends upon the careful calculation of armament norms and other indexes by which their commanders are expected to perform, even in peacetime, or their epaulets are removed.[33]

What Pipes wanted to warn the West about was the fact that, if deterrence failed, the USSR would not react with resigned fatalism. Instead, faced with what it judged the almost certain probability of war, Soviet leaders might strike preemptively, getting in the first blow before the West could do so. To Western readers a Soviet fear of our preemption seems unreasonable, but we are not reasoning through the Western end of the telescope, but the Soviet. And the Soviet perspective is that wars should be avoided, if possible, but if they cannot be, then they should be prosecuted without fear or favor.[34] This spells trouble for Western, especially U.S., notions of limited nuclear war, which was touched on before. NATO strategy depends upon escalation across discrete thresholds, from conventional to limited nuclear, and from limited nuclear, to strategic exchanges by the superpowers aimed at one another's homelands. This is not how the Soviets might choose to fight in the event. They might, for example, choose to respond to a NATO "demonstration" first use with a theater-wide cascade of nuclear salvos.[35]

One of the poorly noted issues in this debate was what the Soviets might mean by "winning." It seemed again that the victory, like the eventual triumph of communism over capitalism, was more hortatory than it was an actual prediction. Soviet military apodicta are not weather forecasts. Their seemingly authoritative pronouncements often conceal their actual meanings from outside readers, including the nonprivileged within the Soviet Union. If the Soviets expect to win a nuclear war, they do not expect to win it in the way that Westerners talk about victory in war. In the West, bourgeois civilization being triumphant, winning includes the idea of fighting at acceptable cost. And the trend is toward costs that are less and less expensive in blood and treasure, if U.S. reaction to its Vietnam experience is any indication. The Soviets are not as interested in marginal-utility theory, provided they are obtaining a substantial political payoff from a military intervention. When the payoff is dubious, as it is in Afghanistan, that is another story. The Kremlin hierarchy has apparently decided that the continued occupation of Afghanistan has little utility.

Afghanistan is a somewhat "unconventional" conventional war, however, and a limited one at that. If Soviet marshals and party or government leaders imagine that nuclear war will involve winners and losers, then they must imagine that a nuclear war could start and be stopped short of escalation to strikes against the Soviet homeland. In order to provide for this, the USSR must have strategic nuclear forces and theater nuclear forces that are functionally equivalent to, if not better than, NATO forces at both levels. Some analysts feel that the USSR is, in fact, superior to NATO in strategic and theater nuclear forces at the present time; this discussion will not go into that debate here. It suffices to consider their strategic and theater nuclear forces adequate to possibly deter NATO nuclear escalation in response to a Soviet conventional attack. In other words, the Soviet nuclear forces are counterdeterrents to NATO's nuclear deterrent.[36]

If that is so, then Soviet nuclear strategy takes on a different meaning from the interpretation that Pipes has ascribed to it. Soviet nuclear forces are threats for coercive purposes more than they are blunderbusses for destruction, although to be credible threats, they must also be credible blunderbusses. This makes Soviet strategy more difficult for the West to interpret, supposing this inference to be correct. The West must simultaneously deter nuclear war in two senses: by deterring the Soviet first use of nuclear weapons against NATO and by deterring the conventional war between East and West, which might escalate into nuclear exchanges. If, however, the West has no more than strategic nuclear equivalence with the forces of the Soviet Union, while NATO's conventional forces are planning to fight with a somewhat self-defeating strategy (see above), then deterrence is not as secure as it might seem in peacetime. In a crisis, which is what matters, it could easily break down. It might seem that crisis control would hold because of Soviet confidence, if, as has been said, NATO deterrence is problematic. But problematic NATO deterrence is not reassuring to the Soviet Union under crisis—as opposed to normal peacetime—conditions. Under normal conditions, it will be assumed by Soviet planners that NATO forces are not poised to retaliate on a hair trigger. In a crisis, however, the opposite will be assumed, and Soviet forces will be prepared to retaliate, or even preempt, in the expectation of NATO nuclear strikes. Thus, for example, the dispersal of NATO-theater nuclear weapons from their storage sites, or the movement from garrison of theater-range missiles, might seem like prudent precautions to the West, and equally points of ignition to the USSR.

Finally, Soviet expectations that they might win a nuclear war are unsound scientifically and strategically, because if they do avoid more losses in a nuclear war than NATO does, then they have probably won a prize that is not worth very much to them. An irradiated desert in Western Europe, Chernobyl on a much larger scale, will not appeal to Soviet appetites for forward settlement of their population. A Europe that glows in the dark, as the macabre saying goes, cannot glow very much in the minds of Kremlin planners who would be risking the same fate for their own citizens affected by the long-term effects of spreading radiation. The issue of winning nuclear war does not end here, however.

Although it can be scientifically shown that the effects of nuclear war are such as to preclude a traditional definition of winning, there are still degrees of losing. A Soviet society that is prepared for nuclear war, or better prepared than their Western opponents, has a relatively better chance to save the lives of its citizens and to reconstruct its postwar society. The issue of Soviet civil-defense competency is one that is hotly debated in the West, relative to the Soviet recovery potential in the aftermath of nuclear war.[37] There can, however, be no denial of the effort, by which the United States and most European states (other than Switzerland) are comparatively embarrassed. The U.S. perspective on civil defense probably cannot be changed, but this does not excuse it. It is compounded of fatalism about surviving nuclear war, on the assumption that all nuclear wars will be unlimited, about U.S.-Soviet wars, and about the absence of modern war on U.S. soil. Probably more important than the physical structures that either side has built to protect its population is the attitude of the governments involved toward the protection of their citizens, however improbable it is judged to be. This illustrates the difference between policy science and natural science. The natural-science view looks at the effects of nuclear war and says "Why bother?" Or it might acknowledge that civil defense could in some situations reduce the fatalities attendant to nuclear war, but it would stop short of deciding that passive defenses are worthwhile. The policy-science view emphasizes the responsibility that government has for making its best effort to protect its citizens, even from the worst disasters and those caused by government folly. Civil defense will not give the USSR a war-winning strategy unless the war is very limited, in which case civil defense may not be necessary. It will, however, give the citizens of the state in which civil defense is taken seriously the feeling that their protection is a desirable end in itself. Curiously, democratic societies for the most part seem less interested in having this demonstrated to them than does the authoritarian Soviet Union, which requires less in the way of public affirmation.[38]

This review of science and scientism, of strategy and strategism, is certainly not complete. The paradigm case for both scientism and strategism, as opposed to science and strategy, is provided in the extensive debate over ballistic missile defense and the Strategic Defense Initiative proposed by the Reagan administration. This deserves consideration at greater length than the issues just discussed, and so will receive it.

NOTES

1. According to two of Secretary of Defense McNamara's principal staff, systems analysis had little influence on the conduct of the war in Vietnam, despite its pervasiveness elsewhere in the Department of Defense. See Alain C. Enthoven

and K. Wayne Smith, *How Much is Enough? Shaping the Defense Program, 1961–69* (New York: Harper & Row, 1971), p. 270.

2. For an assessment of U.S. defense decision making in Vietnam, see Robert W. Komer, *Bureaucracy at War: U.S. Performance in the Vietnam Conflict* (Boulder, CO: Westview Press, 1986).

3. For contrasting assessments, see Matthew Bunn and Kosta Tsipis, "The Uncertainties of Preemptive Nuclear Attack," *Scientific American* 249, No. 5 (November 1983): 38–47; and T. K. Jones and W. Scott Thompson, "Central War and Civil Defense," *Orbis* 22, No. 3 (Fall 1978): 681–713.

4. President's Commission on U.S. Strategic Forces (Scowcroft Commission), *Report* (Washington, DC: April 1983).

5. U.S. Congress, Office of Technology Assessment, *MX Missile Basing* (Washington, DC: U.S. GPO, September 1981) reviews preferred Carter administration and other options.

6. For the case that ICBMs have unique properties important for deterrence, see Colin S. Gray and Blair Stewart, "The Virtues of Diversity and the Future of the ICBM," in *Missiles for the Nineties: ICBMs and Strategic Policy*, ed. Barry R. Schneider, Colin S. Gray, and Keith B. Payne (Boulder, CO: Westview Press, 1984), Ch. 2, pp. 7–28.

7. Trident II D–5 submarine-launched ballistic missiles are scheduled to begin deployment in U.S. Ohio class submarines in 1989. They are expected to have accuracies improved over the current Trident I (C–4) estimated C.E.P (circular error probable) of .25 nautical miles. See John M. Collins with Patrick M. Cronin, *U.S.-Soviet Military Balance: 1980–1985* (New York: Pergamon Brassey's, 1985), p. 178.

8. See Ashton B. Carter, "Assessing Command System Vulnerability," in *Managing Nuclear Operations*, ed. Ashton Carter, John D. Steinbruner, and Charles A. Zraket (Washington, DC: Brookings Institution, 1987), pp. 574–78, urging consideration of SSBN vulnerability in terms of the submarines' mission requirements.

9. Bruce G. Blair, *Strategic Command and Control: Redefining the Nuclear Threat* (Washington, DC: Brookings Institution, 1985), p. 189.

10. For discussion of British and French nuclear forces and their targeting, see Lawrence Freedman, "British Nuclear Targeting," and David S. Yost, "French Nuclear Targeting," Ch. 5 and Ch. 6 in *Strategic Nuclear Targeting*, ed. Desmond Ball and Jeffrey Richelson (Ithaca, NY: Cornell University Press, 1986).

11. Soviet SS–25 and SS-X–24 missiles are characterized in U.S. Department of Defense, *Soviet Military Power:1987* (Washington, DC: U.S. GPO, March 1987), pp. 30–31.

12. See Desmond Ball, "Can Nuclear War Be Controlled?" *Adelphi Papers* 169 (London: International Institute for Strategic Studies, Autumn 1981).

13. Problems facing Gorbachev in his effort to change the system are noted in Stephen F. Cohen, *Sovieticus: American Misperceptions and Soviet Realities* (New York: Norton, 1986), pp. 78–82.

14. See Cohen, *Sovieticus*, pp. 134–38.

15. A comprehensive evaluation of the Soviet ground forces is John Erickson, Lynn Hansen, and William Schneider, *Soviet Ground Forces: An Operational Assessment* (Boulder, CO: Westview Press, 1986).

16. Gregory F. Treverton, *Making the Alliance Work: The United States and Western Europe* (Ithaca, NY: Cornell University Press, 1985).

17. See Richard A. Gabriel, *Military Incompetence* (New York: Hill and Wang, 1985).

18. This was during the Cuban missile crisis, when the U.S. Navy implemented an anti-submarine-warfare campaign according to standard operating procedures, but with implications very anomalous for political control of the crisis. See Graham T. Allison, *Essence of Decision* (Boston: Little, Brown, 1971), p. 138.

19. Richard K. Betts, *Surprise Attack: Lessons for Defense Planning* (Washington, DC: Brookings Institution, 1982), pp. 162–65.

20. See William W. Kaufmann, "Nonnuclear Deterrence," in *Alliance Security and the No-First Use Question*, ed. John D. Steinbruner and Leon V. Sigal (Washington, DC: Brookings Institution, 1983), pp. 43–90.

21. Barry R. Posen, "Competing Views of the Central Region Conventional Balance," in *Alternative Military Strategies for the Future*, ed. Keith A. Dunn and William O. Staudenmaier (Boulder, CO: Westview Press, 1985), Ch. 5, pp. 87–132.

22. See William W. Kaufmann, *A Reasonable Defense* (Washington, DC: Brookings Institution, 1986).

23. Gen. Bernard W. Rogers, USA, "Follow-on Forces Attack (FOFA): Myths and Realities," *NATO Review* 32, No. 6 (December 1984): 1–8.

24. Christopher N. Donnelly, "Soviet Operational Concepts in the 1980s," in *Strengthening Conventional Deterrence in Europe: Proposals for the 1980s*, Report of the European Security Study (New York: St. Martin's Press, 1983), pp. 105–36.

25. See Richard Ned Lebow, "Decision Making in Crises," in *Psychology and the Prevention of Nuclear War*, ed. Ralph K. White (New York: New York University Press, 1986), pp. 397–413.

26. The original nuclear winter study was R. P. Turco, O. B. Toon, T. P. Ackerman, J. B. Pollack, and C. Sagan (TTAPS), "Nuclear Winter: Global Consequences of Multiple Nuclear Explosions," *Science* 222 (1983), pp. 1283–300. See also TTAPS, "The Climatic Effects of Nuclear War," *Scientific American* 251 (August 1984): 33–43.

27. Russell Seitz, "In from the Cold: Nuclear Winter Melts Down," *National Interest*, Fall 1986, pp. 3–17. Seitz questions the methodological impartiality of nuclear-winter studies.

28. Stephen J. Cimbala, "Flexible Targeting, Escalation Control and War in Europe," *Armed Forces and Society* 12, No. 3 (Spring 1986): 383–400.

29. Richard Pipes, "Why the Soviet Union Thinks It Could Fight and Win a Nuclear War," *Commentary* (July 1977), pp. 21–34.

30. See Robert L. Arnett, "Soviet Attitudes Towards Nuclear War: Do They Really Think They Can Win?" *Journal of Strategic Studies* 2, No. 2 (September 1979): 172–91.

31. P. H. Vigor, *Soviet Blitzkrieg Theory* (New York: St. Martin's Press, 1983).

32. John G. Hines, Phillip A. Petersen, and Notra Trulock III, "Soviet Military Theory from 1945–2000: Implications for NATO," *Washington Quarterly* 9, No. 4 (Fall 1986): 117–37.

33. On the importance of norms in Soviet operational planning, see John Er-

ickson, Lynn Hansen, and William Schneider, *Soviet Ground Forces: An Operational Assessment* (Boulder, CO: Westview Press, 1986), Ch. 4.

34. See John Erickson, "The Soviet View of Deterrence: A General Survey," *Survival* 24, No. 6 (November/December 1982): 242–51.

35. The possibility of a Soviet theater-wide nuclear response to NATO limited and selective first use is noted in Stephen M. Meyer, "Soviet Perspectives on the Paths to Nuclear War," in *Hawks, Doves and Owls: An Agenda for Avoiding Nuclear War*, ed. Graham T. Allison, Albert Carnesale, and Joseph S. Nye, Jr. (New York: Norton, 1985), Ch. 7, p. 201.

36. Samuel P. Huntington, "The Renewal of Strategy," in *The Strategic Imperative: New Policies for American Security*, ed. Samuel Huntington (Cambridge, MA: Ballinger, 1982), Ch. 1, pp. 1–52.

37. Harriet Fast Scott and William F. Scott, *The Soviet Control Structure: Capabilities for Wartime Survival* (New York: Crane, Russak/National Strategy Information Center, 1983).

38. On this point see Gary L. Guertner, "Strategic Vulnerability of a Multinational State: Deterring the Soviet Union," *Political Science Quarterly* 96, No. 2 (Summer 1981): 209–23.

4

DETERRENCE, RATIONALITY, AND NUCLEAR WEAPONS

Like the Lewis Carroll character who insisted upon believing two impossible things before breakfast, deterrence theorists believe in rationality to prevent war. Deterrence having failed, they also believe in rationality to prevent the war from escalating beyond their control into an all-out holocaust. Of course, it will be contended this is a very conditional rationality, dependent on time and circumstances. Nonetheless, however qualified it is, there remains the dependency upon a rational model of choice, applied to contexts outside of the Western tradition whence it came. This faith in rationality does not always result from exposure to military history or other defense studies, but from the immersion of U.S. strategists in economics and engineering. The application of economic and other mathematically based models to nuclear strategy can, under the proper conditions, enrich our understanding of certain issues. Misapplied, economic and game-theoreticial models of strategy can lead us down the primrose path.[1]

The rationality of economics, for example, is both like and unlike the rationality of strategy. In both cases there are individuals or state actors who are attempting to obtain the most of some desired commodity or state of affairs, or to endure the least miserable of some undesired event or condition. This is the rationality of utilitarianism, as it has trickled down to the twentieth century, much edited from its original formulations by Jeremy Bentham and John Stuart Mill. Utilitarianism was a valuable corrective to theories that posited that individuals either (a) did not know their desired goals or objectives, or (b) if they did, could not establish any consistent preference ordering among them, with some authority telling them what it ought to be. Problem (b) is still with us, as Kenneth

Arrow's modern contributions and Thomas Hobbes's earlier ones remind us.

We will leave aside for the moment the problem of cumulation of individual preferences into collective ones (for example, the state speaking on behalf of its citizens), because it is tricky enough in economics and in politics more so. Let us assume for purposes of discussion that the policy makers of a political community speak for the citizens in general with regard to its foreign-policy responsibilities. There are other issues to bedevil us with regard to the differences between economic and political rationality.

Politics, as Plato and Aristotle struggled to instruct us, begins with an effort to define the good. The good is not just anything that people or states value. The good is that which is genuinely good for individuals and political communities, judged by an objective standard. In Plato's case, the objective standard was that of a designed utopia, with philosopher kings who were educated to distinguish the objective good from the subjective good. Never would ancient political theorists have endorsed the notion that one defines the good by majority vote. This was their omission—not taking into account the need to include in a definition of the good the sentiments of the greatest number, as well as the most learned. This omission occurred in their thinking because they mistakenly chased an objectivity that may be possible in some experiments, but never in political ones.

Conversely, it was the contribution of the utilitarians to introduce the idea of the greater good as being that seen by the greater number, and in so doing, to reintroduce the masses into a political dialogue with the elite. Along with this contribution, however, the utilitarians flattened the idea of the good into a very subjective condition: The good is what the greater number of persons say it is. Now, John Stuart Mill's writing on freedom of expression makes it very clear that he understood that there are absolutes as well as relative goods in society, but we are speaking here of the net impact of utilitarianism, notwithstanding some of the exceptional proponents of it.

This contrast, between the essential idea of the good as something objective, versus the good as something to be determined by cumulation of individually subjective preferences, continues to be important for political thought today. It is especially important for nuclear strategy. The difference between the essentialist and what we might call the instrumentalist view of the good is vital to deciding what it is that nuclear strategy should do. For example, it is customary for strategists to say that the objective of deterrence is to prevent war. Preventing war, however, is part of the definition of deterrence. Therefore, to say that the objective of deterrence is to prevent war is to say nothing very meaningful, especially about how deterrence is supposed to work.

How deterrence is supposed to work is the subject of a great many volumes.[2] To make a long story short, it is premised upon the rationality of the threatener and the rationality of the party being threatened. There are two kinds of threats involved, one a continuing one in the absence of any immediate crisis, and the other, a more specific irritant that may prompt nuclear preemption or retaliation.[3] In other words, simmering within the state of nature referred to as the international system, there is the lingering possibility of legalized resort to violence against one another by sovereign political entities. This lingering patina of latent violence is the "deep structure," as linguists might say, in which the particular patterns of specific crisis and conflict are embedded. The form of this deep structure of latent violence can vary, but its content is quite nicely characterized by Hobbes's description of a state of nature as a "war of all against all." This can be misdescribed as anarchy, which it is not, else nuclear-armed states would have blown themselves to kingdom come decades ago, but it is not a legal order, either. The order is provided by diplomacy and strategy, which succeed to the extent that they are cognizant of this deep structure of latent violence permeating the system. If we think of this deep structure as a kind of jello mold and the diplomatic and strategic relations among states as ships that have comparatively smooth or rocky sailing, we shall not be far off. It is not inevitable that diplomacy and strategy will be so badly bungled that the ships will sink into the jello, but with effort they can, and history records that they have.

Deterrence is founded on the premise that this jello mold of latent violence can be changed in viscosity while the ship is moving and while, if necessary, tail winds are blowing the ships of state in the direction of one another, possibly into a head-on collision. This leads naturally into a commingling of game-theory models and deterrence metaphors, as in "chicken" or "prisoner's dilemma."[4] The language of economics also lends a hand with the assumption of payoffs and values, which can be determined from matrix algebra by applying the proper formula to the correct cell entries. The idea of interdependent payoffs has been borrowed from game theory and applied to nuclear strategy with especially interesting results. What one side gets out of a conflict depends in part upon the actions of its adversary, and those actions are in turn dependent upon the reactions of the first side, and so forth. Sometimes this elaborate minuet is played out solely in the minds of theorists or policy makers without reference to actual events or even plausible ones.

Although proper uses of scientific method are to be welcomed, the application of game-theoretical and economic rationality to nuclear strategy has for the most part been unproductive of strategic, as opposed to economic, insights. This generalization is not offered to disparage the efforts of some very productive thinkers, for those efforts are indeed noteworthy.[5] The problem is that the subject matter does not lend itself to rationalization, that is, to the rationality of means, exclusive of the rationality of ends. And the rationality of ends is frequently not amenable to quantification of the most important issues, including national survival, honor or defeat, however they are defined. This, it will be argued by some readers, is not news. Deterrence theory is neither better nor worse in this regard than other political theories that deal with important but "mushy" variables. Let us get on with the task of pinning numbers on things and not be delayed by metaphysical objections.

The philosophical point, however, about the difference between rationality of means and ends as it applies to nuclear strategy and deterrence, cannot be dismissed so readily,[6] for the rationality of ends is not different from the rationality of means just as a matter of degree, but as a matter of kind. This means that the rationality of ends, as that rationality is applied to nuclear strategy, cannot derive the ends from the means at all, nor can the means be derived from ends with any consistency. By "any consistency" is meant according to any decision rules that have the property of following the same logic from one case to another, regardless of the content of the cases. There are several reasons why there is not a crossnational or transcultural logic of deterrence, except one so general as to be devoid of historical content.

First, there is the problem of ethnocentrism, of the temptation to attribute to one's opposite number in a conflictual relationship the same logic of relating strategy to policy that one follows at home.[7] Sometimes this is referred to as "mirror imaging" of the opponent's strategy through the conceptual lenses of one's own, and this does happen all too frequently. The problem of ethnocentrism, however, is deeper than mirror imaging in the failure to see into the perceptions of the uses of latent violence that are culturally conditioned. Consider, for example, the problem of war termination, of how we would seek to end a war begun for whatever reason, before it escalated beyond the control of U.S. and Soviet policy makers. This has been the preoccupation of academic and governmental policy analysts for some time in the United States, and some considerable thought has been given to how the problem of war termination might be approached, even in nuclear war.[8]

Undoubtedly, the Soviet concept of war termination, especially as it might apply to superpower nuclear war, differs from that of the United States. It differs not only because of disagreements over who gets what share of the international pie, but also because of deeply rooted historical and cultural experiences. As Raymond L. Garthoff has explained, the Soviet view of war termination is bound up with the expectation that the West will attack it, rather than the reverse, and that the war might be a decisive clash for the survival of socialism, not just the USSR.[9] This has very significant implications for the choice of weapons, tactics, and negotiating strategies by Soviet opponents, even after deterrence has failed. It would suggest that, all other things being equal, the Soviets are going to have difficulty receiving a transcultural communication of the Western intent to keep nuclear war limited, although it has started. Albert Wohlstetter and Richard Brody have recently argued very cogently that nuclear war, even in Europe, might remain limited, and that the two superpowers would have very strong reasons for attempting to keep it so.[10] George H. Quester has suggested in a very interesting essay that the two sides might swap doctrine, with NATO desiring to suggest that war could not be controlled, and the USSR that it could.[11] Without denying any of these well-argued positions about what might happen, it must not be taken for granted that the Western position about escalation control will be obvious to the USSR, either through tacit or explicit communication. And the nuclear detonations against Warsaw Pact forces or society will be interpreted by Kremlin leaders not only as the first steps of a collective-bargaining agreement, but as creating some potential for the negation of agreement altogether.

If the first problem with utilitarian rationality as applied to nuclear strategy lies in its potential for cultural bias, the second problem is that the connection between means and ends cannot be established independently of the logic of successive approximation. There is some necessary jargon here, meaning that policy makers in the real world, as opposed to game theorists and economists, rarely have the opportunity to "maximize" their values. Especially in war, they must approximate their desired goals, while paying the costs in blood and treasure and then ending up with some, but not all, of what they wanted. And in nuclear war, should it occur, the maximization of value as traditionally understood in war, meaning victory, becomes an absurdity both logically and empirically. Thus, the connection between means and ends will proceed by successive approximation of the goals that can be obtained under the circumstances—which may include the detonation of nuclear warheads on one's own soil.

Successive approximation of a desired end state is rational, if it arrives at a solution that is acceptable to the parties involved, whether or not it is rational according to the logic of the observer.[12] From the standpoint of science (as misapplied to social phenomena, or scientism) this is heresy. The connection between means and ends must be objectively determined, with reference to the payoff table. The payoff table, however, is itself filled with values that are constantly changing as the war evolves and as policy makers estimate probable outcomes. Now, this might be thought to be manageable within the framework of game theory itself, in the way that admissions officers in universities avoid a fixed reference standard by operating under a "rolling" admissions policy until quotas are filled. The problem here is more difficult than that. Not only are the values for the combatants in the payoff table subject to change as the conflict develops, but the most important value, once war begins, cannot be entered into the table at all (that is, it is exogenous to the model). This most important value, once war has begun, is the degree of control that the two sides jointly can exercise over the process of escalation. Not only is this value unknown, in the two sides' relative appreciation of its merit, but it is also highly dependent upon decisions made before the war began. If even one side, let alone both, has not provided for continuing control over the pace and intensity of escalation and for the strategic command, control, and communications (C3) to maintain that grip through the duration of the war, then the entire payoff matrix is a crap shoot.

Thomas Schelling discusses this issue with reference to the problem of limited nuclear reprisals during war in Europe:

> It would be a mistake to think that conducting war in the measured cadence of limited reprisal somehow rescues the whole business of war from impetuosity and gives it "rational" qualities that it would otherwise lack. True, there is a sense in which anything done coolly, deliberately, on schedule, by plan, upon reflection, in accordance with rules and formulae, and pursuant to a calculus, is "rational" but it is in a very limited sense.[13]

In our terms, one can rationally conduct an irrational war with stupid political objectives and perhaps societally self-destructive. Or, to reverse gears, if the war is likely to destroy our society for the sake of inflicting compensatory damage on the opponent, it is obviously not rational in the proper sense, although the desire for revenge may be perfectly understandable. If real policy makers fighting a nuclear war, or deciding to plunge into one, must proceed by successive approximation of a desired end state that itself is subject to change, then they may be approximating their way into an inferno. To this pessimistic judgment it will be objected that sometimes a nation is attacked and must retaliate, whatever the issue of rationality as described by theorists. Statist political theories even justify revenge for its own sake and for the sake of deterring subsequent attacks. This simplistic answer to a complicated issue does not suffice, however, for it is not obvious that any state undergoing nuclear attack should retaliate with nuclear weapons under all circumstances. It might not always be logical to do so, especially if the state being attacked is grossly inferior to its attacker, and so can avoid suicide only by surrender of important values. The rationality of deterrence does not help us with this problem, except to reassure us that we feel better having gotten even with an unprovoked nuclear aggression against ourselves or against our allies, if only for reasons of carthasis.

The term "unprovoked" leads us to the third major problem inherent in nuclear deterrent rationalities as applied to superpower conflict. An unprovoked attack implies, in the deterrence lexicon, a preventive war that is not prompted by the attacker's fear of being attacked (defined as preemption). A preventive war would be planned in advance in the expectation that if war were not begun now, a future change in the balance of power or intentions of another state could cause that other state to attack. A preventive war is not necessarily an attack out of the blue, which is completely contrary to any anticipations of hostility by the defender. Recall our discussion, above, of the latent potential for violence, our floating jello mold on which the various ships of diplomacy and strategy rest. This latent violence lies beneath the surface of relations between all states, but especially hostile ones, even if they are not contemplating war. If they are, however, then preventive war converts latent violence into a defender's vulnerability, before the defender's expectation of attack can be converted into specific preparedness for it. As Richard K. Betts has explained with reference to surprise attacks, most surprises succeed not because warning was not available, but because of lagging response by the victim.[14] Converting warning into response means, in our terms, understanding the potential inherent in latent violence as it relates to the probability of aggression by one state against another. Earlier we noted the systemic properties of this problem, that an international state of nature puts all nations on guard that they share a security dilemma. That condition is still acknowledged, but more than that is at issue here.

What is also at issue is hinted at in the distinction between preventive and preemptive war, the former a presumably cold-blooded decision, and the latter more likely in the heat of anger, or panic. This distinction is meaningful in an academic assessment, after the fact, of why states went to war. How meaningful it is to the decision makers who must decide for war or peace is questionable. Richard Ned Lebow has studied extensively the crisis preceding the outbreak of World War I and compared it to more contemporary crises, such as the Cuban missile crisis.[15] He has identified a family of crises that he terms "brinkmanship" crises, meaning that the crisis originates in the expectation by one side that it can coerce another in order to prevent (among other things) a future unfavorable balance of power for the first state. In the case of World War I deterrence failed, and the war destroyed three empires. This was a decoupling of political objectives from military strategy, of the most self-destructive sort. Whether the leaders of Germany, Russia, and other states that plunged Europe into war can be deemed subjectively rational is more complicated. They had avoided war in previous twentieth-century crises and had practiced more diplomatic braggadocio than they had effective military maneuvers. This faith in diplomacy, however, was blown over by very inflexible war plans, which allowed for only total rather than partial mobilization, especially in the cases of Germany and Russia. Thus, mobilizations that were thought to be signals of deterrence to potential adversaries were actually interpreted as provocations.[16] The difference between the intentions of mobilizers and the interpretations placed on mobilizations by their adversaries was obscured by the fact that mobilizations were also intended to improve fighting strength if need be. This line, between deterrence and provocation of a potential opponent, is a slippery slope that cannot be factored into rationality models, because the gradient of the slope cannot be known until after deterrence has failed. With the advantage of historical hindsight, we can say that the gradient was too steep or that the policy makers should have measured the slope with more accuracy, but this is difficult, if not impossible, to foresee. And, if we follow the distinction between preventive and preemptive war, what are we to make of the Schlieffen Plan, which Germany devised many years before World War I in the expectation that war would come at some future date with exactly the same cast of allies and adversaries? Was this a preventive war or a preemptive war, since Germany could have avoided war with Britain by not attacking the Belgians, at least for a time?

The answer cannot be provided by deterrence theory, because the distinction between preventive and preemptive war in that theory is one that confuses means and ends. A war is preventive if it is well thought out in advance of any particular incident, and preemptive if undertaken in the expectation of imminent attack. This emphasis of deterrence theory upon the distinction between preventive war and preemption is important to deterrence theorists, because they assume that the first is coldly logical and the second, panic stricken. Thus the first, a coldly logical nuclear surprise attack, is ruled out as impossible by dint of "irrationality." It cannot, however, be established that a preemptive nuclear attack is more rational than a preventive war without reference to values that lie apart from the logic of deterrence theory, including the inherent values that societies place upon their standard of living and societal cohesion, not to say survival. If those values are absolute instead of relative, as they are apt to be, then preventive war is no more irrational than preemptive war, unless preemptive war is undertaken on the basis of evidence that is irrefutable (about the intention of the other side to strike first).

We can never know irrefutably, however, that the opponent has decided to attack us until its missiles have been launched, in which case we are too late to preempt. Since neither can know this, then either side in attacking first is doing something that is not strictly preventive and not strictly preemptive, but a little of both. Perhaps it can be called "anticipatory preemption" but nomenclature is not the issue. The issue is that deterrence logic leads to an assumption that preemption is a logical action between nuclear-armed superpowers, although preventive war never is. In fact, neither action may be rational, or if one is, than both may be. Deterrence theory cannot tell us which is which, because it is neutral (in the sense of oblivious, instead of nonpartisan) with regard to end values, and especially moral values. From deterrence rationality one can derive only the notion that there are degrees of prudent risk that can be "managed" successfully or not, depending on the definition of management that is applied.[17]

RATIONALITY, DETERRENCE, AND MORALITY

The subject of ethics and nuclear war is one to which volumes have been devoted, and it cannot be covered in its entirety here. Nonetheless, it is appropriate to follow our discussion of preventive versus preemptive attack with a consideration of some aspects of this larger issue, as to when, if ever, it would be rational in a moral or ethical sense to wage nuclear war.

Traditional Western thinking, derived from theology in the Middle Ages, has distinguished between the justice of war (*ad bellum*) and justice in war (*in bello*). The justice of war has to do with the reasons for fighting. Justic in war refers to the way in which combat is carried out, for example, in the ability of the disputants to distinguish combatants from noncombatants. The justice of war emphasizes the legality and rectitude of a conflict, determining who is fighting for "right" causes; justice in war tells us what is normal or standard conduct expected of soldiers and what is abnormal.[18]

It would seem evident that justice-of-war questions take pride of place over justice-in-war matters, in the sense that one would first want to determine if the decision to go to war (compared to other alternatives) is right or wrong. If it is wrong, then the methods of conducting the fighting could hardly be judged right. This, however, has not been the practice in international jurisprudence. Instead, the two dimensions are thought to stand separately, and can judge the conduct of soldiers harshly, even if they are fighting in a just cause. We think of uniformed officers who shoot defenseless women and children not as heroes but as criminals who have failed to live up to expectations of how to fight fairly, as embodied in national and international law and custom. Much of this law and custom is of Western origin, and thus ethnocentric to that extent. Having some limitations, however, whatever their sources, is better than having none, and leaders of the West are obligated by precedent to observe the standards of their own legal communities and traditions, whatever others do. Thus, for example, the fact that the Iranian government collaborated with "demonstrators" in seizing and occupying the U.S. embassy in Tehran in 1979 does not justify U.S. retaliation in kind. Nor do the battlefield habits of Iranian and Iraqi commanders, including the alleged use of poison gas by one side, deserve emulation by those with different legal traditions.

With regard to nuclear weapons, however, the Western legal tradition is not much more help than any other. Even if a war justly begun (say, in response to an attack), it seems very difficult to use nuclear weapons in a discriminating way, so as to fulfill the requirements of justice in war. The collateral damage attendant on nuclear detonations would fly in the face of efforts to spare noncombatants or to discriminate cleanly between militarily relevant and irrelevant target sets. Nor is the issue of justice of war an easy one in the case of nuclear retaliation following attack. One has to ask what kind of attack, against which of the defender's values. It must also be asked, What does the defender want to accomplish in response? Thus, the effort to preserve justice in war, in a nuclear conflict, requires advance thinking about justice of war, or whether one would retaliate, and how.

Scenarios are often posited in which the Soviet Union launches an unprovoked bolt-from-the-blue attack on the United States, attempting to destroy as many U.S. strategic nuclear and other military forces as possible. The United States then retaliates in these standard models of superpower nuclear war against a comprehensive target set, including remaining Soviet nuclear forces, other forces, war recovery assets, and command centers. If the USSR were to make such an attack, it would not fulfill the requirements for a just war in the sense of justice of war, unless the USSR were correctly anticipating a U.S. attack and striking in preemption. The Soviets, however, would never be 100 percent certain of a planned U.S. first strike until it was launched. Therefore, if they or we launch retaliatory forces in the expectation of an attack, but before an attack is actually irrefutably confirmed, justice has not been served.

Even if we are unjustly attacked with nuclear salvos in this very simple and hypothetical case, it is not obvious that we should retaliate early and comprehensively. If the two superpowers are evenly matched with regard to strategic nuclear capability, and one preempts the other, the second might not hit back at every conceivable target, despite its instincts to do so. Instead, the second party in this case might strike back initially with a more discriminating response, withholding other forces as an inducement to the attacker to terminate the war before it escapes their joint control, for once nuclear war begins, the logic of justice in war takes precedence. Although the side that struck first might have begun the war with just cause (which would have to meet very exacting standards), it does not follow that it should continue the fighting until arsenals are exhausted. In similar fashion, even if the defender is aggrieved, it is not necessarily the just response to destroy immediately as much of the attacker's value as is physically possible.

This notion, that justice in war can be a pertinent issue, even in superpower nuclear war, is resisted by those who feel that to acknowledge any degree of rectitude in nuclear war makes it more possible, by removing inhibitions against it. This is a very difficult issue, one that everyone hopes to avoid having to face in practice, but not thereby easily dismissed in theory. Can one buy into hell on the installment plan, by getting into small nuclear wars instead of larger ones, or by terminating some nuclear wars short of societal holocaust? Technology will force the question into the consciousness of military and civilian leaders, even if ethical philosophy does not. The future of nuclear-warhead technology, for example, is likely to provide for more accurate targeting of smaller-yield warheads. The same targets that formerly would have required bursts of weapons, with great collateral damage to surrounding forces or society, now might be attacked with small-yield nuclear or nonnuclear weapons. Precision-guided munitions could conceivably be delivered against missile silos, command centers, and other targets, which could then be destroyed by a fraction of the blast and thermal radiation attendant on larger explosions. The kind of dilemma these more discriminating weapons might present for policy makers is illustrated in the neutron-bomb controversy (more properly, the enhanced radiation weapon). This device allows for nuclear explosions in which blast is minimized and opposing forces are destroyed by neutron bombardment, although blast effects are not eliminated. Because incidental property destruction, relative to combat personnel, was minimized, the weapon has been denounced as inhumane and cruel, and its deployment remains controversial in NATO Europe. Opponents of the neutron bomb objected that its deployment would make nuclear weapons seem usable, and thus, nuclear war more likely.

This argument, that more usable weapons make war more likely, must be addressed by deterrence theorists in an unambiguous way. In order to uphold the architecture of deterrence logic, they are going to have to state a clear preference for usable weapons, as opposed to unusable ones, or admit that deterrence rests on a bluff. As we will see, this issue becomes especially problematic for cases of extended deterrence, in which one nation's nuclear force is thought to guarantee a second country against aggression by a third. If nuclear weapons are kept as undiscriminating as possible, on the theory that they will therefore never be used, then we have deliberately omitted from our arsenal options that will spare society possibly avoidable destruction. Nor can the deterrence theorist sidestep the question of whether all nuclear war automatically leads to holocaust, including all superpower nuclear war, because if it does, then the theorist has no choice but to call for abolition of those weapons. It cannot be a measure of deterrence (except for the psychopath) to threaten destruction that is unlimited and to avoid the development of weapons and options that could allow for discriminating attacks. In any case, weapons laboratories and military services on both sides will be hard at work making available usable nuclear weapons, or quasinuclear weapons (nonnuclear weapons with comparable effects). The worst position for the

West to find itself in, morally and otherwise, would be on the receiving end of a discriminating nuclear attack to which it could not respond with other than total war. Then, those in the West who advocated in peacetime that we not acquire any capability for selective nuclear response will almost surely point to our self-induced inflexibility and argue that we should not retaliate at all.

The reverse danger also must be addressed by deterrence theorists, however, that nuclear weapons may become so diversified and compartmentalized that they are used cheaply on behalf of trivial issues, or in place of conventional forces, because the latter have not been adequately provided. The fantasy of dial-a-nuke is just as dangerous as the closure of a box that allows a choice only between "no nukes" or "all nukes." It must never seem to either side that the use of nuclear weapons will be interpreted as an escalation of degree, rather than kind. Instead, in a legal and moral sense, the use of nuclear weapons will be like the use of poison gas, marking off a clear threshold beyond which fewer inhibitions will restrain the combatants in a conflict, and setting a potentially lower threshold for mischief in the next one. The symbolism of the first use of nuclear weapons by a superpower will break precedent and signal that previous expectations about how far either will go are now undergoing reconsideration. Moral philosophers might want to debate whether this symbolism of crosssing the nuclear threshold in anger for the first time since Nagasaki would constitute a violation of just-war tradition in itself. It would change the war into a different kind of war psychologically, in terms of the expectations of soldiers and policy makers who were fighting it, and it would relax an inhibition that until now has been binding on superpowers and other states with the potential to use nuclear forces. In the same way that the first terrorist who assassinated a head of state set a precedent, one that the civilized community cannot endorse in principle, even when the victim is a disreputable scoundrel, so, too, the first use of nuclear weapons since 1945 will set a precedent that others may imitate, to the detriment of civilized life.

Some moral philosophers and other thinkers want to get around this set of problems by arguing that nuclear weapons can be used to threaten, but actually carrying out the threat remains impermissible. This is not acceptable deterrence logic, however it suffices as moral philosophy, for it leaves the problem of maintaining credibility for an incredible threat, that is, one that has been declared immoral to carry out. For Western leaders to maintain such a position for very long would risk alienation of their public support and also risk failure to deter Soviet leaders in a crisis. Strategists and heads of state in the United States and Western Europe will have to decide whether to forego the nuclear option in principle, or, if they cannot, then how to maintain it in a way that is consistent with their traditions of just war and war prevention.

Others might argue that if it is rational to threaten to retaliate with nuclear weapons in response to certain provocations, then it is rational to carry out the threat, even with means that in themselves are abhorrent or irrational. A better formulation of this argument would be to state that the preparation of credible retaliatory options (for the moment leaving aside arguments about what "credible" is) is certainly consistent with the rationality or morality of nuclear threats. Nevertheless, there remains a gap, perhaps one that cannot be bridged, between nuclear threats, however credible, and nuclear retaliation, at least between superpowers. Execution of the threat is difficult to relate to any sensible political objective other than revenge, with the single exception that, should limited nuclear war break out, war termination would be sought through carrots and sticks, including some nuclear retaliation.

One approach to closing this gap between the logic of nuclear threatening and the logic of its execution is to recognize that nuclear weapons have very circumscribed uses in retaliation against other nuclear weapons or as last resorts, if Europe is being lost in a conventional war, and then to say so clearly. Only in the most drastic circumstances, it should be made clear to friend and potential foe, would nuclear attacks be a preferred way of waging war. Nor is it prudent to advertise to the opponent that shortcuts to its strangulation will be used once war begins, such as the prompt decapitation of the opponent's civilian and military leadership. Perhaps, in the event, this would be done, if less desperate options seemed not to work, but to advertise it on the front end of declaratory policy gives the opponent no incentive to limit his attacks. So we will have less control, rather than more, after deterrence fails, and this is perhaps the greatest failure of justice in war—the loss of control and the abdication of responsibility for levels and kinds of destruction. Those who decide for war, even aggressive war by the standards of international law, are not necessarily more immoral, in the proper sense of that term, than those who refuse to limit the destructiveness of war when they can do so, even if the war was imposed on them. Thus, the Japanese attack on Pearl Harbor does not in itself justify the use of atomic bombs against Hiroshima and Nagasaki.

Another contribution to justice in war is to maintain central political control over the uses of nuclear weapons, even after deterrence fails. Once nuclear war begins, conflict is apt to spread to the extremities of military command organizations, each primarily concerned with its own protection and the survival of the forces under its control. Maintaining centralized control over these dispersed forces and commanders will be difficult, and the temptation considerable for force commanders and beleaguered combatants to improvise their own rules of the game. Procedures should be established and rehearsed in peacetime that will guarantee some continuity of central control over nuclear release, even after war has begun. Moreover, it should be made clear to the Soviet Union by the United States, and vice versa, that this is the case, else one side will anticipate a loss of control by the other, and so relax any controls of its own. The difficulty of establishing such controls in peacetime is that exercises cannot simulate the fog of war completely, and no one can anticipate how rapidly expectations will change among leaders and commanders, once nuclear detonations have begun. We are better off for having done the rehearsals, however, although they might be unrealistic, compared to having no advance preparation for continuing control beyond the earliest stages of conflict. Improvising central control under the stress of nuclear war, once that war has spread to U.S. or Soviet homelands, strains the capacities of planners and the credulity of leaders on both sides.

Another issue, related to the question of control and deterrence rationality, is whether it is either rational or moral for deterrence to rest upon the assumption of loss of control over weapons that might destroy civilization. Western strategic thought walks a fine line here, and sometimes stumbles over it, between the "rationality of irrationality" strategies that cover for lack of sufficient forces in crisis management and the requirement for escalation control implicit in deterrence theory and explicit in some government policy statements. Moreover, as the author is reminded in correspondence with Dr. Patrick M. Morgan, a colleague who has written extensively on deterrence theory, if the deterrer can be irrational, so can the deteree. If both are irrational, deterrence fails. The problem is similar to that in economics, with regard to the transaction between producer and consumer rationalities. It turns out that, if consumers are as fully rational as economic theory supposes, then a great many more producers would go out of business. The real marketplace, as opposed to the marketplace of neoclassical theory, is supported by a constant brainwashing of advertising, which compensates for the critical awareness that might lead consumers to reject products that they do not need. If both sides of the relationship are fully rational, which implies that they are making decisions only on the basis of cost effectiveness and not confusing wants with needs, then fewer products are sold; less economic growth results; and employees of the seller's firm are laid off. So economic growth depends upon the persuasion of the consumer that self-satisfaction is as hedonistic as it is economic.

In nuclear strategy, too, the rationalities of the deterrer and the deterree may collide, if both look out for their own best interests, defined without reference to the common good. The jointly interdependent payoff from cooperation may be greater than the payoff from individual value maximization, where nuclear weapons are involved. This is one way in which superpower nuclear exchanges would differ from conventional war in kind, rather than in degree. It seems "better" to retaliate only if the narrow logic of "he will be worse off than I will" is followed, but that logic ignores the comparison between how well off the retaliator is before retaliation, as opposed to afterward. It also ignores the comparison between prewar and postwar states of affairs, including the issue of survival. Herein lies the irony, with regard to U.S. and Soviet strategic nuclear forces, that for either side to launch a first strike would not be rational, if "rational" means to expect to escape devastating retaliation. Once deterrence has failed, however, and one side has been attacked, it is not obviously rational for that side to strike back with a comprehensive attack. If, for the sake of argument, the Soviet Union were to attack the U.S. ICBM force, but ignore other elements of the strategic nuclear triad and U.S. cities, it is not clear that the United States should immediately do likewise to Soviet land-based missiles. What is to be gained by evening up firepower ratios? Perhaps it would be more logical to retaliate against other Soviet targets, including their conventional forces, or against sea-based forces farther removed from population centers than are ICBMs.

EXTENDING DETERRENCE

If the logical burden that deterrence-rationality theory has to bear is substantial with regard to direct Soviet attack on the United States, or vice versa, the burden is even greater when the U.S. nuclear umbrella is extended over Western Europe. Aspersions have been cast on the weakness of deterrence-rationality theory, but this is a good time to note that deterrence is not entirely dependent upon rationality. It also involves credibility, the faith your adversary has that, however illogical it may seem, you will do what you have threatened to do. Unfortunately for the neatness of deterrence theory, but fortunately for the practical usefulness of extended deterrence, credibility counts for more.

This is not to argue, as some have, that there are no rational arguments, in the correct sense, for the U.S. commitment to defend NATO Europe. Indeed there are. The foremost of these is the acknowledgment that the United States is not in Europe just to defend Europe, but to defend North America one step removed. This is perhaps truistic by this time, but easily forgotten amid alliance debates across the Atlantic on burden sharing, or within the U.S. Congress on withdrawing U.S. troops from Europe. The argument that U.S. commitments to defend Europe are selfish instead of altruistic is based upon the very logical premise that Europe entirely in Soviet hands represents a potentially fatal shift in the global balance of power. U.S. presidents cannot talk about balances of power for domestic consumption, of course, and so they tend to use extravagant rhetoric on behalf of other values, but they know the geopolitical equation before they are in office very long, if their advisors are at all competent.

However rational, this self-serving argument has more to do with the defense of Europe than it does with the deterrence of war in Europe. Defense implies forces capable of denial, of physically preventing the opponent from occupying territory or disestablishing governments. Deterrence may not involve denial at all, although NATO deterrence draws upon some denial capabilities. Instead, extended deterrence in Europe depends mainly upon the threat of punishment, and most emphatically nuclear punishment, in response to Soviet aggression, and appears to be succeeding. This threat depends upon its being credible, although not necessarily rational in the sense of economic or political rationality. Henry Kissinger once made an unfortunate speech in Brussels, in which he said that the United States should not make threats it does not mean (nuclear threats to deter conventional war in Europe) or, if it means them, cannot execute, because if it executes, it risks the destruction of civilization.[19]

The only saving grace of this statement was that it was made by Kissinger while out of office, but it still commits almost every sin imaginable from the standpoint of reassurance to Europeans and deterrence of the Soviet Union. The reason is that it confuses rationality with credibility and assumes that a threat that is disproportionate is automatically not believable. USSR behavior before and since makes clear, however, that it regards the threat of NATO nuclear response to conventional aggression very believable. Why? It is so because extended deterrence is made credible in several ways that deterrence rationality cannot fully account for.

The first of these is the idea that Western Europe, or at least some parts of it, constitute a fifty-first state," so tied culturally and historically to the United States that the loss of one would be considered a devastating blow to the identity and security of the other. John F. Kennedy obviously implied something of this kind when he announced, "I am a Berliner" to an adoring crowd of West Germans.[20] Taken as a statement of ethnic identification, this would have set off shock waves in Dublin, but it was a statement about U.S. security commitments, not about cultural heritage, and was so taken by audiences on both sides of the East–West divide in Europe. Of course, Europe is not a state in the same way that Alaska is, and parts of Europe are not equally enamored of the idea that their fate could be decided in Washington instead of in their own capitals. Despite these admonitions, the symbolism of a security identity crossing the Atlantic remains strong, and it is reinforced by diplomatic speeches and military exercises.

The second way in which extended deterrence is made credible, although not necessarily rational, is in the forward deployment of U.S. ground forces near the inter-German border. These forces have some denial capabilities, along with their European counterparts, but their principal function is not denial of territory to the USSR. Instead, it is to become entangled early on in any war between Eastern and Western Europe. The prompt killing of U.S. servicemen makes the war a U.S. war, in the same way that the sinking of a U.S. ship makes any war at sea a U.S. cause. An even better analogy is the sinking of a ship not under U.S. registry, but carrying many U.S. civilian or military personnel; similarly, an attack on West Germany would involve U.S. citizens standing on someone else's soil, but nonetheless victimized. Perhaps, then, the sinking of the Lusitania by Germany in World War I can be likened to the invasion of West Germany by Warsaw Pact forces, even if the balance-of-power argument and the assumption of indivisible U.S. and European interests do not hold.

The third way in which extended deterrence attains credibility without rationality is inherent in the deployment of the instruments of war, as opposed to the military personnel who use them. Of special interest here is the commingling of tactical and theater nuclear forces with the general-purpose (conventional) armies, navies, and air forces of the NATO defenders, raising the immediate specter of escalation. This threat of escalation is brought about in two ways: NATO threatens to use nuclear weapons deliberately in response to Soviet conventional or nuclear attack, or it threatens to become involved in a process of war in which inadvertent escalation to nuclear first use, and then beyond it, might take place.[21] There are some differences of opinion among strategists, in the first kind of escalatory threat, about how much force structure, relative to its opponents, NATO might need. Some NATO planners and military strategists argue for escalation dominance, or forces sufficient to coerce the opponent into war termination on account of their superior survivability and target coverage at every stage of the conflict. Others feel that mere equivalence in theater nuclear weapons of all ranges will suffice. For the second kind of escalation, that which happens by inadvertence, no necessary force mix can be prescribed. As long as nuclear weapons are there and deployed in the path of advancing Soviet ground forces, it will be difficult to avoid having those weapons overrun or granting permission for nuclear release to commanders before their nuclear weapons are lost. Obviously, there may be strong upward pressures from field commanders to SACEUR and then to the North Atlantic Council for predelegation, if things appear to be going badly. What is not entirely clear is how long it will take for authorization and enablement, once it is granted by higher authorities, to flow downward to the besieged commanders. Estimates range from 24 to more than 60 hours for the processing of a single request for a package of nuclear weapons.[22]

This second escalatory pressure, the inadvertent one in which one or both combatants stumble over the nuclear threshold, although not necessarily having anticipated the sequence of events, is "the threat that leaves something to chance," as Thomas Schelling has immortalized it.[23]

NATO threatens very credibly to maintain less than total control over the process of escalation even before the nuclear threshold is crossed, but especially afterward. This argument, that deterrence can be enhanced by a credible threat to lose control of a process of escalation, is part of the rationale for the very forward deployment of battlefield nuclear weapons, such as nuclear artillery and mines. From the standpoint of rational deterrence, these weapons, which are nose to nose with the forward edge of the battle area might seem counterproductive to deterrence, as possibly accidental detonators of the other theater nuclear forces of the two sides, and perhaps their strategic forces as well. The word "accidental" is misleading. What is being threatened is not accidental war but inadvertent war, growing out of a process that is partially, but not totally, under the control of the threatener. If it were fully controllable, then it would be a more rational but a weaker deterrent.

To see this apparent paradox, of more menacing forces because, once engaged, escalation may be less controllable, compare the choice between deploying NATO Long Range Intermediate Nuclear Forces (LRINF), such as Pershing II and GLCM (cruise missiles) on European soil or, as an alternative, in the form of submarine-launched ballistic and cruise missiles assigned to the same targets. The second choice seems more plausible from the standpoint of crisis stability; the sea-based weapons are less vulnerable to surprise attack and so, less dependent upon prompt launch for survivability. Knowing this, the USSR will be less insecure about being caught unawares by prompt launch of sea-based weapons, compared to land-based. This rational argument for the sea-based forces, however, ignores the irrational but credible point about inadvertent escalation, compared to deliberate escalation. Land-based theater nuclear weapons cannot be ignored by advancing Soviet ground forces. Therefore, they will be attacked even during the conventional phase of a war in Europe, in order to forestall the possibility of NATO using them later if need be. The Pershing II and GLCM thus call forth a dilemma for Soviet planners, who must find a way to negate the weapons without provoking Western first use in order to save them. Reasoning through this opacity, the Soviets could decide that the possibility of inadvertent nuclear war was extremely high, although a deliberate first use by the NATO alliance made little sense. And so NATO, by deploying land-based theater nuclear forces capable of reaching the USSR, presents a European-based strategic threat to the Soviets (because the weapons can reach the Soviet homeland), which cannot be got rid of without side payments whose end product is not totally foreseeable or fully controllable.

This last point is crucial for the difference between lay understanding of the term "escalation" and the specialized uses to which it is put by defense analysts. Escalation in deterrence theory refers to a number of processes by which the scope and intensity of war expands, and some of these processes are more foreseeable, and more controllable, than others.[24] It does not, as is commonly supposed, refer to any threat to inflict more destruction on an opponent in battle, which can occur by means of the lateral extension of attrition. In addition, escalation and escalatory threats work on the psychology of opponents more than they work on their capabilities. One is interested not in disarming the opponent militarily or physically, but psychologically. We might call this the agonistic use of deterrence, in which threatened parties can by their compliance have some control over a course of events, but not total control, and the assumption is that the sooner they comply, the more control they may have, or the threatener may have. There is, thus, the pressure of events moving forward faster than the relationship between the parties can be turned toward conciliation, as opposed to increased confrontation. As in all psychological processes, there are wheels within wheels spinning between and within decision makers on all sides, as messages are inferred from the actions of both and from statements that may or may not be understood as intended.[25] Here again, scientism threatens to displace science, and the psychology of deterrence might be misrepresented as a production matrix with simple inputs, outputs, throughputs, and so forth. A process-oriented psychology is more fruitful in understanding how deterrence works, because the policy makers themselves do not fully understand it, blundering from one alternative to another in a crisis, until a satisfactory way out is found.

Consider what might take place, for example, if the United States placed its nuclear forces on a very high level of alert and the Soviet Union, having observed all this with its sensors and other intelligence sources, decided to follow suit. This has never happened in the nuclear age. In previous crises during which the United States significantly raised its level of alert for strategic forces, Soviet forces were not raised to any comparable level of readiness for war, or deployment in the expectation of war.[26] This was true even during the Cuban missile crisis of 1962, and again in the Middle East crisis of 1973. What would happen if both sides simultaneously raised their alert levels from normal peacetime readiness to readiness for war? One can only speculate, but as Paul Bracken has pointed out, under those conditions the two superpowers' warning and response systems might form into one pernicious supersystem of information feedback. In that condition, each side's anxiety would be piqued by the raising of the other's alert levels, step by step, until both found themselves with fully alerted forces, all dressed up and nowhere to go. Their choices would be to de-alert the forces, which is apparently not easy to do, or use them before they risked a loss of readiness to lower than customary peacetime levels.[27]

The lowering of alert levels may be more difficult to do than raising them. Forces and command systems, once poised to retaliate, would have to go through a process of decompression in order to return to day-to-day situational expectations, much as a deep sea diver must rise slowly from the ocean floor to avoid bends. This problem, that de-escalating may be more complicated and therefore more dangerous than escalating, has historical precedent. During the Cuban missile crisis, President Kennedy and Secretary of Defense Robert McNamara found their efforts to keep the crisis under control stymied by standard operating procedures of military organizations. In one specific illustration, U.S. naval quarantine procedures included the assumed right to force Soviet submarines to the surface in the Caribbean, the Atlantic, and even the Pacific, pursuant to the conduct of ASW (antisubmarine warfare) by the book.[28] McNamara's row with the chief of naval operations about procedures to be followed when intercepting ships crossing the blockade or boarding them also illustrated policy makers' concerns that organizational routines not lead to textbook subversion of political objectives. McNamara even wanted to know whether the U.S. Navy had aboard its ships any Russian-speaking officers; he was told by Admiral Anderson that these and other issues relevant to the operation of blockades were all specified in manuals and so would be followed.[29] This was not what the secretary of defense wanted to hear. He was not asking what the Navy would do under normal conditions, but under unprecedented ones.

How organizations might deal with unexpected, as opposed to preprogrammed, stresses is an issue that requires further consideration, and so will receive it in the subsequent discussion of war termination. De-escalating of crisis raises the same fundamental issues as de-escalation of war after it begins. And for nuclear war, or conventional war in which both sides are fighting in the expectation that nuclear escalation might happen at any time, de-escalation poses special difficulties, rooted to some extent in the relationship between policy and organization.

NOTES

1. A useful explanation of this subject is Steven J. Brams, *Game Theory and Politics* (New York: The Free Press, 1975). Of special interest is Chapter 1 on international relations games.

2. For an examination of the logic of deterrence, see *Patrick M. Morgan, Deterrence: A Conceptual Analysis*, 2d. ed. (Beverly Hills, CA: Sage Publications, 1983).

3. An important distinction between general and specific deterrent situations is made in Morgan, *Deterrence*, pp. 27–48.

4. See George H. Quester, *The Future of Nuclear Deterrence* (Lexington, MA: D. C. Heath, 1986), Ch. 2.

5. The well-known works of Thomas Schelling and Albert Wohlstetter are happy exceptions to this generalization; how much they stand out, even today, is testimony to how exceptional they are. For suggestive comparisons between

mutual assured destruction deterrence logic and the law of comparative advantage in international trade, see Michael Mandelbaum, *The Nuclear Revolution: International Politics Before and After Hiroshima* (Cambridge: Cambridge University Press, 1981). pp. 117–46.

6. An excellent study is Joseph S. Nye, Jr., *Nuclear Ethics* (New York: The Free Press, 1986).

7. See Ken Booth, *Strategy and Ethnocentrism* (London: Croom, Helm, 1979).

8. Paul Bracken, "War Termination," in *Managing Nuclear Operations*, ed. Ashton B. Carter, John D. Steinbruner, and Charles A. Zraket (Washington, DC: Brookings Institution, 1987), Ch. 6, pp. 197–216.

9. Raymond L. Garthoff, "Conflict Termination in Soviet Military Thought," in *Conflict Termination in Military Strategy*, ed. Stephen J. Cimbala and Keith A. Dunn (Boulder, CO: Westview Press, 1987), pp. 33–58.

10. Albert Wohlstetter and Richard Brody, "Continuing Control as a Requirement for Deterring," in *Managing Nuclear Operations*, ed. Carter et al. pp. 142–96.

11. George Quester, "Will Washington and Moscow Swap Doctrine?" in *Challenges to Deterrence in the 1990s*, ed. Stephen J. Cimbala (forthcoming).

12. James G. March and Herbert A. Simon, *Organizations* (New York: Wiley, 1958), pp. 136–71.

13. Thomas C. Schelling, *Arms and Influence* (New Haven, CT: Yale University Press, 1966), p. 183.

14. The difference between warning and response is emphasized in Richard K. Betts, *Surprise Attack: Lessons for Defense Planning* (Washington, DC: Brookings Institution, 1982).

15. Richard Ned Lebow, "The Cuban Missile Crisis: Reading the Lessons Correctly," *Political Science Quarterly* 98, No. 3 (Fall 1983): 431–58. See also Lebow, *Between Peace and War: The Nature of International Crisis* (Baltimore, MD: Johns Hopkins University Press, 1981).

16. Barbara W. Tuchman, *The Guns of August* (New York: Macmillan, 1962).

17. This case is most assertively argued in Richard Ned Lebow, *Nuclear Crisis Management: A Dangerous Illusion* (Ithaca, NY: Cornell University Press, 1987).

18. A very good discussion of this and related problems is James Turner Johnson, *Can Modern War Be Just?* (New Haven, CT: Yale University Press, 1984). See also James P. Sterba, ed. *The Ethics of War and Nuclear Deterrence* (Belmont, CA: Wadsworth, 1985). The latter is an anthology containing representative statements and excerpts from diverse perspectives, including that of U.S. Catholic bishops.

19. See "NATO: The Next Thirty Years," speech by Henry A. Kissinger, in *Strategic Deterrence in a Changing Environment*, ed. Christoph Bertram (London: Allenheld, Osmun, 1981), p. 109.

20. Quester, *The Future of Nuclear Deterrence*, Ch. 5, provides an insightful discussion of extended deterrence.

21. The concept of inadvertent nuclear war is discussed in Barry R. Posen, "Inadvertent Nuclear War? Escalation and NATO's Northern Flank," in *Strategy and Nuclear Deterrence*, ed. Steven Miller (Princeton, NJ: Princeton University Press, 1984), pp. 85–112.

22. According to Catherine McArdle Kelleher, "... the operational requirements of bottom-up release border on the impossible." Bottom-up release is that which moves from the corps commander to the higher echelons at which release is granted. See Kelleher, "NATO Nuclear Operations," in *Managing Nuclear Operations*, ed. Carter et al. Ch. 14, pp. 445–69, esp. pp. 458–64.

23. According to Schelling, "it does not always help to be, or to be believed to be, fully rational, cool-headed, and in control of oneself or of one's country." See Schelling, *Arms and Influence*, p. 37.

24. For a discussion of the concept of escalation and some applications to historical cases, see Richard Smoke, *War: Controlling Escalation* (Cambridge, MA: Harvard University Press, 1977).

25. See Ralph K. White, ed., *Psychology and the Prevention of Nuclear War* (New York: New York University Press, 1986), esp. Chs. 18 by Robert Jervis and 19 by Ralph K. White.

26. Bruce G. Blair, "Alerting in Crisis and Conventional War," in *Managing Nuclear Operations*, ed. Carter et al. Ch. 3, pp. 75–120.

27. Paul Bracken, *The Command and Control of Nuclear Forces* (New Haven, CT: Yale University Press, 1983), pp. 59–68, discusses the possibility of mutually reinforcing U.S. and Soviet warnings and alerts.

28. Graham T. Allison, *Essence of Decision* (Boston: Little, Brown, 1971), p. 138.

29. Apparently Navy resistance to President Kennedy's order to draw the blockade line in closer to Cuba forced the president to allow at least one Soviet ship to pass through it. See Allison, *Essence of Decision*, p. 130.

5

DE-ESCALATION AND WAR TERMINATION

We alluded earlier to the need to consider de-escalation, in the context of crisis de-escalation, as related to the problems of managing alerts. Now, extending that problem into the period after arms have clashed, and national honor has been breached by combat casualties, challenges theory and policy still further. We have seen that deterrence rationality is very circumscribed, and that some escape hatches are necessary to enable it to cope with the complexity of actual crisis and war. One of these escape hatches has been to decouple deterrence credibility from deterrence rationality, so that credible threats need not be rational. Recall that this means something more than an absolution from meeting rationality criteria, which economists might set, about utility maximization under conditions of uncertainty. The entire definition of utility in this context is open to question. Once credibility and rationality are treated separately, and they have to be or deterrence will not work in some situations, then we do not expect opponents to comply with our demands because they have calculated their outcomes accordingly, but simply because they are afraid.

Extending our vista into wartime de-escalation, we discover the topic of war termination, of ending wars—including nuclear wars—on terms mutually agreeable to all combatants, and short of exhaustion of their arsenals or destruction of their governments and societies. The discussion here focuses on nuclear war, although wars without nuclear weapons have provided many illustrations of the problems inherent in war termination.[1] As Paul Bracken has rightly noted, the problem of war termination is intimately related to the problem of escalation control.[2] If escalation cannot be controlled, then the pace of military operations eventually outruns the scope of policy objectives, and the definition of winning and losing becomes disconnected from whatever the original wartime objectives were. World War I provides an excellent illustration of the failure by policy makers to ask questions about war termination before the operational issues took on a momentum of their own and, like tapeworms, consumed their hosts.

In nuclear war, there are at least three pertinent issues raised by the subject of war termination. These might be thought of as levels of analysis, or ways of cutting into the problem conceptually. The first is the question of policy guidance and how it is formulated to allow for war termination. The second is command and control systems and their competency for different kinds of control. The third issue is communication with the adversary and the two-way street that is necessary for war termination.

As to the first, policy guidance, it can be said that clear guidance from national leaders about war termination is infrequent, or sporadic. Wars begun with only the foggiest notion of the political objectives for which states were fighting are all too numerous. World War II provides several good examples. The Japanese attack on Pearl Harbor was a very well planned tactical strike, which threw the United States off balance for a short time. It was a strategic disaster, however, mobilizing U.S. anger and revenge and resulting not only in Japan's ultimate defeat but also in nuclear attacks on two of its cities. Nor is this example, of elegance in planning military operations driving the issue of strategic outcomes into the background, an isolated one. Hitler's attack on the Soviet Union in June 1941 was a brilliantly conceived operation and a strategic disaster. It caught the USSR off guard and led to impressive victories in the immediate theater of operations. The Germans could not, however, exploit that surprise in the early stages of war in order to end the war on any terms other than the destruction of Germany itself. They could not in their wildest dreams have hoped to occupy the entire Soviet Union and subdue its entire population, given the remaining forces arrayed against the Nazi regime on all fronts. Somehow, the pertinent questions were never asked, at least by Hitler, who in a classical example of reasoning backward proposed to dismember the USSR and thus induce Britain to sue for peace (for fear of being isolated). Hitler apparently counted the United States of America as an inconsequential piece on the board, and assumed Japanese fidelity to the Axis cause would last forever. More likely, he simply did not think through the situation at all, because doing so would have called the entire Barbarossa operation into question.

Of course, another possible motivation for Hitler's invasion of the Soviet Union was his pessimism about the possibility of a protracted two-front war against England, allied with the United States and the Soviet Union.

The Nazi dictator might not have considered the United States as a significant military power in the short term, but in an extended conflict U.S. potential, combined with British determination, would be more meaningful. The invasion of the USSR before defeating Britain thus presented Hitler with a hopeless position. Some analysts have supposed that the German army was addicted from Moltke the elder to Guderian to an offensive operational doctrine and that this doctrinal bias influenced German prewar preparations prior to World War I and World War II. Perhaps this is so, although there is some controversy among scholars about the extent to which German doctrine was really "offensive" strategically, as opposed to operationally. In other words, tactical and operational offensives may be part of a grand strategic agenda that is ambitious or modest in its politicomilitary objectives. Revisions in NATO and U.S. Army doctrine have in recent years reflected the recognition that the side on the strategic defensive may, nonetheless, exploit aggressive and fast-moving operational and tactical maneuvers. The Schlieffen Plan, by which Germany went to war in World War I, is customarily thought to be an ambitious one, but it might also be argued that it was motivated by the political realism of avoiding an extended two-front war in which Germany would have to fight both France and Russia simultaneously. Here is a critical issue for students of war termination, to distinguish the expectations of policy makers about terminating short wars, versus longer wars, against the same adversaries. It is often noted that the major combatants in World War I planned for short wars, and thus became overly dependent upon mobilization plans that contributed to crisis instability. Granted this supposition, historians must still address the dilemma that policy makers surely faced at that time, that a longer war was possible and, if so, then the geopolitical allocation of resources and allies would weigh in the balance more than the speed of mobilization timetables. In a short war, for example, the United States would count for nothing; in an extended war, as we know, it was decisive. However sensible the Schlieffen Plan might have seemed from this perspective of geopolitics and alliances, it still lacked strategic, as opposed to operational, soundness. What was Germany going to do after France had been knocked out of the war and Russian offensives in the East blunted? The kaiser had no hope of invading and occupying England, nor of investing Moscow. What-if speculation with regard to history is always intriguing, and there have been some imaginative what-ifs about the Ludendorff offensives of 1918, in the sense of, What if they had succeeded? Suppose they had, in the sense that France might have capitulated, but not England and the United States, with their inexhaustible reserves. And Lenin's expectation that he could take the Soviet Union out of the war and get away with it depended upon the erstwhile allies of Russia holding

COLORADO COLLEGE LIBRARY
COLORADO SPRINGS
COLORADO

the ring in the West. If the latter collapsed, the USSR would have to reconsider whether Brest-Litovsk was an acceptable peace settlement, since the Germans would certainly be reconsidering it.

Hitler might be considered an extreme case of geopolitical ambition, but if we flip the chart around and ask if the allies did any better, the answer is, Not really. The wartime objective of the allies was unconditional surrender, which was a vague formula devoid of real policy content. It left unspecified a number of very important issues related to the fate of the postwar world, issues that would create difficulties among the United States, Britain, and the Soviet Union at the Yalta and Potsdam conferences. Each member of the anti-Nazi coalition had its own objectives, of course, and conflicts were inevitable. Even allowing for that, hard questions were not always confronted. Stalin can be forgiven for wondering why it took until June 1944 for a second front to be opened with the Normandy invasion, for he was not fully aware of the disagreements between British and U.S. planners, for several years, over priorities among theaters of operations and timing of campaigns. Even more fundamentally, it was ruled out of order, at least in U.S. policy discussions, to consider what the postwar world might be like if the USSR became an adversary instead of an ally. Franklin Roosevelt simply assumed that his well-known charm would work its wonder on Stalin, and perhaps it did in personal relations, but it had no apparent effect on Stalin's definition of Soviet policy objectives.

Policy goals can be modified in the face of operational setbacks. Sometimes history is rewritten, so that what armies can in fact attain, the state decides it really wanted in the first place. In Korea, the U.S. government settled for half a loaf as consistent with the original policy objectives of blunting the North Korean invasion, although not consistent with the revised and more ambitious aim of reuniting Korea under U.N. supervision. In Vietnam the objective became "peace with honor," meaning a phased withdrawal of U.S. forces, which avoided a surrender until those forces were fully extricated from the combat zone, and the defeat would be South Vietnam's alone. The Vietnamization program of phased withdrawal of U.S. forces was an operational plan to solve problems in U.S. public opinion, not a war-termination strategy, except by coincidence. No one believed that the United States, having withdrawn its forces, would be permitted by the Congress or public opinion to reintroduce them. Certainly, the North Vietnamese Politburo did not believe it and, in the final analysis, it was their perception that counted.

It might be thought that states will modify their policy objectives in the face of certain defeat for their armed forces, but this is very scenario dependent on who their leaders are and how much control those leaders have within their own government. Toward the end of World War II, efforts to obtain a Japanese surrender were hampered by the opposition within the Japanese armed forces leadership to any negotiated peace. Even after Emperor Hirohito had decided that surrender must be offered, factions opposed to that decision tried to circumvent it and to continue the war, even to desperation. Hitler did continue the war to desperation, although some of his minions made apparent efforts to contact Western intelligence sources, in order to determine whether the United States and Britain might make peace separately from the Soviet Union. Losers are not necessarily more willing to modify their goals than are winners. Once losses accumulate beyond a certain point, desperation may replace calculation, or divisions within the loser's government may make compromise impossible. Fred Charles Iklé has characterized this as the dilemma of "hawks" versus "doves" in a state that is losing a war, but does not know how to get out of it.[3] Hawks tend to believe, in principle, that more fighting will improve the situation, whereas doves focus on conciliation. Frequently, neither is well informed about how the enemy will read the signals correctly, if at all. Nor are the hawks always military leaders and the doves civilians; not infrequently it is the reverse, with military planners hoping to preserve some sense of organizational integrity and purpose, and therefore opposing further senseless violence. The U.S. Army leadership in Vietnam, for example, came to share the feeling that continuation of the war would be destructive of organizational cohesion, as did much of the French army leadership in Indochina and in Algeria. Military leaders can see the costs to their organizations when civilians cannot, the latter demanding victories on the battlefield to compensate for policies poorly thought out.

In some cases, disagreement may be as poignant within the military hierarchy as it is between military and civilian leaders. During the Korean War General Douglas MacArthur wanted permission to bomb across the Chinese border in retaliation for Chinese attacks against U.S. forces. By the logic of the battlefield, MacArthur had a strong case. Chinese forces were operating from sanctuaries at low risk of retaliation against their support and supply bases outside Korea. The political constraints imposed on the war by the Truman administration did not, however, allow for risking a major war with the People's Republic, and so MacArthur was denied the satisfaction of striking back at the source of his frustration. This frustration eventually led to his dismissal, and that dismissal was the signal that the president and his advisors had thought through the issue of what the United States was fighting for and decided it was not fighting to stamp out communism in Asia, but for something more specific. The Chinese, too, signaled by diplomatic and military actions that they considered their intervention to have objectives short of declared war with the United States, for which Peking found it as difficult as Washington did to write a credible policy story, or an endgame.

As suggested by the Korean intervention, limited war in the nuclear age poses special problems for the definition of wartime objectives and for efforts to terminate limited wars between superpower allies or others. There are two very distinct dangers here. The first is that a conventional war in Europe or elsewhere, in which U.S or Soviet forces are involved, may escalate into a nuclear exchange. The second and more probable is that wars may remain limited to conflicts outside the superpowers' immediate spheres of control, therefore being less manageable from Washington or Moscow.[4] In the first case, for a war in Europe to remain truly limited the superpowers would have to impose restraints on their own objectives and those of their allies. It will be difficult for them to do this, unless the war is in its early stages and has not yet crossed the nuclear threshold. One can imagine circumstances under which conventional war breaks out in Europe and remains stalemated, followed by an armistice that provides a basis for settlement (but on what terms?).[5] It is easier, however, to imagine conditions under which control breaks down, and the probability is that it would, unless both sides somehow got cold feet during the war, despite their hot blood in having started it.

So the second kind of limited war, involving countries not allied to superpowers, or nonstate actors like the Palestine Liberation Organization or the Polisario movement, is more probable. The Iran–Iraq war, which at this writing has been going on for seven years and shows no sign of abatement, provides an interesting case study in limited war in the nuclear age. Of course, the war is limited in the sense that the superpowers are not directly engaged. It has also been limited, however, by the capabilities of the two sides, neither being able to destroy the armed forces of the other, occupy completely its opponent's territory, or unseat its government.[6] It might be argued that, in terms of societal resources committed to the war, for Iran and Iraq it is more like total than limited war, but this is more arguable for Iran than for Iraq. Other limitations have been imposed by the wariness of both sides about expanding the conflict to include the major powers of Europe or the United States and the USSR. Attacks on shipping through the Persian Gulf risk expansion of the conflict beyond the ability of Saddam Hussein or Ayatollah Khomeini to control it. In April and May of 1987, Kuwaiti ships arranged to sail through the Gulf under Soviet and U.S. flags. While this did not provide complete immunity from Iranian attacks, it certainly signaled to Tehran the risk of provoking an entirely different kind of conflict, should it go too far. Unlike the case of Europe, however, war in the Gulf might involve tacit collaboration between the superpowers, rather than their collision. The Soviets pose a long-standing threat to Iran that has not been lost on the regime in Tehran, which is not much friendlier to them than it has been to the United States. The USSR and the United States might at least cooperate tacitly to the extent that they would not allow any conflict between Gulf or other Middle Eastern states to involve their forces directly, whatever aid and "fraternal assistance" they otherwise provided. The October war of 1973 might have created a precedent in this regard. Although the United States during that crisis placed its forces on a DefCon 3 alert, there is no indication that the Soviet Union followed suit, suggesting that whatever Moscow expected to happen, it did not expect nuclear war.

COMMAND ORGANIZATIONS

The first issue in war termination is objectives and the ability to limit them, at least to less than total conquest, in contests between superpowers, and isolating the Soviet Union and United States from others. The second issue is the question of command systems or organizations and their capabilities for war termination under what would be the most stressful conditions imaginable, nuclear crisis or war.

The U.S. command and control system for the management of nuclear-force operations has evolved from a simple to a complicated one, with multiple missions and conflicting imperatives.[7] The command system must prevent unauthorized or accidental launch (loosely termed "negative control") and provide for prompt and effective retaliation, once duly authorized commands have been received ("positive control"). In peacetime the U.S. strategic command system can easily accomplish both objectives. During a crisis tensions are created in fulfilling simultaneously the two imperatives.

As is well known, military organizations, including those that have been created to manage the nuclear forces of the United States and the Soviet Union, are tasked for war, although their primary mission may be deterrence. Thus, the expectation that war may be imminent upstages peacetime priorities. From a low level of vigilance, the system "turns on" in progressive stages of higher and higher alert. At each elevation in the alert thermometer, so to speak, the emphasis on negative control becomes less urgent and that on positive control more important. As a crisis deepens, each side fears more the loss of its forces in a surprise attack, compared to the possibility of accidental or unauthorized launch.

It may be that the problem of surprise attack has been overrated in the nuclear age. (A subsequent chapter will address this issue specifically.) Nevertheless, U.S. strategic nuclear forces have, since the 1960s, been sized and exercised on the assumption that many of them will be lost in a first strike and some surviving fraction will have to retaliate. Less attention has been paid to the survivability of commanders and command centers, compared to forces, but they, too, are thought sufficiently vulnerable that many will not survive. Therefore, attention has been paid to improving the survivability of commanders, command posts, and communications, in order to ensure that retaliation under the worst conditions of confusion and disorganization is still possible. The Reagan administration's improvement program for command, control, communications, and intelligence (C3I), for example, is intended to improve postattack communications between National Command Authorities and the force commanders by deploying the Ground Wave Emergency Network (GWEN) and the MILSTAR generation of satellites.[8] These and other C3I improvements will enhance the probability that the U.S. command system will be able to survive long enough to guarantee retaliation against a large Soviet target set.

This survivable command system is not necessarily adequate for war termination, however, should political leaders on either side desire to bring it about after nuclear warheads have begun detonating. Once communications channels and command posts have been disrupted or destroyed, the expectations of national military and political leaders will change. Standard operating procedures of large command organizations cannot be revised instantaneously, and large changes in previously learned behavior will only disrupt whatever efficiency remains. Under attack, command systems (if one can speak of them organically) will be primarily concerned with their own survival, and secondarily with whatever missions they can carry out, having survived. This may lead to pathological behavior in terms of organizational, as opposed to suborganization or unit, goals. When a command organization such as that of the United States includes multiple layers of civilian and military personnel, who must coordinate their activities by rote instead of improvisation, the expectation that the command system can be "tuned into" war termination must be built in ahead of time, that is, before war begins. This might not be thought a worthwhile exercise by persons who abhor the thought of any nuclear detonations on U.S., Soviet, or other soil, but that is beside the point of the present discussion, conceding as it does the preference for "no war" as opposed to "some war." The question here is what to do if "some war" starts and there is a need to turn it off quickly.

The Hot Line provides one illustration of a device by which national leaders can communicate their intentions to terminate a war, even after deterrence has failed. Of course, to be useful for this purpose, it must survive during the early phases of war, and it is unlikely to survive attacks directed specifically against it. Indeed, attacking the Hot Line would be one signal that the attacker had no particular interest in terminating the war, short of all-out destruction—as would other attacks on the command system itself, as opposed to attacks on forces that destroyed command systems incidentally. If, for example, the Soviets attacked Washington—or the United States, Moscow—the consequences for the command systems on either side would be drastic, especially if neither had anticipated the attack and prepared its leadership for it. The Soviet Union has apparently done far more than the United States has to provide survivable leadership facilities around Moscow and elsewhere.[9] These facilities might be useful if the USSR had strategic warning of attack and if the attack did not include options specifically tailored to destroy the Soviet leadership and its principal command facilities.

The last noted objective, destroying the Soviet leadership in its command bunkers around Moscow and elsewhere, was apparently included in U.S. strategic nuclear war plans during the Carter administration, and perhaps earlier.[10] This countercommand targeting apparently evolved from two directions. First, it was felt to be an expedient way of defeating the Soviet Union or forcing it to end a war on U.S. preferred terms, on the assumption that the USSR hierarchy valued its own survival more than anything else that might be included in U.S. target sets.[11] Second, it was thought that fears for their own survival would help to deter Soviet leaders from embarking on a war in the first place. If the Soviet leadership imagined that the U.S. SIOP (Single Integrated Operational Plan for nuclear war) included warheads addressed directly to their mailboxes, they would avoid attempts at provocation or crisis coercion that might unleash destructive retaliation aimed at them personally.

The assumption that the Soviet leadership would fear for their own lives and be more deterred than otherwise may illustrate the tendency of theorists to be too clever by half. Apparently there was some recognition of this, for the highest Soviet leadership levels were thought to be included in "withholds," or force packages that would be used in the later stages of war, after other options had failed to win or terminate it.[12] Whether slow death as opposed to prompt destruction was a reassurance to Soviet leaders is a subject on which they have not pronounced. The entire countercommand-attack concept was the result of mirror imaging Soviet interests in command destruction that have been alleged by U.S. deterrence strategists and other military experts.[13] Soviet interests in destroying the command systems of their opponents in conventional war have been acknowledged by their military writers, and the assumption has been made that they would also be interested in counter-C3 attacks in nuclear war. Perhaps they would be. The issue of war termination, however, is something that their leaders, as well as ours, must think about, and thinking about it must lead to concern in Moscow as well as in Washington that a countercommand attack could outsmart itself.

It could do this by forcing the *de facto* control over nuclear forces down the chain of command to lower-level military commanders instead of higher-level political and military authorities. This might not make much difference in how either side would fight at the outset of war, but if either side wanted to quit, it would be terribly important to establish who still had nuclear weapons and could fire them. Suppose, for example, that the president of the United States and most of his cabinet had been killed in early Soviet attacks on Washington. How would surviving military and civilian authorities authenticate their right to control forces, and to whom? Obviously these procedures are shrouded in secrecy, for they protect the U.S. command system from a true decapitation attack, but they also risk continuing a nuclear war at a time when whatever central policy makers still lived would want to turn it off. Moreover, as Paul Bracken has noted, targeting a leadership is not really comparable to attacking a list of addresses or persons, as such. It is, in essence, an effort to destroy the coherence of an organization.[14] The coherence of an organization depends upon procedures that can be reconstituted, after they have been disrupted, by those persons who have survived the initial attacks. Whether U.S., or Soviet attacks could kill members of the Politburo or cabinet would be less important than whether they could disrupt the standard operating procedures of the U.S. Strategic Air Command or the Soviet Strategic Rocket Forces. If so, it would not be necessary to kill the leadership, for they would be at the mercy of any successful attempt to immobilize their retaliatory forces.

The ability of command systems to reconstitute themselves, like an amoeba, has been demonstrated historically. Perhaps the most pertinent example in recent history was the Soviet high command after the invasion of the USSR on June 22, 1941 by Hitler's armies. The surprise of the German attack, despite previous intelligence warnings made available to the Soviet high command, disrupted the USSR command system and immobilized effective response for weeks. Information from critical sectors of the Soviet western border was either unavailable or distorted, and it took far too long to learn which commanders were incompetent and to replace them.[15] The speed and destructiveness of the German advance simply overran the capacity of the Soviet system to cope with it, and Stalin's prewar purges of much of the military command left the armed forces without their best leadership at a time of maximum peril. Once the initial period of the war was survived, however, the Soviet leadership, including Stalin himself, put together a very competent command system that combined flexible adaptation to fluid combat conditions with a very skillful exploitation of Soviet military and societal strengths. The command system with which the USSR finished the war was a very far cry from the one with which it began the war, and the system that provided for eventual success in the Great Patriotic War became a model for the postwar command structure, down to the present.[16]

If U.S. and Soviet command systems could survive repeated nuclear attacks, the possibility of extended or protracted nuclear war would present complications for planners on both sides. Again, like war termination, this is an issue that to the lay audience seems repulsive, but for nuclear strategists the question is germane. Weapons and command systems that were adequate for a short war might fall short of the requirements for fighting a long one. This might influence deterrence in a crisis, if one side felt comfortably superior to the other in extended, as opposed to short, war-fighting capability. Qualitative differences in forces and command systems might mean more than quantitative differences, with regard to the issue of postattack reconstitution and extended conflict. Mobile ICBMs and sea-launched missiles would be more useful than ICBMs based in fixed silos. Bombers, which were eclipsed during the 1960 and 1970s in much strategic thinking because of their slow flight times compared to missiles, might become more important in extended war scenarios, if their airfield and supporting infrastructure could be reconstituted.[17] Moving both superpowers in a direction away from forces dependent upon prompt launch, like ICBMs in silos, and toward more dependency upon forces that can be delayed and withheld, might improve crisis stability, as well as making protracted war possible. Not too much should be made of the possibility of protracted nuclear war, however, if the expectation is that it could be conducted for many weeks or months at full salvo levels against U.S. and Soviet homelands. This is highly improbable. Any extended war would be protracted only if the U.S. and Soviet leaderships exercised restraint in their choices of targets and in the collateral damage attendant to their attacks.[18]

COMMUNICATIONS

Suppose that U.S. and Soviet leaders did exercise such restraint. This would open the possibility of war termination, but by no means guarantee it. Soviet and U.S. leaders would need to communicate with one another in order to arrange a cease-fire for nuclear forces, and then conventional forces, if possible. If the war had begun in Europe, troops occupying hostile territory would somehow have to be returned to their original positions, at least eventually. It would be a long way to go back to the *status quo ante*, but the alternative, since each side would still have nuclear weapons that it had not yet expended, would be worse.

The first communications requirement for ending the war would be authenticated, survivable leadership. Leaders on each side would have to be identified as competent negotiators on behalf of their governments, not only by their foreign opponents but also by their domestic political *confrères*. The U.S. presidency may now have devolved onto the secretary of education as the sole surviving cabinet member, if that person is alive and can be established as the next in line for the presidency. That person, however, and the same holds for many cabinet members, may have no information, even in peacetime, about U.S. war plans and no notion of what options are available for striking back. So actual military command would probably devolve from the National Command Authority (the president, the secretary of defense and/or their successors, together with the Joint Chiefs of Staff and their successors) onto the surviving unified and specified commanders who held custody of U.S. nuclear weapons. These include the U.S. commanders in chief for the Atlantic, for Europe, for the Pacific, for the Strategic Air Command, and others.

In theory, U.S. nuclear weapons cannot be fired unless presidential authorization is obtained and electronic codes transmitted through the appropriate channels. This model of a neat, hierarchical chain of command is probably more descriptive of what would happen in peacetime than it is an accurate description of wartime events. In practice, commanders who held nuclear weapons would not want to see them destroyed in preemptive attack, and so would request early release authorization from the appropriate authorities. Contingent approval for the use of certain limited packages of weapons could be granted in order to avoid the use-them-or-lose-them dilemma. Once granted, contingent authorization would be interpreted liberally, if forces feared that their own destruction was imminent. At sea, the absence of electronic locks (Permissive Action Links) is compensated for by more elaborate requirements for concurrence among many different persons aboard ship before launch is enabled, even after launch is authorized. Although some analysts have expressed concern that U.S. nuclear weapons deployed at sea might be more loosely controlled than others, in practice the dilemma is not qualitatively different. Electronic locks prevent accidental and unauthorized launches, not strikes for which contingent permission has been granted or assumed. Nuclear-force commanders do not intend to be caught with their forces subject to preemption, and signals and photographic intelligence that suggest this possibility to them will be rapidly followed by urgent requests for contingent release.

In other words, the wrong problem has been addressed by persons who worry that the United States will be unable to retaliate in some fashion in response to successful surprise attack. The more subtle and pertinent issue is whether any constitutional response is possible under all conditions of surprise attack. Probably it is not. A complete bolt-from-the-blue Soviet attack on Washington would not allow for more than a simple and brutal response, and time for consultation among more than a few key civilian and military leaders in the executive branch would not exist. A protracted crisis, followed by an extended but limited nuclear war, would be another story, and U.S. officials could find themselves subjected to congressional pressure to terminate the war or to end a stalemate by winning it in some decisive way. As we saw in Vietnam, the U.S. public is impatient with stalemated wars. The British House of Commons leadership is, of course, fused with the cabinet in a way that differs from the U.S. model of two independent branches, so friction about prolonging and ending the war in that case might all take place within one branch, rather than between two. In either the British or U.S. sense of the term, the cabinet might easily disintegrate politically during the attempt to terminate a nuclear war before it slipped totally out of control, and one can imagine a spectrum of hawks, doves, and in-betweens within the majority party or presidential party itself.

The Soviets, too, would have to be concerned with the problem of leadership struggle, the longer the war continued. Here their World War II experience might be misleading, because the longer that war went on, the more effective Soviet forces became, relative to their opponents. A different experience in World War I, however, ultimately brought down the entire Russian regime, and the Kremlin leadership would certainly recall the czar's fate in the aftermath of a costly protracted war. Succession struggles might ensue within the Politburo, while the fate of Europe was being decided on the battlefield and at the conference table, with hawks clamoring for even more escalation and doves demanding an end to the war on whatever terms were available. Those seeking to unseat the Soviet leadership could argue that the war should not have started, or, having been started, should not have been fought in the way it was being fought. A succession crisis within the Soviet leadership during a nuclear crisis or extended war, even a conventional war in which Soviet forces were engaged, is perhaps more likely than it is in the Western democratic governments of Britain and the United States. In the latter cases, the sagacity of leadership policies might be at issue, but an intrawar change of horses would not fit historical precedent.[19]

Assuming the problem of stable and authenticated leadership could be resolved on both sides, a second issue would be the existence of channels through which they could communicate. If numerous detonations of nuclear weapons had already occurred on either Soviet or U.S. territory, then communications equipment could be destroyed and links disputed. The Hot Line is an example of a link designed to work if it is not directly attacked; if it is, other means of communication will have to be improvised, and destruction of the Hot Line may be interpreted as suggesting disinterest in war termination.[20] Postattack satellite links and their ground stations might also be destroyed and their destruction interpreted as an antitermination stance.

If nuclear war had begun but not yet spread into the homelands of either superpower, and each wanted to stop the war before crossing the threshold of homeland exchanges, then channels of communication would certainly exist physically. The problem would be in using them and in each side being convinced that the messages being sent were not deceptive feints, but actual invitations to negotiate. Obviously, such initiatives would have to be accompanied by reassurances that forces ordered to stop firing would do so, and this might be more of a problem for NATO than for the Warsaw Treaty Organization. If a war that begins with an uprising in Eastern Europe and then spills over into Western Europe is being de-escalated, does Eastern Europe count as the Soviet "fifty-first state," and West Germany as the U.S. counterpart? Probably not, for the superpowers' homelands could be "sanctuarized" while attacks proceeded against the territories of their allies, although such an expectation, for obvious reasons, could not be discussed openly, within either alliance, before the war.

Channels remaining open, and messages being sincere, there would still be problems of putting flesh on the bare bones of "we want to quit" entreaties. Whose forces will be stood down, and at what pace, while giving up or holding onto what objective? How will the status of surviving but not expended nuclear forces be ascertained objectively? There are answers to these questions, of course, but the point will be for the two sides to arrive at them under the duress of war, and not in the comparative calm of peacetime. Salient points and thresholds will have to be established by tacit agreement as much as by explicit negotiation. Some fighting in peripheral areas will just have to wind down, and war at sea may not be turned off as quickly or as securely as war on land. Whatever the truce or cease-fire terms may be, there will be persons in each government who are unhappy and may contest them, so each leadership will have to be certain that back channels are not used by dissenting elites in order to sabotage any agreement. Elements of trust that had not been developed between heads of state before war began (or else why did deterrence fail?) would have to be improvised or negotiated around. Verification of arms-control agreements has sometimes been done without dependency on mutual trust, as by satellite inspection of missile fields, and so might verification of war termination. In such cases, each side would have to agree not to continue attacks on its opponent's means of verification, including satellites, if ASAT or other antisurveillance attacks were under way already.

In addition, there would have to be some expectation that neither superpower would be vulnerable to strategic deception while war termination was being worked out. Strategic deception implies a deception in which the balance of power is turned fundamentally against one state on account of its willingness to stand down its forces.[21] Thus, the inability to photograph a Soviet rifle squad or two would not make much difference in resolving a conflict in Western Europe, but the inability to know the whereabouts and tasking of several army groups (fronts) might. Even if war termination preceded the detonation of any nuclear weapons by either side, this would not necessarily make politicians' tasks easier. A very dangerous situation could arise in which negotiations for war termination began while the war remained conventional, as both sides positioned their nuclear forces for immediate retaliatory strikes, just in case the other side failed to cooperate (a classical prisoner's dilemma).[22]

The trick for both sides would be to convert a potential prisoner's dilemma, in which the incentives favor noncooperation, into an actual positive-sum game in which both can enjoy winning outcomes. One possibility is to go beyond direct trading of valued territories or other objectives, to an effort to "expand the pie" by opening up the larger subject of peace settlement in the postwar world. This happened in a comparatively minor way (minor, that is, only in comparison to this thankfully hypothetical scenario) after the superpowers narrowly avoided a nuclear clash over Cuba in 1962. The period following October of 1962 was one in which both U.S. and Soviet leaderships resolved never to be the prisoners of events during a future nuclear crisis, whatever was at stake, and to open up permanent peacetime channels for exchanging views between national leaders (the Hot Line). Following war in Europe or elsewhere that remained at the conventional level, despite direct combat between U.S. and Soviet forces, against all odds, the postwar reflections might be sobering. All during the war, policy makers in Moscow and Washington would have been reflecting on the imminence of their personal and societal obituaries and, having escaped that fate, might want to institutionalize permanent escape.

The above arguments involve some supposition, as does all argument about nuclear thresholds and nuclear war. And there are admittedly large assumptions that must grace any theory of war termination that promises to help superpowers end a war that they have, despite all misgivings, nevertheless plunged into. War termination is better than fatalism, however, and for it to happen after war has begun, it has to be thought out beforehand. We have seen that the three constituent elements of war termination—objectives, command systems, and communications—cannot be taken for granted, especially not in nuclear war. If these elements are not rehearsed in peacetime, they will not be available in wartime. Grim as it is to contemplate, small nuclear wars are preferable to larger ones when so much is at stake, provided this argument is not used to justify nuclear war as preferred to peace. This last error would confuse relative issues with absolutes, as deterrence rationality can sometimes do.

NOTES

1. Fred Charles Iklé, *Every War Must End* (New York: Columbia University Press, 1971).

2. Paul Bracken, "War Termination," in *Managing Nuclear Operations*, ed. Ashton B. Carter, John D. Steinbruner, and Charles A. Zraket (Washington, DC: Brookings Institution, 1987), pp. 197–214, esp. p. 198.

3. Fred Iklé asks the interesting and pertinent question, as to whether hawks or doves are the real traitors, in *Every War Must End*, pp. 60–83.

4. See Robert E. Osgood, "The Post-War Strategy of Limited War: Before, During and After Vietnam," in *Strategic Thought in the Nuclear Age*, ed. Laur-

ence Martin (Baltimore, MD: Johns Hopkins University Press, 1979), Ch. 4, pp. 93–130.

5. Possibilities for termination of war in Europe are discussed in Gregory F. Treverton, "Ending Major Coalition Wars," in *Conflict Termination in Military Strategy*, ed. Stephen J. Cimbala and Keith A. Dunn (Boulder, CO: Westview Press, 1987), Ch. 6, pp. 89–108.

6. Background on this conflict is provided in Ralph King, "The Iran–Iraq War: The Political Implications," Adelphi Papers, 219 (London: International Institute for Strategic Studies, Spring 1987).

7. Background on the U.S. strategic command, control, and communications system (C3) can be found in Bruce G. Blair, *Strategic Command and Control: Redefining the Nuclear Threat* (Washington, DC: Brookings Institution, 1985).

8. An assessment of Reagan C3 modernization programs is provided in Blair, *Strategic Command and Control*, Ch. 8. See also Desmond Ball, et al., *Crisis Stability and Nuclear War*, a report published under the auspices of the American Academy of Arts and Sciences and the Cornell University Peace Studies Program, January 1987, p. 21.

9. U.S. Department of Defense, *Soviet Military Power: 1987* (Washington, DC: U.S. GPO, March 1987), pp. 25–26.

10. Countercommand attacks are discussed in Jeffrey Richelson, "The Dilemmas of Counterpower Targeting," in *Strategic Nuclear Targeting*, ed. Desmond Ball and Jeffrey Richelson (Ithaca, NY: Cornell University Press, 1986), Ch. 7, pp. 159–70.

11. This argument defeated itself in supposing that the asset most precious to the Soviet Union was preservation of its leadership and control, and that attacking its central command, or suggesting its vulnerability by attacking other command targets, would motivate it to comply with U.S. demands. If the assumption about the centrality of preserving command viability (in the Soviet hierarchy of values) is correct, however, then attacking it motivates them to cease all restraint, not enforce limitations. See Colin S. Gray, "Targeting Problems for Central War," in *Strategic Nuclear Targeting* ed. Ball and Richelson Ch. 8, pp. 171–93. See also Stephen J. Cimbala, "Countercommand Attacks and War Termination," in *Strategic War Termination*, ed. Stephen J. Cimbala (New York: Praeger, 1986), Ch. 7, pp. 134–56.

12. Desmond Ball, "The Development of the SIOP, 1960–1983," in *Strategic Nuclear Targeting*, ed. Ball and Richelson Ch. 3, pp. 57–83. See also Leon Sloss, "The Strategist's Perspective," in *Ballistic Missile Defense*, ed. Ashton B. Carter and David N. Schwartz (Washington, DC: Brookings Institution, 1984), Ch. 2, pp. 39–41.

13. Soviet interest in command suppression is noted in Fritz W. Ermarth, "Contrasts in American and Soviet Strategic Thought," in *Soviet Military Thinking*, ed. Derek Leebaert (London: Allen and Unwin, 1981), pp. 50–72, esp. p. 66.

14. On the difference between targeting groups and organizations, see Paul Bracken, *The Command and Control of Nuclear Forces* (New Haven, CT: Yale University Press, 1983), pp. 90–97.

15. Performance of the Soviet command system in the decades preceding World War II is assessed by John Erickson, "Threat Identification and Strategic Appraisal by the Soviet Union, 1930–41," in *Knowing One's Enemies: Intelligence*

Assessment Before the Two World Wars, ed. Ernest R. May (Princeton, NJ: Princeton University Press, 1984), Ch. 13, pp. 375–423.

16. Harriet Fast Scott and William F. Scott, *The Soviet Control Structure: Capabilities for Wartime Survival* (New York: Crane, Russak/National Strategy Information Center, 1983), especially the concluding chapter.

17. Christopher I. Branch, *Fighting a Long Nuclear War* (Washington: National Defense University Press, 1984). National Security Affairs Monograph Series 84–5.

18. The notion that a protracted nuclear conflict would have to be a limited one is discussed in Ashton B. Carter, "Assessing Command System Vulnerability," in *Managing Nuclear Operations*, ed. Carter et al. Ch. 17, pp. 555–610.

19. See Stephen M. Meyer, "Soviet Nuclear Operations," in *Managing Nuclear Operations*, ed. Carter et al. esp. pp. 482–84.

20. Bracken, "War Termination," in *Managing Nuclear Operations*, ed. Carter et al. p. 204.

21. An insightful application of deception to the problem of nuclear war is Leon Sloss, "Impact of Deception on U.S. Nuclear Strategy," in *Soviet Strategic Deception*, ed. Brian D. Dailey and Patrick J. Parker (Lexington, MA: D. C. Heath, 1987), Ch. 20, pp. 431–48.

22. For discussion of the prisoner's dilemma in the context of nuclear strategy, see George H. Quester, *The Future of Nuclear Deterrence* (Lexington, MA: D. C. Heath, 1986), pp. 31–33.

6

MISSILE DEFENSE: RATIONALITY OR ESCAPISM

The application of a certain kind of rationality to strategic nuclear deterrence reached its apogee with a speech by President Ronald Reagan on March 23, 1983. Reagan called for a research program that might lead to the eventual deployment of a ballistic missile defense (BMD) system, eventually making nuclear weapons obsolete.[1] The president's speech, as is well known, stirred controversy on both sides of the Atlantic, and the controversy is not done yet. All sides of the debate converged to argue the pros and cons of nuclear deterrence with defenses, without defenses, and with defenses on the drawing boards but not yet deployed.

The putative rationality of BMD and other strategic defenses lies in the assumption that defenses can change the basis of deterrence stability. Instead of relying upon offensive retaliation after being attacked, both superpowers could protect their societies and forces with defenses. Defenses would eventually be superior to offenses, thus making offensive first strikes nonpaying propositions. The related assumptions are that offensive first strikes might be paying propositions now; that defenses are necessary to turn potentially attractive first strikes into unattractive ones; and that defenses can be deployed and maintained at a marginal cost no greater than the marginal cost of improving offenses.

How can the above arguments be described as within the tradition of deterrence rationality? Are not the deterrence rationality of mutual assured destruction or mutual vulnerability and the logic of SDI diametrically opposed, since the first bases deterrence on the threat of retaliation, and the second on the ability to deny any gains from a first strike? The answer is that the logics are not dissimilar, just the policy prescriptions drawn from the logic, and the policy prescription is in turn embedded in other and sometimes unarticulated premises that are not always made explicit.

MUTUAL DETERRENCE

The missile defense debate, in earlier decades and now, has hinged on whether defensive technologies will become more powerful than offensive ones. If, for example, space-based laser battle stations can be parked in orbits and intercept ballistic missiles in the earliest stage of their flight, then defenses will be superior to offenses, and first strikes nullified in their significance. It has been assumed by advocates of defenses that, in the event defense technologies become so competent relative to offensive ones, strategic stability will be improved.

Opponents of defenses disagree that the deployment of defenses, however competent they are relative to offenses, will improve stability. In their view, it will detract from stable deterrence, at worst, or have no significant impact, at best. Deterrence is thought to rest on the shared vulnerability of Soviet and U.S. cities to retaliatory strikes, regardless of the competency of surprise first strikes. If populations and economic values are kept vulnerable to retaliatory strikes, and forces survivable against preemptive attack, then deterrence remains stable, in the view of those who oppose BMD.

In both cases, BMD proponents and opponents base their arguments on what it is rational for an attacker to do, rational in the economic or cost-effective sense, or rational in the game-theoretic sense of payoff tables and investment functions. In the antidefense argument, it does not pay to deploy defenses, since they cannot make any difference unless they are so good that they upset the entire balance of stable deterrence. This they might do by proving to be good enough to deny either side its retaliatory strike after its opponent has struck first. In that instance, defenses would be counterproductive to stability.

In the prodefense argument, similar rationality assumptions prevail. According to Ambassador Paul H. Nitze, the Reagan administration would insist that any deployable defenses meet two principal criteria: They must be cost effective at the margin, and they must be survivable.[2] The second seems self-evident, although it has implications that are not, as we shall note. The first criterion is more interesting for present purposes.

COST EFFECTIVENESS AND BMD

What would cost-effective defenses mean? The problem with cost effectiveness in economic reasoning is that it all depends upon the definition of effectiveness, which in economic theory may be self-evident in profit.

In political theory it is anything but. Is the performance of government to be measured, for example, by consumer satisfaction with commodities and prices, or with the faith that voters have in the integrity of the political process? Is a higher GNP worth more than a fairer distribution of wealth or income? Establishing criteria by which to decide among these end values, as opposed to instrumental or means values, demands more than comparisons of marginal utility.

Defenses that were cost effective at the margin might mean one of several things. First, it could mean that defenses, once they have been deployed, should not be more expensive to augment or improve than it would be to improve the offenses that oppose them. Second, it could mean that even before they are deployed, investments in defense should pay larger deterrence and arms-control dividends than further investments in offensive force modernization by the same side; that is, U.S. defensive investments should have superior utility to U.S. offensive investments. Third, it could mean that the marginal cost of adding to defensive-force structure is less than the marginal cost of adding to offensive-force structure, whatever their assumed deterrence impacts. Fourth, it could mean that the marginal utility of expenditures for defenses is superior to that of adding to existing offenses, but not necessarily better than adding new generations of offenses.

Nor is this all, although enough has been said to indicate that it is already the proverbial can of worms. The marginal utility of U.S. defenses, compared to Soviet offenses, is almost impossible to establish, for several reasons.

First, there is the problem of comparing apples and oranges. The conversion of dollars into rubles, or vice versa, is difficult enough, and done only with formulas that are extremely arbitrary. The deeper problem is that the U.S. and Soviet economies differ in structure, in kind rather than in degree. What is the "opportunity cost" paid by the USSR for building more tanks and fewer hospitals, compared to the opportunity cost paid in the United States for the same substitution? The answer depends upon the societal values placed by the Soviet Union and the United States on peacetime health care, compared to peacetime defense preparedness. Unless those desired objectives can be quantified in some unambiguous and culturally neutral fashion, the outputs associated with those objectives cannot be compared for marginal cost efficiency.

Second, there is the problem of absolute versus relative distinctions. In the Soviet Union one can take for granted that leaders place a nearly absolute value on national defense, in a command economy that allows them to establish defense as first among equal claimants. This results from their experiences in the Second World War, which are still burned into their memories, institutional and personal. There is nothing like being invaded and pillaged by Nazi troops to remind one of the price for deterrence failure, combined with misguided placatory diplomacy. In the United States, on the other hand, Fourth of July speeches notwithstanding, defense does not have the same absolutist valuation, for the very reason that U.S. history does not replicate Soviet history. U.S. forces have for the most part fought elsewhere, not in defense of their own soil. The most destructive conflict fought on U.S. soil was the Civil War, which is still being fought out politically, although peacefully, according to some cynical U.S. observers. The Soviet decision-making process certainly makes room for other than defense claims on the budget, and one can talk about a Soviet "military industrial complex," which competes with other sectors for shares of the pie. Relative to their U.S. counterparts, however, Soviet military and heavy industry "metal eaters" receive first shares of the pie, not leftovers. Even within the public sector, which itself constitutes only about 25 percent of the U.S. gross national product, defense in peacetime often fares poorly.

Third, and related to the second point, commercial societies also value political decision making that is pluralistic, meaning that power is dispersed, sometimes to the point of inability to reach any policy consensus. Widely dispersed political power goes hand in hand with strong private-market forces. Thus, the market for U.S. goods is predominantly driven by consumer demand (at the receiving end) and advertising (at the producing end). U.S. federal, state, and local governments, taken all together, might disperse funds equivalent to one-third of the gross national product. In Europe, higher proportions of GNP go through the public, as opposed to the private, sector, but no West European economy approximates the Soviet model. Concentration of Soviet political and economic power at the center, although it should not be exaggerated, is necessary to ensure continuity of party rule over other sectors that might be tempted to challenge that rule, including the armed forces, technocrats, and others.[3]

Thus, comparisons of the marginal cost effectiveness between U.S. ballistic missile defenses and Soviet offenses are bound to be misleading or self-defeating. The two economies defy comparison, and we have noted a number of problems inherent in attempting to measure cost effectiveness or even to define it unambiguously. There is another and more fundamental problem, however, which involves the logic of cost effectiveness as a criterion for deciding upon strategic programs.

Cost-effective strategic programs are those that are necessary to deter war and are not superfluous for that task. The problem is in deciding what deters and identifying the wars that would have broken out in the absence of a particular category of weapon. Will U.S. strategic ballistic missile defenses, for example, deter wars that the Soviet Union would otherwise undertake or contemplate more seriously? To answer this is to move from the criterion of cost effectiveness to the arena of strategy, in order to revisit first principles about what pays and what doesn't in nuclear deterrence and war, if it comes to that. To anticipate, we will find that additional weapons systems may have little or no bearing on deterrence, unless and until cities can be made defensible; that it is irrational to threaten to attack cities, but very believable, and therefore the threat ought to suffice for deterrence, under most conditions; that if it is thought necessary to deploy BMD, then the consequences will not be simple to interpret or to project into the future. More on all of this follows.

U.S.–SOVIET STRATEGIC NUCLEAR DETERRENCE: NECESSARY AND SUFFICIENT CONDITIONS

What will active defenses, including BMD, add to deterrence? Nothing, if deterrence is already stable, but we have seen that deterrence rationality cannot guarantee that. So deterrence might fail, along the lines of a two-sided crisis that gets beyond the control of policy makers, or an escalation from conventional war, despite all efforts to prevent it.[4]

Under these conditions, of spiraling crises or escalation rather than preventive war, defenses might contribute to deterrence in any one of several ways. First, they might increase the survivability of one side's strategic retaliatory forces against any first strike the other might contemplate. Second, defenses could introduce ambiguity and uncertainty into any aggressor's attack plans, even if their precise contributions to the survival of forces or societal assets were unknown. Any uncertainty makes a first strike less likely. Third, defenses, if deployed by both superpowers to protect their forces and cities, could change the basis of stable deterrence from deterrence based on retaliation to deterrence based on denial. Defense-dominant deterrence is preferable to offense-dominant deterrence, so the argument goes, because defenses protect people against the effects of weapons, instead of striking at innocent people in revenge for being attacked. As Donald Brennan, the late noted strategist, frequently said, "We should prefer live Americans to dead Russians."

These arguments on behalf of transcending deterrence based on offensive retaliation actually depend on a logical pattern of inference, similar to that held by opponents of defenses. Both pro-BMD and anti-BMD arguments assume a willingness to treat the costs of war in terms of marginal utility instead of absolute disaster. If the USSR could come off with relatively fewer casualties, compared to the United States, or with more surviving forces, then it might preempt. Defenses would complicate the Soviet attack plan and limit damage if they did attack. Therefore, defenses are necessary.

The counterpoint is that U.S. missile defenses will provoke Soviet countermeasures, inducing another ratchet in the arms race.[5] Therefore, defenses are not only unnecessary but also dangerous, for they upset previously established superpower expectations of mutual vulnerability.[6] No defenses are needed, because the surviving destructive power of each side's arsenal, after absorbing a surprise attack, is more than sufficient to destroy the other's society.

Both sets of arguments depend upon national leaders in the Kremlin and in Washington making fine assessments of differences in arsenals and deciding, on the basis of those assessments, to go or not to go with the most important decision of their tenure of office, and perhaps of their country's entire history. In fact, whether defenses are deployed may make little difference in the probability of nuclear war between super-powers, because there is so much "slack" in the size and diversity of their arsenals. This slack means that neither can deploy a defense that is perfect or nearly perfect; enough leakage of attacking warheads through the defense, however many layers it has, will wreak unprecedented societal destruction. Conversely, if offenses are drastically limited by the U.S.- Soviet treaty arrangement, then defenses become more important, and, if offenses are nearly eliminated as envisioned in the Reagan strategic concept, then defenses become the basis of stable deterrence—or unstable deterrence, if they do not work.[7] This is the irony of the negotiations between U.S. President Ronald Reagan and Soviet General Secretary Mikhail Gorbachev at Reykjavik, Iceland, in 1986. The Soviets wanted the United States to limit research and development on SDI in return for a willingness to drastically reduce strategic offensive forces. In return, the United States apparently agreed to discuss cutting in half both sides' inventories of offensive strategic ballistic missiles within five years, and, further, to the possible elimination of all strategic ballistic missiles within ten years.[8]

NATO European allies of the United States were understandably con-cerned about these proposals, which were followed up in 1987 to become the basis for further negotiations on strategic arms control. The reduction of both sides' offensive ballistic missile forces would leave the strategic balance more reliant upon bomber-delivered and sea-based weapons, plus defenses in whatever inchoate state they might exist. The Soviet side at Reykjavik may have underestimated the determination of President Rea-gan not to yield on SDI, and the U.S. side may not have understood fully the kinds of concessions the Soviets would expect for agreeing to dis-mantle so many of their modern ballistic missiles. If, however, agree-ments were worked out for disarming even half of each side's ballistic missile force, then the task for even partially competent defenses, relative to attacking offenses, is that much easier. Now one begins to see the prospect of arms reductions in offenses, followed by the gradual deployment of defenses. If the defenses are nonnuclear, what is wrong with that?

What is wrong is that, as offenses get lower and lower and ultimately approach zero, then even defenses become trump cards. Say, offenses are reduced to several hundred strategic warheads for each side. Then a defense that is "only" 25 percent effective is much more meaningful, compared to a defense that is 25 percent effective against 10,000 warheads. In other words, we are back to the distinction between relatives and absolutes again, and with a vengeance. A partially effective defense, of no importance against large offenses, becomes a vital force against small offenses. Once defenses take on this importance, another arms race, this one in qualitative innovation in defenses, begins. Defenses may be racing one another in the same way that offenses have, ever since the two superpowers acquired nuclear weapons, but with a difference.

The risks are grave for either party if it cannot guarantee retaliation after being the victim of a first strike, and that first strike becomes easier, because the number of the defender's aim points is smaller. Of course, the attacker's warheads are less numerous, too, and if the arms reductions are carefully calibrated, then each side may have insufficient warheads for a first strike, speaking mathematically, allowing that the first striker would undoubtedly want to retain a reserve force for any following strikes, if necessary.

In other words, the destination proposed by the Reagan strategic concept, of preeminent defenses and comparatively weak offenses, may not be the destination most conducive to stability, even if we can get there. And getting there is a big if.[9] To get there, to a supposedly benign condition of very competent nonnuclear defenses and relatively incompetent nuclear offenses, U.S. and Soviet leaders must pass through intermediate difficulties, much like the oft-described problem of "midcourse discrimination" for BMD between decoys and real warheads. While partially effective defenses are being deployed, individually or jointly, by the superpowers, each will attribute to the other's defenses more capability than it actually has. And each will estimate very conservatively its own capabilities. Consequently, each will want to allow a margin of safety in the number of offensive warheads remaining in the arsenal, so that whatever is left after the opponent's first strike could still retaliate and create unacceptable damage. The more pessimistic we are about their defenses, the more we will be motivated to offset that pessimism with our own countermeasures in additional offenses or in countermeasures to outsmart the defenses. This, too, seems like the typical "prisoner's dilemma" in which the incentives to cooperate (deploy defenses, reduce offenses) are smaller than the incentives to cheat (deploy defenses, maintain offenses). Proponents of defenses, however, would consider the prisoner's dilemma analogy a false one, because in the long run, they would argue, a superior basis for strategic stability will result from deploying defenses, to the advantage of both sides.[10] Notice, however, that the argument for how to get there then depends on a driving assumption, itself unvalidated, that the destination, once arrived at, will be more benign than the present condition.

It is not clear that this is so, that a defense-dominant world will be more stable than an offense-dominant one. The confusion in some arguments about this issue is a fundamental one, between defensive versus offensive *technology* on one hand, and defensive versus offensive *strategies* on the other. Under present conditions of dominant offensive technologies, a defensive strategy pays dividends: Neither superpower can contemplate a first strike that effectively disarms its opponent. Conversely, under a future condition in which defenses are deployed along with offenses, either side might consider the possibility of a first strike, if its defenses were good enough to absorb the opponent's retaliatory strike. In other words, defensive technologies might make possible an offensive strategy, especially if offenses are not totally disarmed. Even more frustrating is the recognition that, even if offenses are drastically disarmed, defenses are not necessarily more stabilizing. We are not talking here of two superpowers with their own version of the strategic Maginot Line, forced by the supremacy of defensive technologies to rely upon parrying the opponent's thrust to restore the status quo. What happens with regard to each side's defenses is the beginning, not the end of the war. Let us assume that both the United States and the Soviet Union have cut in half their strategic offensive warheads, to approximately 5,000 force loadings on all launchers. And let us further assume that each side has deployed a defense based on earth or in space, or both, which is potentially 25 percent effective against the other's full first strike. Do these 25 percent shields deter attack, or invite it? The numerical situation lends itself to either argument, unfortunately. The defenses are deterrents of attack, or incentives to attack sooner, depending on the state of political relations between the superpowers. Under normal peacetime conditions, the defenses create additional complications for military planners. When crisis seems to be sliding into war, however, then each side's defenses invite defense suppression as soon as possible, else the surviving defenses, combined with one side's first strike, could nullify the retaliatory strike of the other. Defense suppression has received comparatively little attention from deterrence arguments about SDI and BMD, but it alludes to the second of Nitze's two stated criteria: that the defenses must be survivable.

Of course, survivability is a matter of degree. Defenses are survivable to the extent that the offense is willing to pay the price to attack and destroy them. This concept of an attack price is very important.[11] The first striker does not have an unlimited arsenal; some missiles will have to be reprogrammed on account of reliability failures, and withholds for war termination or for use against third parties must be provided for. In the canonical case of attack against missile silos, for example, some easy points are won by debaters who assert that, if missile defenses are deployed to protect silos, then the attacker can simply add warheads intended for the same target, and eventually destroy it by exhausting the interceptors that might save the target. This is too simplistic, however, as a model of what would happen, for only a certain number of an attacker's warheads could be detonated over the same spot within a finite time frame (unless the attacker were willing to risk self-destructive side effects, including fratricide or disruption of guidance for some "smart" warheads). Moreover, in the case of U.S. ICBMs, which are thought to be vulnerable to a Soviet ICBM first strike, by the time more than three Soviet RVs could be detonated over each Minuteman ICBM silo, the silos would either be empty (on account of launch on warning or launch under attack) or nonfunctional for other reasons. In all likelihood, confirmation of Soviet attack by the dual phenomenology of space- and ground-based sensors would lead to NCA authorization for prompt launch of U.S. ICBMs; without question, they would be launched, if they could be, once any detonations on U.S. soil began.[12]

Defenses of dubious survivability might tempt preemptive attack even more than would doubtfully survivable offenses. Offenses like ICBMs in fixed silos may be thought nonsurvivable against sufficiently dedicated attacks, by some analysts. Unless, however, the attacker can remove its cities from their hostage condition by deploying city defenses, destroying the opponent's strategic forces does not gain anything meaningful. The attacker's loss exceeds any putative gains, not by the logic of cost effectiveness (which would simply compare net surviving warheads), but by the intrinsic value of cities, or civilizations, which would be destroyed in retaliation. In fact, without city defenses, the attacker might as well turn its weapons on its own cities, at least having the perverse satisfaction of disallowing the "pleasure" to the opponent. Once effective defenses for cities have been deployed, however, the game changes, because now either side might assume it could protect enough of its society after the opponent's forces had been largely destroyed.

Defenses are not more destabilizing under all conditions, however, than improved offenses. Much depends upon the tasking of defenses and the standards of survivability that they must meet. If defenses must only survive attacks that it would be reasonable for either side to launch against them, as opposed to back-of-the-envelope attacks devised for worst-case scenarios, then they contribute to uncertainty and perhaps to stability. In one model of how the United States might deploy BMD, for example, analysts suggest a three-stage system in which boost-phase, late-midcourse, and terminal interceptors are combined with a variety of sensors and decentralized battle management.[13] This might be called a pragmatist's approximation of workable missile defense, as opposed to the scientists' dream of a perfect defense. In this approximation, suggested by noted U.S. space scientist Robert Jastrow and others, space-based kinetic-kill vehicles are directed against launchers in the boost phase and the bus that dispenses warheads in the postboost phase. Late-midcourse interception is accomplished by ground-based ERIS (exoatmospheric reentry intercept system) rockets that also launch homing interceptors into the path of the target, destroying it by impact or collision. This proposal includes a terminal interceptor that is also ground based (HEDI, for high endoatmospheric defensive interceptor) and an Airborne Optical System (AOS) which would help to detect and discriminate warheads in late midcourse.[14] The proposal by Jastrow and colleagues avoids for the moment the problem of midcourse discrimination (of warheads from numerous decoys, which would undoubtedly accompany them), allowing for later development of laser- and particle-beam applications for solution of the discrimination problem. So deployed, they contend that this system would be about 93 percent effective against a Soviet attack with about 10,000 strategic warheads. Even if the system falls far short of its claims, and other interim systems have been proposed, the point is that down-tasking of the system places fewer demands upon its components and reduces the dependency of U.S. strategy on denial, as opposed to retaliation. Partially effective defenses, if they could thin out any attack enough to make first strikes improbable, but still not threaten the opponent's second-strike capability, might then contribute to stability, instead of detracting from it. This is against conventional wisdom, which has suggested that if either side deploys defenses and offenses together, it is moving toward a first-strike capability. This is not necessarily the case, however, and it depends on how good each side's offenses and defenses are expected to be. Defenses that are too good could be destabilizing, if they were deployed in addition to offenses that were vulnerable to first strikes and primarily useful as first-strike weapons. Suppose, as an illustration, that the United States reversed its earlier decision to de-emphasize silo-based ICBMs and deploy mobile land-based missiles in the 1990s, scrapping Midgetman and tripling the deployment of MX/Peacekeeper in silos. Then it deployed defenses that not only protected retaliatory forces, but also had some ambiguous capabilities against Soviet countervalue retaliation. Now the going gets sticky, for the USSR, viewing with some jaundice the combination of U.S. modern ICBMs along with potentially anti-second-strike BMD, must now be concerned about its deterrent. This is a very important difference between active defense and passive survivability measures to protect the U.S. land-based missile force. The active defenses under certain conditions threaten Soviet retaliatory capability, and so would an improved system of theirs, vis-à-vis ours. Making missiles mobile, however, improves their survivability without adding to the arsenal a capability to deny to the Soviet Union a retaliatory strike, on which its deterrent depends. Mobility without defenses is like a warhead sponge, soaking up Soviet RVs in a first strike without necessarily denying their assured retaliation. Defenses of ICBMs in fixed or mobile basing add to the sponge a more menacing cast. If the sponge can squirt back, it can, along with sufficient counterforce capabilities, amount to a first strike. U.S. policy makers, observing the unfolding of Soviet research and development on BMD-capable technologies, will be no less concerned about the possibility of preemption-*cum*-BMD than their Soviet counterparts. Much, then, depends upon how much prompt counterforce remains in the inventories of both sides' strategic forces.

Nor should the entire onus, even hypothetically, be put on the United States in developing worst-case scenarios for BMD. After all, the USSR has the world's only deployed BMD system now protecting Moscow and its environs, and despite Soviet declarations that SDI is a threat to peace, they are modernizing their own BMD system, not removing it. This Soviet posture reflects many different motives, including their wariness of British and French nuclear forces and their potential growth, even if the United States deploys no strategic defenses. Still, the Gorbachev regime is at some pains to argue that the United States should destroy SDI in its infancy, while the USSR deploys new classes of interceptors, radars, and ground-based lasers, in some instances acknowledged by all sides of the U.S. arms-control debate as violations of SALT II.[15] If the USSR is really concerned that BMD represent a categorical threat to peace, then Soviet leaders can contribute to a peaceful world by offering to dismantle their system in return for U.S. offensive-force reductions, or some other trade-off. The Soviets, however, have not shown any interest in dismantling their BMD system, and for the very plausible reason that their system is not caught up in the same trap of pseudoscience and pseudorationality as the U.S. SDI proposal. The USSR is not claiming that its system can protect its entire society (disallowed by the ABM Treaty in any event), nor that the Soviet Union considers it likely that any technology can make nuclear-armed ballistic missiles obsolete. Instead, the Soviet system performs the very practical function of contributing to the protection of Soviet leadership. For the USSR, with a history of succession crises and no constitutional tradition for the transfer of power, this protection is supremely important. No member of the Politburo would sleep well, knowing, or fearing, that a small nuclear attack by an nth-country arsenal (say, Israel) on Moscow could decapitate the Soviet leadership and transfer *de facto* control of the regime to military leaders in their command bunkers. Although the regime would survive such an attack and destroy any aggressor other than the United States with a fraction of its arsenal, control might pass, even temporarily, from the hands of key party and government leaders. Under some conditions the USSR might find it (ironically) advantageous that not all members of the Politburo are in Moscow most of the time, especially candidate members.

The Soviet BMD system might also figure in their plans for conventional war in Europe, should deterrence fail there. If NATO conventional defenses halted the initial Pact offensive and forced the war into a stalemate, then a Soviet BMD system that protected the western military districts of the USSR would provide confidence to them that they might initiate the limited, theater use of nuclear weapons in Europe. A west-of-the-Urals Soviet territorial BMD system could be devised by the 1990s, building upon their existing air-defense surface-to-air missiles (SAMs), modern interceptor aircraft, additional radars of the Krasnoyarsk level of technology, and other components.[16] Although of modest value against a full U.S. retaliatory strike (involving at least 3,500 surviving warheads in a worst-case scenario for the U.S. side and probably many more, of disparate penetration capability), such a jerry-rigged BMD could be deployed by the USSR if it could develop the battle-management/command-and-control software.[17] This would not be a welcome development from the British or French standpoint, which is one of the reasons for their ambivalence and that of other Europeans toward SDI. The Soviet limited BMD or ATBM (antitactical ballistic missile system, which unlike a strategic BMD system is not prohibited by the ABM Treaty) could, however, also create difficulties for NATO strategy, in addition to creating complications for British and French targeting plans. Although Soviet intentions with regard to theater BMD systems are not fully known, it is suspected that their plans for conventional war in Europe are based on a desire to avoid nuclear escalation. Soviet theater BMD systems, by making NATO escalation of some kind less credible, might pose complications for the Western alliance's defense strategy, as discussed below.

Before discussing the implications of SDI for NATO, it might be useful to note one irony of the "great debate" sparked by the Carter administration over the targeting of Soviet leadership in U.S. nuclear-war plans. The British and French nuclear deterrents have relied on this threat tacitly, if not explicitly, for many years. What else could the Kremlin fear from those forces, in addition to collateral societal damage, but its own survival and possible loss of control, however temporarily? This would be paranoia by Western standards, but the Soviet view should not be assumed as identical to the Western one, for reasons already noted. The difference between tacit threats to Soviet leadership previously posed by British and French deterrents, versus explicit threats appearing in U.S. confidential documents and then leaked to the press, is the amount of ambient noise generated on the U.S. side of the Atlantic. This appears to be a U.S. tradition, to hold a widespread debate in the news media on matters of high sensitivity in national security policy, whereas in Britain the press, in general even gamier than its U.S. cousins, is much more discreet about intelligence and security issues. Soviet leaders know that British and French nuclear arsenals are not pointed at targets west of the inter-German border, unless accidentally, and they also have figured out whose hides are at risk if those deterrents are detonated. This is precisely why a small nuclear force, if it can penetrate to its targets and those targets are highly valued intrinsically (as seats of government usually are), can be very menacing. In particular, with reference to the USSR, the nuclear forces of Britain and France, small only in comparison to U.S. and Soviet forces, loom large in Kremlin planning.

NATO STRATEGY AND BMD

The foregoing discussion brings us to the matter of the NATO alliance, NATO strategy, and missile defense. We will not review the entire issue of past and present NATO strategy here; excellent surveys of that are available.[18] SDI has special implications for NATO strategy, however, and vice versa.

First, SDI creates concerns in Europe about U.S. nuclear-deterrence guarantees (extended deterrence) and about alliance solidarity. If the United States deploys a territorial BMD system for North America, this might allow it to withdraw from European security issues behind a "Fortress America" complex. Or, opposite but equally of concern to Europeans, is the possibility that U.S. leaders might be too complacent about nuclear first use in Europe, optimistic that they can rely on their SDI to deter Soviet escalation to strategic, as opposed to theater, warfare.[19] U.S. leaders are understandably irked by these seemingly contradictory complaints, but the concerns are not as antithetical as they might appear. Both spring from political rather than strategic-theoretical logic. The United States has historically tended to take as much or as little of European conflicts as it desired. The period following World War II is an exception. Moreover, important intellectual and political actors in the United States are once again calling for a reduction of the U.S. contribution to European defense, in soldiers and in dollars.[20] Initiatives by U.S. congressional leaders, from Mansfield to Nunn, are reminders that even globally minded legislators, to say nothing of their narrower contemporaries, could be persuaded to put NATO on more of a pay-as-you-go basis. We have already seen that, underlying much U.S. deterrence logic, there is the economic genre of analysis in which cost–benefit metaphors substitute for strategic thinking. And so, quite logically, Europeans wonder whether persons who do their strategic sums the way Bob

Cratchit compiled his accounts can be depended upon to see the intrinsic issues in the defense of Europe, as opposed to the marginal utility issues.

Consider, for example, the voluminous debates in the United States over burden sharing in the Western alliance, quite understandable from the standpoint of accounting and budgetary considerations, but quite beside the point from the strategic standpoint. The Soviet Union is not deterred from war by the distribution of fiscal inputs or even by their size, but by what comes out of the pipeline in the way of forces, their training and readiness, and the potential for their modernization relative to Pact forces. U.S. strategic analyst Edward Luttwak once combatively entitled an article, "Why We Need More Waste, Fraud and Abuse in the Pentagon" to make the point that Congress had a fixation on Pentagon accounts, to the detriment of Pentagon strategy.[21] Colin S. Gray, a native of the United Kingdom who has established a high visibility among U.S. nuclear strategists, has also noted the U.S. propensity to avoid serious questions of strategy and to emphasize economic rationality as a substitute.[22] In short, Europeans can be forgiven for suspecting that any peace shield behind which the United States was truly safe from nuclear weapons might be a way out of Europe, instead of a way in. This fear is called "decoupling" in the jargon of strategists, suggesting, as it does, that the NATO defense commitments resemble railway cars linked together more or less dependably. Extending this metaphor, one might argue that many alliance debates revolve around who is the locomotive, and who is the caboose, but since the departure of General de Gaulle those debates have become more muted.

The opposite fear held by Europeans, as opposed to fear of decoupling, is that the United States will propel the entire alliance into war, when Europeans prefer to avoid it, or into peacetime confrontation, when Europeans prefer détente. The United States might do this, from the perspective of some Europeans, if it had deployed missile defenses that provided credible protection for the U.S. homeland, whether or not Europeans were similarly protected. And even if they were, they might not have the faith in that protection that their U.S. allies, did, since Europeans are closer to Soviet territory, and so threatened by many more weapons systems of shorter range and quicker reaction. Even without the SDI issue, the question of U.S. precipitation of war in Europe, or unnecessary peacetime confrontation, arose over the "572" Pershing II and cruise-missile deployments, which NATO undertook pursuant to a decision reached in 1979. Although the initial interest in deploying these Long Range Intermediate Nuclear Forces (LRINF) came from European leaders, such as former West German Chancellor Helmut Schmidt, by the time the decision came to be made, there were some cold feet. So, NATO embarked on a two-track policy, in which the USSR would simultaneously be offered the sticks of Euromissile deployments, and the carrots of arms-control negotiations to preclude NATO Euromissiles and Soviet SS–20 missiles of approximately similar range.[23]

Nor was this all. Not only did NATO cling to détente and deterrence at the same time with regard to the Euromissiles, but, according to its flexible-response doctrine, it also regarded those missiles as denial forces, intermediate between short-range nuclear missiles and U.S. strategic nuclear weapons. Thus the Euromissiles were accounted for by simultaneous and conflicting deterrence, denial, and détente rationales.[24] Further to this confusion, the missiles became hostages to the thaw in U.S. and Soviet relations that took place after the Reagan-Gorbachev summit at Reykjavik in 1986. By early 1987 the USSR was proposing that both sides agree to essentially the same formula proposed by President Reagan as the "zero option," but rejected at that time by the Soviets and by some U.S. NATO allies. An agreement by both sides to eliminate LRINF based in Europe seemed almost unavoidable in 1987. Whether the negotiators' hopes were fulfilled or not, the missiles that had once been judged essential were now advertised as expendable, however much advocates of the original decision to deploy might now argue that those deployments, in fact, motivated Soviet cooperation. It appeared that the Euromissiles were not only deterrence, détente, and denial forces, but also destructive forces.

One of the reasons NATO was willing to let go of its hard-fought decision to deploy Pershings and cruise missiles was the controversiality of those deployments within European parliaments and among the public at large. Especially embarrassing was the uproar in the Federal Republic of Germany, where the peace movement seemed to have strongest roots in parliamentary opposition (the Greens) and where the Kohl government, a supporter of the 572 decision, won reelection but remained of two minds about the Euromissiles. They were regarded as necessary to induce Soviet arms-control cooperation, but not desirable from the standpoint of any necessary contribution to deterrence. Quite the contrary, they were presumed to be provocative to the USSR and destabilizing of détente, so therefore a political time bomb for the Christian Democratic party leadership. They could neither repudiate the missiles openly nor get rid of them expeditiously, a fate similar to that of those whose relatives arrive for dinner rather unexpectedly and then stay for the weekend. Meanwhile, the USSR, sensitive to a potential vulnerability in the NATO and especially FRG public-relations jugular, mobilized one of its most intensive disinformation campaigns against the missiles.[25] Fortunately, from NATO's standpoint, the USSR overdid its merchandising and so turned off some ambivalent clientele groups with regard to its position against the deployments, but the political furor of 1983 was surmounted by NATO only momentarily. The missiles were clearly going to come out sooner or later, unless the Soviets did something terribly provocative to justify completion of the Euromissile deployments, which were proceeding at a drip-drip pace, suggesting that NATO was using prospective deployments coercively as much as previous deployments were being used strategically. Indeed, the USSR, if it proved to be willing to limit its SS-20 IRBMs to 100 warheads deployed in Soviet Asia, would be providing for the West a very attractive offer, given the disarray over the 572 deployments and the conflicting rationales. The Soviets, by adopting their own version of the zero option and obtaining Western acquiescence to it before Reagan left office, might have resolved the issue of NATO alliance solidarity, which the proposed deployments threatened to disrupt. Undoubtedly, Mr. Gorbachev intended no such bonus for NATO solidarity, but he exhibited in 1987 a perceived need for U.S.–Soviet strategic and theater nuclear-arms agreements and was prepared to pay the price of any side payments to NATO unity. This might be thought identical to an argument that the 572 deployments served as bargaining chips in that well-known arms-control phraseology. Perhaps they did, but an additional point is noteworthy here. NATO got itself onto a hook by proposing a strategically vague and politically contentious enhancement of its theater nuclear forces at a time when the proposed deployments were marching against the clock of Jimmy Carter's political demise. With the departure of Carter and the advent of Reagan, at least until 1984, U.S.–Soviet relations changed for the worse on arms-control issues. And the Reagan administration, having at first resisted negotiations to reduce INF along the lines of preferred Carter approaches, ended by conceding more in 1987, much to the apparent distress of some of the U.S.'s European allies.

The first set of issues, then, lies in the conflicting motives of Europeans and their fears, not illogical but still frustrating, of the collapse of détente and of U.S. isolationism. The second set of issues is more narrowly based on strategic and military doctrine, having to do with assumptions about whether U.S. strategic or European theater missiles would improve or weaken deterrence.

The essential controversy here is ironically not about the possible failure of SDI, but instead about its possible success. Success in this sense means that some U.S.- or European-based BMD system would work as a technology, with some capability to thin out Soviet conventional or nuclear ballistic missile attacks. Why would the systems be more controversial if they worked than if they did not?

The reason for this irony, of effective technologies creating more political difficulties than ineffective ones, is that effective theater or strategic defenses collide with NATO's dependency upon the threat promptly to escalate to nuclear war any conventional war, if it is losing. If, however, the Soviets follow any U.S. BMD or NATO ATBM deployments with their own comparable systems, then NATO may be deterred from nuclear escalation. This returns the issue to the balance of Western and Eastern conventional forces, which is thought to favor the Pact, although not as much as some pessimists might argue.

Some have suggested that missile defenses might make Europe "safe for conventional war," but this exaggerates their probable impact. The probability is that, long before strategic BMD are available for deployment, theater ballistic missile defenses will be deployed in Europe. Their effects will not be to eliminate the possibility of nuclear escalation by either side, but to complicate prevailing estimates about force balances and denial capabilities. NATO antitactical ballistic missile defenses, for example, could be useful in denying a free ride to Soviet conventionally armed, short-range ballistic missiles targeted against NATO air defenses, airfields, nuclear-weapons storage sites, command and control centers, and other important and time-urgent targets.[26] Soviet theater ballistic missile defenses might deny to NATO some selective nuclear options that it would otherwise have and some conventional deep-attack options incorporated into NATO Follow-on Forces Attack (FOFA) declaratory strategy. FOFA will be highly dependent upon the development of improved sensors and processors for real-time reconnaissance and information analysis, plus more commonality among NATO members' electronic security measures and electronic countermeasures (ESM and ECM, the former protecting its own communications and the latter disrupting those of the opponent).[27] The obsolescence of nuclear weapons as components of deterrence of war in Europe is no more at hand than the obsolescence of strategic nuclear weapons. The future is more likely to see a commingling of improved very "smart" nonnuclear offenses, combined with selectively deployed theater antimissile defenses, the latter growing out of air-defense technologies already deployed (for example, Patriot). The Soviets are certainly in a good position to deploy more of their mobile and highly competent SAMs forward, with their divisions and allied Pact divisions in East Germany and Czechoslovakia, along with improved short-range conventionally armed, but nuclear-capable, ballistic missiles (SS–21, SS–12/22, and SS–23). Each side could conceivably become less reliant upon early nuclear use in a conventional war, which would certainly be desirable, but neither could afford to factor out of the equation entirely the possibility of nuclear escalation, if only to hold its own allies in line.

A more complicated issue for the United States alone, as well as for alliance relations, is the relationship of strategic air defense to ballistic missile defense. Deployment of U.S. strategic BMD will drive Soviet countermeasures toward air-breathing systems, such as bombers and cruise missiles. Therefore, improved atmospheric defenses will have to follow deployment of BMD, or the BMD investments will be offset, probably at lower marginal cost. In Western Europe, theater BMD and air defenses may grow up together, because air defenses have a head start. Theater ballistic missile defenses may not be as vulnerable to air-breathing offenses, comparatively speaking, as are strategic BMD based on other technologies. Atmospheric defense technologies have been tested and deployed, although little remains of the once very extensive U.S. strategic air defense system.[28]

Important as these technological issues may be, of primary importance are the political issues. Two of the most urgent are alliance cohesion, already alluded to, and the character of U.S.–Soviet political relations. The irony of proposals for deployment of U.S. and Soviet strategic BMD is that, if the level of trust on both sides is sufficient to allow for mutual and verifiable deployments, then the level of trust is adequate to bring mutual reductions in offenses through arms control, and without BMD. If, on the other hand, there is insufficient trust to allow for mutual and verifiable offense-constrained defense deployments, then unilateral BMD deployments simply risk starting another round of the arms race.[29] And if adequate trust exists for U.S. and Soviet deployments of strategic BMD systems, then suspicious U.S. allies in Europe will ask for similar kinds of protection, or alliance cohesion will melt down. If U.S. allies in Western Europe are protected, the Soviets will be faced with similar demands from their Warsaw Treaty Organization confrères. To complicate matters further, the balance between NATO and Pact conventional forces capable of attacking or defending Europe without nuclear weapons will be harder to evaluate after defenses are deployed. The net assessment will be more dependent upon new technology and research innovation, subject to the usual interbloc intelligence rivalries.

It took no small amount of pulling and hauling to get NATO consensus on the declaratory strategy of flexible response in 1967, and only the withdrawal of France from the NATO military command structure made that consensus possible. Flexible response is doctrinally coupled to forward defense, meaning that no declaratory strategy can concede West German territory at the outset of any conflict, in order to trade space for time. Further, the NATO flexible-response strategy presupposes that escalation can take place in very graduated steps, as opposed to sudden eruptions. The pace at which both sides ascend the ladder is not fully controllable by NATO, however, and flexible response becomes inflexible stalemate, at a higher level of violence, if the USSR refuses to acknowledge intrawar deterrence. In addition, there is not a transatlantic consensus on the role of conventional forces in NATO strategy, as to whether they are trip wires or genuine denial forces, or both. The U.S. propensity for grumbling about burden sharing assumes that they are truly denial forces, but the status of U.S. and NATO strategic and theater nuclear forces, compared to Soviet forces, makes that assumption improbable. Improving the efficiency of infrastructure and logistics and sharing the burden for those improvements equitably seems laudable in its own right, but it has little strategic significance if conventional forces are trip wires only. On the other hand, if they are also denial forces, then the operational strategy for denial of Soviet objectives must be credible. A credible operational strategy for NATO conventional defense might include ATBMs, but it is not dependent upon them, and deployment of ATBMs (or a U.S. SDI) is not the most pressing weakness in NATO's conventional deterrence. What SDI or ATBM can do for NATO deterrence is to put back into NATO strategy some of the "flex" that would be subtracted from it if the Soviets initiated ATBM deployments as a counter to NATO's threat of escalation. Thus, Soviet ATBM might pose a threat to flexible response to the extent that flexible response depends upon early (ballistic) nuclear first use to remedy conventional deficiencies; but if NATO strategy is not so dependent, and it need not be, then NATO ATBM might not be advisable even if the Soviets deploy their own. As in strategic ballistic missile defenses, so in theater systems for the same function; the best reaction to an opponent's deployment of new or upgraded defenses might not be one's own defenses, but better offenses to assure penetration of its defenses.

In this regard, the technologies for making the front ends of ballistic and cruise missiles very smart and very invisible (as in stealth technology) may prove to be the trumps in future generations of offense–defense competitions. It would not do for the superpowers to disinvest in conventional defenses, in order to build SDI and SDI-ski, and then find that smarter offensive ballistic and cruise missiles (aided by smart reconnaissance platforms based in space) made those defenses obsolete. There is some hubris in supposing that smart warfare will favor the defense, because the USSR is always placed in the role of notional adversary, preferring to attack by surprise. Smart warfare may favor the attacker, not the defender, even in exercises devised from the standpoint of Western experience and measuring rods. If defenders can profit from a more transparent battlefield, which will allow for conventional deep strike against Soviet second-echelon formations, for example, cannot the USSR benefit from the same technology to destroy mobile targets in the NATO rear at the outset of war? It would seem that technology eventually serves as an equalizer between defenders and attackers, although smart technologies may be trumps compared to other technologies—for example, fast interceptors and maneuverable satellites.

We have spent much time on the alliance end of the SDI issue, because the United States is not accomplishing much if it is defending itself alone, or deterring war on North America without also deterring war against Europe. In fact, U.S. policy aspires to do more, even to deter coercion based on Soviet manipulation of any perceived asymmetry in the conventional or nuclear balance. Withal, coercion is certainly more the day-to-day risk compared to an actual outbreak of war on the Central Front, and the Soviet calculus of risk taking partakes of coercion sooner than war. Europeans on the front end of Soviet coercive pressures and (often at the same time) entreaties toward détente cannot always fully appreciate the more detached U.S. view of strategic rationality. People in the United States fail to understand the European paradox of greater nearness to the Soviet Union sometimes inducing less fear of actual war. NATO's problem is to make deterrence rationality, which is itself not fully consistent with other criteria for rationality, compatible with the political imperatives of reassurance, and nonprovocation. This implies reassurance to the European allies of the United States that war is a distant possibility, and an avoidance of provocative behavior that might motivate the Soviet Union to attack. That NATO has partially juggled all of these balls without completely dropping any one of them is a tribute to its endurance, however defective the structure of deterrence rationality on which it depends.[30]

NOTES

1. The conclusion of President Reagan's March 23, 1983 address to the nation (now known as his "Star Wars" speech) is reprinted in Arms Control Association, *Star Wars Quotes* (Washington, DC: Arms Control Association, July 1986), pp. 118–19.

2. Paul H. Nitze, "On the Road to a More Stable Peace," U.S. Department of State, *Current Policy*, No. 657, February 29, 1985.

3. For perspective on Soviet decision making, see Richard F. Staar, *USSR Foreign Policies after Detente* (Stanford, CA: Hoover Institution Press, 1985), pp. 21–42, and David Holloway, "Doctrine and Technology in Soviet Armaments Policy," in ed. Derek Leebaers, *Soviet Military Thinking* (London: Allen and Unwin, 1981), pp. 259–91.

4. An informative discussion is Fen Osler Hampsen, "Escalation in Europe," in *Hawks, Doves and Owls: An Agenda for Avoiding Nuclear War*, ed. Graham T. Allison, Albert Carnesale, and Joseph S. Nye, Jr. (New York: Norton, 1985), Ch. 4, pp. 80–114.

5. Robert S. McNamara, *Blundering into Disaster: Surviving the First Century of the Nuclear Age* (New York: Pantheon Books, 1986).

6. Spurgeon M. Keeny, Jr. and Wolfgang K. H. Panofsky, "MAD Versus NUTS: Can Doctrine or Weaponry Remedy the Mutual Hostage Relationship of the Superpowers?" *Foreign Affairs* 60, No. 2 (Winter 1981–82): 287–304. Advocates of M.A.D. appear not to recognize the danger of too much of a good thing. By arguing that technology imposes a relationship of mutual vulnerability upon the superpowers, they downgrade the importance of policy choices, regardless of technology, by implication.

7. For SDI near-term technology prospects, see Strategic Defense Initiative Organization, *Report to the Congress on the Strategic Defense Initiative*, Washington, DC, April 1987.

8. On the proposals made at the Reykjavik U.S.–Soviet summit, see Secretary of State George Shultz, "Nuclear Weapons, Arms Control and the Future of Deterrence," U.S. Department of State, *Current Policy* No. 893, pp. 3–4.

9. Keith B. Payne and Colin S. Gray, "Nuclear Policy and the Defensive Transition," *Foreign Affairs* 62, No. 4 (Spring 1984): 820–42. A more palatable form of this argument for those suspicious of Reagan administration motives is Alvin Weinberg and Jack N. Barkenbus, "Stabilizing Star Wars," *Foreign Policy* (Spring 1984): 164–70.

10. An argument to this effect is made by Keith B. Payne, *Strategic Defense: Star Wars in Perspective* (Lanham, MD: Hamilton Press, 1986), Ch. 6.

11. The concept of an attack price is explained in Ashton B. Carter, "BMD Applications: Performance and Limitations," in *Ballistic Missile Defense*, ed. Carter and David N. Schwartz (Washington, DC: Brookings Institution, 1984), Ch. 4, pp. 110–120.

12. Difficulties in launching U.S. ICBMs under attack are discussed in Ashton B. Carter, "Assessing Command System Vulnerability," in *Managing Nuclear Operations*, ed. Carter, John B. Steinbruner, and Charles A. Zraket (Washington, DC: Brookings Institution, 1987), Ch. 17, pp. 578–82; and John D. Steinbruner, "Launch Under Attack," *Scientific American* 250 (January 1984): 37–47. Whether the USSR could count on preventing U.S. ICBMs from being launched under attack depends upon Soviet ability to attack other elements of the U.S. strategic triad and strategic command and control, as well as the ICBMs themselves. Nor is it obvious to conservative Soviet planners that U.S. ICBMs, except under bolt-from-the-blue conditions in which no strategic warning is available, will remain in their silos until Soviet warheads begin detonating.

13. John Gardner, Edward Gerry, Robert Jastrow, William Nierenberg, and Frederick Seitz, *Missile Defense in the 1990s* (Washington, DC: George C. Marshall Institute, 1987).

14. See Strategic Defense Initiative Organization, *Report to the Congress*; and John Gardner et al., *Missile Defense in the 1990s*, Part Two.

15. Development of Soviet missile defenses is described in Sayre Stevens, "The Soviet BMD Program," in *Ballistic Missile Defense*, ed. Carter and Schwartz pp. 182–220.

16. For a current U.S. intelligence assessment of Soviet BMD programs, see Robert M. Gates, "The Soviets and SDI," Appendix in Gardner et al., *Missile Defense in the 1990s*, pp. 45–52.

17. Survivable U.S. warheads following notional Soviet attacks are indicated in Desmond Ball, "Development of the SIOP, 1960–1983" in *Strategic Nuclear Targeting*, ed. Demond Ball and Jeffrey Richelson (Ithaca, NY: Cornell University Press, 1986), p. 81.

18. See Stanley R. Sloan, *NATO's Future: Toward a New Transatlantic Bargain* (Washington, DC: National Defense University Press, 1985).

19. On European concerns with regard to SDI, see Lawrence Freedman, "The Star Wars Debate: The Western Alliance and Strategic Defence: Part II," in *New Technology and Western Security Policy*, ed. Robert O'Neill (Hamden, CT: Shoe String Press, 1985), pp. 149–65.

20. An argument that NATO is economically dysfunctional for the United

States is made in Melvyn Krauss, *How NATO Weakens the West* (New York: Simon & Shuster, 1986).

21. For a fuller account of Luttwak's views, see Edward N. Luttwak, *The Pentagon and the Art of War* (New York: Simon & Shuster, 1984).

22. A forceful critique of U.S. concepts of crisis management appears in Colin S. Gray, *Nuclear Strategy and National Style* (Lanham, MD: Hamilton Press, 1986), Ch. 6.

23. David N. Schwartz, *NATO's Nuclear Dilemmas* (Washington, DC: Brookings Institution, 1984), pp. 193–251, reviews these issues succinctly.

24. Leon V. Sigal, *Nuclear Forces in Europe: Enduring Dilemmas, Present Prospects* (Washington, DC: Brookings Institution, 1984).

25. See David S. Yost, "The Soviet Campaign against INF in West Germany," in *Soviet Strategic Deception*, ed. Brian D. Dailey and Patrick J. Parker (Lexington, MA: Lexington Books/D. C. Heath, 1987), Ch. 17, pp. 343–374.

26. Dennis M. Gormley, "The Impact of NATO Doctrinal Choices on the Policies and Strategic Choices of Warsaw Pact States: Part II," *Adelphi Papers*, 206 (London: International Institute for Strategic Studies, Spring 1986), pp. 20–34.

27. General Bernard W. Rogers, "Follow-on Forces Attack (FOFA): Myths and Realities," *NATO Review* 32, No. 6 (December 1984): 1–9, is an authoritative statement of NATO doctrine by the then Supreme Allied Commander, Europe (SACEUR). For a critique, see Steven L. Canby, "New Conventional Force Technology and the NATO-Warsaw Pact Balance: Part I," in *New Technology and Western Security Policy*, ed. O'Neill, pp. 66–83.

28. U.S. strategic air defense forces are described in Caspar W. Weinberger, *Annual Report to the Congress, Fiscal Year 1988* (Washington, DC: U.S. GPO, January 12, 1987), pp. 213–14.

29. For more discussion of this point, see McNamara, *Blundering into Disaster*, p. 106 and passim.

30. An argument made at greater length in Stephen J. Cimbala, *Extended Deterrence: The U.S. and NATO Europe* (Lexington, MA: Lexington Books/D. C. Heath, 1987).

7

DETERRENCE, RATIONALITY, AND POLITICAL CONSISTENCY

One of the hallmarks of rational policy is consistency between what is intended and what is actually done. Nuclear strategy can be evaluated in terms of the consistency of the faces it shows to its diverse audiences. There are essentially four of these faces: declaratory policy; operational or employment policy; force development or acquisition policy; and arms-control policy.[1] Declaratory policy is the publicly proclaimed doctrine by which strategy is explained to the public and other audiences outside the community of high policy makers and strategic specialists. Operational or employment policy is embodied in actual war plans drawn up by the appropriate civilian and military authorities. Acquisition policy determines what forces we buy and deploy. Arms-control policy intends to reduce the risks of nuclear war, to diminish the consequences of war if it occurs, and to limit the growth of arms inventories by superpower competition. Some inconsistency among these varieties of policy is to be expected; drastic or gross inconsistencies send conflicting messages to allies and potential adversaries, as well as to the people of the United States.

We will look at several issues that provide a focus on the degree to which U.S. declaratory, operational, and acquisition policies are consistent or inconsistent, for the United States itself, and by implication for the NATO alliance. The issues are the doctrine of assured destruction, the problem of force acquisition and "servicism," and the question of prompt or delayed counterforce missions for strategic forces. Most of our discussion will focus on the relationship between declaratory and operational policy, or the congruity between what we say we will do and what we actually plan to do. Whether we can actually do either what we say or what we plan for depends upon the forces and other capabilities actually purchased and deployed, so some of the pressures on acquisition policy are noted. The larger context for acquisition policy is, of course, the entire U.S. domestic-policy-making process, a subject much too extensive for comprehensive study here; but some characteristics of U.S. defense organizations are pertinent to the decisions about forces acquired, and thus capabilities made available to support declaratory and operational policy. Arms-control policy receives separate treatment in another chapter.

ASSURED DESTRUCTION

U.S. strategic nuclear forces have for many years been sized against a worst-case threat of surprise attack. A worst-case threat means that the forces would be caught while on day-to-day rather than generated alert, the latter implying that they have been forewarned that war is imminent and are poised to retaliate. Former Secretary of Defense Robert S. McNamara indicated a tendency in conservative force-structure planning for the worst, when he determined force size according to a "greater than expected" threat, following which the United States should have a capability for "assured destruction" of the Soviet Union as a modern society.[2] This criterion for force sizing was supposedly related to the amount of damage the United States could do, even after absorbing a surprise attack against its retaliatory forces and other targets. McNamara's notion of a greater than expected threat undoubtedly annoyed some strategic doves, just as his notion of assured destruction later frustrated hawks, who saw it as a way of limiting, not increasing, the growth of force structure.

McNamara's debates with his critics were informed less by strategic rationality than by competing managerial rationalities. McNamara's approach was to assert that any rational Soviet leader would be deterred at the prospect that the United States could assure, following any Soviet first strike, a retaliatory strike that would destroy from one-fourth to one-third of the Soviet population, and one-half to two-thirds of its industrial society.[3] These numbers were arrived at by inferring what would deter a Soviet leader from what it was reasonable to assume would deter any U.S. president. The assured destruction criteria could be criticized from a liberal standpoint as involving too much overkill, and by conservatives as not promising to destroy the Soviet military arsenal.

McNamara did not come to assured destruction easily. He began his tenure of office with an excursion into what came to be called no-cities doctrine, or what is correctly termed counterforce. In a noted speech in Ann Arbor, Michigan, in 1962, the secretary of defense contended that, to the extent possible, nuclear weapons would be used in a future war just as conventional weapons might be:

The U.S. has come to the conclusion that to the extent feasible basic military strategy in a possible general nuclear war should be approached in much the same way that more conventional military operations have been regarded in the past. That is to say, principal military objectives, in the event of a nuclear war stemming from a major attack on the Alliance, should be the destruction of the enemy's military forces, not of his civilian population.[4]

In this instance McNamara was attempting to bring declaratory policy, or what was promulgated by officials in public forums, into consistency with the administration's objectives for actual targeting policy and war plans. Having inherited from the Eisenhower administration war plans that it felt were not sufficiently discriminatory among kinds of targets and attack strategies, the Kennedy national security team sought to provide options for the president other than immediate, all-out retaliation against Soviet cities.

The attempt to reconcile these divergent strands of policy, declaratory and operational, was an acknowledged failure by 1966, when McNamara began to emphasize assured destruction and capabilities for countercity retaliation to the near exclusion of counterforce strategies.[5] His reasons for this shift in declaratory policy, while operational planning went in the opposite direction, were complicated, but they boiled down to strategic reasons and fiscal reasons. McNamara's strategic reasoning was that force deployments in excess of what was required for assured destruction would stimulate the arms race and motivate Soviet leaders to follow suit. His fiscal reason was that the armed forces saw earlier city-avoidance statements as an invitation to request more strategic counterforce than the secretary wanted to purchase. Thus, his shift in declaratory policy accomplished an objective in acquisition policy, by holding down the growth of strategic budgets and forces. It had wider repercussions than that, however, for it grew from an expedient declaratory to a partial cap on force acquisitions during the latter 1960s and the 1970s. McNamara's explanations of assured destruction also provided the strategic rationale for the momentum behind U.S. approaches to negotiations for the reduction of superpower strategic armaments, the Strategic Arms Limitation Talks (SALT).[6]

In part as a result of McNamara's explanations of declaratory policy, the United States did not acquire the forces necessary to fulfill his aspirations as stated at Ann Arbor in 1962. There were other reasons for this outcome, including Soviet claims that ample U.S. strategic counterforce (especially prompt counterforce in the form of ICBMs) could be used for first strikes as well as retaliatory strikes. This Soviet concern, although it seemed disingenuous to U.S. observers at the time, was probably as sincere as the Soviet fear of surprise attack was canonical, ever since the experience of Operation Barbarossa in 1941. The USSR, however, was also playing to U.S. allies' misgivings about counterforce doctrines, knowing that Europeans were sensitive to suggestions of limited nuclear wars that might be fought on their soil and only on their soil.

McNamara left the matter of assured destruction as a conceptual framework, which guided subsequent thinking on force acquisition and arms-control policy, but not for employment policy (targeting). Here, there is a more linear trend, from the early 1960s to the present, in the development of the U.S. Single Integrated Operational Plan (SIOP) and the policy guidance from which it derives. That trend has been toward the development of more numerous and more selective nuclear options for the use of U.S. strategic forces, if deterrence fails.[7] As the United States has talked itself away from increased versatility in war-fighting options as a matter of declaratory policy, it has sought that very same versatility in its targeting plans. Furthermore, force acquisitions have seemed to provide more variety and size than is necessary to fulfill the requirements of declaratory policy, and less than is necessary to satisfy all the options demanded by target planners. While the exercises of target planning and attendant policy guidance involve a multiservice cast, the forces procured and deployed have survived the political weeding process to the extent that they fulfilled individual military service roles and missions.

U.S. NUCLEAR FORCES

In addition to having declaratory, operational, acquisition, and arms-control forces, the United States also has the bureaucratic forces of the Army, Navy, Air Forces and Marines, the last notionally included within the Navy table of organization, but with a very different tradition. In the case of strategic retaliatory forces, the Air Force has custody of the long-range strategic bomber forces and the land-based strategic missile force (ICBMs), in addition to cruise missiles deployed on bombers (ALCM for air-launched cruise missiles). The Navy has its Poseidon ballistic missile submarines (SSBNs) and cruise missiles that are being deployed on submarines and surface ships, in addition to nuclear bombs, which can be delivered from carrier-based aircraft. The Army has had propriety custody of ballistic missile defense (BMD) since the 1950s, although this is likely to be challenged as the BMD technology is deployed in space, which is the traditional proving ground for the U.S. Air Force, already in charge of North American Air Defense Command (NORAD) and Strategic Air Command (SAC), and playing the dominant role in Space Command. The Army insists upon pride of place over tactical air defense for its ground forces, while strategic air defense is the property of the Air

Force (and the Navy develops and deploys state-of-the-art fleet-air-defense technology on its Aegis-class cruisers and Arleigh-Burke-class destroyers.[8]

As Samuel Huntington has noted, the forces that are actually purchased by the U.S. Congress and deployed with U.S. armies, navies, and air forces are the result of servicism, not strategic analysis.[9] The forces that are most valuable to the military services, which must compete in the rough-and-tumble of the domestic budgetary process for their preferred shares of the defense pie, are those forces that cannot be duplicated in another service. So the Navy prefers capital ships, especially large, nuclear-powered carriers, and the Air Force fighter aircraft that can fly at Mach 2.5, and the Army tanks in which one can ride in comfort at 40 miles per hour (no doubt in order to avoid potholes). Thus, the U.S. strategic forces, determined by the same process required for the justification of other forces, are subject to the same sentiments of ownership, notwithstanding their strategic relevance.

Consider, as illustrative of the importance of servicism in the acquisition process, the role of the manned strategic bomber in U.S. deterrence policy. Since the arrival of ballistic missiles, the role of bombers has been subject to dispute. Obviously land- and sea-based ballistic missiles (ICBMs and SLBMs) would take over the targeting of many objectives formerly assigned to bombers. Bombers had the disadvantage of being slow, compared to missiles, but the comparative advantage of diversity in means of weapons delivery (cruise missiles, gravity bombs, and short-range air-to-ground missiles). Missiles, even with the improved accuracies of the 1980s, would not be as accurate as some bomber-delivered weapons, but the bomber-delivered weapons would have to penetrate Soviet air defenses to reach their assigned targets, and the missile would be opposed (as of the early 1980s) by a single Soviet BMD system of 64 interceptors surrounding Moscow.

The Air Force has argued that bombers perform a unique function in the strategic inventory, in addition to their contribution to its synergistic survivability. This contribution to the survival of the U.S. strategic triad as a whole comes about as a result of the diversity in basing modes and in operational assumptions about command and control for bombers, as opposed to missiles. What complicates the Soviet attack plan also complicates the U.S. response plan, if the diversity in U.S. force structure is viewed not as a quantity of objects to be destroyed, but as a large central nervous system with distributed ganglia, and at the end of each ganglion a military force with its own special organizational norms, traditions, and standard operating procedures.

In the case of bombers compared to strategic missiles, for example, the command and control procedures for assured survivability differ considerably. Bombers can be launched even before attack on the United

States has actually been confirmed, under a procedure termed Positive Control Launch (PCL). The bombers go to a predetermined point outside hostile air space and loiter for a certain time, awaiting a signal telling them to continue to their assigned targets. If no signal is received, they return to base.[10] This capability for being recalled gives the bomber force a flexibility that missiles do not have, for the missiles have not been built with a capability for destruction by remote control after they have been launched. This capability for the bomber force has not been used casually, however, indeed, it has never been completely "scrambled," in the vernacular. SAC moved to a DefCon 2 state of alert during the Cuban missile crisis, one step before forces are actually deployed for combat and (in the case of nuclear forces) considered subject to imminent attack.[11]

Compared to the procedures for command, control, and communications (C3) with bombers, the arrangements for ICBMs are much more straightforward. Land-based strategic missiles like the U.S. Minuteman are kept in a high state of peacetime readiness for immediate launch; the name Minuteman was not chosen coincidentally. Fast-reacting ICBMs could be launched promptly after authorized commands reached the silos, and U.S. ICBMs can be retargeted in a very short time by Command Data Buffers, if the appropriate intelligence is available. The disadvantages of ICBMs are that they are deployed in fixed silos, and thus the basing mode cannot be moved out of harm's way. Increasingly accurate Soviet ICBM warheads threaten to destroy much of the Minuteman force in a preemptive attack, and this is one reason that the U.S. Air Force is now developing a mobile ICBM (Midgetman) for deployment during the 1990s. The Soviets, in turn, have already deployed one strategic ICBM in a mobile basing mode (SS–25) and will soon deploy another (SS–24), the latter a MIRVed version.[12]

Under the worst-case scenario of a Soviet bolt from the blue that first launched SLBM attacks against U.S. bomber bases and then attacked U.S. ICBMs with Soviet ICBMs, the survival of U.S. land-based missiles would be dependent upon launch on warning/launch under attack, or prompt launch (now the accepted terminology). This might be difficult to do, if the attacker used SLBM detonations over the ICBM fields to create pindown effects preventing prompt launch.[13] A bolt from the blue against ungenerated U.S. forces is improbable, however, compared to the much more likely scenario of an attack during a crisis, in which case U.S. forces would be alerted. Soviet submarines would have a tougher time getting close to some of their preferred launch points off the U.S. Atlantic and Pacific coasts, and some of them might suffer attrition from ASW efforts pursuant to the U.S. maritime strategy. In addition, Soviet attacks on U.S. ICBMs and bomber bases would have to be timed very carefully; there is a trade-off for them in choosing between simultaneous or sequential detonations of their ICBMs and SLBMs against the appropriate

U.S. targets. If the USSR land- and sea-based ballistic missiles are launched simultaneously, then more U.S. ICBMs will escape destruction, for the Soviet SLBMs will arrive sooner and so warn U.S. defenders of impending attacks on ICBMs. If, on the other hand, Soviet SLBMs and ICBMs are launched in sequence, in order to arrive at the same time, then the massive launch of their ICBMs will be detected within minutes and so reduce the surprise component of their SLBM attacks. In that case, more U.S. bombers would escape destruction.[14]

PROMPT VERSUS SLOW COUNTERFORCE

U.S. strategy pessimists can contrive scenarios in which the USSR destroys the bulk of the U.S. ICBM force and thus removes the largest amount of the prompt counterforce. So disarmed, in these scenarios, the United States capitulates, having only its bombers and submarines with which to retaliate. With ICBMs eliminated, so the story goes, the United States would be denied weapons with which to strike back at Soviet forces in an accurate and timely fashion. It could retaliate against Soviet cities, but so could the Soviets, following a U.S. retaliation, strike its cities. The U.S. retaliation might then be withheld by a president who calculated that his counterforce weapons had been subtracted from the inventory and there was no point in destroying Soviet cities, if their destruction provoked the destruction of U.S. cities.

Scenarios of this type are technically deficient and strategically misleading. They exemplify strategizing and scientism, instead of science and strategy. There are several reasons. First, the United States would not be bereft of counterforce weapons after the best first strike that the Soviet Union could make, even against ungenerated U.S. forces. One-third of the U.S. bomber force is on strip alert at all times and would be airborne before any SLBMs could strike their bases, assuming that U.S. satellite detectors functioned properly and strategic communications "connectivity" were not severed. The U.S. strategic bomber force carries approximately one-half of the total megatonnage in the U.S. arsenal. Not all the surviving bombers would penetrate to their targets, in all probability; there would be some attrition by Soviet air defenses. Not all bombers, however, need to penetrate in order to destroy the appropriate targets. Air-launched cruise missiles have been deployed with the B–52 force and will be deployed for the B–1B force, as its major role shifts in the 1990s from penetration to standoff cruise-missile carrier. U.S. strategic cruise missiles will also be deployed on submarines and surface ships; these will be varieties of Tomahawk land-attack cruise missiles with nuclear warheads, which will be difficult to distinguish from sea-launched cruise missiles with conventional warheads (TLAM-N, as opposed to TLAM-C). The lighter weight of nuclear compared to conventional warheads will give the former a greater range of several thousand kilometers. Although slow in speed compared to ballistic missiles, cruise missiles are extremely accurate, and their second-strike counterforce capability against OMT targets (Soviet general-purpose forces, including those organized and equipped for transition to nuclear combat) is not to be belittled. U.S. ICBMs are thought to be especially useful against two classes of time-urgent targets: Soviet ICBM silos and command bunkers for their military and political leadership.

The first objection to the artificiality of the ICBM vulnerability scenario was that the United States has plenty of slow counterforce likely to survive any Soviet first strike, much of it extremely accurate. The second point relates to the strategic sense of prompt retaliation against the Soviet ICBM force and command system. There are two issues here, and both involve misconstructions that confuse real war with war on paper. The first issue, that of statistical combat between Soviet and U.S. ICBM forces, revolves around comparative indexes of warheads, throw weight, reliability, and kill probabilities for the two sides. Obviously it is important to walk through these numbers, in the same way that one walks through a military or command-post exercise for the vicarious experience. Having done the exercise, one has a better sense of how inaccurate any prewar estimates might be, how much the fog of war would cloud the sand table.[15] Unfortunately, this is not always the reaction. Some analysts get bogged down in arguing about postattack firepower ratios, as if the exercise numbers represent a real world instead of an artificial construct, useful as it is. Real Soviet planners will probably make very conservative assumptions about the probable success of their preemption, given the uncertainties attendant on attacks on flight trajectories and under operational conditions never approximated in preceding tests. If U.S. figures show that the USSR in a surprise first strike could destroy some 90 percent of the U.S. ICBM force, then the Soviets might assume that, *ceteris paribus*, they will destroy 60 or 70 percent of it at best.

Or, they might assume that they have no way of calculating any estimate of U.S. ICBM survivability, given the uncertainty of U.S. political behavior in addition to the statistical uncertainties of ICBM duels.[16] Would the U.S. president, or his alternates in case of his unavailability, leave the Minuteman force sitting in its silos, once reliable warning of impending attack on American ICBMs had been received? Perhaps they would, or confusion and indecision would reign, and so allow the Soviet missiles more time to arrive at their assigned targets. A prudent Soviet planner, however, could never make assumptions as optimistic as these. Soviet leaders would have to estimate what they would do in a worst case, and a worst case for their preemption would be a U.S. launch on warning, immediately after their launch is detected. Now, American analysts will object that it is not U.S. policy to launch on warning in this fashion, but that is not the most important issue here. The important issue is what the Soviets will assume about U.S. behavior, not what Americans, under normal peacetime conditions, assume about it. A Soviet leader would have to assume conservatively that the U.S. ICBM force will be on its way to the Soviet Union as soon as a Soviet launch has been detected, even though this might not happen in fact.

Suppose that these uncertainties do not deter the Soviets. There is still the question of whether the United States needs to retaliate promptly against Soviet silos and command centers. And, if it does, are ICBMs the most effective forces with which to do it? Surviving U.S. ICBMs are not necessarily assigned their optimal targets if they are directed at the Soviet ICBM force, depending on how much of the Soviet force is left over after their first strike and how fast U.S. ICBMs can retaliate. After 1989 the United States will deploy Trident II (D–5) submarine-launched ballistic missiles with accuracies sufficient to attack hard targets in the USSR, including their missile silos. These sea-based weapons might be better choices for some hard targets than ICBMs, since, among other things, the U.S. ICBMs will be coming from very predictable trajectories (over the Pole), whereas the SLBMs might attack from any azimuth on the compass. Much depends upon the surviving Soviet BMD and air defenses, together with their selection of ICBMs to be included in the initial attack.[17]

The other unique attribute of ICBMs, their ability to promptly destroy Soviet command bunkers, is a mixed blessing, for if they do, they contribute to a Soviet leadership more uncertain in composition, and less available for or interested in war termination. Thus, prompt destruction of the Soviet leadership, or even some of its key components, could initiate a "going out of business" sale for later efforts to turn the war off, with the result that it could not be stopped until arsenals were exhausted.[18] U.S. efforts to destroy the Soviet command structure would probably also be misguided about how vulnerable to destruction the Soviet C3 system might be, since the USSR has made extensive preparations for the survival of its postattack civilian and military leadership.[19] Nor is it clear that the command structure has to be attacked rapidly rather than slowly, in the latter case holding the threat of destruction over its head while allowing for negotiation and the possible cessation of the fighting, or at least a moderation of its severity.

Speaking frankly, if either the United States or the Soviet side in a nuclear war were committed to destroying the central nervous system of its opponents—that is, the state—it would have to face the inescapable fact that the society would in all probability have to be destroyed along with it. The Soviet and U.S. governments exist not only at the national (central) levels, but at the regional levels as well. In the United States alone, there are thousands of independent governmental units, and the

Soviet system has numerous regional components also. This has not gone unnoticed by U.S. target planners, apparently. In past discussions some may have proposed selective targeting of certain Soviet nationalities other than Russians, on the theory that this would embolden revolution by non-Russian nationalities against their Russian ethnic masters, perhaps to the extent of secession from the USSR itself.[20] The very concept of ethnic targeting is repugnant and smacks of genocide, but in a perverse way it acknowledges the diversity of Soviet nationalities and, by implication, the visibility of public authorities other than those located in Moscow. Indeed, the durability of the Soviet state is rooted in party, state, and internal-security (KGB and other) webs of personnel, which are in contact with citizens at every level. It is difficult to imagine that this fabric could be destroyed while leaving much of the society intact.

Of course, the notion of countercommand attacks might mean something different, implying an effort to lop off the heads of the very top party and governmental leadership in the hope that this would bring about confusion in an acephalous Soviet opponent. In order for this to happen, however, the military leadership would have to be decapitated too, or the result of party/state leaders' destruction would simply bring about the long-feared advent of Bonapartism in Moscow. U.S. planners cannot view with optimism the replacement of the Soviet civilian leadership by a military one, for there is no evidence of any consistent civil–military cleavage within the Soviet leadership on defense issues that could be exploited to U.S. advantage, were the civilians displaced. However targeting plans are devised, it appears that attacking the Soviet command system is tantamount to destroying its society or putting into place a leadership that is even more unlikely to sue for peace on U.S. terms than the peacetime leadership.

There is more to be said about countercommand attacks, but for the moment we are considering the issue only because parts of the U.S. force structure are justified with reference to this mission. The countercommand mission, like the prompt counterforce mission, may have more to do with strategism, rooted in servicism, than it has with strategy. And the MX are suggestive in this regard. The Carter administration wanted to deploy 200 MX in a "racetrack" configuration known as MPS (for multiple protective shelters), in which mobility and deception would ensure survivability. The Reagan administration rejected the Carter plan and proposed, following the Scowcroft Commission report in April 1983, deployment of 100 MX (now called Peacekeepers) in Minuteman silos. The U.S. Congress rejected this and agreed to only 50 silo-deployed MX, and the U.S. Air Force has recommended that the second 50 be deployed in a rail-garrison mode, meaning on train cars from which they could be launched after being moved from one location to another.

Thus the Carter administration favored survivability, and the Reagan program the availability of prompt counterforce for matching Soviet counterforce capabilities. Moreover, the Reagan administration proposed a modernization program for the ICBM force, which would emphasize the mobile Midgetman missile and limit MX deployments to 100. Then, in something of a self-contradiction, the administration proposed, during arms-control negotiations with the Soviets in 1986, that mobile missiles be banned in future deployments by both sides. Meanwhile, the Reagan administration had agreed with its NATO European allies to deploy the Pershing II missile in West Germany, which had capabilities considered equivalent to strategic by the Soviet Union, since it purportedly threatened important command targets in their western military districts.[21] So, within a period of two administrations, the United States had emphasized ICBM survivability, which seemed to weaken the imperative for prompt as opposed to delayed counterforce, and then ICBM prompt counterforce capabilities, whether or not survivability could be expected to meet minimum standards of political and technical acceptability.

It turned out, ironically, that whereas in the 1960s U.S. defense officials proclaimed the obsolescence of the bomber force and the advent of the missile era, it was rediscovered in the 1980s that bombers have useful and unique properties. Missiles based in silos, the backbone of a survivable retaliatory force in the 1960s, had become liabilities that might invite attack by the 1980s. Proposals were made to "take the MX out to sea" by deploying numerous additional strategic missiles on submarines, although the United States would have to build many more submarines than it has now in order to add the MX force to the planned Trident force of the 1990s.

Meanwhile, as enthusiasm for the MX waned on account of the controversy about its basing mode, Trident II escaped comparable scrutiny from arms-control advocates. The comparatively smooth sailing for Trident II was due to the MX having acquired a lightning-rod status, and the old adage, "out at sea, out of mind" was applied to Trident II. The fact that Trident II missiles with D–5 warheads would pose a threat to the survival of Soviet ICBMs, if tasked for that mission, was pushed back into the recesses of the public debate, at least until the next decade. Military planners recognized that, as a matter of strategy, not all Trident II missiles deployed on a force of approximately 20 ballistic missile submarines in the 1990s would be tasked for prompt counterforce missions. Part of the role for strategic SSBN is to "lurk and murk" invisibly in the open oceans as a last strike force after other components of the arsenal have been launched or lost. Britain, too, has now committed itself to the Trident II, thus posing for the USSR a sea-based ballistic missile threat to military and other targets that is out of range of Soviet preemptive attack.

Here again, sand-table models of the strategic balance suggest that the United States and the Soviet Union should both do away with their land-based missiles and base their strategic weapons at sea, where they are assuredly survivable and less provocative. The strategic world, however, is more than the arms controllers' world, even if the Soviet arms controllers were to see the world in the same way that U.S. arms controllers did. Sea-based strategic counterforce might be perceived by the USSR to be more menacing to stability than land-based strategic counterforce. The first reason for this possible Soviet perception is that they have invested most of their strategic offensive rubles in land-based systems, which carry about three-fourths of their preattack warheads and most of their megatonnage. Soviet investments in modern submarine and bomber forces have lagged behind U.S. commitments to the same forces for most of the nuclear age, although Soviet bomber modernization is now apparent and they lead the United States in raw numbers of ballistic missile submarines. (They trail in warheads based at sea, however.)

Soviet objections to sea-based strategic counterforce are more than self-serving. From their perspective, weapons systems that they can control reliably are more dependable than those over which control is attenuated. And submarines, once they are on patrol, present a situation of attenuated control that might make Soviet planners very reluctant to base most of their survivable warheads there. Geography favors U.S. emphasis on sea-based forces and Soviet preference for missiles dispersed throughout its large land mass. U.S. cynics have argued that the bulk of the Soviet force is on ICBMs because the USSR has no intention of riding out any attack; ICBMs are the primary first-strike counterforce weapons. This may not be true in the future, however, when both sides have deployed advanced and stealthy cruise missiles along with ballistic missile defenses. Then the surprise attack may come slowly, from the sea or air, instead of from ground-based missiles that are launched through space and return into the atmosphere. A surprise is a surprise, since the issue is whether the defender detects the surprise in time to do anything about it, and not primarily how fast the event happens. Disposing of this cynical assessment of Soviet reluctance to make greater commitments to sea-based forces leads to a more plausible assessment, rooted in the Soviet leadership and its character.

As the United States has learned, strategic or other submarines cannot be kept on the same short leash that other weapons platforms can be. Their safety from preemptive destruction lies in either of two strategies. The U.S. strategy is to hide them in the open oceans. The Soviet strategy is to protect them in bastions close to Soviet shores by using land-based naval aircraft, surface ships, and attack submarines. So, clustered within the protective womb of home waters, Soviet SSBN will be very difficult to destroy before they can receive orders to launch their missiles, and their modern SLBMs can reach continental U.S. targets from these home waters.[22] Expert assessment is that the oceans will remain sufficiently opaque to anti-SSBN ASW so that U.S. submarines will not be vulnerable to catastrophic surprise attack, either. Simple arithmetic shows that either superpower, with even a fraction of its modern submarines surviving any surprise attack, could inflict unprecedented retaliatory destruction on its opponent, probably sufficient to deter all but those who were beyond deterrence.[23] U.S. maritime strategy for conventional war has been criticized, in fact, because of its potential for leading into nuclear exchanges as Soviet SSBN are sunk by NATO attack submarines pursuing an aggressive forward strategy.[24] Although this risk cannot be ruled out, assuming these U.S. maritime operations take place after the outbreak of war in Europe, the small number of SSBN that either superpower would need to guarantee assured destruction of the opponent's largest cities might restrain any hair-trigger responses. In fact, this might be the largest drawback of U.S. and Soviet BMD deployments—that they would call into question the obvious societal devastation that can be inflicted by either side with only half its surviving SSBN force on patrol. Reduced confidence in the submarine-based retaliatory strikes might lead to increased worry about the consequences of preemption by the opponent against other forces. One of the reasons that the United States at the present time does not fear overmuch the loss of its ICBM force to a Soviet first strike is that even the most successful such Soviet campaign would leave the USSR open to retaliation that its leaders could not conceivably justify to their population (witness Chernobyl).

The command and control problems with regard to ballistic missile submarines are certainly more complex than they are for the land-based missile force, but not unexpectedly so, given the difference between land- and sea-based missions. And the bomber force command and control issues are the most complicated of all.[25] Nuclear weapons based on submarines do not have electronic locks, and some experts have proposed putting them there, although the U.S. Navy is strongly opposed. The Navy reasons, with some justification, that the best guarantee for the security of nuclear weapons lies in the screening and training of personnel, and not in the mechanics of codes and ciphers. This argument often results in two sides talking past one another, because one side is worried about accidental or unauthorized launch in peacetime, whereas the Navy is more concerned with its effectiveness in carrying out assigned wartime missions. Missiles with armed warheads cannot be launched from U.S. submarines without authorization from the National Command Authority or their successors in wartime, in the form of an Emergency Action Message that would reach the submarine by one of several pathways. If no message were received and the submarine felt it was under attack, it could defend itself without firing ballistic missiles at land-based targets. Were it apparent that war had begun and no clear instructions had been received, despite repeated attempts to clarily its mission, then under certain very restrictive conditions, the missiles could be launched. Apparently some eight officers aboard an American SSBN, including the captain and launch control officer, would have to perform certain functions within a prescribed time interval in order to retaliate without explicit instructions from NCA.[26] The probability of unauthorized launch under these conditions seems remote, compared to the probability of being attacked while seeking clarification of orders (by moving toward the surface to receive additional communications).

And on the Soviet side, it is doubtful that the Politburo worries overmuch about defecting submarine commanders, however entertaining novels based on this premise might be. The concerns would be more technical—as to whether the roving submarines would get precise orders, or get them garbled and so foul up the details of a complicated war plan that might have to be altered from its original script. The Soviets have been through this before, during June and July 1941, when German attacks forced them to regroup and rethink their operational and strategic priorities for the defense of the USSR. Hitler's legions made mincemeat of Soviet first-echelon defenses, and stunned Red Army commanders reeled back in confusion, without dependable communications and immediately available reserves.[27] Its navy might not win the next war for the USSR, but it could contribute to losing it by an adventurist strategy (from the Soviet standpoint) of attacking U.S. carrier battle groups and convoys in the mid-Atlantic, instead of forming a protective cordon around its strategic submarine force. So control over maritime forces, and especially over those with strategic ballistic missiles, would certainly be a priority in the Kremlin. It is not inconceivable that the Soviet SSBNs have two chains of command for authorizing launch of their nuclear-armed missiles, one running through the regular military chain of command and the other through the KGB.[28]

By the 1990s, U.S. and Soviet triads may become quadrads or pentads, with the deployment of strategic cruise missiles on aircraft and maritime forces (surface ships and submarines). Cruise missiles with their characteristics of high accuracy, comparatively slow speed, and (ultimately) low visibility to radar are candidates for a status that is *sui generis*. Their high survivability and versatility make them very attractive as second-strike weapons, and their comparatively slow speeds less obviously useful as first-strike weapons. Evolution away from ballistic and toward cruise-missile development could, however, lead to deployment of enhanced cruise missiles that are brilliant as opposed to smart, and therefore extremely accurate and devious with regard to avoidance of detection. If so, they will acquire a two-sided technical cast as candidate weapons for preemption and retaliation, with no obvious distinction between the two missions in some basing modes. This will further confound the neat distinction between offense and defense, and further encourage servicism, for each of the U.S. and Soviet services will undoubtedly want its own cruise missiles under its (bureaucratic) territorial control.

NOTES

1. On the distinction between U.S. strategic nuclear declaratory and employment policies, as it applies to doctrine, see Aaron L. Friedberg, "The Evolution of U.S. Strategic 'Doctrine'—1945–1981," in *The Strategic Imperative: New Policies for National Security*, ed. Samuel P. Huntington (Cambridge, MA: Ballinger, 1983), pp. 53–99.

2. Alain C. Enthoven and K. Wayne Smith, *How Much Is Enough? Shaping the Defense Program 1961–69* (New York: Harper & Row, 1971), p. 179.

3. Enthoven and Smith, *How Much Is Enough?*, pp. 207–8.

4. As quoted in Lawrence Freedman, *The Evolution of Nuclear Strategy* (New York: St. Martin's Press, 1981), p. 235.

5. See Henry S. Rowen, "The Evolution of Strategic Nuclear Doctrine," in *Strategic Thought in the Nuclear Age*, ed. Laurence Martin (Baltimore, MD: Johns Hopkins University Press, 1981), pp. 131–56. This is an extremely important assessment of the McNamara strategy, and the discussion of McNamara's interest in nuclear flexibility offers some counterarguments to conventional wisdom about his strategy (pp. 148–49).

6. Colin S. Gray, *Nuclear Strategy and National Style* (Lanham, MD: Hamilton Press, 1986), pp. 169–200, offers insightful comments on the weaknesses of U.S. concepts of escalation control.

7. Desmond Ball, "Counterforce Targeting: How New? How Viable?" *Arms Control Today* 11, No. 2 (February 1981), reprinted with revisions in *American Defense Policy*, ed. John R. Reichart and Steven R. Sturm (Baltimore, MD: Johns Hopkins University Press, 1982), pp. 227–34.

8. On the size and capabilities of U.S. strategic nuclear forces relative to those of the USSR, see John M. Collins with Patrick Cronin, *U.S.-Soviet Military Balance: 1980–85* (New York: Pergamon Brassey's, 1985), pp. 53–65.

9. On "servicism," see Samuel P. Huntington, "Organization and Strategy," in *Reorganizing America's Defense*, ed. Robert J. Art, Vincent Davis, and Huntington (New York: Pergamon Brassey's, 1985), pp. 230–54.

10. Positive control launch for the U.S. strategic bomber force is discussed in Ashton B. Carter, "Assessing Command System Vulnerability," in *Managing Nuclear Operations*, ed. Carter, Steinbruner, and Zraket (Washington, DC: Brookings Institution, 1987), Ch. 17, pp. 582–89.

11. See Bruce G. Blair, "Alerting in Crisis and Conventional War," in *Managing Nuclear Operations*, ed. Carter, Steinbruner, and Zraket Ch. 3, pp. 75–120.

12. U.S. Department of Defense, *Soviet Military Power: 1987* (Washington, DC: U.S. GPO, March 1987), pp. 30–31, discusses the SS–25 and SS–24 (SS–X–24 to designate that it was not yet deployed at the time of publication).

13. John Steinbruner, "Launch under Attack," *Scientific American* (January 1984): 37–47.

14. President's Commission on U.S. Strategic Forces (Scowcroft Commission), *Report* (Washington, DC,: April 1983), p. 7.

15. See Stephen J. Cimbala, "What Price Survivability? Progress vs. Perfection," *Armed Forces and Society* 13, No. 1 (Fall 1986): 107–24.

16. Pessimistic assessments of U.S. vulnerability were provided by Paul H. Nitze, "Assuring Strategic Stability in an Era of Detente," *Foreign Affairs* 54 (1976): 207–33. Soviet problems in countersilo targeting are discussed in Barry R. Schneider, "Soviet Uncertainties in Targeting Peacekeeper," in *Missiles for the Nineties*, ed. Schneider, Colin S. Gray, and Keith B. Payne (Boulder, CO: Westview Press, 1984), pp. 109–34.

17. William C. Martel and Paul L. Savage, *Strategic Nuclear War: What the Superpowers Target and Why* (Westport, CT: Greenwood Press, 1986), esp. pp. 83–110; Martel, "Exchange Calculus of Strategic Nuclear War," in *Strategic War Termination*, ed. Stephen J. Cimbala (New York: Praeger, 1986), pp. 3–30.

18. On the prospects for decapitation attacks, see Paul Bracken, *The Command and Control of Nuclear Forces* (New Haven, CT: Yale University Press, 1983), pp. 232–37. See also John D. Steinbruner, "Nuclear Decapitation," *Foreign Policy* 45 (Winter 1981–82): 16–28.

19. An argument that Soviet civil defense programs might make a difference in intrawar deterrence and postattack superiority appears in T. K. Jones and W. Scott Thompson, "Central War and Civil Defense," *Orbis* 22, No. 3 (Fall 1978): 681–713.

20. See George H. Quester and David T. Cattell, "Ethnic Targeting: Some Bad Ideas," in *Strategic Nuclear Targeting*, ed. Desmond Ball and Jeffrey Richelson (Ithaca, NY: Cornell University Press, 1986), pp. 267–84.

21. Benjamin S. Lambeth, "What Deters? An Assessment of the Soviet View," in *American Defense Policy*, ed. John F. Reichart and Steven R. Sturm (Baltimore, MD: Johns Hopkins University Press, 1982), pp. 188–98, is especially helpful.

22. On Soviet SSBNs and U.S. antisubmarine warfare, see Donald C. Daniel, *Anti-Submarine Warfare and Superpower Strategic Stability* (Urbana: University of Illinois Press, 1986), esp. pp. 145–60.

23. If each superpower retained an assured destruction capability of 200 megaton equivalents (MTE) following a surprise attack in 1985, the United States would have needed an average of 8 submarines (within a range of 7 to 9) and the USSR 12 (within a range of 8 to 18). See Daniel, *Anti-Submarine Warfare and Superpower Strategic Stability*, pp. 8–9.

24. Barry R. Posen, "Inadvertent Nuclear War: Escalation and NATO's Northern Flank," in *Strategy and Nuclear Deterrence*, ed. Steven E. Miller (Princeton, NJ: Princeton University Press, 1984), pp. 85–112.

25. See the chapter by Ashton B. Carter on commands-system vulnerabilities, cited in Note 10.

26. American SSBN procedures for launch are for obvious reasons described less than completely in the open literature. The more important issue is the rules of engagement under which these and other nuclear armed submarines are operating during crises. See Demond Ball, "Nuclear War at Sea," *International Security* 10, No. 3 (Winter 1985/86): 3–31.

27. See Bryan I. Fugate, *Operation Barbarossa: Strategy and Tactics on the Eastern Front, 1941* (Novato, CA: Presidio Press, 1984).

28. Stephen M. Meyer, "Soviet Perspectives on the Paths to Nuclear War," in *Hawks, Doves and Owls: An Agenda for Avoiding Nuclear War*, ed. Graham T. Allison, Albert Carnesale and Joseph S. Nye, Jr. (New York: Norton, 1985), pp. 167–205, notes that the Soviet military was not assigned custody of nuclear weapons until 1954. There are separate command and control links between the political leadership in Moscow and Soviet nuclear forces, one for the military and the other for the KGB (p. 188).

8

EXPECTED AND
UNEXPECTED WARS

The rationality of U.S. and NATO nuclear strategy, in terms of the quality of means and ends and the relationship between them, has been considered from various perspectives. One additional perspective remains, and that is the question about the kind of war that can be expected, should deterrence fail. This question must be faced, however uncomfortable it may be, because deterrence can fail in unexpected ways. Once that has happened, war can take surprising forms.

There is an old chestnut to the effect that soldiers always prepare to fight the last war, and that politicians always expect the last war, plus one. Most often, however, no one knows what war to expect, or how to define clearly the concept of victory or defeat, until the clash of arms has settled the issue of what is possible. What is possible depends upon what the home front will tolerate and how competent are the various armies in contention. Prewar expectations often clash with the actual turn of events. The U.S. Civil War, for example, is often written of as the first modern war, a nineteenth-century war that prefigured the shape of war in the current century. This was in part because that war saw the first truly effective use of certain technology, like the telegraph and repeating rifles, but it was not exclusively the reason. The biggest surprise that happened in the Civil War was that the better army did not win, because the war was not short. And in a protracted war, as opposed to a short war, industrial power and economic sustainability proved to be decisive. Superior generalship did not provide victory for the South; it simply postponed a defeat that was made inevitable (it now appears after the fact) by the superior resources of the North. And in World War I, sustainability and attrition became more decisive than prewar expectations of superior strategy, rapidly applied. As attrition became more important to the outcome, the advantage for the defense became more obvious: Frontal attacks on heavily defended positions were unproductive, and no-man's land became a euphemism for graveyards of frustrated attackers on the Western Front.

In similar fashion, the early battles in the American colonies' War of Independence against Great Britain favored the ultimate losers of that war, not the winners. The quality of U.S. army regulars improved as the war went on, but George Washington complained consistently about the militia (probably overmuch). Nevertheless, the British could not win the war quickly and decisively with the forces they were prepared to invest in it, and, in an extended war, they could not hold out in the face of the colonists' determination and opposition to British policy at home.

Further to the issue of winning the early war but losing it ultimately, Hitler's invasion of the Soviet Union in 1941 resulted in an early string of very impressive victories. These early victories, however, could not be turned into a rout of the entire Soviet army, nor into the collapse or surrender of its government. Hitler followed the example of Napoleon to the letter, even launching his invasion on the same day of the month, June 22 of 1941, 129 years after the French emperor crossed the Nieman river into Russia. And in both cases, general staffs and other advisors who dutifully followed their leaders had premonitions of disaster awaiting those who would attempt the conquest of so vast a nation. In deciding upon the fateful invasion of Russia, Napoleon convinced himself and then sought to convince others that Czar Alexander was both hostile and afraid of France. His advisor and ambassador to Russia, Caulaincourt, attempted to instruct him otherwise:

No, Sire, because while recognizing your military talent, he has often pointed out to me that his country was large; that though your genius would give you many advantages over his generals, even if no occasion arose to fight you in advantageous circumstances, there was plenty of margin for ceding you territory, and that to separate you from France and from your resources would be, in itself, a means of successfully fighting you.

Caulaincourt goes on to quote the czar to the effect that "it will not be a one-day war," and these words proved prophetic.

More was at issue in this conversation, of course, than the length of any war between Russia and Napoleonic France, for the length of the war would determine the kind of war that it was, and what it was being fought for. The fates were doubly unkind to Napoleon. Like Macbeth, he was led into overly ambitious and ultimately self-destructive objectives, and like Macbeth, he used others only as echo chambers for his own ambitions, discounting those parts of their predictions that did not fit into his visionary future.

Even worse for Napoleon, his armies were not defeated in battle in the traditional way, but worn out in a debilitating retreat from Moscow to the crossing of the Berezina. The *grande armée* that could not be defeated in great battles could be disintegrated by the cumulative effects of wear and tear on its internal combustion, so that Napoleon's soldiers were reduced to cannibalism on their way out of Russia. Hitler, too, destroyed the world's most powerful war machine to date, the *Wehrmacht*, in expecting to bring about the rapid collapse of the Soviet Union, as Napoleon had expected the czar to surrender once Moscow was occupied. Hitler's generals shared the delusion of Bonaparte, or at least some of them did, that once Moscow was in enemy hands, resistance in the USSR would cease.[2]

Hitler and Napoleon also made another error of judgment, related to their expectation that war would be short instead of long. Neither sought to mobilize the disaffected Russian population against its autocratic rulers. Whether either could have succeeded in doing so is debatable, but the fact that neither seriously tried is remarkable, and both Nazi German and Napoleonic French armies suffered significantly for it. So did the U.S. government in conducting its counterinsurgency campaign on behalf of South Vietnam from 1961 to 1965. The U.S. strategy was to reinforce the government of South Vietnam, but the popular disaffection against that government was never turned around. As a result, the Viet Cong and North Vietnamese forces were able to exploit a social and political environment hostile to the United States, which soon found itself not the protector of South Vietnam but the destroyer of its society, while its opponents posed as defenders of the people and ultimately received more popular support.

Thus, protracted conventional wars have some similarities to revolutionary wars and civil wars (and to revolutionary civil wars, which wars sometimes are). The skills of the combatants matter less than the will and determination of the population at large, which in turn depends on motivations, perceptions, and allegiances that defy easy quantification. After Napoleon invaded Russia, his failure was assured when the czar took the offensive in what we would now call the "propaganda battle" and convinced his followers that Napoleon's armies represented the embodiment of evil, a force against religion as well as state. It took time for this effect to make a difference, but time was what the czar had and Napoleon did not.

Protracted war changes the equation of generalship, of military expertise and campaign analysis, relative to the tenacity of the hold a regime has on its population, and on its ability to draw upon its resource base even after it appears to be exhausted. The Russians were technically defeated when Napoleon occupied Moscow, but they refused to know it. Commanding General Kutuzov was overly cautious, and probably missed a chance to destroy the *grande armée* as it retreated from Moscow. Indeed, Kutuzov has come to be synonymous with dilatory for Western readers of the Soviet military experience. Although the Russians were not defeated by Napoleon, it is not on account of their superior military art. The Russians did not plan in advance to withdraw and to surrender Moscow; this strategy was forced upon them by their initial failures. It can be said, however, that Kutuzov understood the societal conditions in which the war was being fought better than Napoleon did, since the latter clearly failed to anticipate either the sociopolitical or the meteorological climate (partisan warfare or the Russian winter) in which the war was being fought.

Napoleon and Hitler might be considered extreme examples of personality disorders superimposed on authoritarian political systems, with disaster inevitably waiting around the corner. Consider, then, another set of expectations about short as opposed to long war, which then colored the judgment of the character of war as well. World War I illustrates, as no other, that long wars, at least long wars fought in the twentieth century among major powers, are different in character, as well as in length, from short wars.

Few if any of the members of the Triple Alliance or the Triple Entente went into World War I expecting a protracted war, lasting four years and ultimately collapsing the German, Russian, and Austro-Hungarian empires. This was nothing less than a remaking of the political map of Europe, and more than that, if the consequences of the October Revolution are added. The question of what the major powers were fighting for was very different, once it became clear that the war could not be ended quickly. In one of the most remarkable episodes in modern history, both democratic and autocratic societies kept fighting a stalemated war for several years without recognizing that the stakes of that conflict had changed fundamentally in the process. Woodrow Wilson's hyperbole that the world should be made "safe for democracy" was misplaced historical summation, for the democracies were as much to blame for the stupidity of the carnage as were the autocracies. Not only were there no good reasons for starting the war, there were even fewer for continuing it.

As the war continued, its character changed, from a contest of armed forces to a contest of social wills. How ironical it was that this enduring bloodletting would follow from mobilization plans on all sides, which helped to precipitate war. Prewar mobilization planning in Russia and Germany, the two keys to what we now call stable deterrence, was based on the assumption that a delay of several days to a week could bring about defeat.[3] Actual events could not have differed more from prewar expectations than tragedy differs from comedy. Germany finally resorted to unrestricted submarine warfare in an attempt to disrupt the British economy and to force its frustrated people, and therefore its government, to sue for peace. The British returned the favor with their blockade. These tactics by both sides testified to their recognition, after several years of armed conflict, that the war of barbed wire and trenches on the Western Front could not be won.

Prior to their attack on Pearl Harbor, Japanese leaders who were following a strategic rationality should have asked how that attack would be followed up, and how they could prevail in an extended war against the United States. They did not, and their political system, like that of the imperial participants in World War I, was the cost. The Japanese might have intended their attack to surprise and to stun U.S. policy makers, who would then, according to Japanese reasoning, accommodate Japanese imperial ambitions in the Pacific. Such a war of limited aims was not in the cards, however, from the U.S. perspective, and in retrospect it is not easy to see how the Japanese could have mistaken U.S. resolve, if they in fact did mistake it.[4]

FEROCITY AND INTENSITY

Not only do the stakes of the game change in a protracted war, compared to a short one. The conduct of the war itself is shaped by the duration of the conflict. Wars that go on for years require that the home front be mobilized, and some of the methods used to mobilize mass popular support are less than charitable to the image of the opponent. Germans are depicted as "Huns" in the First World War or "Krauts" in the Second; U.S images of the Japanese culture, and theirs of the United States, were so extremely stereotyped prior to World War II that bigotry was substituted where information was lacking. As wars are extended, this problem becomes more acute, leading to diabolical images of the enemy, or even suspicion between allies in the same coalition.

The on-again off-again relations between Hitler and Stalin prior to 1939, culminating in the Molotov–Ribbentrop agreement, required that popular images of enemies and friends change to match the sudden reversals in alignment sought by leaders.[5] Having endured a dubious cohabitation for two years, the Germans and Soviets parted company following Hitler's invasion of the Soviet Union, but popular images lagged. The feelings of the decades preceding 1939 had to be brought back into popular consciousness by Nazi and Soviet propagandists. Nor were they alone. U.S. Communists, who from 1939 to 1941 had refused to entertain any serious criticisms of Hitler's motives, decided after June 1941 that he was the devil incarnate, against whom any expedient alliance would suffice.

Once at war, Nazi and Soviet combatants fought with an intensity that may not be equaled again in conventional war. The more atrocities committed on either side, the greater the determination of the opponent to match them in kind. This is not to deny that both sides' regular armed forces fought bravely, and often according to traditional international conventions of war. For the most part they did so, but the departures from comity were frequent and significant. There was no quarter given and none asked, especially among the German *Einsatzgruppen* who accompanied the regular German divisions and whose job it was to massacre Soviet civilians, nor by the Soviet partisans as they harried retreating German forces in 1944 and 1945.

Civil wars that are protracted may involve special brutality. Nationals are fighting nationals, and extended family kin frequently have divided political loyalties. Thus the Korean war, which at one level was a war between the United States and the Soviet Union (with U.N. legal cover in the U.S. case, and Chinese surrogates in the Soviet), at another level was a bitter civil war among Koreans. And it was fought bitterly by ROK and North Korean troops, each fighting to preserve its home territory against an invader from the south or north. Even apart from the disagreements between the two Koreas, entry of the People's Republic of China into the war ensured that it would be protracted and probably stalemated, unless the United States was willing to wage a declared war on China. This the United States was not willing to do, for the very reason that it was not in Korea to fight China, but to defend South Korean independence and territory. The war dragged on years after the fighting had stabilized around the line of the 38th parallel, near the status quo ante, and the casualties of this skirmishing, after the essential political issues were clearly decided, were heavy.

As extended wars become more ferocious and exacting of blood and treasure, the costs become harder to justify, especially where mass publics have some say in the direction of their government. Even if they do not, however, if conditions are bad enough and there seems little hope of relief, they can bring the government to a halt. This is what happened in Russia in 1917. The czarist system was a hollow polity with little basis of broad popular support; allegiance to the czar was more a personal than a systemic commitment. When the system began to fall apart under the stress of war, the czar abdicated, and without the czar the system had no roots, only terror and habituation, which in the end proved to be insufficient. Conversely, Lenin and his followers may not have followed the theoretical Marxist script to its literal end, but they did understand that power is based on the ability to get things done. And so they withdrew from the war that had devastated Russian society, albeit at an extremely high price at Brest-Litovsk. The protracted struggle of World War I, and in particular the humiliation inflicted on Russian armies by the Germans, had turned the Russian people against their system as a symbol of incompetency. Once focused on governmental performance, the spotlight could not be darkened, and both Kerensky and Lenin in turn were illuminated by its glare. The one proved insufficient, the other more than sufficient, to persevere through adversity.

That is what protracted wars fundamentally are, adversity, burned into national consciousness forever as great triumphs if they are won, or humiliating defeats if lost. That is why the French and Germans fought three wars in 1870, 1914, and 1941—or, from a long-range standpoint, they fought one war with two pauses. After 1870 the defeated French vowed to remember Alsace and Lorraine, and after 1918, Hitler remembered where Germany had been forced to sign the armistice and repeated the gesture in 1940. After World War II, Germany was divided into two states and, if the Soviet Union has its way, will remain in that condition for at least the rest of this century. One has to go no farther than a single cemetery outside Leningrad to understand and appreciate why the Soviet Union will never again be caught unprepared for war, if it can help it. One might comment, à propos these illustrations, that the war in 1870 does not fit, because the Prussians won it quickly and decisively; but the Franco-Prussian war of 1870 was only the frosting on the cake, the culmination of the maturation process by which Bismarck's Prussia became the German empire that took itself into World War I. Bismarck's politicomilitary strategy assured that Prussia could gradually build up to this denouement, by first striking against Denmark, and then against Austria, the latter four years before the final curtain against France. In each case Bismarck used skillful diplomacy to isolate his intended victims from outside assistance, and so prevented himself from getting into a multifront, protracted war.[6]

This ability to isolate an intended victim from outside help, before pouncing on his armed forces and defeating them, often separates those who win wars quickly from those who are stuck in protracted and losing struggles. Hitler failed to reckon with the problem of leaving England undefeated, and nonetheless launched his attack on Russia. The U.S. bombing of North Vietnam, beginning in 1964 (Operation Rolling Thunder), was supposed to coerce Hanoi's leadership into desisting in their support for the war in South Vietnam, but bombing losses were replaced by North Vietnamese improvisation and aid from Communist allies whose territories were sanctuaries. After the Japanese attack on Pearl Harbor, Hitler gratuitously declared war on the United States, thus ensuring a coalition of overwhelming preponderance against him. The Japanese in World War II attacked the United States in the Pacific, counting on Hitler's forces to prevent the USSR from encroaching on Japanese imperial conquests at a later time. In the American Revolution, the British did not count on French assistance for the rebels.

Perhaps the most classic illustration of a "perfect" war plan for a quick victory that failed to work is the Schlieffen Plan adopted by the German general staff in 1914. Actually, the plan was in the works for many years previously, and had it been executed literally, it might just have worked as designed. This issue has provided fuel for a great many academic disputations. What is less frequently argued about, but more crucial, is what the Germans would have done then. Having subdued the French, were they in a position to attack England, or coerce a British surrender? It seems unlikely, and if they had been able to do either, what would they have done about the United States? Now, looking eastward, suppose the Germans had subdued the British and obtained from London a favorable peace settlement, ceding everything between Berlin and the English Channel to the kaiser. What about the Russians? Could the Russians have withdrawn from the war, under any leadership, with Germany astride all of Western Europe? Again, it seems unlikely, and the chaos in St. Petersburg might quickly have subsided if victorious Germans in the West were seen mopping up in the expectation of moving east (as they indeed did in World War II). Czar or Lenin, tiredness of the war was in some proportion to the ability to drop out of it unilaterally, and this Lenin could do only because his former allies in the West were holding the ring and taking the beating on their territories instead of his.

Where the Schlieffen Plan was defective, then, was not in the tactical or operational sense of how many divisions should be allotted to Von Kluck's sweeping right wing, or whether several of them should have been withdrawn by the younger Von Moltke to send east at the most inopportune time. The larger mistake made in the Schlieffen Plan was the assumption that France could be defeated and then, *without* England being eliminated, the Germans could turn around and defeat the Russians, and *then* return (with the Russians forever quiescent) to defeat England again. (And what of the United States in this calculation?) In other words, the Schlieffen Plan might have been very sensible, or at least operationally thorough as a theater campaign plan, but that is not the equivalent of a strategic war plan—that is, a plan for victory by which the winner is better off than before war started. The longer war is continued, the harder it is to make a case that victory at acceptable cost is possible, so the costs rise as the commitment deepens. Eventually the costs become so unbearable, relative to the dividends, that public opinion demands an exit (as in Vietnam, or in Indochina in 1954), but even then, it must be "peace with honor," not an abject surrender. If the war is continued past the point at which sacrifices can be related to any sensible political objective, as in World War I, then the fighting and its costs become the issues, and the original political issues for which the war was fought, if they are remembered at all, suffer meltdown. Thus, in the U.S. Civil War, the issue became secession itself, preserving the Union, and in Lenin's withdrawal of the Soviet Union from World War I, the issue was survival of the new Soviet state, at whatever temporary price. Few states fight, as Nazi Germany did, until their entire country is demolished and their political system overthrown, although some fight very close to that threshold.

POSTNUCLEAR WAR

The most surprising thing about World War III might be that it, like World War I, is not short. So now, as they did prior to World War I, the major powers, in this case the nuclear-armed states, have made plans for a knockout blow appropriate for a short war. This is true of U.S. and Soviet war planning, although Soviet rhetoric sounds more reluctant to acknowledge it, as well as the war planning of Britain and France.[7] The Soviet case has some distinct features, so we will emphasize Western expectations first, noting Soviet characteristics when appropriate.

The nuclear arsenals of the two superpowers are basically designed to attack large and categorical target sets, and in a relatively short time. In the case of the U.S.' strategic command, control, and communications (C3) system, its flexibility has been improved significantly since the 1974 "Schlesinger doctrine" was promulgated.[8] These refinements, however, are further to the prosecution of a short war, not a long one, because deficiencies in the command system would preclude conduct of a protracted nuclear war, according to the authoritative study by Bruce G. Blair for the Brookings Institution.[9] In truth, no one really expects the U.S. strategic command system to "endure," nor is this particularly disquieting, from the standpoint of how a protracted war is envisioned by most observers. The idea that the United States and the Soviet Union could throw even half of their total strategic and theater nuclear arsenals at each other, without destroying their societies in the process, is self-evidently silly. This, however, is not the shape that an extended or protracted war is likely to take, if it occurs.

Instead of a large emptying of their nuclear arsenals in blind fury, within twenty minutes to half an hour, Soviet and U.S. leaders might take tactical nuclear strikes, in or outside Europe, and withhold the remainder of their nuclear arsenals while conventional war began. Warsaw Pact conventional forces would press forward in the northwestern, western, and southwestern TVDs (theaters of military action), prodding NATO from the tip of Norway to the Mediterranean, and in the Pacific, coercing Japan and South Korea. The conventional war in Europe might be punctuated by small nuclear strikes on NATO defenders at battalion or division level, but more destructive attacks could be withheld, in order to preserve the economic assets of Western Europe for future Soviet use. Similarly, selective attacks, mostly conventional, but some with tactical nuclear weapons, could begin at sea. Naval warfare in the Mediterranean or Norwegian Sea would involve U.S., other NATO, and Soviet forces equipped with conventional and nuclear weapons, and some of both might be exploded against targets of opportunity.

Such a conflict would confound the prewar expectations of strategists and policy makers alike. It would be a far cry from the computerized simulations of choreographed nuclear ballet, in which one side launches a large first strike against the entire force structure of its opponent, the second side retaliates against the remaining forces and cities of the first, and the first side then mops up the remaining societal assets of the second. These standard scenarios appeal to those who are fatalistic about any war involving U.S. or Soviet nuclear weapons used against one another, on the assumption that fatalism about controlling war helps to deter it. Other standard scenarios, more typical of textbooks at staff and command colleges in the West, assume that battlefield "packages" can be exchanged, after which losses are totaled up and fighting stops. Real war might be messier, involving ugly exchanges of nuclear weapons against forces, cities, petroleum dumps, nuclear power plants, farms, factories, transportation nodes, and schools, in a pattern unrelated to rhyme or reason. Far worse than a war that ends in several hours with nuclear winter, in which temporary suffering is followed by blessed extinction, this war involves no eschatology, only months or years of misery, protracted destruction, deprivation, and mutilation.

The conventional forces of both sides would be more important to the outcome of such a conflict in its early stages, and the largest nuclear forces would be withheld as the ultimate weapon, to be used to deter any effort to overthrow either the Soviet or U.S. regime. Short of that, NATO and Pact armies, navies, and air forces will vie for space and territory in three dimensions, and nuclear weapons will be part of that contest, but not all of it. Chemical and biological weapons will be available, and perhaps used, if not against superpower homelands, then against their allies on either side who cannot retaliate. The coherence of command systems and their ability to extract resources and commitment from their peoples, over a period of many months if not years, may have more to do with who prevails in such a conflict than with who has more nuclear weapons left at the end.

To the extent that the superpowers and other nuclear-armed states are dependent upon nuclear weapons to destroy the cities of an opponent, they must withhold those assets as threats to coerce the opponent, instead of wasting them early in war. The largest counters would probably be withheld as potential strikes against central command systems and the most important cities, while smaller nuclear forces and conventional forces fought for supremacy, or to stalemate. One can imagine a scarred moonscape in Western Europe, pocked with the craters of conventional and tactical nuclear explosions, a European Vietnam, with limited chemical use as needed for attaining special military objectives, and possible small-scale uses of toxins, so as not to contaminate friendly forces along with hostile ones. A devastated Europe might be rebuilt, along Soviet Socialist or capitalist lines, depending on whose stalemated conventional and tactical nuclear forces give way first, or whose governments capitulate.

Although the Soviet Union is thought more sensitive to the problem of extended war than is the West, there would be no more rehearsal for this kind of war for them than for NATO. It would be unprecedented, a war of pain and nerve, more than a war over territorial conquest, with global conventional and nuclear skirmishes taking place simultaneously with fitful efforts to negotiate and fight for advantage. New technologies would contribute to the possibility of an extended instead of a short campaign, including limited ballistic missile defenses, proliferated cruise missiles, and dispersed command and control systems operating on partial "crash" under the direction of fragmented or no authorities. A regionalized war, one in which the outcomes in the Pacific might not mirror those in the Atlantic, is a very plausible expectation, and victory on one side of the prime meridian might occur simultaneously with defeat in another.

In such a coercive, fragmented, and extended war, the breaking of will and the endurance of societal pain would be as important as who had the larger box score of casualties inflicted or divisions put out of action. The home front might disintegrate, or parts of it rise in rebellion. The Soviet Union cannot forget that its Kronstadt sailors played an important part in toppling the czar, as did the soldiers who left the front and returned to the capital, joining forces with hungry and desperate workers. Europe full of vagabonds who no longer care where national boundaries begin and end, who seek to reunite dispersed families and to find displaced coworkers, amid chaos and rubble, with shattered work and life routines, would resemble the First World War extended another ten years. While Eastern and Western Europe resembled a desert, Soviet and North American territories might resemble pincushions, in which navies and air forces had struck partial blows against conventional and nuclear projection forces, while refraining from invasion or all-out nuclear attack.

NATO, with its plan for nuclear escalation, ultimately to the use of U.S. strategic nuclear forces, is poorly prepared for this kind of war, as is the Soviet Union, with its plan for rapid and decisive conventional victory in Europe. Neither would have anticipated a long-drawn-out and inconclusive bleeding of the social and military fabric, rending armies and navies into isolated islands of combat, beyond the total control of central commanders—like unsupervised vicious children loose in a playground, sinking ships, blowing up bridges and air bases, playing at destruction, maiming civilization, but stopping short of destroying it, because those ultimate weapons still remained under the control of increasingly desperate central authorities. The task would not be to win such a war, but to end it on some terms that were mutually acceptable, before tired and desperate National Command Authorities in Moscow or Washington decided to exhaust their arsenals, preferring the sleep of cremation to slow death of their societies.

This vision is horrifying but realistic, precisely because this extended nightmare deviates no more from current peacetime expectations than did the peacetime expectations of the czar, the kaiser, and the Western democracies prior to World War I. There a homogeneous set of European empires undid their own civilization, replacing it (from their standpoint) with pandemic democratic barbarism. So, too, the First World states of Eurasia could exhaust their war machines and societies, so that the new world below the equator emerged to supplant the old one, but only after much of the new world (in the Middle East, for example) had served as part of the global battleground for the First World. Indeed, it is quite likely that this global epidemic of conventional-*cum*-nuclear struggle between superpowers and their allies could have begun in the Persian Gulf, with an Iranian attack on a Soviet or U.S. vessel; from there to war in Europe, and from war in Europe to global but not unrestrained war, if unrestrained means holding back some nuclear weapons in reserve, but not otherwise limiting brutality.

To say that Western societies will be poorly prepared for such a conflict is to fault them very little, relative to what we can reasonably expect from them. It is the exceptional case that finds that peacetime preparedness for wartime sacrifices is not begrudged to policy makers by their electorates. This is true also for natural and manufactured disasters, from hurricanes to Bhopal, in which people who would not adjust their behavior under normal conditions will suddenly do so with alacrity. After Chernobyl it is not at all clear that the Soviets cope with unexpected disasters any more effectively, so it would not be farfetched to suppose that wars of global scope would present even more imposing problems. Of particular concern to this writer is the peacetime emphasis in the West on wars that are strictly conventional, or apocalyptically nuclear, to the near exclusion of ambiguous cases that are partially conventional and partially nuclear. Yet U.S. doctrine for war at sea and Soviet doctrine for conventional war in Europe make the prospect of a mixed conventional nuclear war as realistic as the prospect of conventional-only global wars.

NONNUCLEAR WAR

Little can be done to anticipate the scenario outlined above, since it has no precedent, but some military analysts have thought about the possibility of protracted war without nuclear weapons, including wars involving the United States and the Soviet Union. Suppose that war broke out in Europe, became stalemated, and the use of nuclear weapons was somehow avoided. What kinds of planning have been done by either side for such a conflict, and who would prevail? Granted, the continuation of any war in Europe for an appreciable length of time, say, beyond a week or two, without the use of nuclear weapons is a large assumption. The assumption might not be so grandiose if the United States and the Soviet Union were to follow through with their plans to withdraw significant numbers of nuclear weapons from Western Europe and the European USSR, especially the so-called Long Range Intermediate Nuclear Forces, such as the Soviet SS–20 and the NATO Pershing II and ground-launched cruise missiles. However, even after all long- and short-range INF were withdrawn from range of European targets by both sides, there would still be substantial nuclear weapons, in the NATO case roughly 4,300, delivered by aircraft, artillery, and missiles of battlefield range.[10]

NATO's dependency upon nuclear weapons deployed in Europe is the problem in keeping any war there conventional. It is a problem from the standpoint of those U.S. and European strategists who want to raise the nuclear threshold so that, if deterrence fails, Europe can be defended without NATO being required to initiate the early use of nuclear weapons. NATO might be reluctant to do this, given the likelihood that many of the weapons would be exploded over friendly territory against advancing Soviet troops. On the other hand, if the threat of early or any first use by NATO is removed from Soviet calculations, then deterrence as a whole might be weakened. A failure of deterrence that permitted a devastating conventional war in Europe below the nuclear threshold is less satisfying to Europeans than it is to the U.S. public. And Europeans fear that a conventional deterrent that does not include a nuclear umbrella will cause it to rain on them, creating another temptation for their allies across the Atlantic to take as much, or as little, of the war as possible.

Actually, the fear of a better conventional defense making war more likely, because of raising the nuclear threshold, may be misplaced. The Soviet estimate of probable success or failure may be more dependent upon how long they expect the war to be and on its presumed effects on their geopolitical position overall. Theorists who are fixated upon where to set the nuclear threshold in Europe may find that Soviet planners are more concerned about the temporal threshold, about how long the war goes on. After all, the USSR is as prepared for nuclear escalation in Europe as is NATO, if not more so. It is obviously not to NATO's advantage to escalate a conventional war into nuclear war, unless the balance of conventional and nuclear forces in Europe changes very much in NATO's favor.

In a long war without the use of nuclear weapons, the West would have several advantages, compared to the East. First, the overall size and strength of Western economics (including Japan in the Western anti-

Soviet coalition), compared to those of the Warsaw Pact, is considerably in favor of the West. A protracted war that goes on long enough for the two sides to mobilize effectively all their resources obviously spells trouble for the Kremlin. As Peter H. Vigor, a noted military historian and Soviet expert, points out, Soviet leaders steeped in Marxism will be especially sensitive to the importance of overall economic strength.[11] Notice that we have specified that superior and larger anti-Soviet economics will be important, if they can be mobilized effectively. The U.S. economy, for industrial mobilization, is not what it once was, and Rosie the Riveter is now Yancey the Yuppie. Overall, Western economics are more service oriented and less manufacturing centered than during the great mobilization of World War II.

Second, the maritime superiority of the United States and its allies, compared to the Soviet Union and its allies, will be important in any extended conventional war. U.S. maritime strength combined with allied NATO navies should be able to prevent Soviet closure of the "Atlantic bridge," which separates Europe from the United States, and so guarantee that reinforcements from the United States will arrive to replace losses in Europe. Here again, the caveat "if they can be mobilized" must be provided, for this would mean a large draft in the United States and a great disruption of social and economic life. It is not self-evident, at least not to Europeans, that the U.S. public in general will consider the need to defend Europe as obvious as strategists do. Assuming, however, that this obstacle has somehow been surmounted, and that cumulative allied merchant marines are adequate in numbers and can move in protected convoys, then sustainability for the NATO conventional war effort can be assured for many months. There is, nevertheless, some controversy about the current U.S. maritime strategy as to whether it emphasizes a risky effort to sink the Soviet navy in its backyard, as opposed to protecting the sea lanes of communication between the United States and Europe.[12] All contenders can agree, however, on the need to protect the SLOCs as a necessary condition, if not a sufficient one.

Third, the longer war in Europe is continued, the more Soviet leaders must worry about the prospect of Chinese intervention on the Soviets' eastern flank. The PRC would not be likely to declare war on the USSR unless the Soviets seemed to be collapsing within their own empire as well as in their war effort. More likely, and still problematic for the Soviet Union, would be Chinese nibbling at the edges of disputed borders, while the USSR was stalemated in the West. As relations are improved between China and Japan, the possibility of a Sino-Japanese collaboration against Soviet interests in North and South Asia will also present itself, once war breaks out. The PRC has already expressed its displeasure with the occupation of Afghanistan by Soviet forces and made their withdrawal an unconditional demand before Sino-Soviet relations can be improved.

Other political and military targets of opportunity would undoubtedly present themselves.

Fourth, a protracted war threatens to weaken Soviet control over its Warsaw Pact allies, some of which are already chafing at peacetime restrictions imposed by the USSR. Rumania refuses to partake of Warsaw Pact military exercises, Hungary experiments with a partially free market economy, and East Germany draws closer to West Germany in terms of economic and humanitarian policies, pursuant to the "Helsinki spirit." The outbreak of war in Europe, assuming the war had an ambiguous cause, could find significant defections from the Warsaw Pact taking place in Poland, for example, and the rise of presently dormant dissatisfaction in Czechoslovakia. In both cases the Soviet war plan would be heavily dependent not only on the close cooperation of forces in both states but also on the absence of any sabotage or nonviolent resistance against troop movements and logistical resupply.[13]

On the other hand, an extended conventional war does not obviously favor the West, if it fails to remain politically cohesive. If the war is not the result of a Soviet bolt from the blue across the North German plain, but instead results from crisis contretemps and confusion, then it may not be obvious who is more to blame for having started it. Either the West or the East could lunge across the inter-German border in the mistaken assumption that the other side had already started war, when it in fact had not.[14] The Soviet plan for war in Europe, meaning conventional war if possible, is thought to be heavily dependent upon surprise, in the classical sense that the defender is caught unprepared and so suffers devastating losses in the early rounds of the conflict.[15] There is a danger inherent in this expectation, however, for NATO as well as for the Soviet Union. For NATO, assuming that the Soviet war plan depends for its success on the use of surprise as a force multiplier allows for Western planners too much complacency, if surprise is missing. For the USSR, a war plan that depends for its success on surprise can go wrong, if the surprise is not effectively followed up, as Hitler discovered to his regret while fighting on Soviet territory.[16]

Thus, although U.S. military planners expect that a long war would be advantageous to the West and detrimental to the Soviets, this is a very scenario-dependent generalization, and the number of scenarios is limited only by the imagination. The problem begins when imagination turns to hope and hope displaces strategy.

The U.S. hope, understandably, is that if war breaks out in Europe, it can be confined there. The European hope, again quite understandably, is that war in Europe will of necessity involve the United States, immediately and unavoidably. This is what NATO is all about. It is not a classical alliance in which the various parties defend one another, but a security guarantee from the United States to Western Europe, which allows the Europeans, in turn, to carry on political pluralism within the shadow of Soviet power. It is this shadow that is cast over Europe in peacetime by Soviet military power, which goes hand in hand with the appeal of détente to European elites and publics. The peacetime protracted conflict that the USSR presents to Europe is its ability to manipulate the thermometer of coercion, when that is useful, and the barometer of détente, when that is preferred. This sometimes growling, sometimes embracing strategy cannot work unless Soviet control over Eastern Europe is secure, and that explains the presence of Soviet troops there more convincingly than any Soviet plan to attack Western Europe.

This last note might sound optimistic for NATO, and it is, if NATO can avoid falling apart from its own divided counsel, not only in peacetime, but on the threshold of war. One of the issues on which NATO divisions are sure to occur is that of nuclear weapons in Europe, especially if they are U.S. weapons. The presence of U.S. nuclear weapons is wanted in Europe to guarantee against any Soviet expectation of a successful conventional war plan. These weapons are not wanted, however, when they become periodic liabilities in European domestic politics. During those times, U.S. frustration expresses itself in journalistic and scholarly demands for a self-sufficient European NATO conventional defense, and there are some proposals for innovative approaches to conventional defense in Europe that involve rethinking of the U.S. contribution.[17] When these proposals build upon the coupling of U.S. strategic forces to European-based nuclear and conventional forces, then they remind Europeans of the costs of U.S. commitments, a potential nuclear war. When reform proposals do away with U.S.–European nuclear coupling, Europeans are frightened that they will do away with deterrence also.

For the West, the problem of protracted war preparedness is limited by the context explained in the preceding paragraph. It would not do to give the USSR any impression that war in Europe could be fought under a nuclear sanctuary, or that conventional deterrence might weaken. It would also be mistaken, however, to suggest to European members of NATO that a nuclear war could be fought in Europe, while preserving U.S. and Soviet homelands as sanctuaries. This sounds as if Europeans would prefer general nuclear war to conventional or limited nuclear war and, of course, that is absurd, as stated. The argument is about the ingredients of credible deterrence. Western preparedness for an extended conventional war would pay dividends, if the Soviets were willing to cooperate by engaging in reciprocal targeting restraint. If they were, however, it would be because they were winning or at least doing much better than NATO was, without using nuclear weapons. If the USSR were losing, there is every reason to believe that it would prefer to use nuclear weapons, although not necessarily strategic and long-range theater nuclear weapons, before yielding important military and political objectives. So it is hard to see how this protracted conventional war scenario between East and West is going to be written to the advantage of the West, unless the Soviets become more interested in extended stalemate for their conventional forces than their doctrine would indicate.

A Soviet plan for conventional war in Europe would be more credible, relative to their current situation, if nuclear weapons were withdrawn from the European continent outside of the Soviet Union. Thus, the interest of some Western politicians and analysts in a Europe free of nuclear weapons is surprising, in the absence of any offsetting improvement of Western conventional forces, or a Mutual and Balanced Force Reductions agreement, which creates true equivalence in forces within the guidelines area (East Germany, Czechoslovakia, and Poland on the eastern side, and West Germany, Belgium, the Netherlands, and Luxembourg on the western). One would like to assume that Mr. Gorbachev's interest in a drawdown of nuclear forces in Europe is unrelated to any interest in coercing NATO Europe with the shadow of Soviet conventional military power. Prudent NATO planners should assume, however, that the political temperature of East-West relations goes up and down, and a nuclear-incompetent NATO force in Europe had better be very competent otherwise. "Otherwise" might include the comparative capabilities of the two sides in chemical and electronic warfare, as well as in the important arts of operational and strategic deception.

CONCLUSIONS

The most surprising outcome for military planners would be a World War III in which, for reasons of prudence or fear, both sides fought a slow and painful protracted war, instead of a fast and furious race to Armageddon. The development of U.S. strategic nuclear doctrine has essentially been about how to conduct the fast, and apocalyptic, war, although declaratory policy since 1974 has called for more selective use of strategic nuclear forces, if deterrence fails. The possibility of extended war that is partly nuclear and mostly conventional has, however, received less attention. This would be "combined arms" with a vengeance, a dispersed global battle of attrition in the midst of fluid political objectives and disaggregated command and control. The war could be ended with Europe in medieval ruins, parts of China occupied by Soviet forces (and vice versa), and the Middle East boiling over with clashes between superpower surrogates. The aftermath of such a war might resemble the problems facing Europe after the Thirty Years War instead of after World War II, only this time the misery would be globally dispersed. Instead of the eschatological nuclear winter expected by scientists, one could find a slow rebuilding process in Europe and parts of Asia, with the First World now very dependent on resources from the Third World, and at prices that would change the postwar balance of economic power. As Western banks put their assets into receivership in the form of careless loans to developing countries in the 1970s, so wars in the developed world, if they are global but still limited, may put Western economic reconstruction at the mercy of providers who were once impoverished. If the new world comes to the rescue of the old, it will not be the first time.

NOTES

1. Nigel Nicolson, *Napoleon 1812* (New York: Harper & Row, 1985), p. 17.
2. Bryan I. Fugate, *Operation Barbarossa* (Novato, CA: Presidio Press, 1984), pp. 311–12 and passim.
3. Barbara W. Tuchman, *The Guns of August* (New York: Macmillan, 1962).
4. For discussion of the concept of limited aims, see John J. Mearsheimer, *Conventional Deterrence* (Ithaca, NY: Cornell University Press, 1983), pp. 53–56.
5. Michael I. Handel, *The Diplomacy of Surprise: Hitler, Nixon, Sadat* (Cambridge, MA: Harvard Studies in International Affairs, 1981), pp. 97–175.
6. This is suggested by P. H. Vigor, *Soviet Blitzkrieg Theory* (New York: St. Martin's Press, 1983), p. 29.
7. On Soviet expectations about nuclear war, see Stephen M. Meyer, "Soviet Nuclear Operations," in *Managing Nuclear Operations*, ed. Ashton B. Carter, John D. Steinbruner, and Charles D. Zraket (Washington, DC: Brookings Institution, 1987), Ch. 15, pp. 470–531.
8. On the Schlesinger doctrine and its implications, see Lynn Etheridge Davis, "Limited Nuclear Options: Deterrence and the New American Doctrine," in *Strategic Deterrence in a Changing Environment*, ed. Christoph Bertram (Montclair, NJ: Allenheld, Osmun, 1981), pp. 42–62.
9. Bruce G. Blair, *Strategic Command and Control: Redefining the Nuclear Threat* (Washington, DC: Brookings Institution, 1985).
10. See Jack Mendelsohn, "Wending Our Way to Zero," *Arms Control Today*, May 1987, pp. 4–9.
11. On this point see Vigor, *Soviet Blitzkrieg Theory*, pp. 1–9.
12. The authoritative public exposition of the U.S. maritime strategy is Admiral James D. Watkins, USN, "The Maritime Strategy," Proceedings of the U.S. Naval Institute, January 1986, pp. 3–17. For a critique, see John J. Mearsheimer, "A Strategic Misstep: The Maritime Strategy and Deterrence in Europe," *International Security* 11, No. 2 (Fall 1986): 3–57.
13. See Robert W. Clawson and Lawrence S. Kaplan, eds., *The Warsaw Pact: Political Purpose and Military Means* (Wilmington, DE: Scholarly Resources, 1982).
14. For comments on the possibility of Soviet "defensive surprise," see Richard K. Betts *Surprise Attack: Lessons for Defense Planning* (Washington, DC: Brookings Institution, 1982), pp. 162–65. Soviet defensive surprise would occur if their attack were motivated more by anxiety than aggressive intent.
15. The importance of the initial period of the war in Soviet doctrine is stressed in Christopher N. Donnelly, "Soviet Operational Concepts in the 1980s," in

Strengthening Conventional Deterrence in the 1980s, Report of the European Security Study (New York: St. Martin's Press, 1983), pp. 105–36, esp. pp. 114–16.

16. Vigor, *Soviet Blitzkrieg Theory,* p. 146. Soviet proponents of strong ground forces have always advocated that they be prepared for either short or long war, but the recent emphasis has apparently shifted toward appreciation of sustained combat capability, or what the United States calls "sustainability." See John Erickson, Lynn Hansen, and William Schneider, *Soviet Ground Forces: An Operational Assessment* (Boulder, CO: Westview Press, 1986), p. 35. Soviet planners may now prefer to fight a war in Europe without using nuclear weapons at all, although they will be prepared for transition to nuclear war if need be. See John G. Hines, Phillip A. Petersen, and Notra Trulock III, "Soviet Military Theory from 1945–2000: Implications for NATO," *Washington Quarterly* 9, No. 4 (Fall 1986): 117–37.

17. For an interesting discussion of NATO alternatives, see Robert S. McNamara, *Blundering into Disaster: Surviving the First Century of the Nuclear Age* (New York: Pantheon Press, 1986).

9

NUCLEAR SURPRISE

To consider the problem of nuclear surprise attack, as it might apply to U.S.–Soviet crisis behavior, this chapter first outlines a taxonomy of kinds of surprise, then studies examples of surprise in previous wars and intelligence failures, and finally reviews other issues bearing upon the relationship between crisis stability and surprise attack. The literature and historical record suggest two disturbing and not fully consistent conclusions. Nuclear surprise attack could be the most rational thing for a state to do, under certain very restricted conditions, although it might result from irrational motives on the part of policy makers. Second, and somewhat inconsistent with the first argument, is the historical record for strategic surprise attacks in conventional wars, which suggests a high payoff for well-executed surprises.

Thus, according to the first conclusion, the decision calculus might tip for nuclear war, if surprise attack could limit retaliation to acceptable levels, whatever "acceptable" was defined to mean. The definition of acceptable might be very subjective, however, relative to the imaginary costs of awaiting attack by the opponent. Preemption could be dictated by subjectively driven misperceptions of an adversary's intentions, which would then lead to an objective assessment that hitting first is better than hitting second. According to the second conclusion, strategic nuclear surprise is appealing, not from desperation but from hope. The hope is that an opponent's forces can be so denuded, or its command system so disrupted, that effective retaliation is not possible. The hopeful attacker, unlike the desperate one, gambles that the odds favor a rapid and decisive knockout blow, a nuclear *blitzkrieg*.

If we consider the first motivation for nuclear surprise, desperation,

in conjunction with the second—hopeful expectation of a decisive blow—
then we have noted the paradox on which deterrence must rest, as long
as there are first-strike forces or incentives. Deterrence lies in creating
the greatest distance between desperation and hope, for when hope is
combined with crisis-induced desperation, the conjunction spells deterrence instability. As noted below, scholarly research suggests a variety
of paths by which crises become unstable, but the notion of crises stability
is itself a contradiction. Crises are, by definition, processes that may
terminate in some disaster, else they are not crises. If they are disaster
prone, then crises are not stable. They are manageable, provided hopes
and desperations pertinent to surprise are kept below the thresholds at
which they will react catalytically with one another.[1]

Unfortunately, U.S.–Soviet strategic nuclear war is not inconceivable.
The verdict of history is not yet in. Although there is no historical precedent for nuclear exchanges, there is precedent for international conflict
between antagonistic political systems. That conflict has often ended in
war. Nuclear weapons have, at least temporarily, changed the relationship between the risks of going to war and the toleration of reversals in
diplomacy and strategy. Now, states might be willing to endure great
loss of face and significant diplomatic reversals, if the alternative is nuclear devastation, but no one can guarantee that this condition will last
forever. History has pronounced harsh verdicts on those who assume that
the past will go on repeating itself. As Ernest May has noted in his
excellent study, *Lessons of the Past*, what political and military leaders
have learned from history is incorrect.[2] The misunderstanding is not
limited to those exceptional cases in which eccentric personalities wildly
misperceive reality. As individuals and in groups, policy makers create
and re-create their own realities from a very selective slice of experience.
Their shared perceptions and expectations form a matrix that is subjective, distorted in some particulars, and open to challenge only with great
difficulty, the longer it is held in place by various intellectual and motivational props.[3]

It seems implausible that U.S. and Soviet leaders would be surprised
by the outbreak of war between them, given the generally anarchic nature
of the international system and the at least abstract possibility that war
can always happen. In addition, the tendency of military establishments
to seek overinsurance against potential enemies is well known. The difference between the expectation of conflict in general and the expectation
of a particular war is a profound distinction with regard to surprise.
Despite their general expectancy of war in the offing, policy makers have
frequently been caught napping with regard to the kind of war that has
broken out, to where it has begun, and to the tactics and techniques of
the opponent. In short, even surprises that might have been expected
have been predicted badly.[4]

In the real world, the matter of successful or unsuccessful surprise is not a simple dichotomy. Surprises happen in lumps. Defenders are caught partially aware and partially napping. Deception hides some important indicators, but not others. Surprise becomes a continuum or sliding scale in many dimensions: it has length, breadth, depth, and other latitudinal and longitudinal variations. Moreover, a small surprise, say at the tactical level, can have ripple effects that cumulate in an effect much more consequential. In other words, tactical innovations are components of strategic surprises.

A common and fruitful approach is to distinguish surprises by their level of impact and intended targets. Thus, strategic surprises are commonly described as those that happen as a result of a defender's misjudgments of the adversary's long-run intentions and capabilities. Tactical surprises are more limited in time and scope to individual campaigns and near-term results. Provided this distinction, as commonly used, is understood heuristically, it presents no difficulties, but especially with regard to the prospect of strategic nuclear surprise, the distinction cannot be pushed too far. In the absence of adequate tactical warning of surprise attack, either superpower would suffer devastating losses. Indeed, some nuclear forces are maintained at high levels of readiness in peacetime in order to prevent tactical surprises that might inflict strategic military and political losses. When these forces maintained at high readiness are dubiously survivable, they are potential detractors from crisis stability.

This situation, of devastating societal losses growing out of tactical surprise, is unprecedented in the nuclear age. Prenuclear tactical surprises would at best promise to open the door for defeat of the opponent's armed forces and political capitulation. The opponent's society could not be got at without stretching the rubber band of surprise for all it was worth. With nuclear forces of the size of superpower strategic forces, failure to respond to tactical warning would cause catastrophic, and perhaps ultimate, losses. This is true even if, following the surprise first strike, the defender can retaliate and destroy the attacker's society. Destruction of the attacker's society in retaliation will not save the defender's forces and society that were subjected to the first strike.

Policy makers in an international system based on sovereign national states might be expected to anticipate surprise in general, as a derivative of the lack of consensual systemic norms and the opportunistic attractiveness of surprise when it succeeds. These expectations may characterize the general mind sets of national leaders, but their specific actions in a crisis are more dependent upon the channels through which they receive information and the kinds of perceptions and expectations they hold about national, and personal, political risks. A general appreciation of the possibility of surprise commonly does not lead to improved abilities to anticipate specific attacks.

The losing side in a war is almost always the victim of some kind of surprise. Any pattern of events that falsifies the expectations of the loser can be loosely fitted into the category of surprise by the winner. Even cultural misunderstandings have been described as important contributory factors to political and military surprise during crisis and war. Accordingly, this chapter's first section offers a provisional taxonomy of kinds of politicomilitary surprise, with some comments anticipating which forms of surprise will be emphasized as pertinent to nuclear surprise.

This is not to exclude other kinds of surprises, but only to pick out a few that have special pertinence for nuclear crises, especially those that might occur between superpowers. There is a danger here, aside from the arbitrary character of any classification. The classification is reified by the investigator, and so real behavior, if not in conformity with categorically expected behavior, is ignored or misunderstood. Errors at opposite ends of this spectrum, of wrong inferences based on confusing categories with reality, are bolt-from-the-blue scenarios, in which crisis momentum "automatically" takes charge of policy makers' decisions. It is a beginning presumption, for the discussion that follows, that either the assumption of bolt from the blue or the assumption of automaticity in crisis momentum is useful only to define hypothetical and extreme points on a continuum of possibilities. Like depression and full employment in economics, unprovoked surprise attacks and momentum sweeping policy makers off their feet occur rarely in nature, and then not according to many expectations implicit in models. Like economists, we, too, consider unprovoked surprises and unstoppable momentum as hypothetically possible, although infrequent, conditions, compared to other possibilities. Between these extremes, of mindless momentum and unprovoked surprise, lie the most interesting, and therefore the most surprising cases. In the final analysis, one is surprised if war, or successful coercion that obtains the same objectives, happens in a way that falsifies policy makers' and analysts' preconflict expectations.

For the reason just noted, economic paradigms of marginal-utility theory, although frequently employed by Western military strategists, may be less pertinent to the problem of surprise than are theories drawn from other disciplines. In particular, the discipline of psychology might provide equally valid insights, compared to marginal-utility analysis, relevant to the problem of preventing nuclear surprise. Historical study of surprise, in nuclear crises and elsewhere, shows that a flawed decision-making process surprises itself as much as deception or espionage create a surprised victim. In the case of U.S.–Soviet relations, nuclear surprise is deemed impossible by many analysts who assess the possibility that either side can successfully apply enough hardware to the task of a preemptive or preventive first strike. It is thought a sufficient deterrent that, absent any protection against retaliation, neither side would dare to contemplate a first strike. This reasoning is further defended by the assumption that since war has not occurred between the superpowers, then deterrence must be stable, or ultrastable (tending toward a stable equilibrium in general, despite small perturbations from time to time).

Deterrence would be weakened if either the United States or the Soviet Union could calculate that it was somehow advantageous to strike the first in a crisis, and if the side striking first then expected to escape all but acceptable retaliation. The potential development of strategic defenses in this century or, more likely, the next, raises complications for this simple but durable model of deterrence by threat of retaliation. Even before defenses have been deployed, policy makers and theorists should question whether superpower nuclear deterrence is as stable as is commonly supposed. The behavior of both U.S. and Soviet leaders is characterized by their undoubtedly sincere acknowledgements that in nuclear war, under present conditions, there can be no winners. These protestations against the possibility of any gains from war are made, however, with reference to a peacetime standard of acceptability, not a crisis or wartime standard. The imperial rulers of Germany, Austria-Hungary, and Russia prior to World War I did not want a general war, which would ultimately destroy their empires, but they nevertheless blundered into what they thought was a limited war, with unforeseen and disastrous consequences. This is most probably how a nuclear war would begin, by escalation from something smaller and more uncertain, diplomatic importunings combined with shootings, mixed signals and confused movements, and policy makers stumbling like inebriated deckhands on a sinking luxury liner. After the fact, it will be small consolation if historians can show that the tides that swamped the boat were not aiming at that boat, specifically.

KINDS OF POLITICOMILITARY SURPRISE

There are at least six different forms of politicomilitary surprises that are possibly pertinent to the problem of strategic nuclear surprise. All of these are touched on later, but some receive more emphasis than others. The basic kinds are grand strategic surprise, a failure to understand the long-run intentions of the opponent and its psychology or culture; military strategic surprise, misjudgment of the military situation and especially of one's own military vulnerabilities, including one's own strategy or theory of conflict; technical surprise, the introduction or adaptive use of military technologies in unexpected ways; intelligence surprise, either passive in the defender's inability to penetrate the secrets of the opponent and so correctly anticipate the outbreak of war, or active, in which the attacker deceives the defender by sending false signals and messages; operational-tactical surprise, or how one side might structure its campaigns in novel fashion in order to bring about strategically decisive results; and systemic surprise, in which the understanding, on the part of one or both sides, of the international system and prewar alignment of international forces proves to be defective.[5] These categories are not mutually exclusive, and it is possible for one side to benefit from more than one kind of surprise in the same conflict. Moreover, none of these forms of surprise, even if it succeeds, can by itself guarantee defeat of the opponent.

This taxonomy of kinds of surprise is obviously not exhaustive, but only indicative of some plausible distinctions pertinent to the subject matter. A more fundamental distinction in theory, although harder to make in practice, is between those strategic surprises that are planned or designed in advance and a set of surprising developments, events that are unexpected.[6] A successful surprise in the first sense obviously involves some component of surprise in the second; the victim's expectations had to be discrepant from what actually happened. Sometimes, however, putative surprisers surprise themselves, and the results are not in keeping with their assumptions about how well the surprise attack will go, or the particular forms it will take. Sometimes attackers are surprised beyond their most optimistic expectations. MacArthur's landing at Inchon was an operation about which almost all of his superiors had grave misgivings; only MacArthur was confident that a seemingly large gamble would pay dividends.[7] Hitler's attack against France in 1940 surprised both the French and the Germans. Although it achieved its operational objective of establishing German control over Western Europe, the Germans were unprepared to exploit their success fully, that is, strategically. The rapid collapse of French resistance led to uncertainty about how to follow it up, and the hesitancy of the German high command allowed the British army to escape at Dunkirk.

In terms of strategic nuclear surprise, this distinction, between deliberately planned and inadvertent surprises, is extremely important. Most experts consider it improbable that a preplanned strategic nuclear surprise attack could work against a superpower. Modern intelligence systems would provide too much warning of attacker preparations, and discovery could invite preemption. More probable is inadvertent war, meaning that nuclear war grows out of a strategy for fighting a conventional war, or that a larger nuclear war grows out of a planned series of limited nuclear exchanges.[8] Inadvertent war crosses the boundary between the premeditated and the unpremeditated, between contract murder and purely spontaneous killing. An example is provided, according to Barry R. Posen, by contemporary U.S. maritime strategy, which would include prompt attacks against Soviet ballistic missile submarines (SSBNs) by U.S. naval forces using conventional antisubmarine weapons.[9] Although the U.S. Navy describes this strategy of attrition against

Soviet SSBNs as a way to induce war termination, Posen contends that it will raise the risks of superpower nuclear war. The attacks on Soviet SSBNs would not be inadvertent, but the escalation from conventional to nuclear war might be.[10] Another illustration of the risks of inadvertent nuclear war is provided by some of the events that took place during the Cuban missile crisis of 1962, which is discussed below. Inadvertent nuclear war could easily have happened during that crisis, and almost did, although deliberate nuclear war was avoided. Indeed, some of the steps taken to compel Soviet compliance with U.S. demands raised the risks of inadvertent war, even as they seemed to be sensible moves to deter a deliberate surprise attack.

THE CUBAN MISSILE CRISIS: A CASE STUDY

That history could be misleading with regard to the durability of deterrence and nuclear surprise is suggested by the Cuban missile crisis of 1962. This narrow escape from U.S.–Soviet nuclear war was trumpeted as a great diplomatic success for the Kennedy administration by its court historians. It was also treated as a successful case of nuclear deterrence by some prominent analysts and strategists. If success is relative, then the superpowers' avoidance of nuclear war over Cuba in 1962 was successful, considering the consequences, had the superpowers used nuclear weapons. Short of nuclear catastrophe, however, there are reasons to doubt that Cuba represented an unequivocal example of successful crisis management.[11]

A different perspective on the Cuban crisis could propose that it was a case of "low intensity conflict" (in currently used terminology) having been escalated into a nuclear confrontation by U.S. unpreparedness for surprise and Soviet miscalculation of U.S. embarrassment after the fact of surprise. Khrushchev's desire to emplace Soviet medium-range missiles in Cuba has been described by some observers as an attempt to rectify an obvious strategic imbalance in favor of the United States, following U.S. pronouncements in 1961 that the missile gap had turned out to be in its favor.[12] Certainly this U.S. declaration represents a dubious diplomatic step, even without its unforeseen and more drastic military consequences downstream. Having rubbed Khrushchev's nose in the facts of his strategic nuclear inferiority, U.S. policy makers should have expected him to respond, not by acceptance of his humiliation but by taking some steps to change the perception of Soviet strategic inferiority. Kennedy's behavior during the Cuban crisis is testimony to the importance of perceptions of the strategic balance by the United States; as the president noted after the missiles were discovered, whether the Soviet deployments in Cuba had actually changed the balance of power was less important than the perception that it had.[13] Apparently Kennedy could not attribute this same perceptual dilemma to Khrushchev, following Deputy Secretary of Defense Roswell Gilpatric's authorized announcement of the missile gap favoring U.S. forces, compared to Soviet ones.

Taking the United States at its word that its nuclear superiority was secure, Khrushchev might not have perceived the deployment of missiles in Cuba as a fundamental threat to U.S. security. Some members of the "ExCom," which gathered to debate U.S. responses to the Soviet challenge in October of 1962, also felt that missiles launched from Cuba were not different in kind from missiles launched from the Soviet Union. Khrushchev could not have hoped to change the strategic balance, as perceived mechanistically, by deploying medium-range missiles in Cuba, where they were not survivable against any U.S. retaliation and would serve to draw fire on the fledgling arsenal of retaliatory forces then being constructed in the Soviet homeland. He might, however, have hoped to change the perceived balance psychologically, by making the United States feel vulnerable to Soviet nuclear weapons deployed for the first time close to U.S. shores, but this psychological gambit could not be pushed too far beyond the balance of force structures itself. U.S. observers who noted the possibility of preemptive attacks from Cuba against U.S. cities disregarded the strategic logic that U.S. experts had come to accept by the beginning of the Kennedy administration: that forces that are not survivable invite attack on themselves and provoke wars under the most unfavorable conditions.[14]

More plausible as an explanation for Khrushchev's conduct is the notion that he sought to create a potential trip wire for future U.S. efforts to threaten or to attack Cuba, while impressing the Chinese with his determination and refuting their claims that he was reluctant to challenge the imperialist foe.[15] Nuclear missiles in Cuba would raise the costs of another Bay of Pigs—indeed, virtually preclude it. Soviet missiles manned by Soviet forces in Cuba would convert a small risk of nuclear confrontation (if the United States invaded Cuba with conventional forces and the Cubans had no missiles) into a larger risk, once the missiles were deployed. If this was Soviet reasoning, it was faulty in its lack of understanding of the U.S. position, once the missiles were being constructed. U.S. historical interests in Latin America, the Monroe Doctrine, and President Kennedy's personal pride mitigated against U.S. acceptance of any Soviet transfer to Cuba of nuclear weapons. Khrushchev was obviously surprised by Kenedy's reaction to the missile deployments, and it is not entirely clear what he would have done, had the construction of missile sites been completed before they were discovered by U.S. intelligence. U.S. conventional superiority in the Caribbean theater of operations was and remains overwhelming. Soviet completion of the missile deployments might have resulted in a worse outcome for them than Kennedy's successful demand for their withdrawal. Once completed, they would provide a U.S. justification for an invasion of Cuba on a massive scale, with the probable support of the then members of the Organization of American States and U.S. European allies. The Soviets could have responded with lateral escalation of the conflict to Berlin or another East-West trouble spot, but they could do little to affect outcomes favorable to the United States so close to its borders.

Seen through skeptical eyes, the U.S. triumph in Cuba seems to provide little precedent for future crisis management. The skepticism is not based as much on the changed U.S.–Soviet strategic-force balance since then, although that change is significant. Instead, the doubt that Cuba provides a useful precedent for crisis management rests upon the substantial evidence of misperception, wishful thinking, and bolstering of minimally acceptable alternatives by leaders on both sides.[16] Moreover, there is the larger issue of the relationship between means and ends, implicit in the tacit and explicit proposals by both sides during the crisis. Kennedy's declaratory threat to launch an all-out attack on the Soviet Union in response to a Cuban missile launch against any point in the Western Hemisphere must certainly be recorded as a disproportionate one. Khrushchev's effort to save diplomatic face by presenting the United States with a strategic reversal in its own hemisphere is also an example of a lack of proportion between means and ends.

Not for the first time, national leaders incorporated their personal ego needs into their decision calculus on behalf of their countries. During the crisis preceding the outbreak of World War I, the kaiser gave a blood pledge to Austria-Hungary of Germany's willingness to support its demands upon Serbia and (somewhat more ambiguously) to support Austria-Hungary in the event that Russia mobilized its forces against Germany's ally. The kaiser and the German chancellor did not evaluate the demands made upon Serbia to see whether any Serbian compliance was possible under the circumstances, or whether Austria-Hungary was deliberately imposing demands that could not be met, in order to provide an excuse for war. Hitler declared war on the United States immediately after receiving news of the Pearl Harbor attack, despite the lack of strategic necessity to do so, in part because of his perception that the "Jew Roosevelt" was a personal enemy, not just a geopolitical adversary. Kennedy's well-known reaction when he was presented with hard photographic evidence of Khrushchev's perfidy in the Cuban missile crisis is all too typical, even if apocryphal: "He can't do this to me."

In terms of the categories of surprise discussed earlier, the Cuban missile crisis offers several variations on a theme. It was not grand strategic surprise; the Kennedy administration perceived the intentions of the Soviet Union in a realistic, albeit pessimistic, way. One might argue that military strategic surprise almost occurred in Cuba. Had the missiles of October not been discovered until November, it is possible that the

United States would have been faced with a *fait accompli*, making necessary either invasion or air strikes to remove the missiles. It is also clear that some component of intelligence surprise clearly took place in Cuba. Soviet intentions were not correctly perceived in several ways. Their reaction to the U.S. announcement of a strategic missile gap in its favor was not to acquiesce, but to attempt a short-term (perceived) reversal of that situation. U.S. intelligence estimates were also burdened by preconceptions on the part of policy makers, to the effect that the Soviet Union would not dare to do something so obviously provocative as putting missiles into Cuba. President Kennedy had staked much of his domestic political reputation on Soviet ability to understand, from his perspective, U.S. interests in keeping Soviet nuclear weapons out of the Western Hemisphere. Intelligence failures, which were not surprises in themselves, also contributed to U.S. surprise at the Soviet decision. Air Force and CIA jurisdictional squabbling over whose pilots would be assigned U–2 reconnaissance missions delayed important overflights that could have discovered Soviet missiles earlier.

The Soviets were also surprised in the Cuban crisis. They underestimated the determination of the U.S. president with regard to removal of their missiles, once those missiles had been discovered. Khrushchev first tried denial, then stalling, and finally complied with U.S. demands only after Kennedy left no doubt of U.S. readiness for military action. The United States engaged in coercion by putting into place the blockade of Cuba, and this coercion was backed up by threats to escalate further, which clearly were credible threats. The ability of the United States to control and to dominate any process of escalation in the Caribbean theater with conventional or nuclear weapons was of obvious concern to the Soviet Union, which had not counted on its missiles being discovered while under construction. After the missiles were discovered and photographs had provided to the United States unmistakable evidence of Soviet deception, the USSR offered to trade removal of U.S. missiles from Turkey for Soviet missiles in Cuba. This may have been an after-the-fact improvisation that was designed to save face for the USSR and to compensate for the surprising (to them) reaction of President Kennedy.

It may also be true that the United States surprised itself, as Harry Truman certainly must have done in reaction to the outbreak of war in Korea in 1950. Kennedy was determined to do something, but what he might do was left open for deliberation by the ExCom of hand-picked advisors, including his brother Robert. The ExCom sorted through options within a context provided by the president, who left the actual choice of options open to discussion and debate. Kennedy's final decision, based on these deliberations and recommendations, evolved during the crisis and reflected his increasingly brittle tolerance for Soviet procrastination and stonewalling. The more it seemed that the blockade might be insufficient to compel Soviet removal of the missiles from Cuba, the more favorably Kennedy regarded the options of air strike and invasion. Soviet intelligence might have drawn the wrong conclusion about Kennedy's experience in the Bay of Pigs. The USSR might have concluded that Kennedy's behavior in that crisis, in which he decided to cut U.S. losses rather than proceed with an ill-fated invasion, would be repeated in 1962. The Bay of Pigs could, however, just as plausibly have produced the opposite effect in Kennedy, a determination to yield in a confrontation with the Soviet Union or its allies, and especially in the Western Hemisphere.

The Cuban missile crisis mixes elements of deliberate, inadvertent, and accidental nuclear war, together with the plausible argument that nuclear weapons had more to do with what-if possibilities in the crisis than they did with coercing Soviet removal of the missiles. U.S. conventional military capabilities were certainly sufficient to accomplish that task, and options were prepared accordingly. Deliberate nuclear war was threatened by Kennedy, if a missile launched from Cuba landed anywhere in the Western Hemisphere, but not as a response to Soviet refusal to remove the missiles from Cuba. Inadvertent nuclear war was a possible outcome of Navy standard operating procedures for forcing Soviet submarines to surface, if those submarines carried nuclear weapons, as some probably did. Accidental nuclear war could have happened if the U–2 that accidentally strayed into Soviet airspace late in the crisis had provoked Khrushchev into nuclear retaliation against North America, or conventional war in Europe that then escalated into superpower nuclear exchanges. One of the lessons that might be learned from the Cuban missile crisis is that force balances have less to do with successful deterrence than is commonly supposed. In normal peacetime conditions, force balances provide a shorthand for tabulating approximate strength and weakness. In a crisis where fundamental interests are felt to be at stake, however, especially fear of nuclear surprise, the images that leaders have of one another's goals, strategies, and mind sets may be equally important. Postcrisis assessments by those political and military principals are equally important, and it is highly instructive to recall that participants in the Cuban crisis did not feel, in the aftermath, that they had won or prevailed, but simply coped and escaped.

LESSONS OF HISTORY

The history of nuclear crises and nonnuclear wars can contribute to our understanding of the problem of strategic nuclear surprise, if properly interpreted. History does not repeat itself in terms of the details of technologies and war plans, although some of Napoleon's logistical difficulties in attempting to invade Russia might have been noted, with educational benefit, by Hitler's planners of Barbarossa.[17] History provides suggestive evidence of the behavior of leaders and decision processes, which can be applied from one case to another. There is always the danger that social scientists will ransack historical evidence to construct analogies, but the comparison and contrast among cases is instructive, if done with recognition of its limitations.

It has been argued, for example, that the "cult of the offensive" characterized the military doctrines of the major European powers on the eve of World War I and that this preoccupation with the offensive contributed to the outbreak of war, as well as to absurd methods of fighting it.[18] The issue of military doctrine is a complicated one and involves at least two levels of analysis, as Barry Posen has shown: assumptions made by military and political leaders about the international balance of power, and the infusion into military organizations of preconceptions in favor or against certain tactics and strategies.[19] Although there are important issues still in dispute with regard to the importance of military doctrines as contributory factors in the outbreak of World War I, what can be said is that the major powers of the Triple Alliance and Triple Entente misjudged one another's capabilities and doctrines. Ernest May's judgment on the ability of intelligence services, prior to the first and second world wars, to forecast enemy intentions or capabilities is instructive:

By the test of whether the right questions were pursued, no government did well either before 1914 or in the 1930s. Some, however, did more poorly than others. Their misdiagnoses were fatal or nearly so, not merely crippling. Broadly speaking, governments of the earlier period were at their worst when estimating capabilities. Governments of the 1930's, on the other hand, made their greatest errors when judging proclivities.[20]

In addition, there was no apparent relationship between the organization of intelligence services and the quality of their performance. Different types of organization have their own weaknesses. May's case study of the performance of Britain in 1911 and czarist Russia and imperial Germany in 1912 finds that neither centralized nor collegial types of organization preclude serious errors in collection and estimation.[21] Britain's collegial type of organization produced military estimates that were grossly in error with regard to publicly available data; according to May, "collegiality encouraged reticence."[22] Centralization of assessment in the Russian system contributed to concealment of information and incomplete analysis of alternatives.[23] The German kaiser excluded from an important meeting persons who would doubt his appraisal of other nations' foreign policies and others who might question Germany's military readiness for war.[24]

Nor was intelligence put to work much more effectively prior to World

War II, although in this instance faulty estimates of intentions were more noteworthy than erroneous appreciations of capabilities. According to Michael Geyer, Hitler's decisions to occupy the Rhineland, or to annex Austria, or to attack Czechoslovakia or Poland, were not based on intelligence information that these were fruitful opportunities. Instead, the führer first decided to attack and then sought confirmatory information to support his decision.[25] John Erickson notes that, although Soviet military-technical intelligence was generally sound and very extensive, the interpretation of German military doctrine presented greater difficulties to the Kremlin. Moreover, Stalin's purges in 1937 and 1938 decimated the Soviet high command and the nation's capabilities in military intelligence. Military intelligence was smashed to pieces, and intelligence officers and agents were recalled in the hundreds and executed. The Soviet diplomatic *apparat* was also disrupted, and the security services given a tighter grip over Kremlin diplomacy at the very time when astute diplomacy might have been worth many divisions.[26] Needless to say, the Nazi and Soviet dictatorships cannot be faulted in comparison with U.S. prewar intelligence competency, or lack of it. According to David Kahn "disbelief in a Japanese attack was reinforced by belief in the superiority of the white race. Americans looked upon the Japanese as bucktoothed, bespectacled little yellow men, forever photographing things with their omnipresent cameras so that they could copy them. Such opinions were held not only by common bigots but by opinion-makers as well."[27]

U.S. assumptions about German capabilities, especially the German air force, may have been as inflated as U.S. estimates of Japanese competency were deflated. It might be supposed that today's technology and intelligence organizations available to the superpowers, compared to those prior to the Second World War, would preclude misestimation so wide of the mark. Technology cannot, however, preclude surprise, and in some ways it may make surprise more probable. U.S. estimates of Japanese capabilities did not include the assumption that the Japanese had developed torpedoes that could be used in waters as shallow as those at Pearl Harbor.[28] Nor were the ranges of Japanese attack aircraft correctly estimated, with devastating consequences at Pearl Harbor and in the Philippines. Applications of radar technology during the Battle of Britain allowed a numerically inferior British force to inflict unacceptable losses on the *Luftwaffe* and cause the postponement of Operation Sea Lion, the invasion of the United Kingdom. Germany's development of V–1 and V–2 rocket technologies were unexpected by the anti-Axis allies prior to the war, and the implications of those technologies were not fully understood, or fully exploited, until after the end of World War II. Modern illustrations of surprise using conventional technology have occurred as recently as the October war of 1973 and the Israeli invasion of Lebanon in 1982. In the latter case, the Israelis eliminated surface-to-air (SAM) missile batteries by employing remotely piloted vehicles (RPV) or drone aircraft to reveal their locations and emissions, so that the SAMs could be attacked by follow-on strikes.

U.S. and Soviet technologies of the present day for warning and reconnaissance might contribute to complacency about surprise or, in some instances, to heightened fears, which help to weaken deterrence during a crisis. Technologies are not isolated from the policy contexts within which they are applied, and it is those policy contexts with which we are concerned at the moment. There is more to say about the relationship between technology and strategic nuclear surprise in the next section. The issue of technology has been mentioned here only to alert the reader that the author is extremely skeptical that a larger amount of technical collection, of which the superpowers certainly have an abundance, necessarily contributes to an improved intelligence estimate or net assessment. This fallibility of estimates based on technical collection is not a result of technological folly per se, although there is some of that in the U.S. (and probably the Soviet) intelligence communities. The more important issue is the interpretation placed on collected materials by intelligence analysts and policy makers. There is the tendency to assume that numerical "bean counts" of missile launchers, aircraft, interceptor aircraft, and other force indicators are somehow the functional equivalent of a net assessment or a shorthand replica of the balance of power.

However important it is, the collection of such indicators cannot substitute for the competency of Western analysts in understanding Soviet military doctrine, and vice versa for Soviet analysts reading U.S. tea leaves. The Soviet perspective places emphasis upon the "correlation of forces," which is a more inclusive and a more subtle concept than the U.S. strategic-balance terminology. In the Soviet perspective, the correlation of forces includes political, military, economic, and societal dimensions of the national military effort in peace and war.[29] The Soviet view of surprise attack is unique to its military doctrine and its geopolitical surroundings, together with Soviet appreciation of their historical experiences. Western analysts have been accused, with justification, of mirror-imaging their own doctrine, instead of interpreting Soviet writers in their own terms.[30] Taking into account the asymmetries in U.S. and Soviet force structures, the two nations' doctrinal differences could prove to be of fundamental significance in determining whether superpower crises can be resolved. As we have seen in the Cuban missile crisis, leaders of both countries had little insight into the motivations of their counterparts. Now that strategic parity has replaced a balance that was very lopsided in the U.S. favor, and at much higher levels of armament, the consequences of deterrence failure and surprise would be much greater. Indeed, in the Soviet view, they could be historically decisive, and this is just one illustration of what the West needs to understand about the

Soviet perspective. Some of the other components of that perspective, but by no means all, are reviewed next.

NUCLEAR SURPRISE AND SOVIET STRATEGY

Surprise, from the standpoint of Soviet military doctrine and strategy, has not always been considered fundamentally important. Since Stalin's death their military writers have more frequently acknowledged the relationship between surprise and success or failure in war. With regard to a U.S.-Soviet conflict in which nuclear weapons might be used, Soviet planners cannot disregard the possibility of a U.S. bolt-from-the-blue attack. Nevertheless, there is evidence that such an unprovoked attack is no longer considered the most likely path by which nuclear war would start.[31]

Soviet expectations about the onset of conflicts that might result in nuclear war admit of other, and more plausible in their view, possibilities. Two will receive emphasis here. The first is the direct confrontation between U.S. and Soviet interests, resulting in a two-sided crisis that might lead to nuclear exchanges. The Cuban missile crisis is a prototype. The second is a conventional war in Europe that might escalate into superpower nuclear exchanges either against their respective homelands or against targets in the European theater of operations.

For many years NATO declaratory strategy essentially treated these two cases as one. In the event of a dash for the Pyrenees or the Channel by the Red Army, as was envisioned in the 1940s and for most of the 1950s, the U.S. strategic retaliatory force would pummel as many Soviet and allied military and nonmilitary targets as could be reached within the appropriate time interval.[32] Early nuclear-age war plans envisioned massive destruction of Soviet nuclear forces in "blunting" missions that might have to be executed preemptively, in the expectation that Soviet conventional invasion of Europe had already begun. For understandable reasons and faced with this asymmetry in U.S. nuclear capabilities, compared to Soviet ones, the USSR in its declaratory doctrine emphasized its concerns with being victimized with a nuclear version of Barbarossa, delivered by U.S. bombers and, later, ICBMs.

During the 1960s, U.S. and NATO declaratory doctrine moved away from massive retaliation and toward flexible response in two senses. NATO deterrence would be predicated upon a triad of initial conventional resistance, deliberate escalation to the use of short- and long-range theater nuclear forces, and, ultimately, the employment of U.S. strategic retaliatory forces. Codified in MC–14/3 in 1967, this strategy, as seen by the United States, but not commonly in Europe, also anticipated flexible employment of U.S. strategic forces, even after war began. Flexible response was perceived by the United States as allowing for partial and disaggregated, but not decoupled, conventional and nuclear responses. By Europeans, it was understood to commit the U.S. strategic deterrent to the defense of Europe at a relatively early stage in any conventional war. At best, from the standpoint of European military planners and political leaders, NATO conventional forces were designed to create a pause that allowed Soviet attackers to reconsider their possible costs if war escalated; the denial role of NATO conventional forces was not their primary mission. Nor were they simple trip wires; they were potential triggers of a chain reaction, which might, although with some ambiguity, culminate in a U.S.-Soviet strategic nuclear exchange, with its obvious societal costs.[33]

This summary oversimplifies a larger reality, which is covered in a number of excellent studies.[34] The point, for present purposes, is that the USSR reacted to NATO and U.S. flexible-response doctrines by acknowledging the possibility, although not the certainty, that war in Europe could begin with a conventional phase. Under some conditions, that phase could be quite extended, and Soviet forces needed to be prepared for the possibility that nuclear weapons would not be introduced early or at all. Conventional war in Europe, from the Soviet standpoint, would, however, be fought in the expectation that the war might go nuclear at any time. This was not necessarily the preferred Soviet way of fighting such a war, but it recognized that NATO policy called for early first use and that it might be advantageous, under some conditions, for the Soviets to anticipate NATO use, and preempt it.[35] Apparently Soviet military studies during the 1970s also pointed to practical difficulties inherent in ground-forces operations, when nuclear weapons are being used in combined arms offensives. Rates of advance for Soviet forces might be slowed by collateral damage attendant on nuclear strikes in the theater of military action (TVD, or TSMA), which would impair the efficiency of operations to the detriment of timetables and norms prescribed by HCOF (High Command of Forces in a Theater of Strategic Military Action) or SVGK (Headquarters, Supreme High Command) commanders.[36]

Soviet writers have also acknowledged an apparent willingness to distinguish among thresholds, even after nuclear weapons have been introduced into a conflict. Such thresholds are not so much the bargaining counters of Western deterrence theory as they are the points of no return for Soviet planners in their escalation calculus. For example, it appears that under some conditions of war in Europe, Soviet leaders might distinguish between theater and strategic nuclear war, the latter involving attacks on the Soviet homeland itself.[37] It would be wrong for Western planners to misconstrue this Soviet perspective as one of negotiation by limited nuclear reprisal, a variant of coercive diplomacy.[38] Soviet leaders would be responding to their estimates of whether it continued to be contributory to the success of their military plans to remain at the conventional level, or to confine nuclear attacks to European, and not also U.S. targets. Soviet strategic and theater nuclear forces have not always provided them with a comprehensive menu in this regard; only in recent years have they deployed capabilities sufficient to cover necessary theater/strategic European targets, while preserving forces to attack the transoceanic TVDs (the United States, Canada, and possibly China) if necessary.[39]

If the Soviets really believe in the possiibility of a conventional option against NATO Europe, then they also believe that the success of this option might trigger NATO (or French) nuclear retaliation. One can with permissible injustice consider that there are two, and only two, types of war between NATO and the Warsaw Pact, in terms of the objectives for which the Soviets would be attacking (assuming away, only for purposes of discussion, the scenario of Soviet attack from fear of NATO attack, in response to the unraveling of Eastern Europe, or other intra-Soviet-bloc causes). The first is a strategic war, defined by the Soviet objective of conquest and occupation of Europe, whether it is accomplished with conventional forces only or by combined nuclear and nonnuclear attacks. The second is a war of limited aims, in which the USSR intends to bite off as much as its forward deployed conventional forces (mainly, the GFSG and Soviet armies deployed in Czechoslovakia) can chew, before NATO can react and regroup.[40] The second might be followed by a temporary or permanent halt to the advances by Soviet/Pact ground forces and a continuation of Korean-style skirmishing while negotiations toward war termination proceeded.

The second type of conflict might be terminated by NATO using its conventional forces alone, and the Soviets might be led to expect that NATO resistance would stop short of the nuclear threshold. This would require complicated signaling, with which Western strategists pretend more expertise than Soviet marshals.[41] Much would depend on what was happening elsewhere in the world, outside Europe. If war in Europe followed or was accompanied by U.S.–Soviet clashes in the Persian Gulf or Northeast Asia, then containment of the fighting to its conventional phase would become more difficult.[42] Indeed, early Reagan declaratory strategies called for horizontal escalation of conflict in Europe to other global locations in which U.S. conventional forces might prevail over Soviet clients or allies. The difficulty with this declaratory doctrine, once war in Europe began, was its irrelevance, unless the Soviets overreacted to it. It could not affect the outcome of ground and tactical air combat on the Central Front, and it could provoke overcompensation if the USSR stumbled into direct conflict with U.S. forces on behalf of Soviet surrogates.[43]

Much Western writing on the possible outbreak of nuclear war assumes a clear dichotomy between conventional and theater nuclear war, and between theater and strategic nuclear conflict. Paul Bracken has shown how unlikely it is that these distinctions can be maintained so neatly, after deterrence has failed in Europe.[44] Once war began, decision makers on both sides of the inter-German border would be anticipating and dreading nuclear escalation. The scale of nuclear use would matter less than its initiation. It is a mistake to suppose that the first use of any nuclear weapons by either superpower would necessarily lead to activation of mutual strategic homicide. Were this so, the task of deterrence would be easy, although fatal if it ever failed. The problem of prewar and intrawar deterrence in Europe is more subtle. Nuclear weapons may be used, but even after they are, there is no necessary outcome that follows any particular pattern of initiation. There is no experience with two-sided nuclear conflict from which to extrapolate. This will be especially daunting to the Soviets, given their insistence upon "normativity" and combat performance standards based on careful historical research and modelling.[45] Thus, the West could find itself playing nuclear brinkmanship, not only before the nuclear threshold is crossed, but after it. The unresolved issue is whether the Soviets would play, too. Western writers might see this as a game with the structure of "prisoner's dilemma" or "chicken," in which both sides had interdependent payoffs, and cooperative incentives were mixed with conflicting objectives. Soviet military leaders, although possibly aware of U.S. game-theoretical constructs as applied to nuclear wars, are not necessarily persuaded of their validity.[46] Even if Western leaders did not, Soviet ones would be asking themselves, "What is the war all about?" and answering the question in terms of a Marxist–Leninist reading of history. They could decide that a decisive clash between capitalism and socialism had now begun, or they could determine that war termination on mutually acceptable terms was the best available option. In this regard, it may be unpersuasive, and possibly injurious to NATO war aims in the event, to broadcast plans for destruction of the highest levels of Soviet political and military leadership. Although it may make sense to permit Soviet leaders to contemplate their eventual destruction if the war cannot be terminated, their contemplation should not be panicked by the expectation that dedicated countercommand attacks are imminent, once war begins.[47]

ESCALATION CONTROL AND LIMITED NUCLEAR WAR

It might surprise the United States if deterrence failed and nuclear first use did not result in escalation to theater-wide or strategic exchanges. The popular image of nuclear war reduces itself to the choreography of a single fuse, which burns rapidly and irrevocably from the first package in the NATO Nuclear Operations Plan until both arsenals are exhausted in countersocietal attacks. There are good reasons for this popular image. Expert testimony by military and political leaders raises doubts that they could control escalation, even if they wanted to. According to Marshal of the Soviet Union N.V. Ogarkov,

As for the hopes of U.S. strategists for the possibility of waging a "limited" nuclear war, today these hopes are completely unjustified and are meant for simpletons. To restrain a nuclear war which has begun within some limited framework will be virtually impossible. No matter how limited the use of nuclear weapons may be, it will *inevitably* lead to the immediate use of the *entire* nuclear arsenal of both sides.[48]

Former U.S. Secretary of Defense Harold Brown described the "immense uncertainties" attendant on limited nuclear attacks, in his remarks at the Naval War College on August 20, 1980: "We know that what might start as a supposedly controlled, limited strike could well—in my view would very likely—escalate to a full-scale nuclear war.[49]

These expressions reflect prudent pessimism in the face of weapons of mass destruction tightly coupled to command systems of untested wartime performance. Thus, it would be no surprise if limited nuclear war escalated into total war; it would be surprising if it did not.

After the nuclear threshold has been crossed, it does not necessarily follow that all bets are off and that policy makers will run for their fallout shelters in the expectation of doomsday. Much depends upon how and why the nuclear threshold is crossed and by whom. The nuclear threshold might not be actually crossed, but gradually and inadvertently circumvented. As Paul Bracken has noted, the problems of command and control for general-purpose forces that are forward deployed with nuclear weapons are more complicated than problems inherent in the control of U.S.-based strategic forces.[50] Short- and medium-range nuclear weapons commingled with conventional forces may be used in ways that are unexpected by theater commanders or by NCA. Extended control over forward-deployed and nuclear-armed theater forces, including naval and air forces, is difficult to maintain. It is not impossible, however, and there would be policy-dependent motivations not to lose control, considering the alternative.

The command system required to stop a war or limit escalation might have to be more coherent than a system that authorized a gross retaliation. Albert Wohlstetter and Richard Brody have argued, against conventional wisdom, that this is not necessarily so. Policy makers might require a much higher standard of proof from warning and attack-assessment systems, in order to justify a larger retaliation, and a lesser standard for a smaller and limited response.[51] There is some debatable evidence of Soviet interest in LNOs (limited nuclear options), although it appears that the interest is not derived from considerations of escalation control, as the West understands it.[52] The behavior of U.S. and Soviet policy makers in previous crises suggests that the first use of nuclear weapons would not necessarily trigger an immediate escalation to massive counterforce or countersocietal attacks. There might be policy makers on both sides making desperate efforts to contain the scope of escalation and to terminate the war before it escaped their control. Policy makers would know that they were racing a clock, with military forces under attack seeking to respond with progressively more convincing levels of retaliation; they would have to impose their controls after the first few exchanges of nuclear weapons or risk losing control altogether.

Soviet leaders have reason to doubt that U.S. and NATO European political leaders would launch immediate retaliatory strikes against forces based in the USSR or against other targets in the Soviet homeland. This statement by the author is not an argument for the incredibility of mutual deterrence; that is a different and more complicated issue. One aspect of that issue is touched upon here: that the first use of nuclear weapons by superpower or allied forces creates, above all else, ambiguity in both sides' expectations for the immediate future. In ambiguous circumstances, Soviet leaders will entertain more than one possible scenario, given their experience with the revolving door of U.S. declaratory doctrines and force-acquisition policies. Meanwhile, the Soviet command and force structure will be preparing for war by grinding through the usual alerting and mobilization procedures, which have been described in some detail for the U.S. case.[53] The better prepared they think they are for any U.S. premeditated first strike or preemption, the more Soviet leaders will be motivated to anticipate conciliatory political and military initiatives to dampen the fighting. This last suggestion goes against the historically common interpretation of World War I: that mobilization timetables felt to be inflexible by political leaders propelled them into conflict that might otherwise have been avoided.[54]

Comparisons between the period preceding 1914 and the present can be suggestive or misleading. Undoubtedly, policy makers can be the prisoners of their own war plans, if they are poorly informed about available alternatives. In this regard, one cannot be consoled by the infrequency with which U.S. presidents have familiarized themselves with the operational procedures of nuclear command and control. Nuclear weapons do make a profound difference, however, compared to 1914. Then leaders misestimated badly the capabilities of their potential opponents, despite comparatively accurate estimates of their opponents' intentions.[55] Soviet and U.S. leaders have information that is all too reliable before war begins, and after limited nuclear exchanges, if escalation is not controlled. They will be operating with a crystal ball, which imposes upon them an awareness of technological realities, if not political ones.[56] Of course, this crystal ball can raise or dampen incentives for escalation. It can motivate policy makers to fear expansion, or to encourage it out of fear that the opponent may achieve decisive results from escalating faster. Nuclear anxiety works both ways, to inhibit and promote escalation, both before and during war.

PREEMPTION

Considerations of escalation control lead naturally into a discussion of the alternative most feared by both sides during a nuclear crisis, especially a nuclear crisis following the outbreak of conventional war in Europe. By definition, a preemptive attack in those circumstances cannot come as a strategic surprise; the outbreak of conventional war provides strategic warning.[57] Strategic warning, however, is not equivalent to tactical warning, which provides evidence that an attack has been launched. Launch on receipt of tactical warning that Soviet strategic forces are on their way is a controversial policy that the United States has never foresworn as an option. A variant, launch under attack, calls for immediate retaliation against a comprehensive target set, after Soviet warheads begin detonating on U.S. soil. The President's commission on U.S. Strategic Forces (Scowcroft Commission) noted that the United States would launch ICBMs after Soviet submarine-launched ballistic missiles (SLBMs) detonated against U.S. homeland targets.[58] Launch under-attack/on-warning options are thought to be necessary for the U.S. strategic bomber and ICBM forces, whereas submarines are considered survivable against preemptive attack.

Discussions of preemption infrequently make distinctions among the types of preemption that might take place. A useful taxonomy, offered only provisionally, might distinguish among preventive war, anticipatory preemption, retaliatory preemption, and launch under attack. Preventive war is almost inconceivable with present U.S. and Soviet leadership structures, unless world conditions are perceived by either side to have deteriorated to the point of desperation (which would, however, provide strategic warning that attack was possible). Anticipatory preemption is what most U.S. analysts mean by preemptive attack. The United States attacks the USSR in the expectation that the Soviet Union has already decided to attack, although tactical warning sensors may not have detected boosters or re-entry vehicles. Retaliatory preemption follows detection of Soviet launch by U.S. warning and attack-assessment systems, although a detailed attack characterization may not be available for many minutes. It is equivalent to launch on tactical warning. Launch under attack would presumably follow a Soviet attack in which at least some warheads struck U.S. stategic forces, and other U.S. forces were then launched in order to provide for their survivability.

Soviet distinctions among preemption, launch on tactical warning/ launch under attack, and second-strike ride-out as available options are noted by Stephen M. Meyer.[59] The Soviet or U.S. decision to preempt (in the sense of anticipatory preemption, discussed above) would have to be based on an expectation that preemption paid dividends, compared to waiting. The U.S. and Soviet calculus on this point might differ, if war in Europe already involved conventional deep strikes into Eastern Europe or into the western Soviet Union. A NATO decision to disperse Pershing II and GLCM or other nuclear-capable launchers and weapons could also suggest to the USSR that these were not moves to enhance survivability, but preparations for nuclear preemption. In this regard, the Soviet perception that the Pershing II was designed to attack important components of their strategic command structure may be more significant than the actual range and accuracy of the missile.[60]

Deciding between preemption and second-strike ride-out involves some of the dilemma nicely characterized by Ashton Carter in his discussion of Type I versus Type II errors, nomenclature borrowed from statistical decision theory.[61] A Type I error would be a decision not to preempt or retaliate when either was called for; a Type II error, when preemption or retaliation was the chosen alternative, but was, in fact, unnecessary. Common sense suggests that the two error probabilities are summative and mutually exclusive; knowing one, you can immediately deduce the other. The world of nuclear decision making is not, however, as neat as statistical decision theory, and the probability of Type I or Type II errors may be determined independently, not interdependently. The priorities of policy makers are what count; in a crisis, their priorities may undergo a "risky shift" or step-level transformation, in which they are simultaneously very fearful of the consequences of war and also very determined not to be coerced. Something of this simultaneity in policy-maker perspective is apparent from records of the Cuban missile crisis, for both Kenenedy and Khrushchev. Both feared the consequences if nuclear deterrence failed, but neither wanted to acquiesce under conditions that would appear to involve personal humiliation or national appeasement. How this joint and independent probability, of fear of consequences and fear of coercion, would play itself out in a situation more complicated than that of the Cuban missile crisis is unknown, but past precedent is not necessarily encouraging.

Consider, for example, the reaction of U.S. principals in 1973 to the Soviet threat of unilateral intervention in the Mideast war, in order (presumably) to rescue the Egyptian Third Army from Israeli encirclement. The United States moved its forces onto a DEFCON 3 (Defense Condition 3) level of alert, and this is thought to have motivated the Soviet Union to take seriously the need to resolve the crisis.[62] Without doubting the seriousness of the crisis, one can wonder what Soviet leaders might have done to carry out their threats, and what the United States would have done in response, which would have provided credible political options favorable to Israeli or Egyptian interests. Soviet intervention into Egypt with airborne divisions would have left those divisions in the midst of Israeli forces, which could easily have fought and defeated them. What would the USSR do then? Naval confrontations in the Mediterranean between U.S. and Soviet forces were certainly possible, but again it is difficult to relate such a direct superpower confrontation to any outcomes that were advantageous for the regional combatants. Quite the opposite is the case. Escalation of the fighting into direct U.S.–Soviet conflict, even without nuclear weapons, would have been to the advantage of neither Egypt nor Israel. Even the regional "winner" could lose in the resulting wider war.

A more plausible analysis of this crisis is that the possibility of a U.S.–Soviet confrontation was used by the superpowers to impose a temporary cessation of the fighting on two allies who were threatening to push extended deterrence too far. The perceptions of U.S. and Soviet leaders, however, certainly included the possibility of direct intervention and war, if matters could not be resolved politically. The 1973 Mideast case may illustrate the risks of extended conventional deterrence when conventional forces to back it up are lacking, as they were felt to be by some policy makers and analysts in 1973 (the United States having no RDF/CENTCOM comparable to its present force).

This independence of perceptions, of the risks of conceding defeat, compared to the risks of nuclear preemption or intervention that risks nuclear war, implies something else. The probabilities attached to the preempt or the wait decisions by policy makers are not independent of the utilities attached to the outcomes of those events. In a situation of mutual deterrence, based on survivable strategic retaliatory forces and vulnerable cities, the utilities for both first and second strike are comparable: Losses in both cases are almost absolute.

If, however, active defenses are introduced into the situation of superpower nuclear deterrence, estimates of utilities, or rather, disutilities (negative payoffs) are more complicated. With defenses, losses are no longer absolute, regardless of the decision to strike first or second. Even a leaky or imperfect missile defense system might be very capable of blunting a retaliatory strike, despite the inadequacy of such a system for absorbing a first strike. Thus, preemption, combined with active defenses, changes the relationship between error probabilities and disutilities. Combined with defenses, preemption might make the probability of erroneous preemption seem less to be feared, because the costs of error are thought to be less catastrophic. This is probably the mechanism by which defenses could contribute to crisis instability, if they were paired with policy makers' expectations that the costs of going second were now drastically different from the costs of going first. Moreover, the better defenses are, the more acute this dilemma becomes. If defenses are sufficiently competent to remove many (but never all) U.S. or Soviet cities from their hostage condition, then the difference between first strike and second strike, however inconsequential it appears in peacetime, will seem enormous during a crisis. Of course, preemption is of less benefit to the attacker if the other side has decided to launch on warning, compared to a situation in which the defender elects to ride out the attack. Defenses might make the defender overconfident of successful ride-out, or the attacker too optimistic about absorbing a retaliatory strike.

The same complexity applies to "point" defenses designed to defend U.S. or Soviet retaliatory forces from preemptive attack. It might be supposed that defenses for retaliatory forces were automatically stabilizing according to U.S. deterrence doctrines, but the relationship between error probabilities and disutilities may defy conventional wisdom. With a retaliatory force protected by active defenses, one side can be more confident in engaging in limited nuclear options, confident of the survivability of its deterrent against preemptive attack. And if the other side also defends its retaliatory forces, then, against conventional wisdom, sub-SIOP skirmishing could become more plausible outside superpower homelands, for example, in Europe. Fears of this eventuality, of tolerable regional nuclear wars fought in Europe behind protected superpower shields, would create serious divisions within the NATO alliance.

If we think of preemption as a continuum instead of an either–or decision, then we can imagine that U.S. or Soviet policy makers could be emboldened to attack, or deterred from attacking, on the basis of the *same range of values* for given variables. This implies something different from the tendency of policy makers to see what they want to see, although that propensity should never be discounted. The problem of inferring incentives for preemption also involves a nonperceptual complication. Even events correctly perceived and adversary intentions correctly understood may lead to preemption because the best *available* information suggests that preemption "pays." Although from a precrisis standpoint such a conclusion by national leaders is an absurdity, during crises their estimates of gains and risks, of costs and benefits, may undergo logarithmic transformations from the precrisis baseline. Thus, superpower leaders could contemplate involving their forces in a Middle East war without the foggiest notion of how that war would turn out to the advantage of their respective clients, or themselves.

This recognition of changing decision matrixes and independent estimates of utilities attached to outcomes has implications for the issue of command vulnerabilty, as perceived by U.S. leaders and policy analysts. Focusing on the possibility of a small nuclear attack that somehow decapitates the United States by destroying its command structure, thus locking strategic forces into position, raises the grossest and perhaps least likely possibility.[63] The more realistic concern may be that a structured and coherent retaliation, against a comprehensive target set as defined by policy decision, may be impossible in the event. In a superpower crisis in which preemption is feared by one side or both, the possibility of disruption of the opponent's command systems looms larger than its virtual decapitation. This conclusion implies that no "cheap shot" can separate U.S. forces from their commanders or from some format for execution of an emergency action message that authorizes retaliatory launch. This is small consolation, however, if the command system is expected not only to provide for prompt and massive retaliation but also to allow for controlled and flexible nuclear exchanges, at either theater or strategic levels. It appears that strategic nuclear flexible response is more a declaratory doctrine than a doctrine that can be implemented by the command organizations of either superpower, assuming that they would even want to.

CONCLUSION

Strategic nuclear surprise has been treated by most scholars and analysts as improbable, relative to other sources of superpower conflict. Several factors account for this. The superpowers have large and diversified nuclear arsenals, which preclude a comprehensive first strike, even one designed to disarm the opponent without attacking cities. Although their command systems are physically vulnerable, compared to the more survivable components of force structures, the requirements of decapitation are by no means technically, or politically, simple. U.S. strategic nuclear forces have been sized for many years on the assumption that they must withstand surprise attacks under the most unfavorable conditions and still retaliate. Academic and other studies of the effects of nuclear war leave many readers convinced that the costs of any superpower exchange are, by definition, going to be disproportionate to any rational political objectives.

These are valid perspectives, but they do not necessarily make strategic nuclear surprise less important. The more implausible surprise seems, the more drastic its consequences, should it occur. Surprise refers not only to the basic decision to launch preemptive or retaliatory forces; under many crisis or wartime conditions, that decision might be expected by the victim. Whether this expectation can be turned to advantage is another issue. If the victim's expectation can be used to convince the prospective attacker that preemption will not pay, then it is a useful anticipation. If, however, the expectation of being attacked leads the proposed victim to jump the gun and preempt, then the awareness of possible attack has defeated itself. This might not seem so by traditional military reckoning, in which postattack firepower ratios are equated to preferred political outcomes, but this equation is different with nuclear weapons. With U.S. and Soviet societies held hostage, the advantage inherent in preemption is a very conditional one. Preemption against the opponent's strategic counterforce base does not provide escape for the attacker from devastating retaliation, although it may attenuate a prepared SIOP into a ragged response against military targets. In the absence of city protection, the hostages remain at risk from a very small proportion of the opponent's arsenal.

The largest surprise in a regional European or global nuclear conflict is that it might be stopped short of U.S.–Soviet countercity attacks against their opponents' homelands. Declaratory policies on both sides have warned that nuclear wars cannot be limited once they are started; preconflict statements probably should take this position. No national leader should stumble into a nuclear war with the expectation that controlling it or ending it will be easy. Once nuclear weapons have been fired by either NATO or Pact theater commanders, however, presumably after release has been obtained from higher authorities, expectations may change. Massive societal destruction, thought to be inevitable in the calm of peacetime, may seem avoidable if policy makers have the incentives and the techniques to prevent it. The existence of the direct communication link (Hot Line) between superpower capitals attests to the value both sides find in providing for clarification of intentions during crises. Whether the Hot Line or other methods of crisis communication can survive direct nuclear attack is probably less important than their symbolism of shared interests in avoiding wars and escalations that need not happen. In this regard, the terms "accidental" and "inadvertent" wars come to mind, except that they may not be distinguishable in a crisis from deliberate attacks, especially by the victim.[64]

This calls to mind an important point about methodology, alluded to in the introductory section. The discipline of psychology holds important insights for those who would improve their understanding of the issue of war prevention, including nuclear-war prevention. We have seen from cases noted above that misperceptions of fact and mischaracterizations of the opponent have contributed to surprise and deterrence failure. It may be that they have contributed more to the slide of crises into wars in this century than is commonly acknowledged. Richard Ned Lebow studied 26 historical cases of crisis within a conceptual framework that yielded insights into three types of crisis in particular: justification of hostility, spin-off, and brinkmanship crises.[65] In the first case, justification of hostility crises, the crisis provides a *casus belli* for war, and the decision for war is made before the crisis begins. Spin-off crises are secondary confrontations that result from a primary conflict elsewhere and/or over another issue. Brinkmanship crises, perhaps most pertinent to the nuclear

age, occur when one state challenges the commitment of another in order
to compel it to comply with demands or abandon a commitment. On the
basis of this study, Lebow concludes that the long-run, underlying causes
of wars are no more important than the proximate, short-run causes,
which can be decisive in themselves.

Whether one agrees with Lebow or not, one can appreciate the contribution he makes to clarification of the discussion. We need to distinguish preconditions of war from the immediate precipitants of it. While
the preconditions, including ideological hostility and large armaments,
may not be very responsive to short-term influences, improved understanding of the precipitants could pay large dividends. The temptation
to nuclear surprise resides in this failure to assume that precipitants are
important as long as the preconditions can be organized successfully.
Thus, mainstream analysis in the West would argue that U.S. and Soviet
arsenals of sufficiently massive size and apparent survivability should
deter even madmen from preemptive attack. The problem, however, may
not be mad leaders within an otherwise sensible system, but the other
way around: a systemic arrangement that hides madness within an apparently sensible set of protocols and balances. How resistant this system
is to bewildered leaders, combined with unprecedented crisis conditions,
is the more important issue. Nor is the problem dismissed as a matter
of preserving deterrence stability in some mechanistic relationship between arsenals. Arsenals are not threatening until they are placed in the
hands of persons whose intentions are assumed hostile by one or more
of their potential opponents. From this perspective, the superpowers
could surprise themselves, not by initiating war in ignorance of its possible
costs, but by groping through a decision process in which the costs were
not fully appreciated and the choices seemed fated, if dreadful. More than
one policy maker in history has excused decisions with a reference to
having had no other choice, and in most of these cases historians have
established that, in fact, other choices existed. Whereas behavioral scientists are inclined to speak of choices as compartmentalized entities,
however, the kinds of choices made by leaders in crises, especially nuclear
crises, may differ. Nuclear crisis has a *Gestalt* all its own, a variety of
existential dread that may draw leaders back from the brink or toward
it, like moths into flame.

Policy makers might surprise themselves by finding ways out of crises
by improvising exits or by finding ways into wars that seemed unnecessary. They might also want war to be limited below certain thresholds,
but be unable to define those thresholds or to communicate them to the
opponent. One of the most underformulated issues in this regard is the
transactional character of the relationship between U.S. and Soviet command systems. In peacetime they are on a low simmer in a posture of
watchfulness and electronic ambience. During a crisis the temperature

is progressively turned higher and the resolution of electronic, photographic, and human intelligence is increased. As crisis conditions seem to deteriorate, the resolution becomes microscopic. At some point microscopic becomes myopic, and the enlargement of a small frame leads to a distorted perception of alternatives.

Thus, national leaders who want to avert nuclear war between the superpowers or their allies need to imagine how they will turn the microscopic resolution to grosser magnification instead of finer, when their instincts suggest that war plans are inappropriate to their objectives. Conversely, military planners need to acquaint policy makers with the realistic, as opposed to hypothetical, options that can be executed by the command system, and at what stages of crisis and war. More than one U.S. president and undoubtedly more than one Soviet party chairman has found to his dismay that preferred options were colored gray instead of black or white.

Avoidance of nuclear war takes precedence over the techniques for controlling and terminating it. Yet these techniques and expectations about escalation control and war termination have a reciprocal effect on prewar planning and force building. Intrawar deterrence requires that both sides have incentives and capabilities for reciprocal targeting restraint. This implies a capacity to preserve or reconstitute viable communications and authenticated national leaderships. Nuclear surprise might be so devastating in its eruption or in its consequences that prewar plans for intrawar communications from the NCA to the Soviet high command remain unused after deterrence fails. This psychological shock to military and political principals, and not the physical damage to U.S. and Soviet command structures, will probably determine the degree of surprise experienced after nuclear attacks.

Most important, the degree of surprise inflicted upon the defender may depend on how well the diplomatic, as opposed to the military, preparations for war are undertaken. Facing a NATO coalition of voluntary national commitments, the Soviet Union, if it felt war was unavoidable, would derive maximum benefit from splitting the coalition politically before war started. A NATO deterrent is only as strong or weak as the cohesion of its political objectives. Crises stress that cohesion, and the imminent threat of war may blow it apart. This might be the largest strategic nuclear surprise of all, resulting from a crisis-born intimidation of NATO by Soviet threats that divide the alliance and induce selective cooperation with Soviet demands. When actual launch of nuclear forces might seem unreasonable for either side, the threat of war might seem plausible, counting on compliance by an adversary that had already provided indications of yielding. Therefore, nuclear threats should not be made lightly and especially not as a substitute for deterrence by conventional forces, where conventional forces are more appropriately tasked (for example, in the Persian Gulf). An overextended nuclear umbrella may surprise its holder by serving as a lightning rod for preemption. In this regard, the study of surprises based on failures of conventional deterrence might hold important implications for understanding the prospects for strategic nuclear surprise. Two such implications stand out. First, as Michael Handel has noted, under the right conditions a greater risk of surprise is actually a lesser risk. Because it seems riskier by the estimates of the defender, a bolder attack appears more improbable to the defender, and therefore, more appealing to the attacker.[66] Second, there will always be signals and cues of various sorts that surprise is afoot. In a formal sense, true bolts from the blue never happen, but bolts from the grey are common enough. In the case of strategic nuclear surprise, no attack seems worth the risk or the cost, which is precisely why, in desperate hours, it might seem attractive to the perpetrator.

NOTES

1. Crises have to do with immediate, as opposed to general, deterrence. See Patrick M. Morgan, *Deterrence: A Conceptual Analysis*, 2d ed. (Beverly Hills, CA: Sage Publications, 1983), Ch. 2.

2. Ernest R. May, *Lessons of the Past: The Use and Misuse of History in American Foreign Policy* (New York: Oxford University Press, 1973).

3. Robert Jervis, *Perception and Misperception in International Politics* Princeton, NJ: Princeton University Press, 1976).

4. See the case studies in Klaus Knorr and Patrick Morgan, eds., *Strategic Military Surprise: Incentives and Opportunities* (New Brunswick, NJ: Transaction Books, 1983).

5. The author is grateful to Daniel Goure for his suggestions with regard to this typology.

6. This distinction is suggested to the author by Patrick M. Morgan in a communication June 10, 1987.

7. See Richard Betts, "Strategic Surprise for War Termination: Inchon, Dienbienphu, and Tet," in *Strategic Military Surprise*, ed. Klaus Knorr and Patrick Morgan (New Brunswick, NJ: Transaction Books, 1983), Ch. 6, pp. 147–72.

8. Helpful clarification of terminology is provided in Paul Bracken, "Accidental Nuclear War," in Joseph S. Nye, Jr., *Hawks, Doves and Owls: An Agenda for Avoiding Nuclear War*, ed. Graham T. Allison, Albert Carnesale, and Joseph S. Nye, Jr. (New York: Norton, 1985), Ch. 2, pp. 25–53.

9. Barry R. Posen, "Inadvertent Nuclear War? Escalation and NATO's Northern Flank," in Steven E. Miller, ed., *Strategy and Nuclear Deterrence* (Princeton, NJ: Princeton University Press, 1984), pp. 85–112.

10. For an overall critique of U.S. martitime strategy and its implications, see John J. Mearsheimer, "A Strategic Misstep: The Maritime Strategy and Deterrence in Europe," *International Security* 11, No. 2 (Fall 1986): 3–57.

11. For an effective general discussion of this subject, see Phil Williams, *Crisis*

Management: Confrontation and Diplomacy in the Nuclear Age (New York: Wiley, 1976).

12. For accounts of the Cuban missile crisis, see Graham T. Allison, *Essence of Decision: Explaining the Cuban Missile Crisis* (Boston: Little, Brown, 1971); Elie Abel, *The Missile Crisis* (New York: Bantam Books, 1966); and Robert F. Kennedy, *Thirteen Days: A Memoir of the Cuban Missile Crisis* (New York: Norton, 1969). Recently declassified materials of special importance appear in McGeorge Bundy, transcriber, and James G. Blight, ed., "October 27, 1962: Transcripts of the Meetings of the Ex Comm," *International Security* 12, No. 3 (Winter 1987–88): 30–92.

13. A summary of arguments that the soviet MRBM deployment in Cuba constituted a real reversal of the strategic balance, rather than a perceptual one, appears in Allison, *Essence of Decision*, pp. 53–54. Missiles sent to Cuba were a significant addition to Soviet forces capable of reaching the United States, according to this argument, since the United States was outside the range of MRBMs based in the Soviet Union and Soviet ICBM deployment lagged behind the U.S. pace. The deployment of 48 MRBMs and 24 IRBMs (intermediate range ballistic missiles) in Cuba would double Soviet first-strike capabilities against the United States. The missiles could attack much of the United States before effective warning was made available, because they outflanked the U.S. Ballistic Missile Early Warning System (BMEWS).

These arguments are plausible considerations for military planners who might worry about Soviet crisis incentives for preemption, but they disregard the importance of the relationship between homeland-based U.S. and Soviet strategic capabilities, which is more important. Also neglected are the differences between second-strike and first-strike weapons in terms of their deterrent value; the Soviet MRBMs and IRBMs in Cuba could have been destroyed preemptively with conventional weapons.

14. Lawrence Freedman, *The Evolution of Nuclear Strategy* (New York: St. Martin's Press, 1981), Ch. 9. Khrushchev's motives for deploying missiles in Cuba, as he explains them, included deterrence of U.S. attacks and posing first-strike threats against even one or two U.S. cities. See Strobe Talbott, ed. and trans., *Khrushchev Remembers* (Boston: Little, Brown, 1970), pp. 492–95.

15. For interesting reflections on Cuba, see Roger Hilsman, *The Politics of Policy Making in Defense and Foreign Affairs* (Englewood Cliffs, NJ: Prentice-Hall, 1986), pp. 2–5, 17–19. Hilsman notes that the two explanations most logical from the standpoint of a rational policy model, a "quick fix" of the strategic balance and a "cold war probe" of U.S. resolve, are logically assailable and inconsistent. U.S. actions in the crisis are no more understandable. Briefings for NATO allies "including those who were probably penetrated by KGB agents" assured that the USSR would receive information about U.S. perceptions of Soviet strategic inferiority. This decision was made "in the full knowledge that the information that the United States knew the true situation would alarm the Soviets and compel them to take some form of countermeasure." (pp. 4–5)

16. For an alternative interpretation of Soviet motivations in the Cuban missile crisis (which is not inconsistent with the author's, but has a very different emphasis), see Richard Ned Lebow, "The Cuban Missile Crisis: Reading the Lessons Correctly," *Political Science Quarterly* 98, No. 3 (Fall 1983): 431–58. Lebow

emphasizes the importance of psychological motivations for Soviet leaders' behavior and the possibililty that their decisions can be understood as characteristic of brinksmanship crises. A principal shortcoming in U.S. (and possibly Soviet) deliberations during the Cuban crisis was the failure to perceive value trade-offs between the costs of conciliation and the risks of escalation. See Robert Jervis, "Deterrence and Perception," in *Strategy and Nuclear Deterrence*, ed. Steven E. Miller (Princeton, NJ: Princeton University Press, 1984), pp. 57–84, esp. pp. 76–77.

17. Martin van Creveld, *Supplying War: Logistics from Wallenstein to Patton* (Cambridge: Cambridge University Press, 1977), pp. 61–74. Napoleon did not neglect logistic factors in planning the invasion of Russia, but his planning was inadequate to the obstacles and limitations created by technical means of that age.

18. A.J.P. Taylor comments, à propos the outbreak of World War I, that "we have tended to look too much for the deeper causes of war and neglect its immediate outbreak. Despite these deeper causes, individual men took the decisions and sent the declarations of war.... If two or three men had acted differently, war would not have occurred at that particular moment." Taylor, *From Napoleon to Lenin*, Historical Essays (New York: Harper Torch Books, 1952), p. 157. This is perhaps reductionist, but it makes a valid point about accountability as perceived by historians and felt by policy makers.

19. Barry R. Posen, *The Sources of Military Doctrine: France, Britain and Germany Between The World Wars* (Ithaca, NY: Cornell University Press, 1984), esp. Ch. 2.

20. Ernest R. May, "Conclusions," in *Knowing One's Enemies: Intelligence Assessment before the Two World Wars*, ed. May (Princeton, NJ: Princeton University Press, 1984), p. 504.

21. May, "Cabinet, Tsar, Kaiser: Three Approaches to Assessment," in *Knowing One's Enemies*, pp. 11–36.

22. Ibid., pp. 16–17.

23. Ibid., pp. 17–26.

24. Ibid., p. 31.

25. Michael Geyer, "National Socialist Germany: The Politics of Information," in *Knowing One's Enemies*, ed. Ernest May, Ch. 11, pp. 310–46.

26. John Erickson, "Threat Identification and Strategic Appraisal by the Soviet Union, 1930–1941," in May, ed., *Knowing One's Enemies*, ed. Ernest May, Ch. 13, pp. 375–423, esp. pp. 398, 403.

27. David Kahn, "The United States Views Germany and Japan in 1941," in *Knowing One's Enemies*, ed. Ernest May, Ch. 16, pp. 476–501; citation from pp. 476–77. Kahn disputes Wohlstetter's contention that the ratio of "noise" to "signals" was responsible for the Japanese surprise at Pearl Harbor (p. 500).

28. Irving L. Janis, *Groupthink* (Boston: Houghton Mifflin, 1982), p. 85.

29. John Erickson, "The Soviet View of Deterrence: A General Survey," *Survival* 24, No. 6 (November-December 1982):242–51.

30. See Fritz W. Ermarth, "Contrasts in American and Soviet Strategic Thought," in *Soviet Military Thinking*, ed. Derek Leebaert (London: Allen and Unwin, 1981), pp. 50–69.

31. See Stephen M. Meyer, "Soviet Perspectives on the Paths to Nuclear War,"

in *Hawks, Doves and Owls: An Agenda for Avoiding Nuclear War*, ed. Graham T. Allison et al. (New York: Norton, 1985), pp. 167–205.

32. U.S. war plans prior to the Kennedy administration are reviewed in David Alan Rosenberg, "The Origins of Overkill: Nuclear Weapons and American Strategy, 1945–1960," in Steven E. Miller, ed., *Strategy anad Nuclear Deterrence* (Princeton, NJ: Princeton University Press, 1984), pp. 113–82.

33. See David N. Schwartz, *NATO's Nuclear Dilemmas* (Washington, DC: Brookings Institution, 1983).

34. Informative discussions can be found in Stanley R. Sloan, *NATO's Future: Toward a New Transatlantic Bargain* (Washington, DC: National Defense University Press, 1985), and Gregory F. Treverton, *Making the Alliance Work: The United States and Western Europe* (Ithaca, NY: Cornell University Press, 1985).

35. The relationship between Soviet and Western expectations with regard to crossing the nuclear threshold in Europe is discussed in Joseph D. Douglass, Jr., *Soviet Military Strategy in Europe* (New York: Pergamon Press, 1980), pp. 110–11. According to Douglass, "in effect, the Soviet approach can be viewed as learning how to fight a conventional war from a nuclear war posture, in contrast to the Western approach of fighting an initial phase of a nuclear war from a conventional posture" (p. 111). Some observers have suggested, however, that the Soviet view is changing, although there is still controversy within the hierarchy. Marshal N.V. Ogarkov, formerly military chief of staff and deputy defense minister of the USSR, apparently favored modernization of conventional forces as a priority compared to nuclear forces. See Dusko Doder, "Ex-Soviet Military Chief Reportedly Back in Favor," *Philadelphia Inquirer* (Washington Post News Service), July 18, 1985, p. 13-A, for an interesting, although debatable, account. Recent changes in the Soviet command structure, with implications for fighting a conventional war in Europe, are noted in John G. Hines and Phillip A. Petersen, "The Changing Soviet System of Control for Theater War," *Signal* 41, No. 4 (December 1986): 97–110.

36. See John G. Hines, Phillip A. Petersen, and Notra Trulock III, "Soviet Military from 1945–2000: Implications for NATO," *Washington Quarterly* 9, No. 4 (Fall 1986): 117–37.

37. See Meyer, "Soviet Perspectives on the Paths to Nuclear War," pp. 184–85.

38. The concept of coercive diplomacy is explained in Gordon A. Craig and Alexander L. George, *Force and Statecraft* (New York: Oxford University Press, 1983), Ch. 14.

39. On Soviet nuclear targeting, see William T. Lee, "Soviet Nuclear Targeting Strategy," in *Strategic Nuclear Targeting*, ed. Desmond Ball and Jeffrey Richelson (Ithaca, NY: Cornell University Press, 1986), Ch. 4; and William T. Lee and Richard F. Staar, *Soviet Military Policy Since World War II* (Stanford, CA: Hoover Institution, 1986), Ch. 8.

40. On possible NATO reactions to Soviet surprise attack, see Richard K. Betts, *Surprise Attack*, (Washington, DC: Brookings Institution, 1982), Chs. 6 and 7; and P. H. Vigor, *Soviet Blitzkrieg Theory* (New York: St. Martin's Press, 1983), Chs. 1 and 14.

41. On the value of games and exercises, see Thomas C. Schelling, "The Role of War Games and Exercises," in *Managing Nuclear Operations*, ed. Ashton B.

Carter, John D. Steinbruner, and Charles A. Zraket (Washington, DC: Brookings Institution, 1987), Ch. 13, pp. 426–44.

42. A useful discussion on this subject is Fen Osler Hampsen, "Escalation in Europe," in *Hawks, Doves and Owls*, ed. Allison et al., Ch. 4.

43. A critique of Reagan strategy on this point appears in Joshua M. Epstein, "Horizontal Escalation: Sour Notes on a Recurrent Theme," *International Security* 8, No. 3 (Winter 1983–84): 19–31. One of the difficulties in applying horizontal escalation to contemporary U.S.-Soviet confrontations is that horizontal expansion of the conflict would occur while nuclear forces of the superpowers were being alerted, with attendant implications for crisis stability, unless the horizontal targets were inconsequential.

44. The command and control of NATO nuclear forces in Europe is examined by Bracken, *The Command and Control of Nuclear Forces*, Ch. 5.

45. With regard to Soviet operational planning for suppression of artillery and other fires, including nuclear ones, see Erickson et al., *Soviet Ground Forces*, pp. 171–75.

46. Western and Soviet approaches to escalation are compared in Paul K. Davis and Peter J. E. Stan, *Concepts and Models of Escalation*, (Santa Monica, CA: Rand Strategy Assessment Center, May 1984).

47. Stephen J. Cimbala, "Countercommand Attacks and War Termination," in *Strategic War Termination*, ed. Cimbala (New York: Praeger, 1986), Ch. 7.

48. Marshal N.V. Ogarkov, *History Teaches Vigilance* (Voyenizdat: 1985), JPRS-UMA–85–021-L, p. 59.

49. Harold Brown, "Our Countervailing Strategic Strategy," *Defense 80* (Washington, DC: Department of Defense, October 1980), p. 9.

50. See Paul Bracken, "Delegation of Nuclear Command Authority," in *Managing Nuclear Operations*, ed. Carter, Steinbruner, and Zraket, Ch. 10.

51. Albert Wohlstetter and Richard Brody argue that protracted U.S.–Soviet SIOP-RISOP exchanges are improbable compared to the more selective and limited nuclear attacks growing out of conventional war in Europe. Moreover, the first use of nuclear weapons might make national leaders more cautious rather than less: "It is most unlikely that Western political leaders who exhibit such great caution in a peacetime crisis or during modest conventional engagements with a lesser adversary would throw caution to the winds when the first nuclear weapon was used by the Soviets." See Wohlstetter and Brody, "Continuing Control as a Requirement for Deterring," in *Managing Nuclear Operations*, ed. Carter, Steinbruner, and Zraket, p. 185. If, however, the USSR is introducing nuclear weapons, rather than the West, there is no reason to suppose that flexible and restrained nuclear wars are any more probable than other kinds. For counterarguments, see Stephen J. Cimbala, "Flexible Targeting, Escalation Control and War in Europe, *Armed Forces and Society* 12, No. 3 (Spring 1986): 383–400; and Cimbala, "Soviet Blitzkrieg in Europe: The Abiding Nuclear Dimension," *Strategic Review* 4, No. 3 (Summer 1986): 67–76.

52. The development of Soviet views on limited nuclear warfare is reviewed by Notra Trulock III, "Soviet Perspectives on Limited Nuclear Warfare." Unpublished paper forthcoming in Trulock, *Soviet Perspectives on Limited Nuclear Warfare*, European-American Institute.

53. See Bruce G. Blair, "Alerting in Crisis and Conventional War," in *Man-*

aging Nuclear Operations, ed. Carter et al., Ch. 3; and Scott D. Sagan, "Nuclear Alerts and Crisis Management," *International Security* 9 (Spring 1985): 99–139.

54. Barbara W. Tuchman, *The Guns of August* (New York: Macmillan, 1962) is an important primary source. There is still considerable controversy about whether war plans of the major powers were among the principal causes of war; the contention that offensively oriented plans and military doctrines contributed to crisis instability is not undisputed. See Scott D. Sagan, "1914 Revisited: Allies, Offense and Instability," *International Security* 11, No. 2 (Fall 1986): 151–75. Controversy surrounds the German Schlieffen Plan, which is frequently misexplained. Schlieffen built upon the *kesselschlacht* (encirclement) doctrine of von Moltke, but attached to it more ambitious objectives. Whereas von Moltke expected German forces and resources to be adequate for a war of limited aims against France and Russia, followed by a negotiated peace, von Schlieffen believed that Germany could totally defeat France and Russia in a two-front war. See Larry H. Addington, *The Blitzkrieg Era and the German General Staff, 1865–1941* (New Brunswick, NJ: Rutgers University Press, 1971), pp. 6–17. Richard Ned Lebow notes that the German chancellor and the kaiser "possessed neither the courage nor good sense to alter their policy in mid-crisis," and their actions on the eve of war were marked by "irresolution, bewilderment, and loss of self-confidence." See Lebow, "Windows of Opportunity: Do States Jump Through Them?" *International Security* 9, No. 1 (Summer 1984): pp. 147–86, esp. p. 166.

55. May, "Cabinet, Tsar, Kaiser," *passim*.

56. Albert Carnesale, Paul Doty, Stanley Hoffman, Samuel P. Huntington, Joseph S. Nye, Jr., and Scott Sagan, *Living with Nuclear Weapons* (New York: Bantam Books, 1983), esp. pp. 43–44.

57. Richard K. Betts, "Surprise Attack and Preemption," in *Hawks, Doves and Owls*, ed. Allison et al., Ch. 3.

58. Some observers feel that the United States has a *de facto* launch on warning or first-strike doctrine. See Robert C. Aldridge, *First Strike: The Pentagon's Strategy for Nuclear War* (Boston: South End Press, 1983); and Daniel Ford, *The Button* (New York: Simon & Schuster, 1985). Launch under attack occurs in response to tactical warning that attack is in progress; there is some doubt that it can be accomplished for portions of the U.S. strategic force. See Carter, "Assessing Command System Vulnerabilities," in *Managing Nuclear Operations*, ed. Carter et al., pp. 578–80. The United States might have as little as ten minutes, following Soviet ICBM launch against U.S. silos, to execute LUA successfully; see John Steinbruner, "Launch under Attack," *Scientific American* 250 (January 1984): 37–47; and Office of Technology Assessment, *MX Missile Basing* (Washington, DC: U.S. GPO, 1981), pp. 147–64 (authored by Ashton Carter). LUA differs from positive-control launch for the bomber force; PCL can be undertaken even before an attack has been confirmed, because bombers can be returned to base. See Carter, "Assessing Command System Vulnerabilities," p. 583. Apparently, U.S. normal peacetime levels of alert (DEFCON 4 and 5) permit ICBM launch-crew members to sleep on duty; a DEFCON 3 message "literally might awaken the Minuteman launch crews, an obvious precondition for rapid firing of the forces" (Blair, "Alerting in Crisis and Conventional War," p. 85. See also President's commission on U.S. Strategic Forces (Scowcroft Commission), *Report* (Washington: April 1983).

59. Meyer, "Soviet Perspectives on the Paths to Nuclear War," pp. 177–80.

60. John Erickson, "The Soviet View of Deterrence: A General Survey," *Survival* 24, No. 6 (November/December 1982): 242–51, esp. pp. 246, 248.

61. Ashton B. Carter, "Sources of Error and Uncertainty," in *Managing Nuclear Operations*, ed. Carter et al., Ch. 18, pp. 626–33.

62. See Barry M. Blechman and Douglas M. Hart, "The Political Utility of Nuclear Weapons: The 1973 Middle East Crisis," in ed. Steven E. Miller, *Strategy and Nuclear Deterrence* (Princeton, NJ: Princeton University Press, 1984) pp. 273–97. The U.S. response to a unilateral threat of intervention by Soviet conventional forces was to threaten "incalculable consequences," meaning that inadvertent nuclear war was felt to be a possible outcome of any such Soviet action (p. 282). Undoubtedly, the USSR took this responses seriously as an indication of U.S. annoyance; whether they were actually intimidated is less certain.

63. Carter, "Assessing Command System Vulnerability," pp. 560–67, reviews a national list of U.S. strategic C^3I targets. See also William C. Martel, "Exchange Calculus of Strategic Nuclear War," in *Strategic War Termination*, ed. Stephen J. Cimbala (New York: Praeger, 1986), Ch. 1, p. 16, Table 1.4.

64. Paul Bracken, "Accidental Nuclear War," in *Hawks, Doves and Owls*, ed. Allison et al., Ch. 2.

65. See Richard Ned Lebow, *Between Peace and War* (Baltimore, MD: Johns Hopkins University Press, 1981); and "Decision Making in Crises," in *Psychology and the Prevention of Nuclear War*, ed. Ralph K. White (New York: New York University Press, 1986), pp. 397–413. Other influential applications of concepts from psychology to crisis and deterrence problems include Robert Jervis, *Perception and Misperception in International Politics* (Princeton, NJ: Princeton University Press, 1976); Alexander L. George and Richard Smoke, *Deterrence in American Foreign Policy: Theory and Practice* (New York: Columbia University Press, 1974); Irving L. Janis, *Groupthink*, 2d ed. (Boston: Houghton Mifflin, 1982); Joseph de Rivera, *The Psychological Dimension of Foreign Policy* (Columbus, OH: Charles E. Merrill, 1968); several studies of the Cuban missile crisis, including Allison's *Essence of Decision*, cited above; and Knorr and Morgan, *Strategic Military Surprise*, cited above. On deterrence and rationality in particular, see Patrick M. Morgan, *Deterrence: A Conceptual Analysis*, 2d ed. (Beverly Hills, CA: Sage Publications, 1983), Chs. 4 and 5.

66. Michael I. Handel, *Perception, Deception and Surprise: The Case of the Yom Kippur War* (Jerusalem: Hebrew University of Jerusalem, Jerusalem Papers on Peace Problems, 1976), p. 16. According to Handel's Paradox No. 2, "The greater the risk, the less likely it seems, and the less risky it actually becomes. Thus, the greater the risk, the smaller it becomes." See also Patrick M. Morgan, *Deterrence: A Conceptual Analysis* (Beverly Hills, CA: Sage Publications, 1983), pp. 182–83; and Robert Jervis, "Deterrence and Perception," in *Strategy and Nuclear Deterrence*, ed. Stephen Miller, pp. 57–84, esp. pp. 74–76.

10

ARMS CONTROL AND U.S. NUCLEAR STRATEGY

Nuclear deterrence does not depend totally upon rationality; if it did, it would be much more fragile. Still, the discussion of nuclear strategy as strategizing, as a best-guess approximation to real strategy making, is an appropriate prelude to the subject of arms control. Arms control is a subject to which almost everyone gives lip service, but which few have taken the trouble to understand. The general public confuses arms control with disarmament, and even specialists lament the fact that arms control has not brought about large reductions in superpower nuclear forces. Arms control has been abandoned even by some of its strongest advocates, when it could not produce outcomes that were desired for the sake of what they symbolized, instead of what they could contribute to U.S. nuclear strategy.

The purposes of arms control are, as already noted, to limit the risk of unwanted war, to reduce the costs of war if deterrence fails, and to limit arms races. Now, the beginning of wisdom on this topic is to recognize that not all wars occur on account of deterrence failures. Nor can all wars be prevented by arms control. Of course, those wars not prevented by arms control could have been prevented if states were totally disarmed, and so could any wars, but then disarmed states would not survive for long in the present and recent past international system, so they would be historical anomalies, or curiosities. And arms control is not disarmament, anyway. An example of a war that could not have been prevented by deterrence was Hitler's aggression against Poland, then Western Europe, and finally against the USSR in World War II. It is customary to attribute Hitler's aggressive designs to the mistaken appeasement of the German dictator by his eventual opponents at Munich.

This, however, is a misreading of Hitler's objectives, which were not satisfied with a political or diplomatic extension of German influence in Western Europe, but eventually included total military subjugation of Eurasia. Hitler's timing might have been influenced by the status of his adversaries' military preparedness and the firmness of their political resolution, but Hitler wanted war, and peace was for him an unwelcome interlude before the clash of arms proved the inherent superiority of the German system and people.

The example of Hitler might seem extreme, but others have been beyond deterrence at one time or another in history. So to task arms control with the prevention of those wars on which policy makers are bent, for the sake of motives that are statist, personal, or some mixture of the two, is unfair. This much we can learn from the history of deterrence failures in conventional warfare, although the prenuclear history must be carefully transferred into the nuclear age, and only with amendment. Although prenuclear history can help us to see why deterrence failures occur, conditions now differ, especially in crises involving the nuclear superpowers and the possible use of their own military forces against each other. It is to that special problem that nuclear arms control should be primarily addressed, although the equally serious problem of proliferation deserves worldwide attention. We might say that the problem of U.S.–Soviet arms control is the immediate issue and the problem of proliferation is the long-run issue. The second issue is related to the first by dint of necessity, for if the first is not maintained at least in equilibrium, then the second issue, proliferation, is more difficult to handle. Superpowers running an unrestrained arms race are not in a good position to persuade others to do without nuclear weapons.

What follows will not review the history of U.S.–Soviet arms-control negotiations in detail, since that has been done elsewhere.[1] The emphasis in this discussion will be placed on mismatched expectations and other misunderstandings about what arms control can accomplish. The United States approaches arms control in its characteristic national style, and that style, together with the unavoidable features of the U.S. policy-making process in general, exerts a substantial influence on arms-control policy.[2] Some of what is said below will not be acceptable or pleasurable reading for arms-control specialists, nor for some professional U.S. military strategists. Nothing said is intended to call into question the professional competence of individuals, or the commitment of national military and political leaders to a safer world, in principle. That the task is frequently gone about so wretchedly is a problem of poor understanding, not felonious intent.

NUCLEAR NUMISMATICS

The first problem with superpower arms control negotiations is that they have been conducted as if two traders with hoards of rare coins were negotiating about which they would be willing to swap or do without. The U.S. and Soviet arsenals are not properties in the same way that parts of a Monopoly board are. They are not traditional weapons for seizing a hill or boarding a ship. They are shadows of death pointed at civilizations, including noncombatant civilizations. This is the very reason for their importance, and treating nuclear weapons as simply more destructive versions of other weapons obscures this point. Thus, SALT and START negotiations are not only about which side will emerge with the larger comparative indexes of counterforce, survivable warheads, or throw-weight. They are also about the gap between the superpowers and the rest of the world, including the allies of the two nuclear-armed giants. Witness the anxiety of European members of NATO during the 1970s, especially the West Germans, at the prospect of SALT having established formal strategic nuclear parity between U.S. and Soviet forces.

Nuclear weapons are hegemonic weapons for the Soviet Union and the United States and, to give them up or reduce them drastically, each or both will have to accept the possibility of reducing its global influence, relative to that of competitors. The major reason for having nuclear weapons in the abundance that the United States and the Soviet Union have come to possess them is for their peacetime, rather than wartime, uses. Nuclear weapons are the ticket of admission to the big leagues, and the biggest league of all is the superpower level of competition. Peacetime coercion and influence are the payoffs from nuclear weapons, and as the French have shown in their military investment policies of the 1980s, these peacetime payoffs from having nuclear weapons in significant numbers are considerable. The independent strategic nuclear force of France has provided consultative access to important alliance decisions, even while preserving a strategic independence, to a point, of the two superpowers. Only the United States and the USSR, however, can expect to have the diverse and survivable strategic nuclear forces of their current sizes and to pay for their expensive upkeep. This maintains a nuclear hegemony over other states, including their "allies" in the West or fraternal Socialist comrades in the East. Superpower nuclear forces are hegemonic forces only to an extent, however; nuclear weapons are not a universal solvent for lack of coherent policy. And the more important distinction between superpower and other nuclear forces is in the diversity and survivability of their delivery systems, not their weapons. The weapons themselves are relatively inexpensive.

If the U.S. and Soviet nuclear forces are in part hegemonic forces with regard to other aspiring or existing nuclear powers, then drastic reductions in those forces, unless carefully thought out, could reduce stability instead of increasing it. Arms-race stability has both vertical and horizontal dimensions. The vertical dimension is the piling up of superpower inventories beyond those levels necessary for stable deterrence. The horizontal dimension is the proliferation of nuclear arsenals worldwide. Both vertical and horizontal dimensions also apply to the problem of crisis stability. The superpowers have, after several decades of consultation and negotiation, developed a dialogue on important issues of nuclear strategy. And they have institutionalized expectations and procedures to prevent a crisis from getting out of hand as a result of misunderstanding about one another's intentions. Like disputatious spouses, they often communicate very well with one another without the necessity of speaking a single word. The Soviets deploy a certain new radar or missile, which they know eventually the United States will detect, and when the predictable issues are raised in the Standing Consultative Commission, the Soviets respond with their prepared rationale, which receives the expected U.S. skepticism, and so forth. This continuing dialogue is not just talk for its own sake, as is sometimes supposed, for it establishes a fabric of shared connotations and meanings that outlives the terms of individual U.S. presidents or Soviet party general secretaries.

This institutionalization of expectations, about the continuation of an arms-control conversation according to commonly understood denotations and connotations, should not be confused with other things. Institutionalized expectations are not the same as agreements, although they are probably preconditions for agreements. A results-oriented Western culture is always asking for perpetual progress, preferably progress that can be charted and measured in increments. Other cultures are often more tolerant of cyclical processes, in which progress and regress alternate on single issues, but the process of negotiation continues over the long run. The U.S. public, news media, and Congress have been led by their culture to expect the arms-control "batting average" to improve, or to draw the conclusion that the effort is wasted. The same frame of mind runs U.S. business into obstacle courses in Japanese culture, where the sense of hurriedness to conclude a deal is in contrast to the Japanese preference for courtesy and familiarity before real bargaining begins.

Indeed, the U.S. notion of bargaining is that borrowed from labor–management negotiations, as they are conducted between the United Auto Workers and General Motors, but this is not the Soviet notion of arms-control (or any other) bargaining. Labor–management negotiations involve two parties from the same cultural background who are negotiating about how to divide the pie. In arms-control negotiations, the question is more often, What is the pie? or Whose pie is it? These latter questions bedevil U.S. negotiators who are representing NATO in issues such as the deployment of theater nuclear forces in Europe. Even the SALT I and II negotiations took place in a formally bilateral, but actually multilateral, framework, since the European NATO states are always looking over the shoulders of U.S. arms-control negotiators, in case the U.S. should conclude an agreement that is to their (Europeans') disadvantage. A perfect example is provided by the negotiations between U.S. President Ronald

Reagan and Soviet General Secretary Mikhail Gorbachev at Reykjavik, Iceland, in 1986. There, the U.S. president apparently agreed to future negotiations about strategic arms reductions, on the basis of an intended objective of 50 percent reductions in both sides' strategic nuclear forces within five years, and total elimination of their strategic ballistic missile forces within ten.[3] Some leading Europeans were annoyed and alarmed that the United States would go so far, even in principle, in the direction of denuclearizing their arsenals, before consulting their allies about the implications for extended deterrence in Western Europe.[4]

STRATEGIC DIVERGENCE

If the first source of confusion about arms control is idiomatic, in the misplaced expectation of bargaining over marginal increments of valued objects, the second confusion is about the character of Soviet, as compared to U.S., strategic doctrine. The topic of strategic doctrine is itself controversial, and one might say with only slight exaggeration that the United States has no single doctrine for the use of strategic nuclear forces, or for the use of forces in general. Some of the reasons for this state of affairs have been described in earlier discussions of servicism, but the problem of getting at a consensual U.S. strategic military doctrine is as nothing compared to the reconciliation of differences between U.S. and Soviet understandings.

No reconciliation may, in fact, be possible, but an improved appreciation of the Soviet perspective on strategy, as it relates to the prospects for nuclear arms control, is necessary. It is necessary whether or not agreements on arms reductions can be reached in the near term. The same misunderstandings of Soviet strategy that make arms control discussions so tedious might also lead to crisis instability and ultimately to war. Thus, the Soviet view of strategic doctrine is worth noting for reasons of pragmatic as well as academic interest. In addition, clarification of the U.S. understanding of Soviet reasoning may in turn lead to the clearer perception by the USSR of Western analytical thinking, which must strike them as confusing, or confused, more often than not.

The first issue having to do with Soviet nuclear doctrine or strategy is that when Soviet military writers refer to strategy, they mean strategy in the fullest sense, or the connection between force and policy. This they have learned from Lenin and Clausewitz, as well as a pantheon of home-grown Soviet military theoreticians and leading party spokesmen.[5] From this commitment, to the tight rather than loose connection between force and policy, all else follows. Peace and war are not antithethical states of affairs, but alternating faces of a cotinuous political process. The peace-time political struggle, as the term "peace" is understood in the West, is of a piece with the wartime contest, although the means differ. The object of Soviet strategy, in peace or in war, is the mind of the opponent, represented by the opponent's military commanders and political leadership. If necessary, the opponent's commanders and leaders can be destroyed but, more frequently, they can be influenced.

It follows from this understanding of war and peace that no war, including nuclear war, is the end of history. The only historical eschatology acceptable in the Marxist catechism is the eventual triumph of communism, which cannot be prevented by accidents of war or diplomacy. Wars that are poorly fought, however, or diplomatic blunders that contribute to inexpedient wars, can be avoided. Stalin's errors in failing to anticipate Hitler's attack on the USSR in 1941, and his failure to prepare the Soviet armed forces for the form of that attack and its disastrous impacts, are cited by his successors as personal blunders, not historically determined mistakes. This sense of history as unfolding according to script is made compatible with its seeming opposite, the requirement for Soviet leaders to assist history by making the correct political decisions and military judgments. This seeming inconsistency in Soviet strategy partakes of some of the same strategizing earlier attributed to Western military thought, but from a very different historical and cultural stance.

The compatibility between historically determined triumph of the Communist system and the voluntaristic assistance provided by Soviet marshals is more apparent than real, considered, as it must be, within the overall framework of Soviet geopolitical ambitions and historical experience.[6] What is being prophesied in Marxist-Leninist political thinking is the eventual triumph of a certain way of producing and distributing things, not the final conquest of the entire planet by Soviet armies. In fact, Soviet historical experience suggests to them that their forces have fought very effectively on the defensive, when Russia or the USSR has been invaded, but with mixed results when on the offensive, from the Crimea to Afghanistan. So, theirs is a waiting game, and its is from Marx that Soviet leaders derive the certainty of their victory, which is a displacement of one model of economic development by another and superior model. Needless to say, and much to the posthumous embarrassment of Marx and Lenin, capitalism does not appear to be in its death throes; to the contrary, it jiggles along, consuming its way into some form that is more postindustrial welfare state than it is warfare state. If Marx could be returned alive to witness twentieth-century capitalism, at least in its U.S. variety, he might decide that the game was not worth the candle, capitalism having turned itself into a litigious service station. This is speculative, however, and Marx will never resolve it for us.

What is less speculative is that the USSR is not in a hurry to resolve its issues with the capitalist world by conducting an ultimate and decisive clash of arms, and certainly, any decisive confrontation is to be avoided, unless and until capitalism has begun to show signs of its own terminal decay. Moreover, were the Soviets to contemplate aggressive war against the United States or Europe, it would be more likely to follow the political defection of one or more members of NATO from the alliance and the defector's invitation to the USSR for a treaty of friendship or something similar. Without a change in the political constellation between Eastern and Western Europe, a Soviet attack on Western Europe would be a gambling of Socialist imperium on a very risky throw of the dice.

This recognition, that the USSR is unlikely to attack the West unless the political terrain has been properly prepared beforehand, leads to another. The overall strategic position of the USSR, relative to that of the United States and its allies, is inferior and in danger of weakening. Now, this assessment will produce immediate howls of disbelief from Pentagon pundits and NATO threat assessors, but consider. Against the Soviet Union in the political firmament are aligned, actually or potentially, the United States, NATO Europe, the People's Republic of China, Japan, and the nuclear arsenals of France and Britain, the former not being included in NATO planning, but a counter on the board for the Soviets to contend with, nevertheless. If this correlation of forces faced the United States, we would certainly be expecting the worst, should a major war break out. The Soviets have, despite their commitment to a proper understanding of history, ignored the elementary law of conservation of enemies. From Stalin's time to the present, they have antagonized potential neutrals or even allies. Consider the 1970s, in which the Soviets can be said to have advanced their cause in Angola, Ethiopia, Mozambique, South Yemen, and other targets of opportunity, not to mention U.S. concern about the future direction of the regime in Nicaragua. The Soviet chess masters, however, while sweeping these pawns from the board, lost two much more important pieces, the PRC and Egypt, which have encumbered their policy decisions on more important fronts ever since. This is not the way to play "the great game," as the British used to call it, and the Kremlin's military might is for naught if it continues to turn potential gains into losses in other important regions.

Thus, another characteristic of Soviet military doctrine, its emphasis on the importance of defense, is misunderstood in Western representations of the Soviet perspective. The Soviets are on the defensive in the sense that the correlation of forces globally, including the correlation of military forces, is moving against them, although not irrevocably. Starting from this defensive position, they adopt an offensive approach to military operations, to wit, hitting the opponent very early and with as much muscle as is possible under the circumstances. This leads to an emphasis on preemption, on striking at the forces of the opponent in nuclear as well as conventional war, if it seems apparent that the opponent is planning to attack. Never again will the USSR suffer the surprise and humiliation of Barbarossa, at least not if it can be helped.[7] An interest in nuclear preemption is taken by Western observers to be a Soviet commitment to starting war on the smallest provocation, but in fact, the interest in preemption reflects the expectation of being surprised, and the determination to do something to prevent it or mitigate it. The Soviet interest in ballistic missile and atmospheric defenses has been a constant preoccupation of its leadership, very much in contrast to the episodic ups and downs of U.S. interest, precisely because the Soviet leadership feels that war might be started despite their efforts to avoid it.[8]

Further to the issue of Soviet expectations of war, as related to their military doctrine, is the question of whether they expect to win a nuclear war with the West.[9] Perhaps no issue has stirred so much controversy within the U.S. strategic community, which is forever parsing Soviet military writings in the hope of resolving the issue of their leaders' intent once and for all. Soviet active and passive defenses, however, including civil defenses, are clues to their way of thinking about all war, even nuclear war of the most destructive kind. A Marxist state exists in a hostile world, by definition; therefore, it may be subject to attack at any time. Preparedness cannot be overdone, only complacency. From this standpoint, peacetime preparations for wartime survival of the Soviet command structure, which might seem ominous (or farcical) from the Western standpoint, make perfect sense as seen from Moscow. Peacetime war preparedness, including preparedness for the worst of wars, reinforces in the public mind the conviction that the state will protect its armed forces and society from destruction, whatever the cost proves to be. To do otherwise is to acknowledge that the applecart of history, supposedly moving toward fulfillment of Soviet global objectives, can be overturned by imperialist strategy.

Having gone this far with what might be termed "hawkish" misconceptions of Soviet strategy, we might turn to the "dovish." These might seem more innocuous, but no such judgment is offered here. All misconceptions of Soviet strategy serve the cause of misunderstanding, at a minimum, and create potential causes of war beyond the minimum.

The first of these dovish U.S. misconceptions of Soviet strategy and doctrine is the expectation that the USSR will come to endorse mutual vulnerability of U.S. and Soviet societies as the key to stable deterrence. The idea of mutual vulnerability of societies is an abstraction that appeals to Western strategists who have confused a condition that is unavoidable with current technology, on one hand, with a Soviet or U.S. preference for that condition, on the other.[10] Mutual assured destruction or mutual vulnerability became a U.S. declaratory but not operational policy for a time during the 1960s, when U.S. leaders sought to get superpower arms-control talks moving and to limit the growth of U.S. strategic forces beyond perceived essential military requirements. It was important to establish, in the U.S. debates over the concept of assured destruction, that there was a point beyond which additional strategic nuclear forces, over and above those already deployed, were superfluous for destroying meaningful targets in retaliation for Soviet attack.

This perfectly laudable sentiment, that the military services should be restrained in their appetitive instincts for forces that policy planners regarded as unnecessary, became a touchstone that took on more symbolic baggage than the concept could handle. In particular, it mystified the Soviets in the 1960s as to why anyone would prefer to leave a society vulnerable to enemy nuclear attack, and to the contrary, they have worked continuously, amid the ups and downs of arms-control negotiations, to build active and passive defenses in case deterrence fails. The United States interprets this Soviet defense building as evidence of hostile intent, whereas the USSR wonders how any people with minimum exposure to military history could prefer to leave their society exposed to unprecedented destruction. Especially after the SALT I agreement was concluded, the United States assumed mistakenly that the USSR had now subscribed to mutual vulnerability, that it would lose interest in ballistic missile defense for its territory and leave its society forever vulnerable to U.S. retaliation, consoled by the recognition that ours was, too. Any Soviet military leader who said such a thing would be expelled from the Malinovsky Tank Academy at the first opportunity.

Ironically, the United States has never fully subscribed to mutual vulnerability as a deterrence doctrine for operational war planning. Its importance was that it was adopted by an important network of domestic U.S. policy activists, who used the argument of mutual vulnerability and reasoned from that erroneous premise (about Soviet acceptance of it) backward to a conclusion that superpower arms agreements should be based on that premise. U.S. force building was somewhat constrained in the 1960s by mutual vulnerability doctrine, but in the next decade the concept of mutual vulnerability had to contend with an interest in limited nuclear options in case deterrence failed, and also with the evolution of multiple-warhead (MIRV) technology, which threatened to destabilize the strategic balance. U.S. arms-control advocates of mutual vulnerability perhaps unintentionally misrepresented Soviet interest in forestalling a U.S. breakthrough in BMD, as an expression of Soviet disinterest in the same mission. The Soviets do not view their BMD as threatening to stability, only ours, because they do not perceive themselves to be attacking first, but under attack and retaliating (including preemption when war is deemed unavoidable). Defenses from the Soviet perspective are a necessity, whether their society is vulnerable or not; in fact, the more vulnerable it is (because of the larger size of the U.S. arsenal), the more necessary Soviet defenses are. This is the opposite of the U.S. judgment, which is that the larger the opponent's nuclear forces, the more superfluous defenses are. We need not belabor the point that this difference in perception of the competency of defenses, relative to the size of offenses, relates to the U.S. proclivity for strategizing, illustrated earlier. Defenses that are not perfect, or at least cost effective at the margin in this view, are not worth building. The Soviet view is that scenarios are not all predictable, deterrence can fail, and defenses, together with survivable and accurate offenses, are the best form of insurance. Thus, the USSR has apparently reacted, to the extent that it has reacted at all, more to U.S. actual planning and deployment than to U.S. declaratory policies.

Notice, as a very important parenthesis, the differing views about war and its causation, represented in these differing U.S. and Soviet perspectives on active defenses and societal vulnerability. For the USSR, it is important to distinguish formal causes of wars from efficient ones, as Aristotle might have done. Formal causes are those variables at the left side of an equation that drive the solutions at the right side, and in the equations of historical cause and effect, capitalism causes war. In the U.S. perspective, war results from accident or misunderstanding, an interruption of normal peaceful relations, more or less idiosyncratic. Each war has a different efficient cause, the particular constellation of factors that bring it about, but no formal cause, as in the Soviet view. Thus, for Western writers, World War II was caused by German and Japanese aggression, each for its own motives, and earlier or later wars would have other explanations. From the Soviet perspective, however teleological it is thought to be, the particular causes reflect superstructure that is an outgrowth of substructure, or foundation, based in class conflict. Now, when mention is made of the importance of class conflict in war causation, there are hoots and jeers among Western readers, who consider themselves too sophisticated to take seriously that outmoded literature about the conflict between bourgeoisie and proletariat. That, however, is too literal and too misleading a reading of Marx, Lenin, and their Soviet archivists. The idea of class causation for war, including nuclear war if it happens, is, from the Soviet perspective, rooted in the nature of capitalism, not dependent upon the good or bad faith of U.S. leaders. Since this is a logical argument (meaning formal and deductive) and not an empirical one, it cannot be faulted; since it is also a theological argument, of a secular faith, it must be fulfilled to the extent that Soviet power and doctrine can do so. Therefore, Soviet doctrine must insist that war with the capitalist West will be started by the West and probably on account of a crisis that we, and not they, allow to get out of control.[11]

A second U.S. and Western dovish fallacy about Soviet military doctrine is that the USSR has become seriously interested in (and prefers) limited nuclear war, including limited war in Europe, and that a significant probability exists that such a war might be contained without expanding into central homeland-to-homeland U.S.–Soviet exchanges. Including this view in an inventory of dovish fallacies is somewhat artificial, since many of the U.S. analysts who argue this position are not dovish about U.S. defense or foreign-policy issues in general. They believe, however, that the Soviets, as a result of their growing awareness of the devastation attendant on any direct homeland nuclear exchanges, and as a result of their improved capabilities for selective nuclear use as opposed to indiscriminate strikes, could be motivated to practice intrawar deterrence and reciprocate Western autolimitation upon the scope and destruction of nuclear attacks.[12]

The problem with this view is not whether it is a narrowly correct reading of Soviet intentions, but the assumption of reciprocity on the part of the United States or NATO, granted the supposition that the Soviets are interested in limited nuclear war. The trouble is that the USSR cannot be sure which of the many Western ideas about limited nuclear war it is dealing with. At least five generic ideas can be identified, although they are not as separable in reality as they are in theory. The first is limited nuclear war as an alternative to total nuclear war. The initial interest in deploying tactical nuclear weapons by some U.S. scientists was based on a belief that weapons of low yield and limited range were the equivalent of improved artillery, without the collateral damage of larger strikes, and so not threatening to entire societies, as larger attacks would be. The second idea of limited nuclear war, somewhat related to the first, is that it is an alternative to conventional war, in that tactical nuclear weapons would provide, for the defense in Europe, force multipliers that would offset NATO inferiority in numbers of personnel and equipment.

A third understanding of limited nuclear war was the notion that tactical or other nuclear weapons in Europe were not there for their denial capabilities, but for their deterrent value. This deterrence would continue into war, for after war began and tactical nuclears were exchanged, the imminent prospect of escalation would force the attacker to reconsider and halt the attack. Of course, not all the options for escalation would necessarily be NATO's to choose, and especially not once the USSR acquired and deployed its own arsenal of tactical nuclear weapons. The Soviets could still, however, be deterred from extending tactical into strategic nuclear war by the connection between U.S. nuclear weapons deployed in Europe and those U.S. strategic forces poised to retaliate in North America.

In addition, and subsequent to the conclusion of SALT I and some initiatives by Europeans, the notion of limited-nuclear-war forces as balancers below the level of U.S.–Soviet strategic parity became widely discussed. It will be contended by some advocates of the NATO two-track decision in 1979 that this is not so, and that the Pershing II and ground-launched cruise missiles (GLCMs) of theater range were designed to couple the U.S. strategic deterrent to European defense. That further coupling was needed to make credible the U.S. extended deterrent was not clear, nor was it clear why 572 Pershing II and GLCM, as opposed to some other number, would do the job. The fact remains, however much its authors might in the present climate now want to disown it, that there was a feeling among some Western military and political leaders that the Euromissiles of the West were necessary to balance the SS–20s deployed by the Kremlin, else theater nuclear deterrence would be unbalanced.[13]

Fifth, and finally, there is the idea of limited nuclear war as the "manipulation of risk" or the "threat that leaves something to chance," in Thomas C. Schelling's phrase, the notion that the mere presence of nuclear weapons creates an uncertainty that is deterring, because neither side can preclude the possibility of escalation, however uncertain it is. What is at issue when nuclear weapons are introduced into conventional war is that a salient threshold has been crossed, which was not crossed before, and this psychological firebreak immediately changes expectations as to what the war is all about.[14] Thus, neither side, having distributed nuclear weapons within the force structure of its general-purpose forces deployed in Europe, can know with a high degree of confidence the precise path that the confrontation will take, and one of those paths, willy-nilly, could lead to the use of U.S. and Soviet strategic nuclear forces. The Soviet Union seemed to give some credence to this argument, without intending to do so, when it criticized the limited-nuclear-options declaratory policy of former U.S. Secretary of Defense James R. Schlesinger, following his explanation of it in 1974.[15] Schlesinger's suggestion that U.S. strategic nuclear forces might be used in a more selective and discriminating way implied that they might be called upon earlier in war, and that the United States might move up the ladder of escalation more rapidly than the Soviets had previously assumed in response to an attack on Western Europe.

Having reviewed these partly distinct and partly overlapping notions of limited nuclear war, as they have appeared in the strategic pronouncements and academic literature of the West, we can appreciate the intent of each on its own merits. The problem for the USSR is deciding which among these is the rationale that matters most in the crisis of the moment, for in situations other than crises they are not going to be considering the use of nuclear weapons. The Western notions of limited nuclear war present to the Soviets two very different and somewhat contradictory notions of deterrence, as deterrence appears in the relationship between theater-based and U.S. strategic nuclear forces. The first notion is that the West will be able to coerce the USSR at every step of the escalatory process, by having forces that are at least equivalent to and preferably superior to Soviet forces. The second notion is that the loss of escalation control will engulf both sides in an escalatory process that results in a higher loss for both that each would prefer to avoid, given the chance to decide the issue coolly and rationally. The problem with the escalation-dominance approach is that it is apt to be transitory, applicable only when one side has a temporary advantage in deployments of nuclear forces with certain attributes (as the Soviet SS-20 seemed to have, until NATO began the 572 deployments). The problem with the loss-of-control rationale is that it is hard to orchestrate for an entire alliance like NATO, and threatening to lose control over a process that is two-sided creates an incentive for the opponent to exploit postattack problems of coordination.

The third dovish assumption about Soviet doctrine that may be invalid is that the USSR is an essentially satiated power, which seeks no encroachment on the fundamental interests of the West. This assumption ignores the possibility that there may be a substantial gap between Soviet declaratory and operational policy, as there is in the U.S. case. Certainly, the Soviets are not reckless in their probing of Western resolve and resistance, as shown in their preference for using surrogates and allies instead of their own forces, whenever possible. In addition, threat assessments of Soviet military capabilities that make them appear to be ten feet tall, when in fact they are six and one-half to seven, are counterproductive to the serious evaluation of the threat and estimation of the correct responses. The USSR is not a satisfied power in the sense that it accepts in principle, as opposed to in practice, the international status quo. Soviet ideology maintains that the international status quo is by definition illegitimate, and historically due for its eventual overthrow. The USSR is not, however, about to bring nuclear destruction down on its own head in order to hasten the day, preferring the expedient approach of feeding to the West the appropriate cues for its self-delusion. Thus, the Soviet peace offensives against the 572 deployments and SDI, however valid the cases for each might be, were part of the longer-term pattern of Soviet deception that is built into their military and intelligence system, as well as into their foreign policy.[16] Soviet strategic deception appears in three generic forms, conducted for the most part by three different organizations. Active measures are intended to influence foreign public opinion, political decision makers, and other elites. Counterintelligence neutralizes the efforts of foreign intelligence services. *Maskirovka* includes efforts at camouflage, concealment, cover, and other protective and deceptive activities related to the armed forces and their war plans.[17]

The Soviet propensity for deception pays great dividends in peacetime, and especially when the audience for which the deception is intended is so willing to be convinced. This must be said of U.S. hawks as well as doves, for the USSR has used deception against those in the West who are inclined to underestimate Soviet strategic nuclear capabilities, and against those who might overestimate them. The infamous fly-by of bombers in 1955 over the reviewing stand in Moscow in order to create a

Western perception of a larger-than-life Soviet bomber force is one illustration. Another is the attempt by Khrushchev to bluff U.S. political leaders and military estimators into assuming that he was deploying a large ICBM force in the early 1960s, when in fact the force turned out to be MRBMs aimed at NATO. William R. Van Cleave has noted that, if the USSR ever seriously contemplated nuclear war against the United States, the latter should expect deception to be an important component of the Soviet plan. In his analysis, the USSR might not wait for the crisis generation of U.S. forces to maximum alert, when they were most survivable, but strike in surprise in order to catch them at low ebb. A surprise attack would also catch U.S. command, control, and communications (C3) systems in a posture of lower readiness to respond, and might disconnect some of the more important force commanders from their warning and assessment information, or from their responsive forces.[18]

The point is worth making that nuclear surprise has received less attention than surprise in conventional war, on account of the Western, but not the Soviet, doctrinal propensity for fatalism about reducing the consequences of war if deterrence fails. The point about strategic nuclear surprise, improbable as it might seem under peacetime conditions, has another implication. U.S. or NATO vulnerability to nuclear surprise might be less sensitive to the relative size of U.S. and Soviet forces, and more sensitive to the expectations that policy makers hold, than is generally appreciated. The important component of those expectations, for traditional Western crisis-stability theory, is the perceived difference, by U.S. leaders, between the costs of waiting to ride out a Soviet first strike, and their expected gains from launch under attack or preemption. If the difference between expected gains from LUA and expected losses from second-strike ride-out is very great, the temptation to launch under attack or on warning of attack is strong. It was noted earlier that the U.S. ICBM force might have to be launched under attack or on warning (prompt launch) in order to save it from nearly total destruction. Conversely for the Soviet Union, the expected gain from preemption, if war seemed imminent but possibly avoidable, would have to be weighed against the expected losses if they waited and were struck first. What this means is that forces that need not be launched promptly to survive attack create a smaller gap between expected gains from striking first and anticipated losses in striking back. This estimate by either side, of expected gains compared to expected losses, applies, however, not only to force balances but also to their command and control systems. If either expected its opponent to attack its central command systems as early and as heavily as it could, its expected losses from waiting will seem catastrophic, and expected gains from striking first (perhaps at the opponent's C3 system) will appear more attractive. (Later we will suggest that there is more to the problem of nuclear surprise than the set-piece attacks with which crisis-stability analysis has customarily been occupied.)

ARMS-CONTROL OPTIONS

If the foregoing observations about arms control and Soviet strategy are à propos, what are the objectives that arms control can accomplish, and with what approaches?

First, arms control can reduce the probability of unintended war, war by accident or miscalculation. The Direct Communications Link (Hot Line) for crisis communication between U.S. and Soviet leaders is an important illustration, as is the Prevention of Nuclear War agreement, which requires notification of tests and exercises that might be misconstrued as threatening by either side. The Hot Line has been upgraded to include facsimile capability, and Senators Sam Nunn and John Warner have proposed that Nuclear Risk Reduction Centers be created in Moscow and Washington for communication between Soviet and U.S. military specialists (now established).

Second, forces should not be deployed in a manner coducive to preemptive attack, either by threatening it or inviting it. The MX/Peacekeeper missile deployed in fixed silos violates both canons, and submarines that are routinely deployed so that their missiles are within minutes of striking central strategic C3 assets, including national capitals, also contribute to potential crisis instability. So do potential or proposed deployments of space- or ground-based antisatellite weapons (ASATs), which might attack the early warning and communications satellites of the other side.[19]

Third, arms control should not attempt to bite off more than it can chew in the way of negotiable and verifiable arms reductions. The concept of reducing by half the superpowers' strategic nuclear arsenals, or ultimately eliminating them altogether, has a superficial appeal, but the how of such reductions may be as important as the how many. Strategic delivery vehicles are not equally threatening to crisis or arms-race stability, even considered apart from the doctrinal cocoons in which they are nurtured. Missiles in fixed silos are more destabilizing than mobile missiles, and those deployed at sea are preferable from a crisis-stability standpoint to those deployed on land, with some reservations. Bombers are vulnerable to first strikes unless they are alerted very early in a crisis, but once alerted, they are very flexible and need not be committed irrevocably to retaliation. Submarine-launched ballistic missiles are very survivable, but communications with the submarines preclude much in the way of high-fidelity, two-way comparison of the actual situation with intended plans. Cruise missiles can be delivered from a variety of platforms and over different ranges, and they can be made very survivable even on land, but certainly at sea or in the air. They, however, carry either nuclear or conventional warheads, and thus risk inadvertent crossing of the nuclear threshold, once war has broken out, and they resist simple means of verification that their payloads are nonnuclear.

Fourth, it is often said, somewhat to the consternation of this author, that arms-control agreements, especially U.S.–Soviet strategic agreements, are meaningless, because they simply ratify the existing strategic balance at the moment. Said differently, this is a contention that SALT I or SALT II failed because they did not bring about large reductions in the nuclear forces of either side. This assessment of SALT, however, ignores the fact that the USSR, if not the United States, moves very slowly and cautiously into arms reductions with its superpower adversary. Arms-control proposals, in order to be appealing to the Soviets, cannot expect that they will yield any of their important strategic nuclear systems without what they consider to be equivalent compensation. The Soviets read their fine print, and, as they proved in grain deals during the early 1970s, they are also skilled negotiators.[20] If the USSR is able to strike agreements that allow it flexibility to build forces as it had originally intended, then the West has acquiesced to those agreements and should not complain if the Soviets take full advantage of any loopholes. In addition, ratification of the existing strategic balance is preferable to mindless expansion of both sides' inventories, and it is certainly mindless to add forces that provide redundant, as opposed to necessary, coverage of retaliatory targets. It is probable that both Soviet and U.S. war plans already provide for redundancy against the targets that would matter in a general nuclear war, although there is always the demand from conservative military planners for additional weapons to target the "relocatable" forces of the opponent. One of the ironies of both sides' growing interest in mobile ICBMs, as opposed to those based in silos, is that the deployment of mobile missiles, although more stabilizing in principle, may promote military interest in postattack reconnaissance and strike systems for the protracted phases of a nuclear war. There is a tendency within the U.S. arms-control community to emphasize as the sole criterion of stability the relationship between the attacker's warheads and the defender's potentially vulnerable aim points. Thus, multiple-warhead (MIRV) ICBMs are thought to be destablizing, and single-warhead ICBMs stabilizng, exclusive of how they are based. Single-warhead ICBMs, however, if they are made mobile, raise other issues pertinent to stability. Single-warhead missiles lend themselves to some selective nuclear options better than do multiple-warhead missiles, and so might be launched sooner in a selective attack, in the mistaken impression that the opponent would interpret the attack as limited.[21] In addition, the ability to survive preemptive attack is stabilizing, but mobility also confers the potential for fighting long after the opponent's first strike has been survived. The prospect of extending the war into phases beyond the first few salvos might be destabilizing. If both superpowers have forces with large numbers of sea-based cruise missiles, survivable bombers, and mobile missiles, some of which will have stealth characteristics, then stability will no longer depend upon which side expects a quick kill, but which anticipates being able to prevail in a longer struggle. The present situation is one in which both superpowers have partially vulnerable forces that depend upon quick reaction for survival. This is far from ideal, but it may not be much worse than a situation in which both feel confident that most of their forces can fight an extended war and still have significant numbers of forces left.

Fifth, and most fundamental from a political standpoint, one's theory of arms control is related to one's theory of deterrence. If one's theory is that the ability to destroy cities in retaliation is what is necessary and sufficient for deterrence, it follows that arms control need accomplish only very limited objectives. Keeping both sides' forces limited to countervalue retaliation and immune from counterforce first-strike capabilities should do the trick, if both can be interested in such an approach; however, if either side's theory of deterrence is more demanding of military performance, then arms control faces tougher sledding. In the extreme case, expectations that the U.S. or the Soviet force should be able to survive repeated attacks and endure in a war that lasts several months will create an adverse climate for arms-control achievements. The forces that must fight to the death cannot easily be constrained by mutual trust, which to some extent lies at the base of arms control. It is not trust in shared ideology or doctrine, but trust in the other side's knowledge of our competency and in their common sense. Mr. Khrushchev saw this common sense clearly during the Cuban missile crisis of 1962, and we have to hope that his successors, and those of John F. Kennedy, will do likewise.

NOTES

1. Albert Carnesale, *Learning from Experience with Arms Control*, Final Report submitted to the U.S. Arms Control and Disarmament Agency, John F. Kennedy School of Government, Harvard University, September 1986.

2. Colin S. Gray, *Nuclear Strategy and National Style* (Lanham, MD: Hamilton Press, 1986), pp. 201–38.

3. Secretary of State George Shultz, "Nuclear Weapons, Arms Control and the Future of Deterrence," U.S. State Department, *Current Policy*, No. 893, pp. 3–4.

4. For more discussion of this, see Stephen J. Cimbala, *Extended Deterrence: The U.S. and NATO Europe* (Lexington, MA: D.C. Heath/Lexington Books, 1987).

5. An overview of the development of Soviet military strategy is provided in Condoleezza Rice, "The Making of Soviet Strategy," in *Makers of Modern Strat-*

egy, ed. Peter Paret (Princeton, NJ: Princeton University Press, 1986), pp. 648–76. Rice's essay focuses on the period between World War I and World War III; for earlier Russian military thought, see Walter Pintner, "Russian Military Thought: The Western Model and the Shadow of Suvorov," pp. 354–75 in the same volume. See also Norman Stone, "The Historical Background of the Red Army," in *Soviet Military Power and Performance*, ed. John Erickson and E.J. Feuchtwanger (Hamden, CT: Archon Books, 1979), Ch. 1, pp. 3–17, and John Erickson, "The Soviet Military System: Doctrine, Technology and Style," Ch. 2, pp. 18–44, in the same volume.

6. An excellent explanation of the relationship between Soviet ideology and foreign policy is provided by Vernon V. Aspaturian, "Soviet Foreign Policy," in *Foreign Policy in World Politics*, 6th ed., ed. Roy C. Macridis (Englewood Cliffs, NJ: Prentice-Hall, 1985), Ch. 5, pp. 170–243. An important collection of essays on Soviet military strategy past and present appears in Derek Leebaert, ed., *Soviet Military Thinking* (London: Allen and Unwin, 1981), in which the chapters by Stanley Sienkiewicz, Fritz W. Ermarth, and Raymond L. Garthoff are especially pertinent to the discussion in this text.

7. See John Erickson, "The Soviet View of Deterrence: A General Survey," reprinted in *Nuclear Weapons and the Threat of Nuclear War*, ed. John B. Harris and Eric Markusen (New York: Harcourt Brace Jovanovich, 1986), pp. 170–79.

8. Soviet planners, however, anticipate contingencies across a spectrum from surprise, out-of-the-blue launch on tactical warning/launch under attack, and second-strike retaliation. See Stephen M. Meyer, "Soviet Perspectives on the Paths to Nuclear War," in *Hawks, Doves and Owls: An Agenda for Avoiding Nuclear War*, ed. Graham T. Allison, Albert Carnesale, and Joseph S. Nye, Jr. (New York: Norton, 1985), pp. 167–205.

9. The Soviet view of any war with the United States or NATO is undoubtedly a cautious one. See Benjamin S. Lambeth, "Uncertainties for the Soviet War Planner," *International Security* 7, No. 3 (Winter 1982/83): 139–66. An estimate of Soviet war-fighting and war survival capabilities is provided by Harriet Fast Scott and William F. Scott, *The Soviet Control Structure: Capabilities for Wartime Survival* (New York: Crane, Russak, 1983).

10. Allison, Carnesale, and Nye, eds., *Hawks, Doves and Owls*, p. 228.

11. Khrushchev's expectations about U.S. behavior during the Cuban missile crisis are noted in Strobe Talbott, trans. and ed., *Khrushchev Remembers* (Boston: Little, Brown, 1970), pp. 488–505.

12. Albert Wohlstetter and Richard Brody, "Continuing Control as a Requirement for Deterring," in *Managing Nuclear Operations*, ed. Ashton B. Carter, John S. Steinbruner, and Charles A. Zraket (Washington, DC: Brookings Institution, 1987), Ch. 5, pp. 142–96.

13. See Leon V. Sigal, *Nuclear Forces in Europe: Enduring Dilemmas, Present Prospects* (Washington, DC: Brookings Institution, 1984).

14. For fuller development of this argument, see Thomas C. Schelling, *Arms and Influence* (New Haven, CT: Yale University Press, 1966), pp. 105–16.

15. Lynn Etheridge Davis, "Limited Nuclear Options: Deterrence and the New American Doctrine," in *Strategic Deterrence in a Changing Environment*, ed. Christoph Bertram (Montclair, NJ: Allenheld, Osmun, 1981), pp. 42–92.

16. See the collection of studies on Soviet deception in Brian D. Dailey and

Patrick J. Parker, eds., *Soviet Strategic Deception* (Lexington, MA: D.C. Heath/ Lexington Books, 1987).

17. This distinction follows the suggestion by Richards J. Heuer, Jr., "Soviet Organization and Doctrine for Strategic Deception," in *Soviet Strategic Deception*, ed. Dailey and Parker, pp. 21–53.

18. William R. Van Cleave, "Surprise Nuclear Attack," in ibid., pp. 449–66. See also Earl F. Ziemke, "Stalingrad and Belorussia: Soviet Deception in World War II," in *Strategic Military Deception*, ed. Donald C. Daniel and Katherine L. Herbig (New York: Pergamon Press, 1982), pp. 243–76; and Russel H.S. Stolfi, "Barbarossa: German Grand Deception and the Achievement of Strategic and Tactical Surprise against the Soviet Union, 1940–41," pp. 195–223 in the same volume.

19. See Colonel Robert B. Giffen, USAF, *U.S. Space System Survivability: Strategic Alternatives for the 1990s* (Washington, DC: National Defense University Press, 1982).

20. Experience in negotiating with the USSR and lessons learned therein is discussed in Leon Sloss and M. Scott Davis, eds., *A Game for High Stakes: Lessons Learned in Negotiating with the Soviet Union* (Cambridge, MA: Ballinger, 1986).

21. The "footprint" of multiple, independently targetable re-entry vehicles (RV) dispensed by the bus in the postboost phase of launch limits the ability of the attacker to target widely separated objectives with a single launcher. One would also not want to waste clusters of warheads attacking an objective where one will suffice.

11

FORCE AND POLICY IN THE NUCLEAR AGE

The relationship between force and policy is at the heart of strategic thinking as opposed to other kinds of contributions to foreign policy studies. Strategy offers a lucid connection between means and ends. This implies that the ends of policy should be clearly formulated, and the means should be appropriate to them. Moreover, in a democratic society, both ends and means must be understood by the public at large and its elected representatives. Although the details may be classified or obscure, the general relationship between governmental policy and military force must be clear, at least in any system where military effectiveness depends upon legislative appropriations.

In the United States, the development of nuclear weapons has not been followed by a nuclear strategy that is a strategy in the proper sense of the term, for reasons already noted. The disconnection between force and policy is papered over by substituting hypothetical scenarios and deductive argumentation for the hard issues and facts of war. Some of these hard issues must now be raised. Most notably, the character of U.S. government discussions about nuclear strategy has tended to call for increasingly improbable and politically unsupportable options. Policy makers call for selective and calibrated use of nuclear weapons, including strategic weapons, under conditions that—if they came to pass politically—would preclude such selective uses. While strategy suffers, the marketing of weapons systems for deterrence of improbable wars continues apace. The U.S. defense community has become absorbed in the same public-relations focus, for the same audience of media and congressional news junkies, as has the rest of the federal bureaucracy.

Perhaps the overarching issue is whether nuclear weapons are irrelevant to strategy or transcend it. Deterrence may not be a military strategy at all, but only a psychobabble of academic concepts designed to provide a patina of credibility for what is incredible. This is certainly the verdict of some traditional military historians and of some antinuclear skeptics, and one can go part of the way with this skepticism. To gleefully cast nuclear weapons and deterrence theory adrift from strategy, however, leaves the United States and NATO in a position of practicing of necessity what is defined as strategically impossible. And the theoretical skepticism about deterrence, well founded as it is, cannot be taken too far. Deterrence has, after all, operated with regard to the use of conventional forces, even before nuclear weapons existed. So nuclear weapons require that we continue to partake of deterrence rationality, but with less innocence, for nuclear-weapons technology places in the hands of policy makers the instruments of their own national and societal destruction. The last sentence also helps to mark off the difference between nuclear-deterrence theory and economic theory, in terms of their differing rationalities. In neoclassical economic theory, aggregates determine the trends, and individual "irrational" consumers do not much affect the predictions derived from theory. In nuclear strategy, on the other hand, a micromistake by a single policy maker can have macroconsequences, including the destruction of civilization. Admittedly, this last is the extreme case, but nuclear weapons require that we look into extreme cases. The parallel in economics would be the collapse of one bank leading to the destruction of an entire national banking system, or the imposition of one tariff leading to the development of a mutually suicidal international trade war. The extrapolation from a wrong nuclear decision to an international catastrophe is thus no more illogical than the escalation from the Smoot-Hawley tariff to an international economic depression.

Of course, the public debate is oblivious to distinctions such as these. People in the United States want to be told all of the following, depending on which day of the week it is: that nuclear war cannot be fought or won, unless the United States is attacked, in which case the United States will "prevail"; that U.S. armed forces should not be committed to conflicts in the Third World, unless they can achieve a decisive victory in a day and a half, and then without casualties; that defense systems should be cheaper and more effective in combat; that our allies can carry more of the burden of Western defense, and the way to make them do more is to withdraw from Europe; that a missile defense will shield the United States from the consequences of war if deterrence fails, which, of course, it never can.

The relevance of strategic thinking in the U.S. executive and legislative branches, relative to the force structure that is finally deployed, and against the kinds of wars it can actually be expected to fight, is nil. Each administration in the White House wants to pass the problem of defense on to its successors without engaging in any war that is unpopular, or popular but not "winnable," or popular and winnable, but not well timed for the rest of the administration's policy agenda. As for the U.S. Congress, its policy agenda during the past decade, with reference to military affairs, has emphasized investigatory purges of the intelligence community; legalistic wrangling over the costs of toilet seats and hammers; posturing for constituents at home about waste, fraud, and abuse, while demanding additional weapons-system contracts for their districts; using the defense budget as a *cause célèbre* against which other axes can be ground, including efforts to revive domestic policy agenda of the 1960s under other guises. Most depressing of all is the extent to which Congress is now beholden to the campaign donations of political action committees (PACs) for its survival, leading to a situation that might make Edmund Burke resign from the legislature, were he able to get elected.

In this military psychodrama that passes in Washington for strategic argument, what can be said about the effects of nuclear weapons and deterrence theory on U.S. strategy, relative to the challenges strategy must meet?

First, and this judgment is intentionally harsh, the United States has no coherent and workable strategy for the defense of Western Europe. It may have a more or less coherent declaratory policy, but this is far from having a cohesive operational strategy. NATO's current strategy is to get involved in a conventional war and, when it is apparent that NATO is losing, to escalate to the use of nuclear weapons (which?). The entire flexible-response strategy is a peacetime fig leaf to conceal the unwillingness of the United States and its alliance partners to take seriously the possibility of war in Europe. Drowning in their shared *Gemütlichkeit* of postwar affluence and the spewing of programs from the "positive state," the public, both in the United States and in Europe, considers the prospect of war in Europe to be almost negligible. Moreover, to the extent that people do believe in it, they rely upon a most improbable nuclear strategy to bail them out, if conventional deterrence fails. NATO and U.S. strategic and theater nuclear forces are not meaningfully superior to those of the USSR and its allies, and therefore they do not compensate for the insufficiency of ground and tactical air forces on the Central Front and on the northern and southern flanks.

Into this nonstrategic void of NATO strategy, opportunists and force builders with strategic aspirations will tread. If NATO does not have a credible strategy, the U.S. Navy offers its own, which at least has the virtue that it takes the idea of war termination seriously.[1] The U.S. maritime strategy has been bashed by critics of all persuasions, but some of this is lightning drawn by a former secretary of the navy who enjoyed the role of lightning rod. The exuberant Mr. Lehman succeeded in getting the lion's share of defense budgets for general-purpose forces during the first term of the Reagan administration, and other services and defense strategists show expected skepticism about the strategy that followed in the wake of these budgetary triumphs. The U.S. maritime strategy appears to be overly ambitious only because the NATO ground and tactical air story in Central Europe is so unambitious. Under the doctrine of forward defense, U.S. and allied NATO ground forces must be deployed far forward near the inter-German border, where they are to provide target practice for Soviet first-echelon forces, and ingredients for the stew of deep penetration and encirclement that the Soviet ground forces are preparing in their conventional war plan against NATO.[2] NATO's rationale for offering up this cannon fodder is that the West Germans demand defense as far forward as possible, in order to avoid the implication that any FRG territory will be ceded to Pact attackers in the early going. This is as unstrategic (or unoperational) an idea as one can imagine, for if Germany is to be defended with conventional weapons, as opposed to nuclear ones, then putting NATO's best divisions forward, where they can suffer heavy early losses, does not make much sense.

The U.S. maritime strategy, on the other hand, offers the very sensible proposition that navies are important to winning the long war, provided the armies and air forces of NATO can avoid losing the short war. The maritime strategy supposes, however, that the U.S. Navy cannot really wait to find out if the Western ground forces will lose the war (on the very plausible supposition that they will). Therefore, the legions of Lehman prepared for an assault into the Norwegian and Barents seas early in any conventional war in Europe, in order to sink the Soviet northern Red Banner Fleet and to cause attrition among Soviet attack submarines guarding their northern bastions in the Kola Peninsula. By so doing, the U.S. Navy would pose a credible threat to Soviet strategic ballistic missile submarines, a threat to change eventually the correlation of nuclear forces adversely, and thus create incentives for the USSR to terminate the war on terms favorable to the West.

Supposing that the sinking of the Soviet northern fleet would cause them to want to terminate the war, as opposed to escalating it, is the Navy equivalent of NATO's flexible-response strategy, which argues for the importance of graduated and total escalation at the same time. This point has been alluded to earlier, and bears reexamining now. The logic of U.S. or NATO nuclear strategy is flawed to the extent that it argues for the simultaneous manipulation of two kinds of nuclear threats: the threat to dominate the escalation process, if necessary by going to the top of the ladder in strategic nuclear forces, and the threat that leaves the precise scope and character of the conflict to autonomous forces, as well as deliberate choices. If the U.S. Navy is attempting to sink the Soviet navy, it cannot then argue that it is practicing the "threat that leaves something to chance," because it has bitten into the forbidden fruit of escalation dominance. Innocence after expulsion from the Garden cannot be claimed. Neither can NATO strategy for war in Europe suggest that the West will fight a piecemeal battle on the Central Front until it loses, and then deter the Soviets from further pursuit of their aggression by threatening strategic nuclear war, if necessary. One cannot threaten to get into a strategic nuclear war that unleashes the U.S. strategic nuclear deterrent accidentally, without mortgaging NATO strategy to the willingness of all 16 member states to accept the attendant risks. And, as is clear from the uproar in Europe in 1983 over the 572 deployments, large numbers of European citizens in NATO member states, and many of their parliamentarians, are not willing to run the risk of strategic nuclear war, or theater nuclear war, or any nuclear war. Having been tutored by Western strategic thinkers to believe that any nuclear war is automatically a holocaust, how could they be expected to take any other position?

Further to the issue of strategic escapism, there is the Strategic Defense Initiative of President Ronald Reagan. Now, this vision of a peace shield that protects the United States from Soviet nuclear weapons is not entirely fallacious, if the shield is meant to accompany a sword of offensive retaliatory forces, in which the basis of deterrence remains firmly planted. And, if one looks at Reagan programs rather than Reagan rhetoric, it is apparent that defense planners did recognize that, even in the afterglow of Reykjavik, offenses could not be totally discarded under the supposition that very competent U.S. and Soviet defenses could take their place. If the European delusion is that U.S. strategic forces, which are merely equivalent to Soviet strategic nuclear forces, can forever deter conventional war in Europe, then its American counterpart, among many misconceptions, is the delusion of escaping vulnerability and returning to the nineteenth century. Few in the American defense community seem to have noticed that if U.S. and Soviet strategic nuclear offenses were disarmed and replaced by space-based defenses, the possibility of a strategic Pearl Harbor would go up, not down. Defensive technologies are not necessarily compatible with defensive strategies, nor offensive technologies with offensive ones. In the case of strategic nuclear weapons, from at least the mid-1960s to the mid-1980s, offensive retaliatory forces made a defensive strategy possible. Neither side could launch a surprise attack and expect to escape devastating retaliation, no matter how good that first strike might be. The deployment of defensive technologies might change that strategic condition, making the world safe for offensive nuclear warfare. This could happen in two ways. First, either side might deploy a defense that could absorb its opponent's retaliatory strike. Second, one side or both might deploy space-based defenses that could suppress the other's defenses very quickly. A Hobbesian condition in space could evolve, from space-based BMD deployments by both sides, in which the premium for prompt suppression of the opponent's defenses, paving the way for an attack on its (now reduced) offenses, was very high. As the payoffs rose for suppression–preemption strategies, the payoffs would decline for second-strike ride-out, especially if the second-strike forces were smaller compared to present forces.

Thus, in strategy, as opposed to strategizing, numbers do count, and redundancy is not necessarily bad, as Edward Luttwak has never ceased to remind us.[3] In the case of strategic nuclear forces, we have seen that the U.S. policy-making process has produced some redundancies and logical contradictions (irrationalities). As the Scowcroft panel noted, however, some of these redundancies have proved to be unintentionally beneficial from the standpoint of sound strategy, which must provide for preferable war outcomes with available resources. The strategizing perspective argues that the only forces that should be deployed are the minimum numbers of systems that can survive a notional Soviet attack, not the worst-case attacks that might occur under real conditions. This also applies to Defense Department explanations of nonnuclear contingencies, as when the U.S. frigate *Stark* was hit by an Iraqi Exocet missile in the Persian Gulf. After all, explained U.S. policy makers and Pentagon representatives, an attack by Iraq was not *expected*. This is reminiscent of Marine Commandant P. X. Kelley's explanation of why, despite repeated intelligence warnings about the possibility of terrorism in Beirut, Lebanon, in October of 1983, several hundred U.S. Marines were blown up in their barracks: No one had warned of a truck-delivered bomb, specifically.

Conventional strategizing is almost as prolific as nuclear strategizing on the issue of expecting only the expected. NATO strategy emphasizes the Central Front in Europe, with comparatively little attention to the northern and southern flanks. The latter, however, are much more vulnerable, because of the friction between Greece and Turkey on the southern flank and the inhospitable sea and land areas in which the battle would take place in the north. The south is probably NATO's Achilles' heel from an operational standpoint, since Greece and Turkey are more likely to fight each other than they are to fight any member of the Warsaw Pact, depending upon the state of their relations at the moment. Of course, the Soviets have their Rumania, and Poland, too, so there is no bonanza in alliance solidarity for either side. Nevertheless, NATO needs to reconsider how much of its investment it wants to use in losing the conventional war in Central Europe, as opposed to stalemating or winning it elsewhere. Lest losing the war in Central Europe be dismissed as academic cynicism, the author reminds readers that he is merely citing the estimate by former SACEUR General Bernard Rogers that he would probably have to request authorization for nuclear release within three days after war breaks out in Europe (by which time the Soviet forces, unless they are very incompetent and have had fewer than seven days to build up, ought to be within spitting distance of Frankfurt or Hamburg).

What alternatives are there to plans for losing quickly on the Central Front, sinking the Soviet navy (with what effect on the ground and tactical air war in Europe?), and threatening nuclear escalation, which the West is no more prepared to carry out than is the USSR? Of course, we have noted the president's effort to transcend deterrence instead of improving it, but that idea will crash into the rocks of NATO alliance cohesion before the United States has got very far with its comprehensive peace shield— which brings us to the real alternatives, as opposed to the mystical ones.

First, there is nothing wrong in principle with forward maritime operations in the Norwegian Sea, or with forward defense as a contributory element to the ground and tactical air war in Central Europe, or with the threat of nuclear escalation as an item in NATO's tool kit. The problem lies not in these constituent elements as they are assessed individually, but in the societal base on which they are required to rest. That base, the understanding of and support for U.S. and NATO strategy by publics and parliaments who see the connection between defense and welfare, is very tenuous, or in some member states altogether invisible.

In a democratic society and especially in an alliance of very individual and temperamental democratic societies, as NATO is, military strategy is as strong as the societal support for it. The most carefully contrived tactics and operations cannot save a strategy that is not supported actively, instead of passively, by the public. Where military strategists can be faulted is in tolerating, and in some cases celebrating, defense programs and policies that create divergence between public attitudes and military programs, between defense needs and perceived societal welfare.

Not all the reasons for the growing divergence between public understanding of and support for NATO military strategy, on one hand, and the military doctrines and war plans developed by civil and military elites, on the other, can be reviewed here, but several with special pertinence to NATO stand out, and must be faced down the road.

The first component of this divergence between military strategy and social expectations is the growing technological cast of U.S. and NATO defense strategies. This was serious enough in the nuclear age, but as we now move into a potentially postnuclear age, in which nuclear weapons of exotic varieties are commingled with more competent and lethal conventional weapons, public anxiety and confusion will be expected to grow. Military contractors and weapons laboratories produce in profusion new devices that promise to remove soldiers from the battlefield and to replace them with robots; to design nuclear weapons that can remove one building and leave the building next to it unscathed; to zap enemy warheads as they arc through space, with lasers, particle beams, or space-based kinetic-kill vehicles. Forgive even the intelligent laity who feel, as a result of this barrage in the trade press and newspapers, that they cannot contribute to understanding of the pertinent issues, and who adopt therefore a sense of hoplessness and abdication.

A second component of social and military divergence, in addition to the esoteric character of emerging technology, is the style of writing about deterrence and defense problems. Much of it is either polemical, designed to hustle a particular policy or program, or very obscurantist, in a style that Douglas Hart has aptly characterized as "hermeneutics," in a reference to theological scholarship. Nor is style the only issue. The substance of much writing on nuclear strategy is devoid of any references to strategy in prenuclear history, on the assumption that there is nothing to be learned from it, when in fact, there is a great deal to be learned from it. Thus, one has the impression, from the literature on nuclear strategy, that history began all over again at Alamagordo, that the past was no prologue, and that the wisdom and foolishness of previous commanders and statesmen could contribute nothing to the solution of problems in the balance-of-terror era. Nuclear "theology" is an à propos label, not only because nuclear theologians use obscure language, but because they are prone to imagine that one can arrest the flow of history at will, representing what they have learned from the past as if it were disconnected from the past, now appearing in the form of nuclear prophecy. Witness, for example, the rediscovery of deterrence in the nuclear era, as if prenuclear ages knew nothing about it, never practiced it, and published no studies relevant to the understanding of it. No real theologian would be so inept; proper reconstruction of the past is their touchstone. But nuclear strategy can rest, at least in the West, on imaginary prenuclear history—for example, the notion that total war begins with the advent of nuclear weapons.

Third, and related to the second, is the way in which Westerners, and people in the United States in general, are educated about strategy and military affairs. U.S. undergraduate education exposes students (sometimes) to introductory courses in history and political science that rarely touch on military history and strategy. Or, if they do, the illustrations are of the "isn't that too bad" variety, proving the depravity and fallibility of the human spirit isolated from the benefit of professorial explanation. And this is the education received by those who continue on to higher learning. At the elementary and secondary levels, what passes for social studies is even more devoid of serious concern with the relationship between the uses of force and the ends of policy. The isolationist strain in U.S. foreign policy, always latent and occasionally very assertive, begins with an educational process that teaches not that military conflict is a natural part of human affairs, but an atypical and avoidable social malady.

Not surprisingly, in view of the above, the term "civil defense" in the United States means bomb shelters and paper plans for "crisis relocation," instead of a civilian commitment to national defense. And this divergence between military preparedness and civil commitment has been accelerated in no small measure by U.S. and NATO hyperdependence on nuclear weapons. A public that expects that civil defense is associated only with nuclear war, and nuclear war with social extinction, is not going to be interested in civilian commitment to national defense, properly understood.

We have enumerated three of the many causes for divergence between military strategy and the societal milieu from which it must draw support. The first task was diagnosis, and the second is prescription. A generic prescription will be offered, without attempting to itemize all the specific implications of it; readers may be willing to supply their own examples if they are sympathetic to the argument in general.

The prescriptive task asks that U.S. and NATO strategy, including nuclear strategy, pay more attention to the societal basis of that strategy. Not passive public acquiescence, but active public commitment to its own national defense, is the necessary condition for closing the gap between apathy and commitment. If people feel no responsibility for their own defense, then it will be difficult to defend them at an acceptable cost.

What NATO appears to be missing is the threat to arm its population, not only its armies, to resist any invader in a protracted struggle. European members of NATO are missing the opportunity to confront the aggressor with the prospect of an armed populace that cannot ever be subdued at an acceptable cost, even if the professional armies deployed at the FEBA (Forward Edge of Battle Area) on "D" day can be. Some members of NATO, such as the West Germans, have the potential to mobilize a very effective territorial armed force within several days, and this is certainly one component of a truly national defense. Other components are needed as well, however, including a civilian population organized before war begins to put up extended resistance, months and years if necessary, after the invader has arrived and set up shop.

What makes this more feasible for defenders subjected to sudden military attack and temporary occupation, compared to the past, is the diffusion of very competent high-technology weapons from the ranks of professional armies into the hands of civilians of all kinds, including terrorists, throughout the world. Terrorists would not be half as successful as they are, were it not for the global open and clandestine arms trade, which provides to them a continuous supply of individual and crew-served weapons. Some terrorists in the Middle East already embark on weapons inventories that would have been the envy of the partisans in Europe in 1945. As the terrorists of the contemporary era have also demonstrated, however, armed resistance to even a benign state takes organization, ideological commitment, and financial support.

Western Europe and its allies, given their resources, should certainly have the financial basis to put into place the equipment and training for national risings against occupying and invading forces, if necessary. Such national resistance and terrorist risings could not be improvised after conventional forces were defeated, unless preparations were already in place. Modern reconnaissance and surveillance methods available to Soviet conquerors of Europe, once they had succeeded, would make resistance difficult, unless it had been organized well beforehand. The how of such organization is not unknown. Cells of resistance fighters could be organized within each town, village, or other political subdivision, prepared to go underground in the event that the aboveground war was being lost. These cells would draw upon stores of weapons and ammunition previously stocked for the occasion. The resistance cells would be linked in DNA-like strands with political and military intelligence "sensors" and "fusion centers," which would provide continuous information about enemy military movements and political decisions.

Along with this, and borrowing from the copybook of good guerrilla fighters, such as General Vo Nguyen Giap in North Vietnam, preparations would also be made to infiltrate leadership cadres of the occupying power with persons trained for that mission in appropriate linguistic and technical skills. Some of these cadres could pose as willing collaborators, all the while feeding information to the resistance about the plans and programs of the enemy. Intelligence and counterintelligence activities that are normally carried on in peacetime by NATO agencies could be extended into wartime against an occupying force, which would be thinly stretched across Western and Eastern Europe and prone to penetration.

The immediate reaction to such proposals is undoubtedly one of disbelief. Before reaching this judgment, the reader is asked to consider the Soviet experience in Afghanistan, in which an unexpectedly strong resistance by essentially nomadic armies against a superpower surprised both Soviet and Western observers. The Afghan *mujahiddin* are lightly armed with captured weapons and other weapons infiltrated across the Pakistani border, fighting against Soviet armored personnel carriers, tanks and, the world's most proficient helicopter gunships, aside from those of the United States itself. In December of 1979, when the USSR invaded Afghanistan to get rid of its bumbling factotum Hafizullah Amin and install the more docile Babrak Karmal, no Western military expert would have bet that in 1988 the war could still be going strong on the insurgent side. Even more, no one would have bet that the Soviet leadership would be looking for a face-saving way out, although they are certainly not about to install any leadership in Kabul with hostile intent toward the USSR.

This resistance by Afghans was accomplished against armed forces smaller and less capable than those with which the Soviet Union would invade Europe, if it came to that. Europe, however, also has a larger population base from which to draw resisters, armed and otherwise, and a stronger base of technical knowledge. Recall the difficulties created for the Polish armed forces by workers' demonstrations and political activities in Gdansk and other cities. These activities shook the foundations of the Soviet glacis in Eastern Europe, and they were accomplished under the watchful eye of Big Brother to the East and the Polish Army at home, which has since intervened to keep things under control. It is popularly supposed that the Polish armed forces under General Jaruzelski declared martial law in 1981 in order to preclude a Soviet invasion, after which the Polish leaders would lose control of the situation. Perhaps there is something to this speculation, but there is also something to the notion that the Soviet Union was not very eager to invade Poland with its own forces. Such an invasion could have set off an indescribable bloodbath, which the Red Army and its Polish minions could have eventually put down, but not at a tolerable cost, for the cost would have been the collapse of détente and the rearming of NATO.

Thus, even if the USSR could be confronted, in every NATO country, with the expectation of dealing with at least 16 broadly based nationalist, antiparty movements, and even better movements for workers' rights, just that alone would be discouraging. Added to this expectation could be the expectation of fighting a Swiss- or Israeli-style population in arms, one that would never let up in its resistance to any occupying force, until it was forcibly relocated or exterminated. This is brutal resistance and it invites brutal responses, as the Afghans have seen and as the partisan forces in World War II learned.

Under present conditions, however, such a postattack resistance in Europe could not be organized after a Soviet attack, but only before it, in the expectation that conventional war is a serious possibility, not a pipe dream. Making Europe into a hornet's nest of civilian resisters who are armed and trained for war on all fronts, willing to risk home and hearth for the sake of national liberation (as did the Vietnamese, and the Irish), would add significant uncertainties into Soviet planning estimates. Their citadel in Eastern Europe is not in the best of shape in peacetime, and could become a bubbling inferno during any attack by them against Western Europe. With resistance flourishing in both East and West, the Kremlin would find its hands full and its perimeters vulnerable to Chinese irredentism and Islamic fundamentalist advernturism. The retort to this scenario is that the USSR has enough high-technology conventional forces to suppress any resistance and enough nuclear weapons to deter outside intervention. But it will have used up many of its best weapons in defeating NATO's regular armies, if it can, so those weapons will not be ready immediately for the task of suppressing national risings and guerrilla warfare against Soviet occupation forces.

This recipe for making Europe an unappetizing plum is not easily followed within a social milieu uncongenial to societywide military prepar-edness.[4] It would be the task of policy makers to explain that this is popular defense in the proper sense, by the people, for their own territory and way of life, in order to deter that war in the first place. Training programs would be based on the premise that properly armed and mo-tivated average people can accomplish larger than average military as-signments. The American Colonies, after all, fought a revolution in which this very force multiplier of popular resistance and guerrilla warfare, together with the usual combat between designated regular forces, proved to be significant. The British did not give up in North America because they had exhausted their ammunition, but because they lost their patience.

The idea is to make the Soviets give up on the idea of conquering Western Europe not only in their peacetime rote military exercises, but, and much more important, to discourage the idea during those moments when harried Politburo leaders might contemplate the extension of the Brezhnev doctrine from the Berlin Wall to Gibraltar. It might seem that this could never happen without nuclear weapons being exploded, and so the end of the world, but the USSR will not necessarily be deterred by that vision alone, especially if they assume the West to be as scared of the apocalypse as they are, or even more so. And as Soviet armies advance across West Germany and the Low Countries, Soviet leaders will be broadcasting news announcements that *they* certainly do not want nuclear war, if only NATO will cooperate, but if NATO does not cooperate, then the USSR is prepared for that war, too.

The war that the USSR is not prepared for is a Europe full of Af-ghanistans or Vietnams, only on a broader scale. What stands between the recommendation and the realization is not the incapability of the West to bring it about, but the unwillingness to do so. Free peoples that are highly educated and affluent have the resources, but perhaps not the willingness, to commit themselves to sustainable national armed risings. Making the game of invasion not worth the candle of Western assets also implies that a prepared resistance would destroy those assets, much as the partisans in the USSR did for Nazi invaders, and as Russian cossacks did for Napoleon. The mistake that some proponents of nation-in-arms preparedness have made is to assume that it can substitute for effective conventional defenses, forward deployed and armed with modern, high-technology weapons. It cannot. The objective is to confront the USSR with a two-front war, not of the geographical kind, but with two different kinds of war, one shorter and more conventional, and the other longer and unconventional.

Confronted with the prospect of its own tables being turned against it, of armed resistance by its "liberated" provinces, even if it can somehow defeat and disarm their very competent standing forces, the USSR should be deterred from conventional (and therefore nuclear) war. If we in the West regard this notion, of prewar preparedness for armed resistance in a protracted struggle, as silly or bootless, we have only to ask ourselves why it has worked so well against us, under conditions much more favorable to us, since World War II.

Part of the answer is that no army has been built, nor bomb invented, that is as strong as an idea that couples absolute commitment to sensible preparedness. Europe need not be turned into a peacetime armed camp in order to prepare itself for a very competent intrawar resistance. The appropriate posture, as the Swedes and Swiss have demonstrated, is neither expensive nor unduly disruptive of day-to-day life. Nor is the knowledge base for this preparedness lacking. What is lacking is the leadership and resolve to undertake the difficult political task of telling democratic electorates unpopular things about the possibility of war and about their personal responsibility for helping to deter it. Allowed to escape from confrontation with this leadership, the public of Europe and its U.S. ally should not be blamed for copping out, in the vernacular. Democracy depends for its survival upon the willingness of elites to hear the voices of masses, and of masses to leave the details of governing to elites. Leaders, however, must also rise above details on occasion, to see the larger picture of threat and menace to national security and democratic civilization, and what can and should be done about it. The prospect of conventional war in Europe should be very deterring indeed, if the conventional war is only the first, and easier, part of the Soviet war plan. The next section draws parallels between unconventional wars, in which major powers face unexpected tactics designed to defeat their conventional tactics, and unconventional resistance, following a conventional invasion of one's own territory, as just described. The parallels are inexact, but suggestive of some historical observations pertinent to present-day Western strategic dilemmas.

WHAT WARS CAN WE FIGHT?

The relationship between U.S. armed forces and their society depends upon the legitimacy of the process by which those forces are selected, and upon public approval or disapproval of the kinds of conflicts to which those forces are committed. No U.S. president, after the Vietnam experience, can willy-nilly commit U.S. combat forces to war without asking these two questions—about the perceived legitimacy of soldier recruitment, and about the public approbation or opposition to military intervention. A further difficulty for present and future presidents is that the issues of input legitimacy, of how military resources including personnel are obtained, are linked to the questions of output legitimacy, or the evaluation of the rightness or wrongness of strategy in combat. In the case of nuclear war, we have been fortunate to have no actual tests of this relationship. We do, however, have examples from conventional war, and they illustrate some of the problematic aspects of this relationship between the ways in which we obtain the pertinent resources for fighting, including personnel, and how effectively we pick our spots, having obtained those resources.

In Vietnam, the polarized nature of the U.S. debate since 1968 has made assessment very difficult. The common assumption that the United States lost the war in Vietnam and that its strategy suffered defeat is more emotional than it is strategic or political. The United States has also been accused of having vague or no war aims, which is not entirely fair, and is a very different matter from lacking the strategy to carry out one's war aims, whatever they may be.

What U.S. politicians, military professionals, and (therefore) the public at large lacked most notably was a realistic appraisal of the kind of war that insurgency or civil war, with or without international overlay, can be. The United States should have known better, from its own Civil War or Revolutionary War. Or it could have asked the British, whose experiences in the Boer War were also indicative. A civil war is fundamentally different from a conventional war, by which is meant a war between regular, uniformed national forces, in which noncombatants are spared as much as possible. Let us call this second kind of war "statist" war, while acknowledging that it involves much bloodshed for noncombatants, but nevertheless is recognizable as different from a nonstatist war, including civil war.

In nonstatist wars, the objectives may not be territorial conquest or defeat of the opponent's armies by our armies, but the gradual erosion of one side's political and military control over the population, and therefore its legitimacy. The U.S. Army in Vietnam fought an effective, statist war, but lost the nonstatist one. It could not be defeated on the battlefield by North Vietnamese regulars or Viet Cong, but it could not prevent the political dry rot inside the South Vietnamese government from bringing about its ultimate demise, in the face of a North Vienamese invasion subsequent to U.S. withdrawal.[5] The U.S. government failed to understand what was happening on account of some misleading analogies with previous conflicts, including Munich (in the mind of Lyndon Johnson and some of his advisors) and Dienbienphu. The first analogy was the favorite of conservatives, the second of liberal critics of the war. Both were misleading. The reason why the first analogy, Munich, was misleading is by now obvious, so we pass on to the second.

Dienbienphu was a misleading analogy because the United States was not in Vietnam, as the French were in Indochina following World War II, in order to preserve a diminishing colonial empire. The French experience that more closely corresponds to the U.S. experience in Vietnam is Algeria. For the French in the 1950s, Algeria was not a colonial war in the way that Indochina was. Algeria was considered by many French political and military leaders, and numerous French citizens, to be an integral part of metropolitan France, a fifty-first state, as people in the United States might call it, and one that could not be separated from Paris any more than the Falkland Islands, say, could be yielded by the British. Whereas many French could be persuaded that Ho Chi Minh was a nationalist patriot fighting a second stage of his war of liberation against the Japanese, they were not so easily persuaded that Ben Bella was. Perhaps the closest U.S. analogy to the French experience in Algeria would be a revolution in Puerto Rico, in which armed rebellion became so intensive that the United States intervened militarily.

Now, at first it seems frivolous to compare Vietnam to Puerto Rico, and logically it is, but the assessment here is that for U.S. leaders and the public alike, Vietnam became like a revolutionary Puerto Rico, or Algeria for France, in their misinterpretation of its significance. Vietnam became invested with the symbolic baggage of a fifty-first state, in which the United States, according to Lyndon Johnson, had to make a stand, or U.S. credibility could suffer worldwide. So the United States over-invested its blood and treasure in that war, without any apparent script for terminating it, in the expectation that South Vietnam could be pro-tected from revolutionary overthrow or North Vietnamese aggression (forever?). More surprising than the misassessment of Vietnam's impor-tance was the misperception by U.S. leaders and the public of what a nonstatist or civil war entails in the way of tactics and reprisals.

A civil war is a war against civilian populations, as much as it is a war between regular combat forces. It is purposely antitraditional, if tradition is to preserve a line of demarcation between combatants and noncom-batants, sparing the latter the sufferings of war to the extent possible. In civil or nonstatist war the population is the target, just as it is in terrorism, and the purpose is the same: intimidation, so that the people either support the insurgents or remain neutral and so provide no effec-tive opposition to them by supporting the government. This is a cruel war, in which there are no "good guys" and "bad guys": All sides are the "bad guys" and use appropriate tactics. There is no morality of civil war, because the war is about morality, or whose civic morality will triumph in the conflict. Thus, civil war is more like the wars between the Roman Empire and its barbarian attackers, or subject populations, than it is like traditional statist wars. The U.S. public was understandably horrified to discover these unpleasant realities on their television screens, knowing little of the actual history of the U.S. or other civil or revolutionary wars.

The Vietnam experience is worth reviewing for two reasons. First, the developed West might learn something from the Indochina wars from 1945 to 1975 about the power of low-technology resistance to high-technology military operations; although cultures are not transferable, techniques cross national boundaries. Second, maintaining deterrence in Europe while increasing U.S. "out of the area" responsibilities strains the credulity, not to say resources, of the NATO alliance across the board.

Nonstatist wars have broken out across the globe like a plague, and they present a most acute kind of dilemma to economically developed, pluralist, democratic societies. Those societies, including most members of NATO, have armed forces that are primarily designed for high-intensity wars against statist opponents in the Warsaw Pact or (in the case of Greeks and Turks) elsewhere. Many of these armed forces are poorly equipped and trained to deal with insurgent conflicts and other nonstatist wars, which are more like police actions than wars of the traditional kind. Moreover, soldiers trained to fight against regular armed opponents often resent being assigned to the killing of populations in general in order to remove sanctuaries from insurgent control. The repugnance of this activity, of making war against innocents in order to isolate the guilty, almost destroyed the U.S. army psychologically in Vietnam, and brought about disgrace on Kitchener during the Boer War. There is no way to fight such a war, however, without these kinds of "dirty" tactics, because nonstatist conflicts are not wars. They are life-and-death struggles over legitimacy, and until legitimacy is established beyond disputes by one side or another, there is no benchmark to distinguish good deeds from misdeeds. Groups such as Amnesty International will point to obvious atrocities, and those misdeeds are properly noted as such, but they are going to recur because they are inherent in, and not unfortunate by-products of, nonstatist wars.

Unless and until there is a major change in the kinds of armed forces obtained by developed states in North America and Western Europe, the probability that these armed forces can or should be committed to nonstatist wars with success is very slight. The U.S. military intervention in Grenada is often cited as the exceptional case of a recent and successful defeat of Communist aggression in the Caribbean, but the military context was one in which the United States could not have lost. Nevertheless, the number of foul-ups in the operational enactment of Operation Urgent Fury suggest that any more substantial operation, say Nicaragua, or Cuba, would present impossible dilemmas for U.S. planners.[6] More typical of the ham-handedness that is apt to result from the placement of U.S. and European high-technology armed forces into Third World nonstatist wars is the debacle in Beirut, Lebanon, in which hundreds of U.S. Marines were killed in their own barracks by a terrorist truck bomb. The failures in the Carter administration's attempted rescue of U.S. hostages in Iran are also illustrative. In some of these cases, of course, there are state actors (for example, the Iranian government or the Lebanese government) involved in a conflict that is nevertheless, in a larger sense, a nonstatist war, as we have defined it, meaning that basic issues of political legitimacy are being fought over with a combination of regular and irregular tactics. This often leads, as in the case of the Iranian revolution against the Shah, to the seizure of the government of a state (Iran) by an antistatist regime; that is, the persons who control the government do not want to play by the customary rules of interstate diplomatic and political intercourse. Instead, they are declaredly opposed to the international order and its current basis of legitimation, which the regime now in control in Tehran believes ought to be derived from the Koran. This control of the apparatus of a state by an antistatist faction also occurred during the Bolshevik Revolution in Russia and for a time in the People's Republic of China. Both Soviet and Chinese rulerships have modified their insistence on how fast the statist order must be crushed by revolutionary forces, and for good reason, since the revolutionary forces in the present world are now not the ones they let loose in 1917, or 1949, at least not exclusively.

What this picture of nonstatist wars means for NATO is that, if conventional deterrence is to be preserved in Europe, then Europeans may have to do more themselves, and the United States may have its hands full outside of Europe coping with the statist implications of nonstatist wars. This will involve a very split personality for the U.S. Army, with one part of it devoted to preparedness for high-technology warfare on the Central Front, and the other part designed for rapid transport and agile fighting in the developing (and developed) societies of the Middle East/Southwest Asia, Africa, and Latin America. We say fighting, although much of what the United States will be doing is paramilitary intervention, in order to forestall the necessity for involvement in a wider war, or because a war is not appropriate given national policy objectives.[7]

Still, this skewing of the U.S. defense effort away from Europe, which may be inevitable, will force Europeans to confront some very hard issues. They will have to choose between a covential-emphasis deterrent or a nuclear-emphatic one. So far they have chosen the latter, but only by the nonchoice of relying on U.S. protection and the cheapest means of defense, so as not to strain budgets overly committed to the positive social state. A United States more preoccupied with its out-of-the-area problems in the 1990s and beyond, including some out-of-the-area problems within its own hemisphere, may, however, invite Europeans to take leadership of their own destiny in NATO. One hears more discussion these days, for example by Henry Kissinger, of a European SACEUR for NATO, and of a new entente between France and Germany, in which the French would commit more of their conventional forces to a prompt intervention in the FRG, following any Soviet attack. There is no question that Western Europe has the resources to provide all the conventional defense that Europe needs, given its abundant collective GNP and the wherewithal to set appropriate priorities.

The phrase "all the conventional defense that Europe needs" was used intentionally in the last sentence. NATO cannot ever exclude nuclear weapons from its deterrence and defense picture, however attractive this option seems from the standpoint of humane values and the horror of nuclear-war scenarios. Because nuclear war in Europe or anywhere else would be horrible, it must be prevented. And the way in which nuclear war in Europe is most likely to come about is after conventional deterrence fails. The statement that conventional deterrence fails refers to conventional deterrence under an unclear umbrella, of course. The reasons why it might fail are many, almost as many as there are scenarios and creative writers, but more important, it has held for four decades in the region in which two world wars have been fought in this century.[8] That is not a trivial accomplishment, and it is certainly due in part to the presence of so many NATO and Warsaw Pact nuclear weapons in the relevant theater of operations.

Thus, however nice it might appear as a gesture toward unilateral arms control, a decision by NATO in favor of no first use of nuclear weapons would weaken deterrence, not strengthen it. A no-first-use policy, if believed by the USSR, might encourage their mistaken calculation that a conventional war in Europe could be won. The calculation would be mistaken because, in the event, the nuclear-armed states of Europe and the general-purpose forces deployed there with nuclear weapons would in all probability factor into the Soviet equation of wartime escalation control. Specifically, Soviet attackers, as part of their conventional war plan, would plan to attack NATO nuclear weapons storage sites and delivery systems as soon as possible.[9] (NFU, after all, allows for second or retaliatory use of nuclear weapons.)

The USSR would want to preclude NATO's opportunity to resort to nuclear escalation and not depend upon NATO's self-deterrence. Perceiving this Soviet decision tree, NATO would in turn take actions to make its forces more survivable, and so prompt Soviet preemption. Although not an inevitable sequence of events, this is an all too plausible one. Nor would its plausibility be mitigated very much by a no-early-first-use policy, a modified version of no first use, which concedes the need for some nuclear deterrence, but hopes for less dependency upon nuclear, as opposed to conventional forces. This writer is not unsympathetic to no early use in principle, insofar as it affirms the importance of having NATO conventional forces that do not become their own nuclear trip wires. It would be a mistake, however, for NATO to adopt a no-early-first-use doctrine, if this meant paralyzing its capacity to take prudent measures for the survivability of its nuclear weapons based in Europe. No early first use cannot be an incentive for the Soviets to begin an attack with conventional forces, while honing the finer points of their theater nuclear-strike plan in the expectation of a NATO first use later.

Admittedly, there is an apparent inconsistency in rejecting NFU and urging European preparations for extended conventional war. Some Europeans would surely be persuaded of the need for an extended war capability, if that war was presumed to remain nonnuclear. Nuclear and conventional weapons cannot, however, be separated so neatly in Europe. NATO conventional forces are something less than a self-sufficient conventional defense, and something more than a trip wire. They contribute to deterrence both by providing denial capabilities against wars of limited aim and by creating a plausible threat of escalation, if conventional denial is not sufficient. Conversely, two sorts of errors to be avoided by armchair strategists are the error of nuclear virginity, of removing NATO's nuclear capacity altogether, or the error of nuclear promiscuity, of supposing that nuclear weapons can be used as deterrent substitutes for those contingencies where conventional forces should do the job. NATO can, of course, improve its conventional forces, and should, according to the recipes provided by expert analysts on both sides of the Atlantic. The minimum essentials in this regard have been well documented: permanent fortifications at the inter-German border; improved operational reserves; an alliancewide commitment to improved sustainability, especially the availability of sufficient ammunition and spare parts; improved protection for NATO tactical air forces, including more blast-resistant hangars and possibly theater ballistic missile defenses; and improved capabilities to see more of the battlefield and to interpret what is seen, via improved sensors and battle-management/command-control technologies.[10] These are improvements on the menu of short-war strategies, and they fall within the existing forward-defense/flexible-response corpus of planning. Beyond these minima, the gradual immersion in popular defense, discussed above, would be contributory to creating the societal base for protracted conflict.

An alternative to an extended conventional warfare capability, albeit underneath a nuclear umbrella, would be a European nuclear force. Such a force could stand independently of the U.S. strategic nuclear deterrent, based on the concept of proportional retaliation: It would not be worth the risk, say, of losing one Soviet city to atomic destruction for the USSR to launch a conventional attack on Western Europe. A European nuclear force would not need to be as survivable against preemption as is the U.S. strategic force. And, as a shared commitment by Europeans to defend themselves, with nuclear weapons if necessary, it would be more deterring than the comparatively "incredible" willingness of the United States to trade New York for Paris or Bonn.

The closest Europe has come to a Multilateral Nuclear Force (MLF) was the proposal by that name sponsored by the United States in the early 1960s. The plan was for a fleet of NATO submarines crewed by multinational contingents, with the idea that no one nation in Europe would have its finger on the trigger, but all would be in conjunction with the United States; thus, MLF would be a true NATO force. This initiative died of European opposition to what appeared to them as a transparent U.S. attempt to deny them access to independent nuclear deterrents; French pique was especially poignant. Another example of multilateral defense arrangements that were proposed but ever implemented was the European Defense Community, which fell to ruin in the out basket of French parliamentary review.

There are several difficulties in principle with European multilateral nuclear forces, in addition to the problems of implementation. First, there is no way to escape at least partial reliance upon U.S. strategic retaliatory power as the equalizer against the notional Soviet threat. However the scenarios are written, U.S. strategic nuclear weapons must be the counterdeterrents of their Soviet equivalents. And, in most scenarios of NATO nuclear first use in response to Soviet conventional aggression, NATO will need to demonstrate the willingness to run up the ladder of escalation faster than the Soviet Union can do likewise. So NATO will depend for its intrawar "compellence" upon U.S. strategic forces, no matter what European forces can do, given the competency of Soviet strategic forces.

Second, the problem of a West German (read, German) finger on nuclear trigger will not go away, no matter how logical the design for any multilateral force. The Soviet Union will view any West German participation in a European nuclear force as a repudiation of the post-World War II agreements on the status of the two Germanies and their relationship to the Eastern and Western blocs. Nor would the French be comfortable with a West German (shared or unilateral) nuclear force. More likely, the French would prefer to extend their own nuclear protection, at least a declaratory one of "enlarged sanctuarization," to the Federal Republic, subject to ultimate French national decision about priorities.

Third, how does Europe create its own regional nuclear force, which is both decoupled from the U.S. strategic nuclear force, and thus more believably used, and at the same time coupled, so that a superior Soviet regional nuclear force cannot intimidate it? NATO doctrine with regard to the control of escalation in the Central European theater of operations already straddles this issue. Admittedly, some of this uncertainty about the process of escalation helps NATO, but some of it is unintended confusion among Western policy makers and military planners. If Europe has a self-sufficient nuclear force, such that it can stand toe to toe with Soviet theater nuclear forces and without requiring U.S. assistance, then that force is decoupled from U.S. strategic nuclear forces. If the force is anything less than self-sufficient, then it remains a U.S. nuclear protectorate, although subcontracted to the Europeans of their own volition.

Subcontracts are subject to breaking at the whim of the prime contractor. The United States could decide that Europe's nuclear force was capable of self-sufficient defense when in fact it was not, and so initiate a U.S. nuclear disengagement from Europe, with the consequence of weakening deterrence.

There is a case, however, for strategic devolution of the responsibility for conventional deterrence and defense to NATO Europe, on behalf of the Atlantic alliance. We have already seen that shifts in transatlantic ambience, U.S.–Soviet strategic nuclear parity, and limitations on resources may cause devolution to happen on a schedule not fully planned by political leaders. The best reason for a strategic devolution in the responsibility for European deterrence and defense is political. Nations that take responsibility for their own defense, to the extent possible, are more likely to have a defense that is supported by and understood by their citizens, on whose behalf the armed forces are purchased and tasked. In democratic Western Europe, public acceptance of national defense programs and strategies must be built upon a public recognition that the U.S. defense commitment to Europe is no longer a tutelary one, as it was in the 1940s, but involves a partnership of independent states capable of making interdependent contributions to collective defense. A partnership is harder to manage than a tutor–student relationship, but the latter arrangement will not work in the 1990s or beyond for NATO. For the United States this means taking European strategic needs and perspectives—however different they may be—seriously, in the context of U.S. defense planning. Consultation of allies will have to precede, rather than follow, unilateral U.S. defense commitments growing out of the usual bureaucratic politics at home. Whether the United States can move from an imperative to a consultative role in NATO Europe will determine the extent of its influence, or lack thereof, in the decades ahead.

NOTES

1. An authoritative statement of U.S. maritime strategy appeared in the January 1986 issue of *Proceedings of the U.S. Naval Institute*, authored by Admiral James D. Watkins, then chief of naval operations.

2. John Erickson, Lynn Hansen, and William Schneider, *Soviet Ground Forces: An Operational Assessment* (Boulder, CO: Westview Press, 1986).

3. See Edward N. Luttwak, "The Materialist Bias: Why We Need More 'Fraud, Waste and Mismanagement,'" in Luttwak, *The Pentagon and the Art of War* (New York: Simon & Schuster, 1984), Ch. 5, pp. 130–56; and Michael I. Handel, "Numbers Do Count: The Question of Quality versus Quantity," in *The Strategic Imperative*, ed. Samuel P. Huntington (Cambridge, MA: Ballinger, 1982), pp. 193–228.

4. For a series of essays about what can be accomplished with civil or military resistance, see Adam Roberts, ed., *Civilian Resistance as National Defense*

(Harrisburg, PA: Stackpole Books, 1968). Of special value is the chapter by Gene Sharp on the technique of nonviolent action and that by Liddell Hart on lessons from violent and nonviolent resistance movements.

5. An informative and strongly opinionated treatment of U.S. decision making in the Vietnam conflict is Robert W. Komer, *Bureaucracy at War* (Boulder, CO: Westview Press, 1986), esp. Ch. 2.

6. Luttwak, *The Pentagon and the Art of War*, pp. 51–57, describes problems with execution of Operation Urgent Fury in Grenada.

7. See Richard A. Gabriel, *Military Incompetence: Why the American Military Doesn't Win* (New York: Hill and Wang, 1985), Ch. 4.

8. For elucidation of the conditions under which conventional deterrence works or fails, see John J. Mearsheimer, *Conventional Deterrence* (Ithaca, NY: Cornell University Press, 1983).

9. Erickson et al., *Soviet Ground Forces*, p. 55, notes that "Soviet tactical doctrine assumes that tactical operations will take place on a nuclear battlefield, or one that may become nuclear at any time."

10. European Security Study, *Strengthening Conventional Deterrence in Europe: Proposals for the 1990s* (New York: St. Martin's Press, 1983), provides a useful inventory of these and other recommendations.

12

CONCLUSION

Nuclear strategists, and policy makers who have had to draw upon the concepts developed by them, have done about as well as can be expected. The real world is not very tractable, and nuclear weapons are not surgical instruments. Accordingly, theories of deterrence applied to the superpowers and their bloc politics fall short of meeting the standards of rational decision making. They do not provide any clear and coherent notion of the ends for which nuclear war could be fought, or for the proportionality of means in using nuclear weapons for political ends, supposing the ends could be defined.

In defense of nuclear strategy, it has been said that it provides an explanation of why the United States and the Soviet Union have fought no wars, at least against one another, since 1945. In the absence of nuclear weapons, we are assured, conventional war between NATO and the Warsaw Pact nations would have erupted in Europe, or Western Europe would have lacked the capacity to sustain itself in the aftermath of World War II. Only nuclear weapons provided the shield behind which the democracies of Western Europe could rebuild their economies and anchor their political fates to the United States, according to this vision.

What is problematic about this argument is that it flies in the face of historical experience. There is little evidence to suggest that Stalin was prepared in 1946, or for that matter in 1949, to send the Red Army foraging across Western Europe. To the contrary, the imminent danger for Europe was the collapse of West European economies, followed by the election into power of Socialist or Communist parties with fraternal instincts for the USSR. That is why the U.S. Central Intelligence Agency invested so heavily in obtaining a favorable outcome in Italian elections during the 1940s. George F. Kennan, the distinguished diplomat and scholar who was the architect of the U.S. "containment" doctrine in 1947, understood this last point quite clearly. Kennan foresaw not the invasion of Europe by the Red Army (which had already happened, as far as the Soviets were willing and able to go), but the self-destruction of free Europe under the shadow of Soviet military power.[1]

The containment doctrine is also the reason for incorporating the Federal Republic of Germany into the Western defense alliance. There was less fear that Soviet forces would come crashing across the inter-German border than there was that Germans living in the West would seek to establish firmer bonds with Germans living in the East. Neither the Soviet nor the U.S. leaders wanted that.

West Germany's disaffection from NATO would remove the United States and its influence from continental European defense issues. And aspirations for reunification, which transcend the boundary between the Federal Republic and the DDR (East Germany), are to the Soviet Union a most disturbing threat. The Germans are in NATO, from their perspective, for the protection that the U.S. defense umbrella can offer; from the perspective of the United States and some Europeans other than Germans, the incorporation of the FRG into NATO keeps the Germans on a short leash, and thereby preserves peace.

It follows from the above, therefore, that the way to disestablish détente and peace in Europe is to encourage revolution within either the Soviet protectorate-glacis in Eastern Europe, or the disintegration of free economies and political systems in Western Europe. Preserving peace, that is to say, depends upon preserving lines of political demarcation, which have been arrived at by dint of much negotiating over several decades and by the costs paid by Soviet, U.S., and other allied armies to defeat Hitler. These arrangments, although unfair to the inhabitants of a divided Germany as they are viewed by many of them, are preferable to any alternatives, from the standpoint of preventing war in Europe. Former U.S. official Helmut Sonnenfeldt was once imprudent enough to state this publicly, and showers of vituperation rained down on his head from then on. It is important, however, for scholars to acknowledge what diplomats sometimes cannot. The beginning of wisdom on the subject of preserving peace in Europe, and avoiding nuclear war, lies in not rattling the cages of political accommodations that have by now proved themselves. This common sense is worth more than all the nuclear-strike scenarios and their attendant mathematics.

The second priority in preventing war in Europe is to avoid having the instruments of war become the causes of it. This means that arms control has two important parts to play, with regard to both conventional and nuclear weapons based in Europe. First, the gross numerical totals could be lower than they now are, and should be. There is little likelihood of

NATO and the Warsaw Pact being able to fight a limited nuclear war in Europe, and there is little point in NATO encouraging such a supposition on the part of its European members. Nor is the Soviet Union likely to believe that nuclear war, once it begins, can be limited, notwithstanding the protestations of U.S. strategists that the USSR is now interested more than formerly in the possibility of controlled nuclear war. On this issue, the Soviet Union is apt to take the position attributed to it only in circumstances when the United States wishes they would not. If the USSR can use nuclear weapons in Europe in a selective way with confidence that the war will not escalate into exchanges against their homeland, they will be doing so because the U.S. strategic nuclear deterrent has lost its efficacy. That is hardly reassuring from the Western standpoint. Admittedly, the number of nuclear weapons deployed by NATO has often been a political as much as a military requirement, as in the Pershing II and GLCM deployments that began in 1983.

Second, in addition to lowering the total numbers of nuclear and conventional forces deployed in Europe, sensible precautions can be taken in the form of so-called confidence-building measures, to assure that war does not break out by accident or miscalculation. Notice that we have said twice around that conventional as well as nuclear forces deployed in Europe can be reduced. Negotiations have until now proceeded on separate tracks, the MBFR talks for conventional-force reductions in the relevant guidelines area, and INF negotiations for the reductions of nuclear weapons in Europe (MBFR stands for Mutual and Balanced Force Reductions talks, under way since 1973). It is well past time for the two tracks to be merged, or at least pass each other like ships in the night. This is against the conventional wisdom that reductions in nuclear weapons deployed in Europe should be offset by increases in NATO conventional forces.

This conventional wisdom assumes that there is some sacrosanct dividing line between European nuclear and conventional forces with regard to the probability of war in Europe and, therefore, the stability of deterrence. Now, there is certainly a clear dividing line between the effects of conventional and nuclear weapons, both physical and symbolic; but we are discussing their deterrent effects, and the supposition of some NATO officials seems to be that if nuclear weapons are withdrawn from Europe, then additional conventional forces, meaning regular army divisions and tactical air armies supplied by the member states, must be provided.

This supposition implies that the probability of war in Europe is mainly dependent on what we in the West have come to call the "military balance," which is a bean count of divisions, ships, tanks, and so forth on each side. This balance is certainly important as a necessary condition for stable deterrence; it should not be so lopsided that it invites attack by either side in the expectation of quick and decisive victory, without using nuclear weapons. This is the danger in nuclear-arms reductions, to which some advocates of denuclearization have never been fully sensitive: If nuclear weapons are almost totally removed, or reductions come close to doing that, then neither side's conventional forces can be grossly out of balance with the other's.

Granted this point about military balances, it is not obvious that NATO conventional forces will be hopelessly out of balance with those of the Warsaw Pact, even if nuclear forces in Europe are reduced to nearly zero, which is not a plausible eventuality. NATO has always understated its conventional war-fighting competency, in order to keep U.S. nuclear weapons deployed in Europe as deterrents to Soviet aggression. This strategy can be said to have worked, if the USSR has ever contemplated any aggression of the kind nuclear weapons were thought to deter: a premeditated, massive attack designed to conquer Western Europe and disarm its nuclear forces before they could be used in retaliation. The cost of using U.S. nuclear weapons deployed in Europe for this purpose was that Europeans tied their political and military fates to the strategic and theater nuclear balances, which were mostly determined by the superpowers and not by themselves. Therefore, the European interest both in arms control and in more capable conventional defenses as deterrents was diminished.

The U.S. response has too frequently taken the form of chiding Europeans for wanting their own strategic nuclear forces (in the case of France) or promising the early use of U.S. strategic forces in lieu of European forces (thus frightening the parliamentary Left in several NATO member states). U.S. nuclear weapons deployed in Europe have also been subject to a variety of command, control, and communications (C3) arrangements that were as supple as the least common denominator of agreement among the participating provider and hosts.[2] It is not inconceivable that, if conventional deterrence failed and Soviet attacks were well planned, NATO nuclear weapons might be locked up for an amount of time sufficient for them to be destroyed by Soviet attackers. This is not necessarily the end of the road for the first use of nuclear forces by the West in Europe, since the supreme allied commander, Europe (SACEUR) wears a second hat as U.S. commander in chief, Europe (CINCEUR) and can ask the president for nuclear release in that role while NATO deliberates. Unless, however, Western Europe were on the verge of collapse under the onslaught of Pact forces, intra-European disagreements within NATO might preclude a U.S. president acting against the interests of Europeans as they saw them. It might be very difficult for a U.S. president to justify to his Congress and public the decision to use nuclear weapons over the objections of the Europeans on whose soil they would be detonated, given the attendant risks of escalation. Moreover, Europeans who suspected the United States of intending to use nuclear weapons on their soil, despite their opposition, might defect politically from the war effort.

What we are seeing, then, is that nuclear weapons are deterrents not of first resort, but only last resort, because the Soviets have them, too, and because nuclear war in Europe cannot be isolated from war between superpowers, involving exchanges against their homelands (or if it could be isolated, then NATO nuclear deterrence is a bluff). Accordingly, we are left with the deterrence provided by conventional forces, in the main, with nuclear forces as a backdrop, not irrelevant to the question of deterring war in Europe, but not as important as other things. Those other things include the conventional military balance that we are used to counting, but they include other and more intangible things as well.

First, as argued earlier, they include a positive relationship between the armed forces of European states and the United States and their societies. Societies and polities that regard their armed forces as necessary evils are not in a good position to deter aggression on the day when deterrence may be called upon to work. The willingness of parliaments and legislatures to commit budgets is one index of commitment to national and European defense, but not the only or most important one. Nor is the willingness of private investors to develop high-technology weapons the best indicator of the relationship between the armed forces and society. Instead, the indicators of the quality of this relationship are the intangible matters of honor and tradition, of respect and veneration, of esteem and self-regard. Military forces that are held in high regard for the function that they perform, and perform that function with professional and personal self-esteem, can be expected to cover themselves with credit in combat.

Second, to say that a strong relationship must obtain between polity and army, between armed forces and society, implies something about each end of that connection: The society must be worth defending; and the armed forces must be imbued with the best values of the society that they are defending, provided those are consensual societal values and not narrowly political ones. We do not, for example, want a British army that is a tool of the Conservative party, or a U.S. army that reflects the political program of the Democrats. We do, however, want armed forces in which the belief is strong that their professional character must reflect the best of national character, that elusive but definitive distillation of national political culture, history, and tradition.

U.S. and European societies that expect their armed forces to exhibit the best of their national character will have to provide a society that can distinguish transcendant political and social values from ephemeral values. In particular, the level of private consumption and standard of living will not be a decisive indicator of national health, although it is customary to suppose that it is. The standard of consumption is less important than the standard of production, both in quality and quantity. It is now established that Japan outproduced the United States and Western Europe in the 1970s—at least, established as economic fact, but still resisted as political fact. As this is written, President Reagan and Congress are busily bashing the Japanese for allegedly illegal or otherwise untoward trading practices, that is, for practicing capitalism. What the Japanese have, in fact, done, if it is studied without ethnocentric blinders, is to combine public and private trading and investment strategies on a global scale. They have decided that the state and the private sector should work together, instead of at cross-purposes, because postindustrial capitalism is more complicated than preindustrial or industrial. The United States and Europe are still figuring this out, although the recognition has dawned that protectionist trade legislation (really antitrading legislation) will not save deficient economic sectors from obsolescence.

Japanese success in the 1970s relative to the performance of the United States and Western Europe is one illustration of the blinders that prevent the latter governments from facing the realities of postindustrial politics and economics. Another and better illustration, from the standpoint of the interdependency of security policy and national economic policy, lies in the OPEC oil embargo of 1973 and its disastrous consequences. Those consequences were devastating for Western economies and for their wage-earning citizens, who could not suddenly quadruple their income in order to pay quadrupled oil prices. Yet the quiescence with which U.S. and European leaders accepted the strangulation of their economies, at the hands of seven shiekhs and their own oil companies, was remarkable. Instead of acting in concert to break this choke hold on their entire economies, the leaders of the United States and Europe pampered and stroked the oil companies, appeased the OPEC dictators (who invested some of their petrodollar profits in anti-Western terrorist organizations), and refused to countenance either serious conservation or its logical alternative—abandonment of environmental restrictions that limited energy production. In short, OPEC demonstrated that in economic matters relevant to national security, they were dealing with a ship of fools.

It is all too easy to blame U.S. and European leaders for this debacle, especially when the Nixon administration was in power in Washington, and the president was personally besieged by Watergate. Still, since the Arab oil embargo grew directly out of the Arab–Israeli war of 1973, it was a clear and explicit national security challenge to U.S. and allied credibility. Excuses, of course, can be made and were. U.S. NATO allies said that the alliance was not designed to deal with out-of-the-area issues, as if out of the area included the suffocation of their own economic health. U.S. officials pleaded that they did not have the equivalent of what is now called Central Command, growing out of the Rapid Deployment Force, for military intervention in the Persian Gulf. In 1987 the United

States did have the Central Command and a potential force of considerable size with which to intervene in the Persian Gulf/Southwest Asia theater of operations. This tempted President Reagan to order the reflagging of Kuwaiti oil tankers as U.S. ships and to provide a considerable maritime escort in order to protect those tankers. Like the oil embargo, all of this supposedly took place in peacetime, meaning that the United States and its NATO allies were not themselves in a shooting war. Iran and Iraq were, however, and that war presented a potentially very direct threat to Western oil supplies and also an indirect one, via catalytic expansion of a wider conflict that might involve the major powers of East and West. British, French, and other European escort services were provided for their tankers plying the Gulf in 1987; the Soviets similarly took care of their own. As in 1973, the situation in 1987 called for the skillful use of coercive diplomacy, using the instruments of war in order to influence the behavior of a potential adversary, while avoiding war if possible. Coercive diplomacy, however, requires that a very favorable set of conditions, in fortuitous alignment at the right time and in the right place, be established for its successful execution (discussed at greater length later).

The reversal inflicted by OPEC was more than economic. It advertised that the Western alliance had been politically divided. NATO allies were unwilling to take decisive action to overturn the embargo, and they were unwilling to develop national resources along lines that would preclude decisive clout for OPEC in the future. And we should not be deceived by the currently discussed oil glut, for this is a temporary shifting of market forces—not political forces—in the Persian Gulf or Middle East. The paralysis of U.S. and European political leaders in the 1970s was the simple failure of the successor generation, of those who inherited George F. Kennan's mantle, to distinguish a serious threat from a hypothetical one. While the Carter administration, for example, was fretting about the rebuilding of NATO, Soviet surrogates obtained toeholds in Central America, West and East Africa, and on the Arabian peninsula. Nor were people in the United States the only ones more willing to discuss familiar problems than confront the less familiar, but more painful. Europeans in the 1980s decided that a natural-gas pipeline from the USSR would be an economic boon for both sides of the East-West divide, and so bought into an arrangement that provided the USSR with much needed hard currency. Granted, the Reagan administration handled this issue poorly, as its predecessors frequently mishandled European sensibilities. Style points the United States may have lost, but on substance it was accurate. European and especially West German dependency upon Soviet exports of natural gas was a strategic as well as an economic issue, and not simply a matter of positive-sum economics. In the end, the United States had no choice but to acquiesce, and the Europeans persevered in their arrangements with the Soviet Union as a resource provider. By itself, the pipeline agreement would not collapse the defense of Europe, just as the U.S. paralysis in the OPEC oil embargo, by itself, would not roll up U.S. power east of Suez; but the two cases are consistent, and negative, in pointing toward national security irresolution, when resolution would require sacrifice of an economic kind from the voters who must be appeased. Not only voters, but also interest groups had to be placated. Thus, when U.S. banks found that their loans to Poland might become political liabilities in the early 1980s, they urged the United States not to respond too harshly to the Soviet crackdown on Solidarity (by using Polish national forces to do their work). After all, we would not want to jeopardize Western investments in Eastern Europe in order to make a simple point about the difference between détente on paper and détente in practice.

From the first issue, of having leaders who perceive correctly the threats to national interests and alliance solidarity, we pass to the second, having armed forces that reflect the best values of those societies. Samuel P. Huntington, many years ago, made the useful distinction between subjective and objective civilian control of the armed forces, and warned of the danger of overdoing the inculcation of civilian values into professional armies.[3] This admonition was well intended, for it would not do to have political officer corps that were so "civilianized" that they forgot their own unique history, tradition, and expertise. The reverse of that admonition, however, that military forces must represent their society's unique values, even in combat, must also be upheld. We do not want the U.S. army to behave like the army of Attila the Hun, and no just because it would create bad publicity, but because atrocities violate an implicit contract between a democratic society and its armed forces. The society does not have any right to demand that its soldiers commit atrocities, and the soldiers have the right to refuse to do so, if some ignoramus demands that of them. War is not atrocity making, or if it is, then it is not war, at least not the kind of war that the U.S. or British societies can support. Soldiers carry values into combat along with their rifles and knapsacks. Those values should reflect the best of a liberal democratic society, not the worst elements of it. This means that military training should partake of civilian education for the officer corps, and not be based upon a scholastic apartheid. Thus, the demands of the U.S. Left in the 1970s, for a removal of ROTC (Reserve Officers Training Corps) programs from universities, could not have been more wrong, from the standpoint of providing officers with truly civilian educations to diversify an officer corps otherwise composed entirely of military-academy graduates.

If the army is to be worthy of the democratic society that supports it, then the society must provide the best that it has for its armed forces. Now, this can be accomplished by voluntary or coercive means, and the recipe will vary, consistent with national traditions and expectations. The United States now has an all-volunteer force, although it formerly had a draft (from 1948 until 1973), but for most of its peacetime history has avoided conscription. The British rely on volunteer enlistments as well. This has led to criticism by some U.S. advocates of conscription, who argue that a society such as theirs cannot be defended by an armed force composed only of volunteers. The concern is that an all-volunteer enlisted force does not provide a representative cross-section of the entire society committed to its national defense, and that the upper classes, in particular, escape their share of responsibility for national defense.[4]

Military personnel issues have many complicated facets, but of this one, the relationship between conscription and national commitment to defense, it may be said that the issue is more complicated than opponents of the AVF (All-Volunteer Force) have maintained. It is not obvious that demographic representativeness within an armed force equates to an inculcation of desirable social values, and especially to a understanding of why we are fighting, and for what. As to the issue of shared risk, forces that are fighting on behalf of national defense, as opposed to an upper-class *junta* that has seized control of the country for its own purposes, are carrying out a mission that presumably has national approval. Of course, the pattern of U.S. intervention in Vietnam falsifies this assertion somewhat, since the Johnson administration sought to raise the ante of intervention gradually and with minimum public fanfare. The public was not brought along on the notion that it was a national war, rather than a war of the Johnson administration. And one result of that mismanagement of escalation and commitment was a widespread perception by the public that the draft was not fair, which was based on the claim of disproportionate sacrifices of social and economic classes. Had Vietnam been a national war, however, declared by the U.S. Congress, with trumpets blaring and "Star Spangled Banner" playing, antidraft resistance, really a surrogate for antiwar resistance, would have been unpopular instead of fashionable.

It is not in how the enlisted personnel are inducted, as much as it is in the traditions and training of the officer corps that military performance consistent with national values can be guaranteed. The U.S. Army chose to court-martial Lieutenant William Calley for the My Lai massacre, not the enlisted men under his command, because officers are held accountable for the conduct of their subordinates. The reciprocal of this, however, is that the subordinates have the right to disobey unlawful orders and can be expected to resist leadership that does not provide a good example. In some European armies, the armed forces maintained an upper-class character long after other institutions had become relatively democratized. As a result, social deference provided much of the important glue of leader–follower relations. Regimental loyalties carried through centuries also provide cohesion among officers and enlisted personnel in European armies, for example, the British. Although the U.S. Army is now trying to create its own version of the regimental system, by increasing the proportion of time that enlisted personnel and officers spend within a single unit, the United States has no tradition of social class, comparable to the European experience. We take it for granted that this is good, yet another illustration of how the new world has improved upon the old.

Leading an army into battle is not the same, however, as practicing any other profession. Armed-forces officers share with other professionals a unique expertise and sense of professional responsibility. In this regard, they are very much like doctors, lawyers, clergy, and so on; but in addition to a shared professional expertise, officers must also have a shared mystique. I cannot think of a better term for it, and the reader is invited to improve upon it. It is the indefinable something that distinguishes Montgomery and Patton from John Doe, and it can be ascertained only after the fact, by combat experience. This is a hard way to find out which officers have the mystique, and so modern armed forces have large personnel-review bureaucracies for deciding who gets promoted, transferred, and retired. In this regard, as well as in their technical expertise, they are like civilian bureaucracies, but here again, there is a substantive difference. The marketing firm that makes an erroneous decision loses some money. The military unit that does not fight cohesively, or according to a proper battle plan, loses the lives of its members, and perhaps vital political assets as well. The volume of complaints from U.S. officers (writing anonymously, which tells you something in itself) about the military personnel system, in such publications as *Armed Forces Journal International*, speaks for the difficulty of making proper decisions in peacetime about officer promotion and selection.

If the test of combat is the test of virtue or vice for officer corps, then it is a fair test if and only if the officers and their men are not stranded on an island of illiterate or no policy guidance. Politicians are apt to turn to armies, fleets, and air forces when they are at a loss to know what else to do, and if the United States is illustrative, when the Department of State seems unable or unwilling to provide useful diplomatic alternatives. Witness the fiasco in sending U.S. Marines into Beirut, with the loss of 241 lives in the barracks bombing of October 1983; or the ill-fated operation to rescue U.S. hostages in Iran, which aborted at Desert One; or the imbroglio between the Reagan administration and Congress over the use of U.S. warships to run picket duty for Kuwaiti oil tankers in the Persian Gulf in 1987. Each of these cases illustrates the propensity of politicians to use military forces in what the press calls peacekeeping missions, but which might better be termed coercive diplomacy. This is, as previously suggested, the use of force to send signals to an adversary or potential adversary that certain behavior had better not happen, or be stopped if it is already happening. In the case of U.S. forces in the Persian Gulf, for example, the escorting of Kuwaiti tankers and eventually placing some of them under U.S. flags was designed to send a message to the Iranians, not to extend their war against Iraq into disruption of oil supplies for consumers in the United States, Europe, and Japan.

The difficulty with using military forces in this way is that it will work only under very specific and favorable conditions, and these are rarely so fortuitously arranged. First, the side seeking to use displays of force to influence the behavior of others must clearly specify the behavior desired on the part of the adversary, and the action that will follow if compliance is not obtained. Second, the side being threatened must understand what is expected of it. Third, the side being threatened must perceive that the threatener can carry out the threat at an acceptable cost. Fourth, the side being threatened must perceive that the threatener is willing to carry out the threat. And fifth, there must be no exogenous force that might prevent the threatener from carrying out the threat, or provide the party being threatened with immunity from response.[5]

It can be seen from this checklist that U.S. policy in the Iranian hostage crisis, the Marine insertion into Lebanon in 1983, and the Persian Gulf escort duty did not fulfill most of these conditions. Even more seriously, with regard to the costs of ignoring the checklist, the United States in Vietnam for nearly a decade mistook what could be done with coercive diplomacy. It might seem imprudent to characterize the war that took place there as coercive diplomacy, and in its later stages it went well beyond that. What is important is that U.S. policy makers got themselves in over their heads in the Vietnam War by following the logic of coercive diplomacy into a dead end. Supposedly, the inch-by-inch increase in bombing of North Vietnam, together with the gradual increases in U.S. personnel commitments, would signal resolve to the North Vietnamese, who, suitably impressed, would agree to end the war on terms favorable to the survival of a non-Communist South Vietnam. In fact, the attempt to influence North Vietnam with coercive diplomacy violated all five of the items on our checklist, and the United States found itself in a major war without having thought through what it would do in such a eventuality. Indeed, President Johnson refused to acknowledge in a legal and constitutional sense that it was a war, referring to the U.S. mission as assistance to South Vietnam against North Vietnamese aggression.

Johnson has become the historical scapegoat for the U.S. intervention in Vietnam, but in truth he was badly misadvised, and by those experts whom a *New York Times* writer would aptly characterize as "the best and the brightest." Drawing upon new ideas nurtured in U.S. universities and think tanks, Kennedy and Johnson advisors felt that a slow squeeze on North Vietnam would eventually get them to call it quits at a price acceptable to the United States. With the advantage of hindsight, we can see that the North Vietnamese were willing to pay a higher price than their U.S. opponents had assumed. Thus, the apparent paradox that, although U.S. forces won success after success on the battlefield, when North Vietnamese forces would stand up and do battle, the United States lost its grasp of the coercive power inherent in the use of force. Ultimately, the North Vietnamese coerced the U.S.; that is, they influenced it to withdraw instead of defeating U.S. forces in battle.

Academics can understand this paradox, between increases in military power and decreases in political influence, but military officers have a hard time with it. In Vietnam, the officer corps felt after 1969 that it was conducting a holding action, not a war, and in a sense they were right. This is a dangerous position for officers who feel entrapped by political decisions that first commit them to battle, and then refuse them the open-door policy to bring the battle to a decisive conclusion. Thus, MacArthur articulated his grievances against the Truman administration policy in Korea, where he was overruled and prohibited from attacking the Chinese mainland. The heroic general felt, as he later told Congress, that in war "there is no substitute for victory," but he forgot that the definition of victory begins with a clarification of the political aims for which a state is fighting. The U.S. Army in Vietnam saw itself trapped between a failed coercive diplomacy and the embarrassment of President Johnson and his advisors, which prevented their withdrawal. There is some vindication for this view, since the president and his advisors repeatedly stressed that earlier commitments now necessitated still additional ones, *ad infinitum*, without making clearer the objectives for which soldiers had been sent there to begin with. This conclusion has been disputed, and there are undoubtedly some memoirs of the Vietnam years in which U.S. officials will claim that there was a clear objective: to prevent South Vietnam from falling into the hands of a Communist government. If that was the objective, however, it was not clear that the way to accomplish it was to re-create the Korean War in South Vietnam, while leaving North Vietnam as a sanctuary from the ground war. Actually, the *Pentagon Papers* make quite clear that U.S. policy makers had as many rationales for the Vietnam war as there were institutional vantage points within the government among its various departments, agencies, and bureaus.

The point of the preceding discussion is to give a flavor for the resentment that U.S. Army officers must have felt after being given a "mission impossible" and then finding that even the largest battlefield successes had no political significance. So, too, the U.S. sailors aboard the frigate *Stark* in 1987, which was struck by an Iraqi Exocet missile, must have wondered why they were on a peacekeeping mission in the middle of a war zone, operating under peacetime rules of engagement that made them more vulnerable to surprise. This was especially remarkable because it repeated the entrapment that occurred in Beirut in 1983, in which U.S. Marine guards were forbidden to prechamber their ammunition and the barracks were placed in a situation of extreme geographical vulnerability. What we are getting at is that war forces should be used as peace forces under very specific and limited conditions, and, in addition to those enumerated under the checklist for successful coercive diplomacy, there is one other. Other things being equal, neutral and multilateral military peacekeeping presences are preferable to one-sided and unilateral ones. The United States in Lebanon and in the Persian Gulf was not perceived as a neutral party, whatever President Reagan supposed. Nor should war be confused with coercive diplomacy to the detriment of military effectiveness, leading ultimately to the demise of morale in the officer corps. Much of the blame for the poor performance of officers in Vietnam lies elsewhere, in the expectation by politicians that armed forces are surgical rather than blunt instruments. This does not excuse the failures of individual officers in their tactical assignments, but it does provide some context for the evaluation of their efforts, and the context is still pertinent, as evident in the above examples from the Middle East.

For the United States, the officer corps has recovered much of its self-esteem by putting the Vietnam experience behind it, helped by a shift in national mood more supportive and understanding of Vietnam veterans and their experience. The war remains a warning against misconceived military interventions, but the public memory, always cinematic, is now becoming more sympathetic toward those individuals and institutions that took part. The danger lying ahead for the U.S. officer corps and its counterparts in Western Europe is the danger of "civilianization" of a postindustrial, technological kind. The U.S. military elite of the future will be more managerial and technical, and less traditionally combat oriented, than its predecessors, according to the concerns of some members of the military reform movement in the U.S. Congress and elsewhere. The image of military technocrats, who are disinterested in the lore of combat and the evolution of tactics, is on the front burner of op-ed columns, television talk shows, and professional literature.

This controversy has probably been hyped by exaggeration and conflicts among leading personalities, at least in the U.S. case, but as a genotypical difficulty, in the sense of organizational ethos and the professional identities that result from that ethos, it is a worthwhile issue. The issue is pervasive across civilian and military institutions. Scholars who feel that their universities have been taken over by administrators, or engineers who see experts on law and finance rise to the top of their organization, feel very much like professional soldiers of the "warrior" tradition, who see their eclipse by military accountants, military technocrats, and military publicists. Neither the military nor other institutions in postindustrial society can escape this increasing complexity in role differentiation; they will have to cope with it. One implication of this is a more complicated process by which the armed forces pick up their social cues about their professional identities and statuses, and the concomitant potential for divergence between armed forces and society that may result.

This problem of social norms and professional identity also affects those institutions outside the government that may be assigned to support military planning or operations, or on occasion assigned their own paramilitary operations. Intelligence agencies are the best example. The U.S. Central Intelligence Agency has had more than one internal upheaval over the issue of roles and missions, and whether paramilitary covert actions should be assigned to intelligence agencies at all. During the 1970s, in the aftermath of Vietnam and Watergate, a more critical attitude toward government and a more intrusive congressional and media culture resulted in a shift in the norms by which U.S. intelligence was evaluated. No longer would intelligence escape detailed scrutiny of its covert operations by the legislative branch, as well as through the executive chain of command. This had morale-busting impacts on some professional intelligence officers, but others adjusted to the new climate. As the Iran–Contra affair during the Reagan administration proved, however, the United States has still not devised an effective and accountable way to conduct covert operations. What is accountably reported is sometimes then disclosed to the media, thus blowing the operation; what is effective is not always disclosed. Congressional propensity for legalism, as in the investigation of U.S. aid to the Nicaraguan rebels in 1987, obscures the fact that intelligence operations cannot be micro managed from a distance. Even higher officials in the executive branch may be knowledgeable about the essence of an operation, and should be, without having to second-guess the details. It is even more improbable that the U.S. Congress can do so. The congressional urge to share the credit for covert actions that work, and escape blame for those that do not, creates an adversarial relationship with the president and his advisors, who must accept accountability for successes and failures. A less media-oriented review process for covert and other U.S. intelligence operations would focus on congressional approval, or lack thereof, for the substance of an operation, with an understanding that in the real world the best-planned military and intelligence operations can succeed or fail by a hair's difference. Otherwise, demoralization of the U.S. intelligence professionals will be as marked in future decades as it was in the 1970s, with the further divergence between the norms of operators and the expectations of society. A democratic society begins with a tacit contradiction in any case, between its demands for openness and its need to conduct some matters of state in secrecy, and sometimes unaccountably. "Henry Stimsonism," of the sort that defines gentlemen as those who do not read each other's mail, is still alive in the ethos of the newly minted U.S. congressman or parliamentary backbencher who has had no exposure to foreign and defense policy issues.

SOVIET DILEMMAS

This problem, of military and societal articulation, is not only a Western one. The Soviet Union faced the issue immediately following the defeat of White opponents by Red forces in the civil war. At the Tenth Party Congress in 1921, Mikhail Frunze and S. I. Gusev introduced 22 propositions on the organization of the Soviet armed forces. This was to be the opening volley of a long-running dispute between Frunze and Trotsky on the nature of the Soviet army, and the first step in the development of a unified Soviet military doctrine.[6] It involved a great deal of arguing about whether there was such a thing as a proletarian army as opposed to a capitalist one, and to what extent the social-class structure of a country would determine the character of its military art. Ultimately, history appears to have vindicated Trotsky, to the effect that certain objective conditions might have as much to do with military operations as the class nature of the armed forces (for example, the size of the theater of operations, the numbers of combatants on each side, the state of technology, and so forth).

During the Eleventh Party Congress in 1922, Trotsky and Frunze conducted an extensive debate, which would seem pointless to Westerners, over this same issue, as to whether strategy, tactics, and military regulations could be included in a unified military doctrine created by the Marxist method.[7] This debate was quite acrimonious, with Trotsky, at the top of his form scoring many points. By 1925 Frunze had replaced Trotsky as Commissar for Military and Naval Affairs and Trotsky had fallen into disfavor. From that day to this, Frunze has been treated as a heroic leader of troops in the Civil War (which he was) and as a sainted theorist of Soviet military science. And contemporary Soviet writers draw upon his thoughts about the importance of the offensive, maneuver warfare, and activity (meaning activism) in their debates about military science and military art.[8] Thus, the issue of Marxist military science came about, not by direct deduction from philosophical apothegms to field regulations, but by blending the insights of Frunze and other theorists into actual Soviet experience. In this larger and more subtle sense than Fruze intended, a Soviet military art and science, if not a proletarian one in the class-exclusive sense that some theorists intended, came about.

Soviet military doctrine, which includes military science and military art, includes the nature of future wars and the means of preparing the armed forces to wage them. By definition, these future wars are predominantly wars against capitalist states, for only historical aberrations (read, Chairman Mao) can produce Communist states that do not see the true historical path leading to Soviet-style communism. These wars between Soviet Communists and capitalists are no longer, however, "fatalistically inevitable," in party nomenclature, and since the Khrushchev years the USSR has acknowledged that Soviet military doctrine admits of coexistence with the West. This coexistence does not imply a consensus between East and West about policy objectives or about the assessment of the global correlation of forces at any point in time. Instead, it means that the USSR must pick and choose the conflicts it gets itself into, for fear that it might be propelled into one it cannot get itself out of. Thus, Marxist theory and Soviet military professional thinking converge on the inappropriateness of military adventurism and on the necessity for well-planned and rehearsed operations to precede any war, even wars the USSR does not want, but cannot avoid.[9]

The Soviet army (collective for armed forces as used in the West) is kept powerless to overthrow the party leadership, not by passing out more guns to the party, but by party control of civil and military education. Those who are promoted into the higher military ranks in the USSR thus have been fully indoctrinated with the necessary suppositions about the nature of the class enemy, the character and causes of wars, and the worldwide Soviet mission on behalf of the ever-present global Socialist proletariat. This is subjective control with a vengeance, and its unrelenting grip on the army is vital, for otherwise it might occur to the leadership of the Soviet armed forces that party hacks were disposable. Thus, also, the KGB and other party security organs are wrapped into the armed-forces structure at every point, so as to provide the leadership with advance notice of any disaffection with the regime. Such disaffection does not lead to promotion, and occasionally it leads to worse things. This is not to say that real disputes about military doctrine do not occur in the USSR; they do, and they are quite genuine in their concern with doctrinal points, provided those points have not yet been settled by the party leadership as dogma. If they have not, one can find Soviet writers on all sides of military strategic and operational issues, and evolutionary trends can also be spotted.

One of those evolutionary trends is a movement away from pronouncements that nuclear war with the United States would be no different from other wars, and toward acknowledgment that the traditional notion of victory in class struggles might not apply.[10] Again, to some in the West this seems to be a belated recognition of the obvious by Soviet political and military leaders, but it is not at all obvious to them, because their Marxist heritage and military experience tells them that fatalism is unphilosophical and does not pay dividends on national self-defense. So, from Brezhnev's speech in Tula in 1977 to the present, the Soviet political and military leadership have departed from the script we might have expected of them, had they not considered the results of studies of the effects of nuclear war, including their own studies. The Chernobyl episode can only have reinforced the facing of technological facts, which require that military doctrine be adjusted to fit them.

This adjustment the USSR has had to make time and time again, from Lenin's New Economic Policy to the admission that traditional notions of military victory might not apply to a superpower nuclear war. Nuclear weapons have brought the USSR back to where Frunze began, with an emphasis upon what we now call combined arms, the offensive, maneuver, and the social base upon which military power is built. The USSR may not have a proletarian military doctrine, but it has a Socialist one, the doctrine of a party/state in which supremacy over the armed forces is assured by indoctrination of military leaders and by internal security elements that operate outside military control. The danger was that these internal security organs would get so out of control that they themselves would assume pride of place over party and armed forces, and had Beria assumed control of the USSR after Stalin's death, this might have happened.

The USSR has therefore partaken of the operational and strategic virtues of military art and science without conceding any deviation from its long-range political objectives, which are ideologically conditioned. And the Soviet armed forces have emerged as the most respected and admired institutions in the USSR, in contrast to an economy that is marked with performance failures and a party leadership which, under Brezhnev, was remarkable for its cronyism, geriatric character, and managerial incompetency. The most vivid contrast in Soviet public awareness of and respect for Soviet institutions lies in the contrast between their attitude toward the security organs and their regard for the armed forces, which won the Great Patriotic War and liberated the Soviet Union from Hitler's juggernaut. The "Checklists" of the KGB may be respected or feared for their power or influence, but never for what they symbolize in the way of national achievements, which are part of Soviet collective memory.

A fair verdict on this Soviet experience is that it has not developed any proletarian military art, but it has managed to fuse ideological, organizational, and operational nuances into a resonably coherent whole. This fusion leaves no doubt over the claims by military leaders to their shares of societal resources, provided they are willing to remain politically subordinate. This they are willing to do, although whether they will forever, if resource-allocation priorities are shifted, is not clear. At the very apex of the Soviet power structure—the Politburo—military, internal security, and party organization are represented as an uneasy three-sided triangle, and government as opposed to party bureaucrats might represent a fourth "interest group," using the term loosely, or power elite. Thus the Soviet leadership commingles civilianized military elites with militarized civilian elites, meaning that the civilianized military elites hold military ranks, but have been infused with party values, while the militarized civilians hold nonmilitary posts, but accept the priority of national defense needs over others.

The Western pattern, too, has been to subordinate military to civilian control, although for obvious reasons the mechanics are different. In the USSR the pattern has been to bring about fusion of civil and military elites within an all-enclosing party envelope. In the West, the diffusion of power, rather than its centralization, has been the preferred approach. The Western approach removes the threat of despotic rule, but at a price. Defense by democracy invites the armed forces to become interest groups, which press their claims for resources in the same budget-making process as other interests. In the United States the individual military services develop bureaucratic imperatives for enlarging their shares of the pie on a permanent basis, while secretaries of defense and presidents come and go with each new election. In the United Kingdom the British permanent civil service provides a buffer between service influence and cabinet influence, but this force is less important in the U.S. situation. Individual services can and do make "end runs" to their preferred congressional committees for support on doctrinal or budgetary matters. Given the worldwide dispersal of U.S. commitments, this means that much of the time in the military planning process is spent cleaning up after the wreckage of the "interest articulation" process, meaning lobbying. The U.S. system of defense organization, at least until recently, contributed to his milieu of every service for itself, although some hope that the Goldwater–Nichols defense reorganization of 1986 will provide more clout for the Joint Chiefs of Staff and the chairman of that group, compared to the individual services and their leaders.[11]

Differences between the Western and Soviet pattern of civil-military relations are not irrelevant to the kinds of strategies that have predominated in each case. The West has come to be as reliant as it is on nuclear weapons, not only to deter surprise Soviet nuclear attack on the United States or its NATO allies but also to deter lesser provocations, including strictly conventional wars outside as well as inside Europe. This nuclear strategizing, as opposed to strategy, holds great dangers in stretching the U.S. nuclear umbrella to the breaking point to make up for the unwillingness of European treasuries and legislatures to support their own defense efforts. No argument is made that Europeans are not already doing a lot, for they are. The point is that they must do more, marginally in terms of additional pounds, francs, and marks, but more than marginally, in terms of thinking through the relation between the citizen and the national defense. Or, they must commit themselves to see the painstaking process of conventional arms control through to its conclusion and, in the interim, maintain parity with their Pact counterparts. Although there is some mistaken sentiment in NATO for conventional arms control as a substitute for conventional rearmament, the two are linked. Only something close to conventional parity can serve as a stimulus for East-West mutual reductions, and as a comfort to the hawkish factions on both sides of the inter-German border. Moreover, the conventional balance becomes more important for deterrence as the U.S.–Soviet levels of strategic and long-range theater nuclear weapons are reduced. As we noted, Henry Kissinger was blunt, if tactless, in telling his European audience in 1979 that the United States should not make threats (meaning nuclear threats) that it did not mean, or if it did mean them, it should not execute, because to execute them would mean the end of civilization. The paraphrase captures the essence of Kissinger's statement, which was probably designed to shock European lethargy.

The problems to which Kissinger has pointed, however, will not go away. As Michael Howard has no aptly noted, peoples who are not prepared to defend their own territories with adequate conventional forces cannot be expected to stand firm when they are theatened with nuclear war.[12] Just so—the real nuclear deterrent in Europe lies first of all in the resistance the USSR can expect from NATO conventional forces, and second in the possibility of escalation, if the resistance proves to be inadequate. NATO cannot do without some threat of escalation, but as things stand now, it is much too dependent on it, and not obviously to its advantage. Nuclear threats appear to be low-cost substitutes for conventional denial forces in the calm of peacetime. When war is actually threatening, however, politicians will wish they had the missing conventional forces already in place, and wonder whether they can credibly threaten to use nuclear forces, which the opponent can match or exceed. Whether those conventional forces will be available in adequate numbers in the 1990s, and beyond, is very dependent upon the issues discussed in this chapter, having to do with the congruity of expectations between the armed forces and the societies that provide for their upkeep. NATO forces in Europe could now reasonably expect that, if war breaks out, their societies expect very little more of them than to die in place. They deserve better, from societies that can afford to do more.

NOTES

1. George F. Kennan, "The Origins of Containment," in *Containment: Concept and Policy*, ed. Terry L. Diebel and John Lewis Gaddis (Washington, DC: National Defense University Press, 1986), Ch. 2, pp. 23–32. There is a substantial danger in the "hindsight" interpretation of what Kennan "meant" to say, and perhaps Kennan's own changes of mind have contributed to it. Compare Kennan's piece cited above with his article, "The Sources of Soviet Conduct," *Foreign Affairs* 25 (July 1947), reprinted in Kennan, *American Diplomacy 1900–1950*

Chicago: University of Chicago Press, 1951). Readers should be wary of deductions from Kennan's writings of decades ago that are applied as measuring rods for the assessment of contemporary problems.

2. Katherine McArdle Kelleher, "NATO Nuclear Operations," in *Managing Nuclear Operations*, ed. Ashton B. Carter, John D. Steinbruner, and Charles A. Zraket (Washington, DC: Brookings Institution, 1987), Ch. 14, pp. 445–69.

3. Samuel P. Huntington, *The Soldier and the State: The Theory and Practice of Civil-Military Relations* (New York: Vintage Books, 1964). Originally published by Harvard University Press, in 1957.

4. For an authoritative study of U.S. options for obtaining military personnel, see Richard Danzig and Peter Szanton, *National Service: What Would It Mean?* (Lexington, MA: D.C. Heath, 1986).

5. This checklist for the successful application of coercive diplomacy is adapted from Alexander L. George, David K. Hall, and William R. Simons, *The Limits of Coercive Diplomacy: Laos, Cuba, Vietnam* (Boston: Little, Brown, 1971).

6. Walter Darnell Jacobs, *Frunze: The Soviet Clausewitz, 1885–1925* (The Hague: Martinus Nijhoff, 1969), pp. 24–25.

7. Jacobs, *Frunze: The Soviet Clausewitz*, pp. 66–88.

8. Condoleezza Rice, "The Making of Soviet Strategy," in *Makers of Modern Strategy: From Machiavelli to the Nuclear Age*, ed. Peter Paret (Princeton, NJ: Princeton University Press, 1986), Ch. 22, pp. 648–76, esp. pp. 653–55. Frunze's assertions that proletarians were naturally predisposed to offensive warfare, and peasants to defensive, is among the many stand-alone citations that can be used against him. This is very much out of context, however, and as the studies by Jacobs and Rice cited previously show, Frunze's larger case, on behalf of unified doctrine and a professional cadre army instead of a militia, prevailed.

9. A very informative dissection of the Soviet military mind set can be found in Nathan Leites, "The Soviet Style of War," in *Soviet Military Thinking*, ed. Derek Leebaert (London: Allen and Unwin, 1981), pp. 185–224. The flavor of adjustment in Soviet military thinking as a result of the deployment of nuclear weapons can be obtained from V. D. Sokolovsky, *Soviet Military Strategy*, 3rd ed. (New York: Crane, Russak, 1975); edited, with an analysis and commentary, by Harriet Fast Scott. Also very useful on trends with regard to operational issues is John G. Hines, Phillip A. Petersen, and Notra Trulock III, "Soviet Military Theory from 1945–2000: Implications for NATO," *Washington Quarterly* 9, No. 4 (Fall 1986): 117–37.

10. See Raymond L. Garthoff, "Mutual Deterrence, Parity and Strategic Arms Limitation in Soviet Policy," Ch. 5 in *Soviet Military Thinking*, ed. Leebaert, Ch. 5, pp. 92–124.

11. For perspective and background on issues in U.S. defense organization, see Robert J. Art, Vincent Davis, and Samuel P. Huntington, eds., *Reorganizing America's Defenses* (New York: Pergamon Brassey's, 1985).

12. For this and other pertinent observations on Europe's defense dilemmas, see Michael Howard, *The Causes of Wars* (Cambridge, MA: Harvard University Press, 1984). Kissinger's remarks were cited previously in Bertram, ed., *Strategic Deterrence in a Changing Environment*, p. 109.

EPILOGUE

Even as we write, there are profound forces that are shaping the wars of the future. The day may not be far off when the superpower balance of terror may seem nostalgic. After all, no wars have been fought between U.S. and Soviet armed forces, or among U.S., Soviet, and European forces, since World War II ended. This is a considerable period of peace, brought about by many factors, but pride of place surely belongs to the balance of terror about which writers have expressed so much (understandable) concern. The reason for this concern is valid. Had the U.S.–Soviet balance of terror failed to deter war, mutual suicide for the combatants, and potentially many others, was the certain result.

Note, however, that this stark and terrifying nuclear duopoly can be compared to the costs and benefits of a state of nature among prepolitical beings. Calculations are very simple, even if the results of calculating wrong are horrendous. And certainly since 1949, if not before, leaders of both U.S. and Soviet military hierarchies have been in no doubt about the disproportionate costs of nuclear war, relative to any conceivable benefits that might accrue from it. As McGeorge Bundy, formerly national security advisor to President John F. Kennedy, once said, even the loss of a single U.S. city to a nuclear detonation would be a disaster without precedent in our history. This reckoning by political leaders, undoubtedly true today, means that deterrence has been judged weak from time to time by U.S. or Soviet analysts, but never by political leaders who faced the responsibility for deciding for war with nuclear weapons.

The simplicity of the balance of terror between superpowers is, of course, made somewhat more complicated by the need to extend U.S. defense guarantees, and therefore deterrence, to NATO Europe. In other areas of the world the United States might conceivably use nuclear weapons; in NATO Europe, it is our declaratory strategy to do so. This strategy serves to perform two functions: it helps to deter Soviet first use of nuclear weapons in Europe, and it provides a capability to NATO for escalation to the use of nuclear weapons in order to stop a Soviet conventional attack that is about to succeed. This second function of NATO nuclear weapons, which is to say U.S. and British nuclear weapons assigned to NATO, is much debated on both sides of the Atlantic.[1] Even first use of nuclear weapons, however, by NATO to defeat a Soviet conventional invasion, on the assumption that escalation to strategic nuclear war is a plausible outcome of first use, does not complicate the stability of the strategic balance overly much. It is still the case that, absent any first-strike capability against the home-based forces of its opponent, neither the United States nor the Soviet Union can expect to attain victory, once nuclear weapons are used. Nor can either count on conventional war taking place below the nuclear threshold. Thus, deterrence in Europe seems likely to hold, provided the simple state of nature in which both superpowers find themselves, one of mutual vulnerability to retaliation against their societies, also holds.

It is the holding of the condition of mutual vulnerability, however, that is doubtful for the future, as opposed to the past, of superpower strategic and political relations. The present discussion, admittedly speculative, but based upon indications already taking place, elaborates on why this might be so. If it becomes possible to conceive of fightable, controllable, and winnable nuclear wars, then the future will differ from the past. Perhaps the right question is not whether fightable, controllable, and winnable nuclear exchanges can be contemplated. Instead, we should ask whether superpower conflict could take place using nuclear weapons in small doses in order to attain limited policy objectives, or if the same objectives might be attained by using strategic weapons other than nuclear.

As to the first, the usability of nuclear weapons in pursuit of discrete policy objectives, weapons laboratories in the United States and presumably elsewhere are already at work on the tools. Research is now being conducted on nuclear delivery systems and weapons that might, for example, explode over a very restricted region of airspace above a target, with very minimal collateral damage to surrounding structures and people. This seems incredible to those of us who grew up in the age of nuclear blockbusters, whose large yields compensated for their poor accuracies, but the trend in both superpowers' forces is clear—toward smaller yields and greater accuracies. Delivery systems have undergone modernization, which also contributes to the feasibility of precisely timed and targeted nuclear attacks. The cruise missile is an example. Of course, future research will have to create even smaller packages of fusion bombs to minimize collateral damage well below current standards, but there is no reason to suppose that such progress in yield reduction, given foreseeable improvements in accuracy, cannot happen.

The second development that might make strategic war feasible is the possibility of conducting it without nuclear weapons.[2] This sounds incredible and is, for the moment, but the future is a permissive one. Here we see on the horizon research and development that will invent new kinds of weapons, instead of miniaturizing the damage attendant to older ones. Lasers, particle beams, precision-guided ballistic and cruise missiles, radio-frequency weapons, and other back-of-the-envelope systems not even tested will surely dot the strategic landscape of the twenty-first century. If this seems fanciful, try to imagine that you are a citizen of the United States in 1917, as the United States declares war against the kaiser, and imagine yourself trying to forecast the military technology of 1980. How accurately can we foresee the technology of 2020 from the present, to say nothing of the technology of 2050?

If we take as an example the development of advanced cruise missiles, pilotless jet aircraft that can be launched from ground-, sea-, or land-based platforms, we can see some of the implications of near-term technologies for future strategic thought and practice. The development and deployment of large inventories of ballistic missiles by the superpowers relegated cruise missiles to a back stage for several decades in U.S. planning. They had a comeback in the 1970s, when improved guidance and engines, as well as versatility, made them seem more attractive as strategic weapons. The next generations of U.S. and Soviet cruise missiles will be faster, stealthier (having lower observables), and therefore harder to detect by radar. They will make possible surprise attacks from a larger variety of delivery systems, and from a wider compass of directions and in three dimensions: land, sea, and air. Moreover, cruise missiles and ballistic missiles with sufficiently smart front ends could attack targets now assigned to nuclear weapons. Although ballistic weapons were the weapons of choice in the 1960s and 1970s, because of their prompt counterforce, secure command and control, and improved accuracies, conditions are now changing. In the 1980s ICBMs became a liability because of their putative vulnerability to countersilo first strikes; sea-based ballistic and cruise missiles and air-launched cruise missiles became more attractive, because they were presumed survivable under almost any conditions.

Cruise missiles have their drawbacks, however, including their tendency to blur the distinctions, now so salient, between conventional and nuclear war and between strategic and nonstrategic war. The first confusion would be a problem for arms control, because the distinction between cruise missiles carrying conventional warheads, versus those carrying nuclear ones, is not easy to make. The second confusion might result from the variety of launchers for cruise missiles and the varying distances over which they could be flying to accomplish their missions. For example, would a ground-launched cruise missile (GLCM) launched from the Federal Republic of Germany and landing inside Soviet territory be a strategic weapon or a theater (nuclear or conventional) weapon? In U.S. nomenclature, a strategic weapon is one that has intercontinental range; therefore, European-based cruise missiles do not count as strategic. In Soviet understanding, any weapon that can explode within the territorial homeland of the USSR is a strategic weapon. Although the Soviet Union has from time to time modified this definition in practice, in order to make arms-control agreements more feasible, the essence of Soviet views has not changed very much. Some evidence for this last statement is provided by Soviet exertions in the area of strategic air defense in the absence of any comparable deployments by the United States, and well after the United States shifted from an exclusive reliance upon bombers for strategic retaliation to a mixed force of land- and sea-based missiles, together with bombers.

The discussion of cruise-missile technology only illustrates the problem. Consider now something more futuristic, the possible deployment by either superpower of Star Wars technology for missile defense. This prospect has been greeted with cheers by Reaganauts and with jeers by opponents of the U.S. president, since Reagan first mentioned the idea in his March 23, 1983 speech. The speech turned into a program and an organization working on the development of technology for defense against ballistic missiles, including the possible exploitation of off-the-shelf technologies as early as the 1990s. The SDI rebate rapidly became a shouting match between those who preferred deterrence as usual, based on survivable retaliatory forces and vulnerable populations, and those who preferred a new concept of Mutual Assured Survival, in which both sides would deploy defenses that would deny any attacker its objectives, and so induce reductions in offensive weapons.[3]

This vision of a world almost disarmed of offenses and reliant upon defenses or security required more than newer generations of weapons. It also required rethinking of the relationship between strategic command, control, and communications (C3) and the missions that are assigned to U.S. strategic forces. Until now, the problem of strategic C3 has been simplified by the absence of effective defenses, pursuant to the ABM Treaty of 1972, which precludes effective territorial BMD systems to either superpower. Thus, if the United States tasked its retaliatory forces for general nuclear response against a variety of military and other targets, it could compute with reasonable accuracy the proportion of that force that would survive a surprise attack and penetrate Soviet defenses. Even without defenses, the problem becomes more difficult if the United States also tasks its retaliatory forces with protracted or limited nuclear-war missions, for either assumption requires continuing control over retaliatory forces and fine-tuned attack assessments in the face of possible attempts to disrupt them.[4] The trend in U.S. declaratory and operational policy since 1974 has been to increase the expectations imposed upon strategic retaliatory forces, in terms of the extent to which they can be used selectively and flexibly.[5] As the expectations for the flexible employment of U.S. strategic nuclear forces have increased, the assumption has been that command-system improvements to support increased flexibility in force employment will follow along. It is not always the case, however, that the command system can adjust rapidly to changes in the expectations of policymakers about force tasking. Nor can command systems compensate for basic limitations inherent in the forces themselves. For example, ICBMs must apparently be launched on warning or under attack, if they are to fulfill their assigned missions. Yet expert analysts have questioned whether this can be accomplished, given the plausible time lines associated with preemptive attack against U.S. missile silos.[6] Nor is it a simple matter to launch and recall the bomber force, if it has been scrambled for its own survivability after an apparent strategic warning of possible attack has been received.

These problems, of survivability and flexibility, become even more complicated and more stressful of C3 capabilities when defenses are added to the equation. There are several levels at which the relationship between strategic C3 and BMD can be discussed. First, there is the need to defend the system against preemptive attack. This is true of the weapons and sensors, as well as the C3 system itself. Second, there is the problem of system integration, of making certain that the various parts of the system act together coherently. This is frequently referred to as "battle managemet" in the C3 literature. Third, there is the problem of vulnerability of deception, either self-generated or imposed by the opponent. And fourth, related to the third issue, is the problem of the system defeating itself by overly complicated architecture, misdesigned rules of engagement, or other means. Within this last category one might include concerns about the system automatically firing at ghosts instead of real targets, and the issue of how much response can be automated in order to carry out boost-phase intercept.[7]

The first problem is that of defense suppression. The opponent may decide to attack the defense first, especially if that can be done "inexpensively," relative to the number of the attacker's weapons required for the job. A space-based defense or its space-based C3 elements might be especially prone to defense suppression, especially if the attacker has speed-of-light weapons based in space. The attacker would still have other problems to solve, so the presumed capability for defense suppression is far from equivalent to a credible first-strike capability. The attacker would need a defense, as well, to absorb the retaliatory strike of the defender, and this defense could be vulnerable to retaliatory suppression. This balance of suppressive survivability has not received as much attention as have other issues attendant on BMD deployment, but it is the issue on which most others are dependent. Not only must the defenses survive attack on themselves. If both sides have deployed defenses, they must not invite attack on each other. They will invite attack if they or their C3 components appear vulnerable to a relatively small proportion of the adversary's total arsenal, or if the newer directed-energy-weapons technologies make speed-of-light destruction a spaceborne reality. Two sides with space-based laser BMD systems, for example, would have excellent weapons for defense suppression, even if they were of limited use of intercepting ballistic missiles. The U.S. and Soviet space-based DEW could disable one another's satellites in the first stage of a preemptive strike, and the fear on the part of each side that its counterpart might do this would erode crisis stability.

The second problem is the problem of system integration or coherence. Any BMD system must combine the effective functioning of weapons, sensors, and the platforms on which they are based. Weapons and sensors must be linked to force commanders and national command authorities. If one part of the system fails, it must not jeopardize the performance of the whole. Of particular concern to BMD planners will be the integration among the various layers of the defense system: boost, postboost, midcourse, and terminal, with the possibility of more than one system for a given layer.[8] The problem of system integration is, in principle, susceptible to solution by one of two competing logics: tight or loose integration. In the former, tight integration, a central brain directs the messages and interpretations that course throughout the entire nervous system. This has the advantage of efficiency, provided the decision-making center does not fail. If it does, everything else does. An alternative is a loosly integrated system, in which parts are tasked to cooperate within a common systems framework. Several aircraft-carrier battle groups tasked for a common mission are analogous. This second kind of system is sometimes referred to as a "distributed" system, meaning that decision and communication nodes are distributed throughout a dispersed network.[9] The advantage of a loosely integrated system is that it is harder to destroy, since some nodes may continue to function, even if others are disabled. The disadvantage is that a loosely integrated system may not be as controllable by policy makers or military commanders who value central control for crisis management, or for war termination after deterrence has failed.

The third problem, relative to the C3 requirements of BMD, is the possibility of deception by the opponent. A BMD system could be deceived in a number of ways, but the most basic is to exhaust its supply of interceptors by forcing it to shoot at false targets. Thus, planners of missile defense systems will be concerned with the problem of discrimination, of distinguishing decoys from real warheads. Simulated launchers, such as dummy ICBMs, might also be used to deceive the defense. Space-based defenses could be deceived by "spoofing" procedures, in which false information is introduced into satellite communications links, distorting the satellite's mission performance.[10] Deception about intentions is as important as deception about technologies and capabilities, if not more so. In the two decades preceding World War II, for example, intelligence failures were more commonly misestimates of adversary intentions than they were wrong assessments of military capability.[11] The U.S. and Soviet BMD systems, if deployed, will still leave open the question of how they are to be used and when. If they are based in space and have presumed capabilities to attack the other side's satellites, worst-case assessments can only dictate that each side should fear preemption.

Nor is the matter of intentions confined to deciding when the other side has launched an attack, or decided to do so. Preparations for dealing with the attack, if it is launched, will have to be made in peacetime. Exercises will have to rehearse what policy makers, including the U.S. president and the Soviet general secretary, will do. So-called command-post exercises are difficult enough now, when the assumption is that of a single gross preemptive strike against the vulnerable components of the other side's arsenal. Defenses introduce additional complexity for planners. On one hand, defenses might, if they survived, buy additional time for warning and attack assessment, in order that policy makers might decide among available options more carefully. On the other hand, the presence of defenses means that a very selective attack against U.S. forces, using only a small proportion of Soviet strategic weapons, is unlikely to accomplish much. U.S. defenses will force the USSR to launch very heavy strikes or none at all. The grosser the size of the strike, the less ambiguity there should be about Soviet intentions. One argument made by some analysts, however, to the effect that an attack on components of the U.S. BMD system is tantamount to a preemptive first strike, or should be so assumed, is obviously not correct. The Soviets might be attacking part of the BMD system in order to create a path for limited strikes as well as larger ones. Or, an attack on the BMD system or part of that system might be an end in itself, in order to establish postattack rights of space occupancy for weapons platforms, communications satellites, or space mines.

A fourth issue is the problem of the system defeating itself, although this does not exclude the possibility that self-defeating systems are also vulnerable to countermeasures of the opponent, which exacerbate the problem. We are concerned with two kinds of self-defeating behaviors. The first is failure that occurs because of the complexity of the linkages among components of the system, their operators, and the preprogrammed decision rules by which components and operators interact. Sociologist Charles Perrow has studied the behaviors of technically complex organizations in order to ascertain the relationship between susceptibility to disaster and intraorganizational behaviors.[12] What Perrow learned about nuclear power plants and other high-technology organizations is that many are risk prone on account of being tightly coupled, meaning that what goes wrong in one part of the organization reverberates onto other parts of the system, with unpredictable results. So, a valve that fails to open at the appropriate time is dealt with in a preprogrammed way, according to the book, but—unexpectedly—the solution to this first problem creates a second, and so on through a chain of errors, until a large disaster has happened. It is important to distinguish these kinds of system failures from operator-error or component failure, to which they are normally ascribed.

A BMD system will certainly be a candidate for these kinds of system failures, in that it can never be fully tested under realistic conditions. The components of the system can be tested through exhaustive simulation, of course, and some of them can be made extremely fault tolerant. The system itself must be used, however, by policy makers who may have no familiarity with the details of the system, and those leaders will depend on system operators to interpret messages of component or system failure. It turns out that there have been many component failures with regard to the World Wide Military Command and Control System (WWMMCCS), including failures that affected its strategic warning and assessment. In 1979 a training tape played into the computers at NORAD simulated a Soviet ICBM and SLBM attack, and it required six minutes to grind through the procedures to establish that the "attack" was an error. The president's National Emergency Airborne Command Post (NEACP) and SAC postattack command aircraft were prepared for takeoff, and the aircraft from the airborne command post of the U.S. commander in chief, Pacific (CINCPAC) did take off.[13]

The interactive complexity of a BMD system of the kind envisioned by some planners, involving five to seven layers of sensors, communications, and weapons (many based in space), would be enormous. It would invite compound synergistic failures of the kind Perrow found typical in nuclear power plants, space programs, and other high-risk technical systems. Of course, some of these system failure propensities can be designed around, but on the other hand, the opponent cannot. And this introduces the second way in which the system might defeat itself.

If the U.S. missile defense system is highly complex and tightly coupled, then it is also coupled, however loosely, to the Soviet system. By the Soviet system we mean not just the Soviet BMD system, if they have deployed one, but the entire complex of Soviet warning and attack assessment that is monitoring what is going on in the U.S. system. As Paul

Bracken has noted, at an abstract but very realistic level, the U.S. and Soviet warning and assessment systems, especially during crisis, are mutually interdependent.[14] This unintended sensitivity of each side to the other's crisis behavior could provoke a war under conditions that are otherwise permissive of deterrence failure. For example, each side's sensitivity to the other's alerting of its retaliatory forces, even if the first alert is precautionary, would be high. Soviet leaders might interpret U.S. moves to make forces more survivable as a step in preparing them for a U.S. first strike. This is the main problem with fear of preemption, which has sometimes been misrepresented as resulting from a bolt-from-the-blue attack, with no warning or indications of preattack preparation by the attacker. In reality this contingency, designed against on account of the properly conservative instincts of force planners, is highly unlikely. Some political crisis or other indicators would suggest, although perhaps not confirm, enemy preparations for attack. And each side might misread the signals of the other. It is not clear, for example, how the Soviet Union reacted to the U.S. worldwide military alert (DefCon 3) in October 1973, during the Arab–Israeli war. U.S. leaders apparently saw the alert as a show of resolve and drew the conclusion that alerts are credible signals of that resolve, which can be used as components of extended deterrence to support allies. Soviet leaders may have felt differently.[15] During the Cuban missile crisis, Khrushchev sent two messages to Kennedy with regard to Soviet willingness to end the crisis, and on what terms. The messages were almost totally different in tone and content, and the United States finally decided to acknowledge the first, which was deemed more responsive to U.S. concerns.[16]

Note that this concern with the synergistic complexity of BMD systems, as a potential contributory cause of failure, differs from the simpler matter of preventing accidental launch of nuclear or antinuclear weapons. Much concern has been expressed, in Congress and the media, about the possibly automatic triggering of a U.S. SDI system by computers. The president or other political and military leaders, it is alleged, might be taken out of the decision loop. Although it is not impossible to contrive a fully automated decision system of this type, it is neither necessary or proper for BMD to operate in this fashion. It is not proper, because the decision to authorize BMD responses to an apparent attack is different from the decision to enable the system to respond, should an attack be launched. The first decision, to authorize response, is a policy decision, certainly conditioned by options programmed into the system in peacetime, but not determined by them. The second decision, to enable the system under certain environmental conditions, can be automated and delegated as far down in the military chain of command as efficiency dictates.

Nor is it necessary to place a BMD system on a hair-trigger response mechanism. It is sometimes contended that boost-phases intercept requires a very rapid response, say, within three to five minutes, for interceptors to destroy attacking boosters before the warheads are separated from boosters in the postboost phase. Therefore, it is argued, the boost-phases responses must be fully automated, even if other layers of the system are not. The term "automated" here is misleading, however, as if the choice is to automate or not to automate, whereas the reality is a matter of degree. The system will be enabled to detect certain threat phenomena and to react to them in various ways. It might not shoot at presumed targets immediately, but only defend itself through passive means, including maneuver and deception. A BMD system that judged that it was under attack, perhaps from close quarry-keeping of space mines or flashes of light from ground-based lasers, could choose among passive and active responses that were stored in its repertoire. Also stored there, however, would be rules of engagement allowing the BMD command system to align environmental stimuli with its memory bank and to select options accordingly. These rules of engagement and the menu of available options for the system would be policy choices, not computer-determined decisions.

The easy case, analytically speaking, is the massive launch of thousands of Soviet re-entry vehicles against U.S. territory, which would make the selection among options relatively simple. The harder cases are those in which the USSR might, as an adjunct to a conventional war in Europe, decide to attack U.S. satellites, or we might attack theirs. BMD systems would have residual ASAT capabilities, as would the Soviet Galosh missile-defense system and other delivery systems. (This is why an ASAT treaty will pose difficulty for superpower negotiators, for not everything that has potential ASAT capabilities will be labeled as such.) A U.S. BMD system might be enabled in response to a conventional war in Europe, with the expectation that authorization to fire the system against appropriate targets was imminent. In this regard the president will have something of the same dilemma that applies to decisions about the readiness and launch of offensive retaliatory forces. In peacetime and under normal noncrisis conditions, negative control prevails, and the system will be in a state of low perturbation with regard to its environment. In a crisis, the number of perturbations increases, and the system becomes more sensitive to them, as noted earlier. Once conventional war has broken out, in which U.S. and Soviet forces have fought, U.S. strategic nuclear forces and missile defenses, if they are deployed, will be poised to retaliate. They will be on generated alert, in military parlance. If, during the time that offensive forces are generated, a U.S. BMD system detects what appears to be a defense-suppression attack, the system, having been enabled, will undoubtedly receive authorization to respond.

Partial attacks against U.S. satellites during conventional war would alert BMD satellites, but not necessarily trigger any response. There would, as yet, have been no Soviet ICBM or SLBM launch to which the U.S. BMD system could react. The Soviet Union might attack U.S. satellites in low earth orbit in order to impede reconnaissance of their conventional land and maritime forces. Or, if theater ballistic missile defenses systems (ATBMs) are deployed in Europe, then either side might attack the other's systems as a precursor to a theaterwide conventional or conventional/nuclear offensive. This, too, would alert strategic BMD communications, weapons, and sensors aboard satellites that attack was possible. It is assumed by some commentators that theater ballistic missile defenses are appealing because they are not prohibited by the ABM Treaty, and because they do not threaten U.S. or Soviet strategic second-strike capability, as do territorial homeland BMD defenses. From a command and control standpoint, however, the matter is not so simple. Theater BMD systems could be the triggers of a strategic BMD alert, which, in turn, led to preemptive strategic BMD attacks against space-based or terrestrial targets. Theater BMD systems, which could be seen as stabilizing from the perspective of force balances, because they would contribute to deterrence of a preemptive attack, could be unstable from a command and control standpoint. They could trigger reactions from strategic BMD systems to which they might be connected either directly or indirectly. Of course, under normal peacetime conditions, this seems impossible or improbable, but the system is turned off then, and when it is turned on or enabled, it will interpret very conservatively any stimuli that appear, even remotely.

In this regard, it is not at all clear that artificial intelligence systems, relative to the biases of policy makers and analysts, will do any worse. There is, after all, a mixed record in U.S. crisis management, and it is not obvious that U.S. defense and foreign-policy crisis management has improved since the terminology took hold of the academic and policy communities.[17] The term "crisis" connotes a short decision time, surprise, and other features of diplomatic-strategic behavior that are thought atypical of day-to-day intercourse among nation states. The same persons, however, who manage the affairs of state under normal conditions will also manage them under abnormal ones. And we have abysmally little information, other than biographical or autobiographical accounts, about the behavior of leaders under crisis circumstances. Of particular importance for this discussion is, the fact that the social-science community is not even agreed upon the most relevant level of analysis from which individual and group decision making can be understood. There are very selective partial approaches and very holistic efforts to understand crisis in historical context.[18] Policy makers do not have to be social scientists, and it would probably be a setback for historians seeking colorful subjects to write about if they were; but the findings of social science can be made very useful to policy makers, if the research studies of decision making in historical context can be projected into insights for future leaders.[19]

Even less is known about Soviet leaders and their decision-making behavior than is known about their Western counterparts. In the case of Western leaders, we have too much information from which relevant evidence must be extracted; in the Soviet case, the problem is finding the evidence. Still, Soviet leaders who have written their memoirs, like Khrushchev, have told us some important things intentionally, and other things unintentionally, about how the Soviet command system would operate in crisis and wartime.[20] Seweryn Bialer has studied Soviet change and continuity in Soviet elites, including their perceptions of international relations and national defense issues. He suggests that despite some accounts of leadership crises in the Soviet Union, an overall assessment of its political system is that it is remarkably stable.[21] According to his analysis, the USSR is best understood not as a totalitarian system, but as a modernizing authoritarian one, but it is not subject to the instability that characterizes other modernizing authoritarian regimes, because of the consensual elite support for the value of order. If this assessment is accurate, then we can expect to see Gorbachev continue at least one trend established under Brezhnev, an emphasis on decision making by collective leadership instead of one-person rule (cult of personality, in Soviet pejorative nomenclature).

The short digression on Soviet elite decision making has a point. If so careful a scholar as Bialer draws swords against the basic description of the Soviet regime that is offered by Western analysts, then a cautionary note about U.S. understanding of Soviet crisis behavior is certainly in order. During a crisis that followed the deployment of BMD by both sides, each could misperceive the BMD-relevant strategy of the other. One side—for example, the United States—might consider that its partially effective missile defenses were a signal of its ability to ride out a first strike and strike back effectively. The Soviet Union, on the other hand, might assume that a partially effective U.S. BMD system could deny their retaliatory strike, following a U.S. first strike. That this notion of a U.S. first strike seems incredible to U.S. planners does not mean that it is unbelievable to Soviet planners. From the Soviet perspective, the United States has endorsed first use as part of NATO strategy, in order to deter conventional war in Europe, which is acknowledged by U.S. and Soviet experts to have a high probability of escalating into theater and strategic nuclear exchanges. There is a more general issue, more inclusive than differences between U.S. and Soviet military doctrine relative to the interpretation of BMD deployments during crises. The more general issue is how much U.S. and Soviet leaders know, and how reliably, about the cost–risk calculus of their opposite numbers. Few if any U.S. experts on the Soviet Union would have predicted Khrushchev's willingness to emplace medium- and intermediate-range ballistic missiles in Cuba. Fewer still would believe that, compared with the regime that followed, Khrushchev's years in power might present fewer dilemmas for U.S. strategy than Brezhnev's.

What assumption, then, would the USSR make about a U.S. BMD misfire that destroyed a Soviet missile test launch or spacecraft? Much would depend upon the general tenor of superpower political relations at the time. From a political standpoint, it might be better to increase centralized control, instead of decreasing it, during a crisis. In the case of the Cuban missile crisis, Kennedy and Secretary of Defense Robert McNamara micro managed the imposition of the blockade set up by the U.S. Navy, in ways that were very contrary to previous naval experience. It seems probable that a future crisis would find leaders more sensitive, not less, to the possibility of inadverent escalation and loss of control. Therefore, the greater danger might not be accidental or inadvertent war prompted by a misfiring BMD system, but a tendency by policy makers to immobilize the system until it was too late. It might be objected here that BMD systems using nonnuclear weapons will not pose any decision problem in this regard, for a misfire is not a nuclear detonation on someone else's homeland or forces. True, but the problem does not end there, for the interpretation by the party on the receiving end of a BMD misfire may be that it is part of a preemptive strike. This is also true for ASAT deployments, which have defense-suppression capabilities.

Thus, BMD technology can contribute to stability or detract from it, depending upon the political context of U.S.–Soviet relations and the strategic understanding that each side has about the other's motives and priorities. The U.S. SDI program is unusual in that it began as a presidential "top down" initiative, whereas the more typical pattern is that weapons technologies are created, then followed by strategic rationales for their deployment. BMD research and development is nothing new for U.S. planners, however, and the United States deployed briefly a Safeguard BMD system before dismantling the site in the mid–1970s (at Grand Forks, North Dakota). The Soviet Union retains its Galosh BMD system around Moscow and is now upgrading it; other Soviet missile defense programs are apparently well along in research and development.[22] The Soviet view of strategic BMD systems is quite likely to differ from the U.S. view, even after they are deployed, and especially if the Reagan view of defenses that make offenses obsolete becomes U.S. tradition. The Soviet perspective is more likely to see offenses and defenses as working together to deter war, by providing a complementary capability to limit damage to the Soviet homeland and to retaliate against any aggressor.[23] From the standpoint of some Western analysts, the Soviets have been overly fascinated with strategic nuclear preemption, but discussions of preemption in Soviet military writing were more frequent when their arsenal was less survivable than it now is. Present-day Soviet planners would have the option, even following a surprise attack by U.S. forces, of preemption, launch on tactical warning/launch under attack, or second-strike ride-out. They might prefer preemption, if they thought war inevitable and if the difference in outcomes, between preemption and launch under attack, seemed significant enough.[24] How Western leaders would estimate this Soviet calculus, of the differences in payoffs between preemption and LOTW/LUA, cannot be known with confidence, but it can be stated confidently that the Western estimate would involve a lot of guesswork.

SMARTER AND SLOWER WARS

The comparative study of strategic doctrine and foreign-policy decision making calls for a more inclusive frame of reference than the discussion presented here. Our concern is the relationship between persons and machines in crisis decision-making situations. Missile defense systems do not change the character of that relationship, and they may add additional complexity to it. This is not, however, an advertisement for the insignificance of technology, only a cautionary note about technology assessments extracted from political context. The relationship between political context and technology assessment looms large in several other issues, in addition to BMD.

A first issue is that the development of smart decision aids may make the peace of tactical engagements faster, but the strategic understanding of war more difficult to come by. Battlefield commanders and policy makers will be swamped with information, the assessment of which will require additional and more complicated programs and algorithms. The prospect that commanders will become the apprentices, and automated decision aids the sorcerers, is a real one. Policy makers will think that they have sufficient information to override tactical decisions in the interest of larger strategic goals, as in the case of Lyndon Johnson selecting bombing targets in Vietnam, or president Carter monitoring the ill-fated Iranian hostage rescue. However, and in counterpoint, tactical commanders may be able to create their own fog of information feedback, in order to create a screen between them and higher levels. The tragic bombing of the U.S. Marine barracks in Lebanon in October 1983 was, in this writer's judgment, not the result of tactical error, but one of strategic misjudgment and military micromanagement. The strategic misjudgment was to give a combat force a peacekeeping mission in a politically untenable situation. The military micro management obscured responsibility for security on the ground by encumbering tactical operations with an elaborate chain of command.[25]

A second issue is the impact upon U.S. and Soviet strategic nuclear deterrence doctrines of the transition to force structures that are more dependent upon cruise missiles and mobile ballistic missiles, as opposed to time-urgent ICBMs deployed in fixed silos. Future cruise and mobile ballistic missiles allow planners additional options, including slowing the pace of war and making strikes and restrikes more fine tuned. These possibilities, of slower and more carefully orchestrated nuclear war fighting, will be increased by the development of the smarter decision aids noted above. Another contributory factor will be defense systems to protect fixed command centers, plus other measures to make command systems survivable. As matters now stand, the United States depends upon prompt response for the survival of its ICBM force, and prompt response requires the survival of ICBM silos and the command centers for those launch vehicles. The Soviet Union is even more dependent upon its prompt-launch capabilities inherent in silo-based ICBMs. This situation, of mutual dependency upon prompt launch during periods of crisis, could trigger war by preemption, despite the fact that both sides were seeking to defuse the crisis. Sometimes this issue is explained as if the problem were the survivability of U.S. and Soviet launch vehicles, but the more serious issue is the vulnerability of the two sides' ICBM command centers, which are few in number and susceptible to preemptive destruction. In addition, destruction of ICBM launch control centers would prevent reoptimization of targeting assignments, in cases where original aimpoints were not attacked successfully.

The transition to smarter and slower strategic systems as the backbone of second-strike capability is not without some risks to stability, however. Command and control for the U.S. bomber force is very complex, and the bombers, once launched to their loitering positions over northern Canada, are in a use-them-or-lose-them position, unless improvements are made in U.S. capabilities for reconstitution. Nor is it certain that, following a Soviet surprise attack that is carefully planned, much of the U.S. strategic bomber force can take off and survive. About 30 percent of it is kept on ground alert, and not all of that alerted force will be airborne before Soviet SLBMs, fired from plausible trajectories off the U.S. Atlantic and Pacific coasts, can destroy many aircraft.[26] As in the case of ICBM launcher vulnerability, too much attention has probably been devoted to the vulnerability of launch vehicles, and not enough to command vulnerability and the complexity of command systems, which must function effectively for forces to carry out their assigned missions. It is also true that U.S. strategic forces and the command systems that support them must work synergistically, if they are launched in retaliation. ICBMs, and SLBMs, for example, will have to cut corridors through the Soviet air-defense systems for U.S. bombers to attack their assigned targets.

Increased emphasis upon mobile or relocatable targets, following initial strikes, also calls for improved decision aids and precision-guided weapons that can be delivered on target, despite the disruption of some C3 elements. As both superpowers deploy more of their warheads on mobile ICBMs, submarines, and cruise missiles launched from aircraft, submarines, or surface ships, crisis-born pressure for prompt launch of retaliatory forces may diminish. On the other hand, a more complicated target set presents itself, not only to the attacker, but to the victim of a first strike that is seeking to retaliate against the postattack counterforce inventory of its opponent. So, the avoidance of prompt-launch dependency may be purchased at the price of creating additional difficulties in limiting the ultimate cost of war, if it occurs. If nuclear attack, in order to locate and destroy mobile targets, must be continued over many days or even weeks, then an incentive exists to deploy more and more redundant forces. It may also happen that space-based systems, either ASATs or missile defenses, may increase interest in prompt launch, while terrestrially deployed systems decrease it. The United States could find that its force restructuring, away from prompt-launch dependency and toward fully mobile and/or concealed second-strike capabilities, was offset by space based ASAT-BMD, which was vulnerable to preemptive destruction.

Of course, all of this begs the more important question, of what the United States and the Soviet Union could disagree about to the extent that nuclear war seemed a sensible way of settling the issue. And the answer, of course, is nothing, if the answer is to be provided by a rational policy analysis. There is no gain, in rational decision theory, that is worth the cost of nuclear war between U.S. and Soviet arsenals. That is precisely the point, however—the war is not between their arsenals, but their policy makers, motivated by complex belief systems, pressured by crises, and imprisoned by force structures and command systems put into place under normal peacetime conditions. No one knows what will happen after U.S. or Soviet leaders are convinced that deterrence has really failed, but, if it does, new technology promises only that war will be more complicated in decades hence, not less costly to society. Thus rational policy models and decision theories can help to explain the causal relationships among variables, but they cannot be depended upon for predictions, especially under conditions that are not typical. Although the "brooding omnipresence" of nuclear weapons, as Stanley Hoffman has put it, is certainly a typical condition, the use of them would not be.

NOTES

1. See Gregory F. Treverton, *Making the Alliance Work: The United States and Western Europe* (Ithaca, NY: Cornell University Press, 1985), ch. 2, pp. 25–58.

2. Carl H. Builder, "The Impact of New Weapons Technologies," in *Strategic War Termination*, ed. Stephen J. Cimbala (New York: Praeger, 1986), pp. 157–73.

3. The Reagan strategic concept is outlined in Paul H. Nitze, "On the Road to a More Stable Peace," U.S. Department of State, *Current Policy* No. 657, February 20, 1985.

4. See the arguments in Albert Wohlstetter and Richard Brody, "Continuing Control as a Requirement for Deterring," in *Managing Nuclear Operations*, ed. Ashton B. Carter, John D. Steinbruner, and Charles A. Zraket (Washington, DC: Brookings Institution, 1987), Ch. 5, pp. 142–96.

5. Desmond Ball, "The Development of the SIOP, 1960–1983," in *Strategic Nuclear Targeting*, ed. Desmond Ball and Jeffrey Richelson (Ithaca, NY: Cornell University Press, 1986), Ch. 3, pp. 57–83.

6. Ashton B. Carter, "Assessing Command System Vulnerability," in *Managing Nuclear Operations*, ed. Carter et al., Ch. 17, pp. 555–610.

7. Theodore Jarvis, "Nuclear Operations and Strategic Defense," in *Managing Nuclear Operations*, ed. Carter et al., Ch. 20, pp. 661–78, esp. pp. 668–70.

8. See Office of Technology Assessment, U.S. Congress, *Ballistic Missile Defense Technologies* (Washington, DC: U.S. GPO, September 1985).

9. On distributed BMD systems, see Jarvis, "Nuclear Operations and Strategic Defense," pp. 668–70. See also OTA, *Ballistic Missile Defense Technologies*, pp. 189–90.

10. See William E. Burrows, *Deep Black: Space Espionage and National Security (New York: Random House, 1986), p. 282.*

11. Ernest R. May, "Conclusions: Capabilities and Proclivities," in Knowing One's Enemies: Intelligence Assessment before the Two World Wars, ed. Ernest R. May (Princeton, NJ: Princeton University Press, 1984), pp. 503–42.

12. Charles Perrow, *Normal Accidents: Living with High Risk Technologies* (New York: Basic Books, 1984).

13. Richard Ned Lebow, *Nuclear Crisis Management* (Ithaca, NY: Cornell University Press, 1987), p. 93.

14. Paul Bracken, *The Command and Control of Nuclear Forces* (New Haven, CT: Yale University Press, 1983), pp. 59–68.

15. Graham T. Allison, *Essence of Decision: Explaining the Cuban Missile Crisis* (Boston: Little, Brown, 1971), p. 223.

16. Allison, *Essence of Decision*, p. 227.

17. For a critical assessment of U.S. crisis management, see Colin S. Gray, *Nuclear Strategy and National Style* (Lanham, MD: Hamilton Press, 1986), Ch. 6.

18. See Richard Ned Lebow, *Between Peace and War* (Baltimore, MD: Johns Hopkins University Press, 1981). Examples of psychological applications to the study of nuclear crisis appear in Ralph K. White, ed., *Psychology and the Prevention of Nuclear War* (New York: New York University Press, 1986).

19. As an example, see the cases in Irving Janis, *Groupthink*, 2d ed. (Boston: Houghton Mifflin, 1982). See also Alexander L. George and Richard Smoke, *Deterrence in American Foreign Policy: Theory and Practice* (New York: Columbia University Press, 1974); and Robert Jervis, "Deterrence and Perception,"

in *Strategy ad Nuclear Deterrence*, ed. Steven E. Miller (Princeton: Princeton University Press, 1984), pp. 57–84.

20. For example, see Strobe Talbott, trans. and ed., *Khrushchev Remembers* (Boston: Little, Brown, 1970). On Soviet decision making in nuclear crisis and war, see Stephen M. Meyer, "Soviet Nuclear Operations," in *Managing Nuclear Operations*, ed. Carter et al., Ch. 15, pp. 470–534.

21. Seweryn Bialer, *Stalin's Successors* (Cambridge: Cambridge University Press, 1980), esp. pp. 143–45.

22. U.S. Department of Defense, *Soviet Military Power: 1987* (Washington, DC: U.S. GPO, pp. 45–61, discusses Soviet space and strategic defense operations. See also Sayre Stevens, "The Soviet BMD Program," in *Ballistic Missile Defense*, ed. Ashton B. Carter and David N. Schwartz (Washington, DC: Brookings Institution, 1984), Ch. 5, pp. 182–220.

23. Raymond L. Garthoff, "Mutual Deterrence, Parity and Strategic Arms Limitation in Soviet Policy," in *Soviet Military Thinking*, ed. Derek Leebaert (London: Allen and Unwin, 1981), Ch. 5, pp. 92–124.

24. Stephen M. Meyer, "Soviet Perspectives on the Paths to Nuclear War," in *Hawks, Doves and Owls*, ed. Graham T. Allison, Albert Carnesale and Joseph S. Nye, Jr. (New York: Norton, 1985), Ch. 7, pp. 167–205.

25. On U.S. experience in Lebanon, see Edward Luttwak, *The Pentagon and the Art of War* (New York: Simon & Schuster, 1984), pp. 50–52.

26. Communications with the U.S. strategic bomber force are discussed in Bruce G. Blair, *Strategic Command and Control: Redefining the Nuclear Threat* (Washington, DC: Brookings Institution, 1985), pp. 196–98.

INDEX

ABM Treaty (1972), 125, 126, 276
accidental/inadvertent war, 92, 180–
81, 185, 200, 225, 255, 285
Afghanistan, 14, 43, 58, 59, 60, 61,
69–70, 168, 240, 241
air defenses, 131–32, 218, 276
Air Force, U.S., 35, 36, 140–43, 146,
184
alerts, 5, 32–33, 93–94, 103, 142, 194,
224, 225, 281, 287
Algeria, 101, 244–45
Allison, Graham T., 3
all-volunteer force, 261
American Revolution, 156, 161, 242
anticipatory preemption, 195, 196
applied statistical models. *See* mathematical decision models
Arab-Israeli war (1973), 14–15, 17,
33, 103, 187–88, 196–97, 258, 281
armed forces. *See* military organizations; *name of specific force*
arms control/race: and accidental war,
255; and arms reductions, 225–26;
and assured destruction, 140; and
the balance of terror/balance of
power, 24–26, 226; and bargaining,
214–15; and the causes of war, 254–
55; confusion about, 211, 215; and

consistency, 137; and conventional
war, 275; and crisis stability, 213–
14, 225; and defenses, 119–20; and
deterrence theory, 227; and expectations, 212, 214; failure of, 226–27;
and the international system, 211;
and limited war, 254–55; and missiles, 24–25, 120–21, 128–29, 147–
48, 225–27; and mutual vulnerability, 214, 219; and NATO, 214, 248–
49; and nuclear numismatics, 212–
15, 255; and nuclear strategy, 211–
27; and policy makers, 212; and
predictability, 25–26; and preemption, 225; and the prevention of
war, 211–12; and the progress/pro-
cess issue, 214; and the proliferation of nuclear arms, 212; purposes/
implications of, 137, 211, 225–27;
and the Reagan administration,
130, 214–15; and Soviet-China relations, 61; and Soviet strategy, 58,
59–60, 214–15, 218–19; and strategic
divergence, 215–25; and strategic
weapons, 276; and trust, 110, 227;
and U.S.- Soviet relations, 130; and
verification, 225–26; vertical/hori-
zontal, 213–14; *See also* SALT

Army, U.S., 101, 140–43, 247–48, 261, 262, 264
Arrow, Kenneth, 75–76
assured destruction, 8, 115–16, 137, 138–40, 218–20. *See also* mutual vulnerability
attack assessment, 23, 279, 280–81
attack price, 122–23
avoidance of war. *See* mutual vulnerability

balance: military, 255–56, 257
balance of power, 13, 14–26, 110, 181–82, 186, 188, 226. *See also* balance of terror/balance of power
balance of terror: definition of, 14; and the escalation-dominance perspective, 17–19; as a replacement for the balance of power, 14–26. *See also* balance of terror/balance of power
balance of terror/balance of power: and the arms race, 23–26; and crisis stability, 23–26; and defenses, 24–25; differences between, 13–26; and limited wars, 14–15; and mutual vulnerability, 16–19; and NATO, 17–18; and predictability, 20–24, 25–26; and quantity of nuclear weapons, 25–26; and strategizing, 13–26; and the two major powers system, 20–21
Ball, Desmond, 33–34
Ballistic Missile Defenses. *See* BMD
ballistic missiles. *See* BMD; missiles
Barbarossa. *See* Operation Barbarossa
bargaining, 214–15
battle management, 277
Betts, Richard K., 81
Bialer, Seweryn, 284
biological weapons, 164–65
Blair, Bruce G., 163
BMD (Ballistic Missile Defenses): and absolute/relative values, 117–18; and air defenses, 131–32; and arms control, 24–25, 120–21; and C3 system, 277–86; coherence/complexity

of, 278, 279–81; and an conventional war 131, 282–83 and cost effectiveness, 116–19; and counterforce, 145; and crisis, 284; and deterrence stability, 115–34; and first strike, 115, 279, 284 and marginal utility, 119; and NATO, 120–21, 127–34, 284; opposition to, 116; and payoff tables, 116; and preemption, 279, 283, 285–86; and rationality, 115–34; and the Reagan administration, 115; and retaliation, 284; and scientism, 71; self-defeating behaviors of, 279–81; and Soviet strategy, 125–26; and strategism, 71; and survivability, 122–24; and technology, 133, 278; and threats, 282; and trust, 132; vulnerability of, 123, 278, 279
Boer War, 246
bolt-from-the-blue, 32, 36, 81, 84, 142–43, 178, 189, 203, 281. *See also* first strike; preemption; surprise attack
bolt-from-the-grey, 203
bombers, 141–43, 147, 149–50, 223–26, 276, 277, 287
Bracken, Paul, 32, 93, 97, 106, 192, 193, 280–81
Brennan, Donald, 119
Brezhnev (Leonid) regime, 59, 284,285
brinksmanship crisis, 81, 192, 200–201
Britain. *See* Great Britain
Brody, Richard, 41–42, 79, 193
Brown, Harold, 193
budgets: military, 128, 257
burden sharing, 128, 132–33, 170
bureaucracies, 5, 22–24, 35–36, 262, 266, 280. *See also name of specific organization*

C3 systems (command, control, and communications): and bureaucracies, 22–24; complexity/flexibility of, 34, 277; and counterforce,145–46; and crisis, 278, 284, 285; and defense suppression, 277–78; and the deployment of nuclear weapons,

256–57; and expectations, 277; and force acquisitions, 142; and the longevity of war, 34, 42, 163, 276–77; and missiles, 53, 277–86; and nuclear strategy, 31; and the payoff table, 80; and preemption, 224–25, 277, 278; and the Reagan administration, 104; and Soviet strategy, 224; stability of, 284; and survivability, 104, 277; and termination of war, 278. *See also* command and control; control

capitalism, 58, 216–17, 220, 258

Carter, Ashton B., 34, 196

Carter (Jimmy) administration: and command and control, 105, 126–27; and counterforce, 146; and the Iran hostages, 246, 286; and missiles, 54, 130; and the oil crisis/embargo, 259; and scientism, 54; sensitivity to Europe of the, 62; and Soviet strategy, 59–60; and strategism, 54; and survivability, 146–47

causes of war, 44, 201, 220, 254–55

Central Intelligence Agency (CIA), 184, 266–67

chemical/biological weapons, 41, 164–65, 171

Chernobyl, 7, 166

China, 20–21, 44, 45, 58, 61–62, 101, 160, 168, 217, 247

CIA. *See* Central Intelligence Agency

cities, 123, 138–39, 143, 164, 199, 200

civil defense, 71, 218, 238–39

civil war, 53, 157–58, 160–61, 244–46, 247. *See also name of specific country*

Civil War, U.S., 155, 162

civilian-military relations: U.S., 260–66; Soviet, 267–71

civilians, arming, 239–42

Clausewitz, Karl von, 12–13, 30, 68, 215

coercion, 26, 70, 133–34, 170, 178, 184, 196, 213, 222–23. *See also* coercive diplomacy

coercive diplomacy, 17–18, 190–91, 259, 263, 264, 265

coexistence, 268

command and control: and the avoidance of nuclear war, 201–2; coherence/stability of, 31–34, 106, 125–26, 145–46, 164, 199, 287; and crisis, 103, 201–2; and defenses, 19–20; and escalation, 19, 37, 40, 41–42, 103–7, 193–94; legal premise of, 31–32; literature about, 33; and nuclear strategy, 30–46; and a nuclear war, 19–20; and peacetime, 33–34, 103, 201–2; and postnuclear war, 164; and "safety catch"/"trigger," 32; in the Soviet Union, 125–27, 145–46, 218, 268–69; and stress, 33–34; in the United States, 31–34, 126–27. *See also* C3 systems; civilian-military relations; *name of specific subject or war*

command organization. *See* C3 systems; command and control

communication: and de-escalation, 107–11; sea lanes of, 43, 168; and termination of war, 98, 107–11. *See also* C3 systems; HotLine

communism, 61–62, 216–17, 268

computers, 62–63, 281

conditional rationality, 2–9, 75

Conference on Security and Cooperation in Europe (CSCE), 62

Congress, U.S., 128, 146, 232–33, 261, 266, 281

conservation of enemies, 217

consistency: and assured destruction, 137, 138–40; and counterforce, 137, 143–51; and declaratory policy, 137–51; and force acquisition, 137, 140–43; and operational policy, 137–51

containment doctrine, 254

continental strategies/strategists, 42–43

control. *See* C3 systems; command and control; control of escalation

control of escalation, 67, 80, 88, 92–93, 97–111, 184, 192–95, 202, 222–23

conventional deterrence, 3, 203, 248

Conventional Deterrence (Mearsheimer), 3

conventional forces. *See also* conventional war; flexible response strategy; force structure; NATO; *name of specific subject*

conventional war: and arms control, 275; and BMD, 131, 282–83; and command system, 105; and conditional rationality, 3–4; and the longevity of war, 43, 45, 221; and the maritime strategy 149; and the maximization of values, 88–89; and payoffs, 88–89; and postnuclear war, 163–64; and revolutionary/civil wars, 157–58, 244–47; and Soviet strategy, 45, 70, 126, 189–92; and statist/nonstatist war, 244–47; and surprise attack, 175; and termination of war, 102. *See also* conventional war; flexible response strategy; force structure; NATO. *See also* nonnuclear war; *name of specific subject*

conventionalization of nuclear war, 7, 138–39

coping, 4–9, 185

correlation of forces, 188

cost effectiveness, 116–19

costs of war, 119, 162, 175, 199, 288. *See also* payoffs

countercity retaliation, 139

counterforce, 137, 138–40, 143–51, 275, 288

Craig, Gordon A., 12

credibility, 57, 89, 90–94, 97, 133, 170, 232, 245

crisis: behavior, 7–8, 22, 67, 103, 201–2, 224, 278, 280–81, 283, 284; brinksmanship, 81, 192, 200–201; and the C3 systems, 103, 201–2, 278, 284; and the causes of crisis/war, 44, 65; de-escalation of, 94; and defenses, 197–98; definition of, 176, 283; and deterrence, 16, 67; and hope/desperation, 176; hostility, 200–201; management, 5, 16, 44, 65, 70, 88, 176, 181–85, 278; and perceptions, 181–83; and predictability, 22, 26, 65; and rationality, 5; and

Soviet strategy, 70, 215; spin-off, 200–201; stability, 23–25, 26, 31, 67, 92, 175–77, 197–98, 213–15, 224–25, 278; types of, 200–201; and warning/assessment systems, 280–81. *See also* Cuban missile crisis; Hot Line; *name of specific subject*, e.g., surprise attack

criteria for deployable defenses, 116

cruise missiles. *See* missiles

Cuban missile crisis: and alerts, 33, 93, 142; and balance of power, 181–82; and bureaucracies, 35; and C3 systems, 33, 34–35, 94, 285; as a case study, 181–85; and coercion, 184; and conditional rationality, 3; and coping, 4–5, 185; and deliberate war, 185; and escalation, 18, 184; and inadvertent/accidental war, 181, 185; and intelligence, 184; and military organizations, 94; and mutual vulnerability, 196; and policy makers, 21, 34–35, 188; and predictability, 21, 284–85; and Soviet strategy, 189; and termination of war, 111, 281; and threats, 184; and trust, 227; and the U.S. Navy, 94, 185, 285; World War I compared with the, 81

"cult of the offensive," 186

Czechoslovakia, 60, 131, 169, 171, 191

deception, 110, 223, 277, 278–79

decision making: crisis, 22; and games, 30, 34, 77–78, 147–48, 192; mathematical models for, 30, 144, 196; and rationality, 288

declaratory policy: and consistency, 137–51; definition of, 137. *See also name of specific policy*

decoupling of NATO strategy, 128

de-escalation: and command systems, 103–7; and communications, 107–11; of crisis, 94; and termination of war, 97–111

defenses: advantages of, 119; and budgets, 128, 257; criteria for deployable, 116; definition of, 90; and deterrence, 119–27; nonnuclear, 120–21; point, 198; quantity of, 121, 122, 212–15; slack in, 120; and Soviet strategy, 217–20; and strategy, 122–27. *See also* BMD; defense suppression; *name of specific subject*, e.g., arms control/race

defense suppression, 122–24, 277–78, 282, 285

defensive surprise: and Soviet strategy, 64

deliberate attack/war, 4, 180–81, 185, 200

denial, 90, 119, 133, 221, 249, 271

détente, 59, 61–62, 128, 129, 130, 134, 170, 254, 260

deterrence: agonistic use of, 93–94; credibility, 97, 170, 232; and defenses, 119–27; definition of, 76; diversified, 56; and ethics, 83–89; extended, 4, 89–94, 127–34, 197, 222, 281; as a national policy, 1–2; and political consistency, 137–51; premises of, 77; and preventing war, 76; and preventive war, 81–83; psychology of, 67, 93–94; rationality, 3–4, 9, 75–94, 97, 134, 137–51, 231–32, 253; skepticism about, 232; stability, 115–34, 179, 255–57; theory, 3–4, 77–78, 82–83, 89–94, 227, 231–32, 233–43, 253; and U.S. strategy, 233–43. *See also name of specific subject*, e.g., arms control/race

Dienbienphu, 244–45

diplomacy, 77, 81, 176, 181, 216, 247. *See also* coercive diplomacy

direct confrontation, 189

diversified deterrence, 56

doves and hawks, 101, 218–19, 220–25, 271

Dunn, Keith, 42

Dupuy, Trevor N., 30

East Germany, 60, 62, 131, 169, 171, 254

Eastern Europe, 43, 58, 60–61, 170, 260. *See also name of specific country*

economics, 75, 76, 77–78, 88, 116–19, 155, 168, 171, 232, 258–60

effectiveness: definition of, 116–17; and political theory, 116–17

egos, personal, 183, 184

Egypt, 197, 217. *See also* Arab-Israeli war

Eisenhower (Dwight) administration, 139

electronic locks, 108, 149

electronic measures, 131

electronic warfare, 171

employment policy. *See* operational policy

ends, 77–78, 79–80, 82, 155, 183, 231

Erickson, John, 187

escalation: and the agonistic use of deterrence, 93–94; and alerts, 94; and command and control, 37, 40, 41–42, 193–94; control of, 67, 80, 88, 92–93, 97–111, 184, 192–95, 202, 222–23: and conventional war, 131; and coping, 5–6; and the Cuban missile crisis, 184; and defenses, 119; definition of, 92–93; and deterrence, 43–46, 92–94; and ethnocentrism, 79; and European war, 42–46; and force structure, 222; horizontal, 42–46, 191; inadvertent/deliberate, 92; and longevity of war, 32, 39–40, 43–46, 221; and maritime strategy, 39–40, 234; polar models of, 41; and policy makers, 193–95; and rationality, 5, 75, 223; and Soviet strategy, 41, 190–91; and surprise attack, 192–95; temporal, 43–46; and termination of war, 97–111; and threats, 234; and values, 40, 80; vertical, 43–46. *See also* escalation-dominance; flexible response strategy; NATO

escalation-dominance, 18–19, 91–92, 222–23, 234–35. *See also* bargaining and escalation strategy

ethics, 83–89. *See also* maximization of values; values

ethnic targeting, 146

ethnocentricism, 78–79, 83

European Defense Community, 250

European nuclear force, 249–51

European war: and continental strategists, 42–43; controllability of, 41–46; and deterrence, 39, 127–34; and escalation, 42–46; European views about, 38–39, 42, 127–31, 134, 167, 168, 169–70, 189–90, 233, 256–57; and force structure, 42–43; and the longevity of war, 41–46, 140; and maritime strategy, 42, 43, 233–35; and nonnuclear war, 166–71; and Soviet strategy, 126, 189–92; and threats, 234; and U.S.-Soviet relations, 132; and U.S. strategy, 233–38; U.S. views about, 42, 62, 127–31, 134, 168, 169–70, 233, 256–57. *See also* NATO; *name of war or type of war*, e.g., World War II or limited war

Europe/Europeans: and civilian-military relations, 270–71; and détente, 128, 130, 134, 170; economy of, 253; NATO role of, 247–48, 251; and nonnuclear war, 170; public opinion in, 251; and SDI, 126; Soviet relations with, 62. *See also* Eastern Europe; European war; NATO; Warsaw Pact; Western Europe expectations: and arms control, 212, 214; and the C3 systems, 277; and NATO, 271; of policy makers, 224, 265, 277; and strategy, 237–39

expected/unexpected wars, 154–73, 236

extended control, 193

extended deterrence, 4, 89–94, 127–34, 197, 222, 281

extended war. *See* prolonged war

Falkland Islands, 4–5

fatalism, 69, 71, 111, 224, 268–69

Federal Republic of Germany. *See* West Germany

ferocity/intensity of war, 159–63

first strike: and assured destruction, 138; and attack price, 122–23; and bombers, 225; and coping, 7; and counterforce, 143, 144, 148; and crisis stability, 24; and defense suppression, 277–78: and defenses, 121, 122, 124; and the ethics of war, 86, 89; and losing, 197; and missiles, 115, 123, 150, 226–27, 275, 279, 284; and mutual vulnerability, 116; and nuclear arsenals, 199; and payoffs, 197–98; and predictability, 21, 23–24; and preemption, 82; and preventive war, 82; and rationality, 4, 7, 21, 89; and retaliation, 179, 288; and Soviet strategy, 70, 194, 224; and survivability, 281; and technology, 235–36; and U.S. nuclear strategy, 103. *See also* bolt-from-the-blue: preemption; surprise attack

flexible response strategy (NATO), 17, 129, 132, 189–90, 199, 233, 234, 249

fog of war, 37, 144

Follow-on Forces Attack (FOFA) strategy, 65, 131

force: and policy, 12, 215, 231–51; and strategy, 215; and threats, 263

force acquisition, 137, 140–43, 194, 202, 219

force balance, 185, 283

force sizing, 138

Force and Statecraft (Craig and George), 12

force structure: and assured destruction, 138; and deterrence, 1–2, 91–92; diversity of, 141; and escalation, 91–92, 222; and European war, 42–43; and manipulation of risk, 222; and missiles, 286–87; and prolonged war, 42–43, 107; and prompt launch, 288; and scientism/strategism, 64; and Soviet strategy, 64; and strategic thinking, 232–33; and survivability, 199; and the U.S. Navy, 43

forces, correlation of, 188

forward defense (NATO), 234, 237, 249

France: and Algeria, 244–45; and command and control in the Soviet Union, 126–27; entente between Germany and, 247; and the ferocity/intensity of war, 161; and the horizontal proliferation of nuclear weapons, 20–21; and Indochina, 244–45; and a Multilateral Nuclear Force, 250; and NATO, 132; and nuclear numismatics, 213; and Soviet strategy, 125, 126; and the Suez crisis (1956), 17; and termination of war, 101. *See also* World War I; World War II

Franco-Prussian war (1870), 161

Frunze, Mikhail, 267

game theory, 30, 34, 77–78, 147–48, 192

Garthoff, Raymond L., 78

gas pipeline, 259–60

George, Alexander L., 12

Germany, 161, 186, 247. *See also* East Germany; Schlieffen Plan; West Germany; *name of specific war*

Geyer, Michael, 187

Gilpatric, Roswell, 181–82

good (in political theory), 76–77

Gorbachev (Mikhail) regime, 59, 125, 214–15, 284. *See also* summits

grand strategic surprise attack, 179, 183

grand strategy, 11

Gray, Colin S., 128

Great Britain: and ballistic missiles, 53–54, 147–48; bureaucracies in, 22; and command and control in the Soviet Union, 126–27; and command organization, 109; and the horizontal proliferation of nuclear weapons, 20–21; intelligence services in, 186; military-civilian relations in, 270; military organizations in, 261; and Soviet strategy, 125, 126; and the

Suez crisis (1956), 17; and termination of war, 108

Greece, 236

Grenada, 246

ground forces, Soviet, 60, 190, 191

Handel, Michael, 203

Hart, Douglas, 238

hawks and doves, 101, 218–19, 220–25, 271

Helsinki Accords (1975), 62

heuristic rationality, 2, 5, 7, 8–9

Hines, John G., 41

history, 176, 178, 185–89, 216, 238

Hitler, Adolf. *See* Operation Barbarossa; World War II

Hobbes, Thomas, 12, 75–76, 77

Hoffman, Stanley, 288

hope/desperation, 176

horizontal escalation, 191

hostility crisis, 200–201

Hot Line, 24, 104–5, 109, 111, 200, 225

Howard, Michael, 11, 38, 271

Hungary, 17, 60, 169

Huntington, Samuel P., 141, 260

Ikl, Fred Charles, 101

inadvertent/accidental war, 92, 180–81, 185, 200, 225, 255, 285

India, 20

Indochina, 101, 244–45

intelligence surprise attack, 179, 184

intelligence systems, 180, 184, 186–88, 223, 240, 266–67, 279

international system, 12–13, 20, 26, 77, 180, 211, 223, 247

Iran, 20, 60, 102–3, 246–47, 259, 262–63, 266, 286

Iran-Contra affair, 266

Iraq, 20, 102–3, 236, 259, 264–65

Israel, 17, 20, 187–88, 197. *See also* Arab-Israeli war (1973)

Japan, 214, 258. *See also* World War II

Jastrow, Robert, 124

Jervis, Robert, 7

Johnson (Lyndon) administration, 244–45, 261, 263–64, 286
justice of war/justice in war, 83–89

Kahn, David, 187
Kahn, Herman, 2, 18
Kaufmann, William W., 64
Kelley, P. X., 236
Kennan, George F., 254
Kennedy (John F.) administration, 90, 139. See also Cuban missile crisis
Khruschev, Nikita, 8, 224, 284. See also Cuban missile crisis
Kissinger, Henry, 90, 247, 271
Komer, Robert W., 42
Korean war, 100, 101, 160, 184, 264
Kuwait, 102, 259, 262–63

ladder of escalation metaphor, 18
latent violence, 77, 78, 81
Latin America, 14, 247
launch under attack, 21, 142–43, 195, 196, 224, 277, 285–86
launch in retaliation, 32
launch on warning, 21, 142–43, 144–45, 195, 196, 198, 224, 277, 285–86
leadership. See C3 systems; command and control; policy makers
Lebanon, 187–88, 236, 246–47, 262, 263, 264–65, 286
Lebow, Richard Ned, 81–82, 200–201
legitimacy, 243–51
limited war: as an alternative to total nuclear war, 221; and arms control/race, 254–55; and the balance of terror/balance of power, 13–15; and the C3 systems, 32–33, 42, 193–94; and conditional rationality, 4; and conventional war, 221; and denial, 221; and escalation, 32, 221; European views about, 140; and extended deterrence, 222; improbability of, 200; and the manipulation of risk, 222; and mutual avoidance, 79; and the nation-state system, 13; and NATO, 42, 221–22; and nuclear winter, 66, 67; and policy makers, 193–95, and scientism, 66; and Soviet strategy, 41, 69, 191, 220–23; and surprise attack, 192–95; and termination of war, 101–3; and victory, 57. See also longevity of war; name of specific war
longevity of war: and the C3 systems, 34, 108–9, 163, 276–77; and costs, 162; and ferocity/intensity of war, 159–63; and nonnuclear war, 166–71; and postnuclear war, 163–66; and preparedness, 170; and societal pain, 165; and technology, 165; and termination of war, 99, 108–9; and victory, 162. See also limited war; prolonged war; name of specific war
losing. See winning/losing
Luttwak, Edward, 128, 236

MacArthur, Douglas, 101, 180, 264
McNamara, Robert S., 94, 138–40, 285
manipulation of risk, 17, 222
marginal utility, 69, 117–18, 119, 178
Marines, U.S., 140–43, 236, 246, 262, 263, 264–65, 286
maritime strategy, 2, 39–40, 43,45, 148–50, 163–64, 168, 180–81, 233–35
mathematical decision models, 30, 144, 196
maximization of values, 79–80, 88–89
May, Ernest, 176, 186
means and ends, 77–78, 79–80, 82, 155, 183, 231
Mearsheimer, John J., 3
Meyer, Stephen M., 196
Middle East, 93, 247. See also Arab-Israeli war; Persian Gulf; name of specific country
military balance, 255–56, 257
military doctrine, 186, 267–68
military education/history, 67–68, 238, 268
military organizations: and an all-volunteer force, 261; and civilian relations, 11, 101, 260–71; and command and control, 87–88, 268–69; compared to other bureaucratic

organizations, 35–36; and the Cuban missile crisis, 94; diversity in goals of, 35–36; and the ethics of war, 87–88; and ethos/identity, 265–66; and force acquisitions, 140–43; and leader-follower relations, 261–62; and the officer corps, 260–66; and personnel matters, 262; preconceptions of, 186; as a reflection of society, 257–58; society's views about, 257–58; Soviet, 267–71; and surprise attack, 176, 179–81, 183–84; and termination of war, 101, 103, 105–6; use of, 262–63; and values, 257–58, 260–66. See also name of specific organization
mirror imaging, 78, 105, 188
missiles: and absolute/relative values, 117–18; accuracies of, 53, 141, 275; and air defenses, 131–32; and arms control, 24–25, 120–21, 147–48, 225–27; and bombers, 141–43; and C3 systems, 53, 275; and the Carter administration, 54; and conventional war, 131; and cost effectiveness, 116–19; and counterforce, 143–44, 145, 149–50, 275; and crisis stability, 92; and deterrence stability, 115–34; and first strike, 115, 150, 226–27, 275; and force structure, 286–87; and future technology, 275–76; and marginal utility, 119; mobility of, 107, 125, 142, 147, 226, 286–88; and mutual deterrence, 116; and NATO, 39, 120–21, 127–34, 170; and necessary and sufficient conditions, 119–27; obsolescence of, 53–57; opposition to, 116; and payoff tables, 116; and preemption, 226–27, 277; and rationality, 115–34; and the Reagan administration, 115, 120, 235–36, 276, 285; and scientism, 53–57, 71; and the Scowcroft Commission, 53–57, 59–60, 195; and second strike, 150; and Soviet strategy, 59–60, 125–26, 218, 219; and strategic stability, 54; and strategism, 56–57, 71; and survivabil-

ity, 21–22, 56, 122–25, 150, 275, 277, 287; technology, 133, 276–77; and trust, 132; vulnerability of, 53–57, 59–60, 122–24, 144, 275. See also BMD; defenses; force acquisition; SDI; name of specific country
mobilization, 81–82, 194
Molotov-Ribbentrop pact (1939), 13
morality. See ethics; maximization of values; values
Morgan, Patrick M., 88
motivation: for executing war plans, 36–37; of policy makers, 212; for surprise attack, 175–76; for war, 157–58
Multilateral Nuclear Force, 249–51
mutual assured destruction: 8, 115–16, 137, 138–40, 218–20. See also mutual vulnerability
mutual assured survival, 276
Mutual and Balanced Force Reductions talks, 171, 255
mutual vulnerability, 16–20, 79, 103, 115–16, 120, 196–97, 214, 218–20, 287. See also assured destruction
My Lai massacre, 261

Napoleonic wars, 13, 156–58, 185–86
national character/values, 257–58, 260–66
National Command Authority. See command and control
nationalism, 63–64
nation-state system, 13
NATO: and alerts, 33; and arming the civilian population, 239–42; and arms control/race, 214, 248–49; and the balance of terror/balance of power, 17–18; and burden sharing, 170; cohesion/dissension in, 17, 45–46, 65, 127–31, 132–33, 170, 202, 217, 235, 237, 259; and coping, 5; credible strategy for, 133; decoupling of, 128; and détente, 129; and deterrence, 248, 255–57; and escalation, 271; and escalation/flexible response strategy, 5, 17–18, 42, 45,

69, 129, 132, 167, 199, 233, 234,
249; European role in, 247–48, 251;
and Follow-on Forces Attack strategy, 65, 131; forward defense of,
234, 237, 249; and France, 132; improvement of, 249; and the longevity of war, 38–39, 42, 221–22;
maritime strategy of, 39–40; and
missiles, 39, 120–21, 127–34, 170,
284; and nonnuclear war, 167–71;
nuclear forces role in, 17–18; and
the oil crisis/embargo, 258; and
postnuclear war, 165–66; and
preemption, 248; and public opinion, 237; purpose of, 169–70; and
retaliation, 189–90; and scientism,
64, 65; and societal expectations,
271; and Soviet strategy, 64, 126,
189–92, 217, 248–49; and statist/
nonstatist war, 246, 247–48; and
strategic defense, 99, 127–34; and
strategism, 64; and technology, 65;
two-track decision of, 128–29, 221–
22; weakness of, 236–37; and West
Germany, 64–65, 254. See also Eu-
rope/Europeans; European war
Navy, U.S., 35, 43, 94, 140–43, 149,
180–81, 185, 233, 234–35, 285
necessary and sufficient conditions,
and missile defense, 119–27
negative control, 103, 282
neutron bomb, 85
Nicaragua, 217
Nitze, Paul H., 116
Nixon (Richard) administration,
258
no-cities doctrine, 138–39
no-first-use policy, 248–49
nonnuclear war, 8, 166–71. See also
World War III
nuclear balance, 23–24
nuclear forces, 17–18, 91–92, 140–43,
249–51. See also force structure
Nuclear Non-Proliferation Treaty,
20
nuclear numismatics, 212–15, 236,
255

Nuclear Risk Reduction Centers,
225
nuclear strategy: conventionalization
of, 7; education about, 238; emergence of, 29; and flexibility, 29–37;
groupings of, 29–31; "into the field",
30; legal basis of, 31–32; literature
about, 238; and longevity of war,
29–31, 37–46; and political consistency, 140–43; purpose of, 253; and
rationality, 3–4, 77–78, 140–43;
technical basis of, 11–12. See also
name of specific subject, e.g., flexible response strategy
nuclear theology, 238
nuclear weapons: diversity of, 237–38;
obsolescence of, 131; proliferation
of, 20–21, 212. See also BMD; missiles
nuclear winter, 66–67, 164, 171
Nunn, Sam, 225

offense, 122–27, 186, 235, 276
officer corps, 260–66
Ogarkov, N. V., 193
oil crisis/embargo, 258–60. See also
Persian Gulf
operational policy: and consistency,
137–51; definition of, 137. See also
name of specific policy
operational-tactical surprise attack,
179–80
Operation Barbarossa, 98–99, 106,
139–40, 150, 156, 185–86, 216,
217

payoffs, 77, 79–80, 88–89, 116, 175,
197–98, 213, 236, 286
peace movement, 129
peace as part of a continuous process,
215–16
peace shield, 235–36, 237
peacetime: and command and control,
33–34, 103, 201–2; and predictability, 22; and Soviet strategy, 223–24;
uses of nuclear weapons, 213
Pearl Harbor. See World War II
Pentagon Papers, 264

People's Republic of China. *See* China
perceptions: and crisis management,
   181–83; and the Cuban missile crisis, 188; importance of, 181–82, 197–
   98; of policy makers, 185; and surprise attack, 200
perfection, 2–3
Perrow, Charles, 280
Persian Gulf, 60, 102–3, 191, 258–59,
   262–63, 265
Petersen, Phillip A., 41
Pipes, Richard, 67, 69, 70
pluralism and policy making, 118
point defenses, 198
Poland, 58, 60, 169, 171, 211–12, 240,
   260
police actions, 246
policy: and bureaucracies, 22; and
   force, 12, 215, 231–51; and means
   and ends, 231; and strategy, 215;
   and termination of war, 98–103,
   111. *See also specific type of policy*
policy makers: expectations of, 224,
   265, 277; motivations of, 212; perceptions of, 185; and personal egos,
   183; and pluralism, 118; preconceptions of, 184; standards that are
   meaningful to, 7; and the use of
   military forces, 262–63. *See also* C3
   systems; command and control;
   name of specific subject, e.g., Cuban missile crisis
political action committees, 233
political consistency. *See* consistency
political objectives: and Soviet strategy, 43–44, 45, 58, 65, 68, 268; and
   the Soviet Union, 268; and victory,
   264; and Vietnam, 157
political power, dispersal of, 118
political theory, 76–77, 80, 116–17
politico-military aspects of surprise
   attack, 179–81
politics: study of, 51–52; and technology, 286–87
Posen, Barry R., 64, 180–81, 186
positive control launch (PCL),
   141–42
postnuclear war, 163–66

preconceptions, 184, 186
predictability, 20–26, 65, 176, 177,
   186, 232, 284–85, 288
preemption: advantages of, 199–200,
   224; and alerts, 281; and arms control, 225; and the C3 systems, 198–
   99, 224–25, 277, 278; as a continuum, 198; and crisis stability, 278;
   and defenses, 197–98; definition of,
   82; and deterrence, 81–83, 197; and
   missiles, 226–27, 277, 279, 283, 285–
   86; and NATO, 248; and nuclear arsenals, 201; and payoffs, 197, 236;
   and preventive war, 81–83; and
   prompt launch, 287, 288; and rationality, 82–83; and retaliation,
   198, 199; and Soviet strategy, 69,
   194, 217–18, 219–20, 224, 285-86;
   survivability, 123, 195, 196, 249;
   taxonomy for, 195; and values, 198;
   and victory, 69. *See also* bolt-from-
   the-blue; first strike; launch under
   attack; surprise attack preparedness, 19, 31, 166, 170, 177, 202,
   218, 238–43, 279
President's Commission on U.S. Strategic Forces. *See* Scowcroft Commission
Prevention of Nuclear War agreement, 225
prevention of war, 211–12
preventive war, 81–83, 119, 195
prisoner's dilemma, 110–11, 121–22,
   192
proliferation of nuclear arms, 20–21,
   212
prolonged war, 31, 36–46 43, 45, 106,
   107, 109, 155–63, 234. *See also* longevity of war
prompt launch, 142–43, 287, 288
provocations, mobilizations as,
   81–82
psychology, 93–94, 178, 200
public opinion, 108, 126–27, 211, 223,
   232, 233, 237–39, 243–51, 261,
   268

Quester, George H., 79

Rapid Deployment Force, 44, 258
rationality: as a basis of discussion about nuclear deterrence, 1; conditional, 2–9, 75; of coping, 4–9; and criteria for, 134; definition of, 1–2, 137; heuristic, 2, 5, 7, 8–9. *See also name of specific subject*
Reagan (Ronald) administration: and arms control, 130, 214–15; and C3 system, 104; and counterforce, 146–47; and defenses, 115, 116, 120, 121, 235–36, 276, 285; and the gas pipeline, 259; and horizontal escalation, 191; and the Iran-Contra affair, 266; and maritime strategy, 233–34; and the Persian Gulf, 259, 262–63; and Soviet strategy, 59–60; and the window of vulnerability, 53, 59–60; and the zero option, 129. *See also* SDI; summits
rehearsals, 88, 111, 279
repugnant missions, 36, 246
resistance fighters, 239–42
response lag, 81
retaliation, 85–89, 119, 179, 189–90, 195, 198, 199, 276–78, 284, 288
revenge, 38, 53, 57, 80, 98, 119
revolutionary war, 157–58, 160–61
Reykjavik, Iceland summit (1986), 120, 129, 214–15, 235
risk: in complex organizations, 280; and deterrence rationality, 83; managed, 83; manipulation of, 17, 222; reduction centers, 225; shared, 261; and surprise attack, 203
Rogers, Bernard, 236–37
Roosevelt, Franklin, 100
ROTC (Reserve Officers Training Corps), 260
Rumania, 60, 169

"Safety catch"/"trigger," 32
Sagan, Carl, 66, 67
SALT (Strategic Arms Limitation Talks), 24, 62, 125, 138, 213, 214, 219, 221, 226
Schelling, Thomas C., 40, 80, 91–92, 222

Schlesinger, James R., 163, 222
Schlieffen Plan, 44, 82, 99, 161–62
Schmidt, Helmut, 128
science, 52, 79
scientism, 8, 51–71, 93–94, 143
Scowcroft Commission (1983), 21–22, 53, 54, 55, 59–60, 146, 195, 236
SDI (Strategic Defense Initiative), 71, 115–16, 120, 122–24, 125, 126, 127–34, 223, 235–36, 276, 281, 285
sea lanes of communication (SLOC), 43, 168
second strike, 4, 150, 196, 197–98, 224, 236, 285–86, 287, 288
servicism, 137, 141–43, 146, 150–51, 215
shared vulnerability. *See* mutual vulnerability
SIOP (single integrated operational plan), 105, 140
SLOC (sea lanes of communication), 43, 168
Sonnenfeldt, Helmut, 254
Soviet strategy. *See name of specific subject*, e.g., Afghanistan
Soviet Union: command and control in the, 125–26; dilemmas in the, 267–71; economy of the, 58–59, 62–63, 268; effect of World War II on, the, 109; and internal controversy, 63–64; and military power/problems, 60–63; military studies in the, 67–68, 268; mind set in the, 67–68; and nationalism, 63–64; and political objectives, 43–44, 45, 58, 65, 68, 268; and the revolution of 1917, 160–61, 247; space program, 63; U.S. analysis of the, 57–71; and valuation of defense, 117–18. *See also* Operation Barbarossa; *name of specific subject*, e.g., escalation
Soviet, U.S. relations, 130–132, 285
spin-off crisis, 200–201
stability. *See specific type of stability*, e.g., crisis stability
Stalin, Josef. *See* World War II

Star Wars, 276
Stark (U.S. frigate), 236, 264–65
START negotiations, 213
state, theories of, 12–13
statistical decision theory. *See* mathematical decision models
statist/nonstatist war, 244–48
Staudenmaier, William 0., 42
stealth technologies, 133
Strategic Arms Limitation Talks. *See* SALT
strategic balance, 147–48
Strategic Defense Initiatives. *See* SDI
strategic devolution, 251
strategic divergence, 215–25
strategic escapism, 235
strategic military surprise, 4
strategic stability, 54
strategic war, 190–92, 274–76
strategism. *See* strategizing
strategizing: and absolute war, 13–26; and the balance of terror, 13–26; and ballistic missiles, 56–57, 71; and the Carter administration, 54; and civilian-military relations, 270–71; and command system, 146; and counterforce, 143; definition of, 11; disservices of, 29; and expected/unexpected attacks, 236; and force structure, 64; and NATO, 64; and nuclear numismatics, 236; and nuclear strategy, 11, 211; and rationality, 8–9; and scientism, 8, 51–71; and Soviet strategy, 57–71, 216; and Vietnam, 52–53
strategy: and cost effectiveness, 118–19; defensive versus offensive, 122–27; definition of, 11, 29; and deterrence theory, 231–32; and expectations, 237–39; and force, 215; grand, 11; and the international system, 12; and latent violence, 77; and means and ends, 231; military, 11; motivation for execution of, 36; and nuclear numismatics, 236; and policy, 215; Soviet definition of, 215. *See also name of specific strategy*

submarines. *See* BMD; maritime strategy
successive approximation, 79–80
Suez crisis (1956), 17
summits, 120, 129, 214–15, 235
suppressive survivability, 278
surprise attack: advantages of, 6; and assured destruction, 138; and bombers, 287; and C3 systems, 103, 108–9; classifications of, 178; and coercion, 178; as a continuum, 177; and conventional war, 6–7, 175; and coping, 6–7; and costs, 175, 199; and counterforce, 148–49; and crisis stability, 175, 224–25; and the Cuban missile crisis, 181–85; defensive, 64; and the degree of surprise, 202; deliberately planned, 180–81; and deterrence stability, 179; and escalation control, 192–95; and the failure of conventional deterrence, 203; grand strategic, 179, 183; and history, 176, 178, 185–89; improbability of, 199; inadvertent, 180–81; intelligence, 179, 184; and intelligence systems, 180, 187; and level of impact, 177; and limited war, 192–95; and marginal utility, 178; and maritime strategy, 148–49; and military organizations, 176; military strategic, 179, 183–84; and missiles, 275; motivations for, 175–76; and nonnuclear war, 169; nuclear, 175–203; operational-tactical, 179–80; and payoffs, 175; and perceptions, 200; and policy makers, 176, 177, 178: politico-military aspects of, 179–81; and predictability, 176, 177; and preemption, 195–99; and psychology, 178; and rationality, 6, 175; and response lag, 81; results of, 177, 180; and risk, 203; and Soviet strategy, 189–92, 224, 285–86; and survivability, 276, 287; systemic, 180; tactical, 177; and targets, 177; technical, 179; and technology, 179, 187–88, 235–36; and termination of war, 108–9; un-

provoked, 178; and winning/losing the war, 178, 179, 189; and World War II, 180, 187. *See also* bolt-from-the-blue; first strike; preemption
survivability: and bombers, 141–42; and the C3 system, 103–4, 107, 144, 218, 277, 287; and the Carter administration, 146–47; and civil defense, 71; and counterforce, 144, 147; and defenses, 116, 119, 122–24; and deterrence theory, 4, 277; estimating, 144; and the ethics of war, 89; and first strike, 281; and force structure, 199; and the Hot Line, 200; and missiles, 21–22, 56, 122–25, 150, 275, 277, 287; and mobility, 146; mutual assured, 276; and nuclear numismatics, 213; and preemption, 123, 195, 196, 249; and Soviet strategy, 285–86; suppressive, 278; and surprise attack, 276, 287; and termination of war, 107
systemic surprise attack, 180

tactical surprise attack, 177
targeting, 146, 170, 177, 202, 287–88. *See also* operational policy
technical surprise attack, 179
technology: and accuracy, 85; air-defense, 131–32; and the balance of power, 188; and BMD, 133, 278; and coping, 8–9; and defenses, 235; defensive versus offensive, 122–27; and the diversity of nuclear weapons, 237–38; and the ethics of war, 85; and first strike, 235–36; of the future, 275–76; and intelligence systems, 187–88; and the longevity of war, 165; and mutual vulnerability, 219; and NATO, 65; and policy makers, 286–87; and politics, 286–87; and postnuclear war, 165; and public opinion, 237–38; and the Soviet economy, 62–63; stealth, 133; and surprise attack, 179, 187–88, 235–36; and Vietnam, 245–46
termination of war: and alerts, 103;

and avoidance of war, 202; and the balance of power, 16; and C3 system, 98, 103–11, 278; definition of, 97; and escalation, 97–111; and ethnocentrism, 78–79; and fatalism, 111; and Great Britain, 108; and the Hot Line, 104–5, 109, 111; and longevity of war, 99, 101–3, 108–9; and maritime strategy, 40, 234; and military organizations, 101, 103, 105–6; and policy, 98–103, 111; and Soviet strategy, 191, 192; and surprise attack, 108–9; and survivability, 107; and trust, 110; and the U.S. Navy, 233. *See also name of specific war*
terrorism, 239–40, 245, 246, 258
theater nuclear war, 190–92
Third World, 14, 61, 232
threats, 77, 86, 87, 90–92, 184, 202–3, 234–35, 263, 271, 282
thresholds and Soviet strategy, 190–91
threshold states, 20
timing, 44, 62, 212
Trulock, Notra R., 41
trust, 110, 132, 227
Tuchman, Barbara W., 44
Turkey, 184, 236
two-front war, 44–45, 61, 98–99
two major powers system, 20–21
two-track policy (NATO), 128–29, 221–22
Type I/Type II errors, 196

unexpected wars. *See* bolt-from-the-blue; expected/unexpected wars; surprise attacks
United States. *See name of specific topic*
unprovoked nuclear aggression, 80–81
uses of nuclear weapons: and deterrence, 85–86; and the ethics of war, 85–86; peacetime, 213; and U.S. strategy, 231–32
U.S.-Soviet relations, 130, 132, 285
U.S.S.R. *See* Soviet Union

utilitarianism, 75–76, 79
utilities. *See* payoffs

values: absolute/relative, 117–18; and
coping, 4; and cost effectiveness,
117; and defenses, 117–18; and deterrence theory, 82–83; and escalation, 40; hierarchies of, 4, 40; and
military organizations, 257–58, 260–
66; national, 257–58, 260–66; and
preemption, 198. *See also* ethics;
maximization of values
Van Cleave, William R., 224
verification, 225–26
victory. *See* winning/losing
Vietnam: and applied statistical decision models, 30; and the Calley
court-martial, 261; as a civil war,
244–46; and coercive diplomacy,
264; and command and control, 52;
and Congress, 261; and credibility
of the U.S., 245; direct involvement
of U.S. and U.S.S.R. in, 14; and
the escalation-dominance perspective, 18; ferocity/intensity of, 161;
as the fifty-first state, 245; force in,
263–64; and longevity of war, 157,
161; objective in, 157, 264; officer
corps in, 264; and policy makers,
286; and public opinion, 108, 244–
46, 261; and strategism, 52–53; and
technology, 245–46; and termination
of war, 100, 101, 245; U.S. failure
in, 52–53
Vigor, Peter H., 40–41, 168
violence, 26. *See also* latent violence;
terrorism

war: as part of a continuous process,
215–16; revenge distinguished from,
38. *See also* specific kind of war,
e.g., conventional war; limited war
war plans. *See* nuclear strategy;
strategy; strategizing
Warner, John, 225
Warsaw Pact allies, 132, 169. *See also*
name of specific country
Watkins, James D., 40

weapons: diversification of, 86;
smarter/slower, 286–88; as a threat,
86; usable, 85–86. *See also* nuclear
weapons; *name of specific type of
weapon*
West. *See* NATO; United States;
name of specific country
West Germany, 62, 64–65, 109–10,
147, 171, 234, 250, 254, 259
Western Europe, 89–94, 90, 233–38,
253, 258–60. *See also* NATO; *name
of specific country*
window of vulnerability, 53–56,
59–60
winning/losing: and Afghanistan, 69–
70; and civil defense, 71; and communism, 216; definition of, 69; degrees of, 70–71; and first strike,
197; and limited war, 57; and the
longevity of war, 162; and the maximization of values, 79–80; and mutual vulnerability, 197; and
Operation Barbarossa, 156; and political aims, 264; and preemption,
69; and scientism, 66, 67–71; and
second strike, 197; and Soviet
strategy, 216, 218; and surprise attack, 178, 179; and termination of
war, 101; warfare with the expectation of, 57
Wohlstetter, Albert, 41–42, 79, 193
World War I: attrition in, 155–56; and
the causes of war, 44; and the cult
of the offensive, 186; and escalation, 194; ferocity/intensity of, 160–
61; and the international system,
26: Lebow's work on, 81; and the
lessons of history, 186; and the longevity of war, 158–59, 160–61, 162;
and mobilization, 194; and policy
makers, 183; and rationality, 81; results of, 81, 160–61, 179; sustainability in, 155–56; and termination of
war, 98, 99–100, 162; and a two-
front war, 44. *See also* Schlieffen
Plan
World War II: and the causes of war,
220; and command organization,

106, 109; and coping, 4–5; and defenses, 117–18; effect on Soviet Union of, 109; and the ethics of war, 87: ferocity/intensity of, 159–60, 161; and intelligence services, 186–87; and longevity of war, 156–57, 158, 159, 161; and the motivation of executing war plans, 36; and

policy makers, 183; and the prevention of war, 211–12; and revenge, 98; and surprise attacks, 180, 187; and termination of war, 98–101, 162–63; and a two-front war, 98–99

World War III, 166–72, 179

ABOUT THE AUTHOR

STEPHEN J. CIMBALA is professor of political science at Pennsylvania State University (Delaware County). He is the author of previously published works on U.S. nuclear deterrence policy, military strategy, and U.S.-Soviet strategic policies. He recently authored *Nuclear War and Nuclear Strategy* (Greenwood, 1987) and was editor of *Challenges to Deterrence* (Praeger, 1987).